PUBLISHERS

Drunk Driving Defense
Fifth Edition
by Lawrence Taylor

With society's increased consciousness of the costs of drunk driving, law enforcement officials have become more and more aggressive in seeking convictions. *Drunk Driving Defense* covers every step of the police action and legal process, from the Breathalyzer and field sobriety tests to witness preparation and jury instruction.

Highlights of the 2004 Cumulative Supplement

Supplement prepared by Steven Oberman

The 2004 Cumulative Supplement brings you up-to-date on the latest developments, including:

- New section discussing *Crawford v. Washington* and its applicability to the DUI case.

- Discussion of effect of new U.S. Supreme Court decision in *Blakely v. Washington* on sentencing in DUI cases.

- New section regarding the Fifth Amendment right to remain silent in civil litigation and its importance to the DUI practitioner.

- Inclusion of the most recent NHTSA document regarding roadblocks: The Use of Sobriety Checkpoints for Impaired Driving Enforcement.

- Updated information on vehicle confiscation and forfeiture.

- New sections discussing the distracted and drowsy driver.

- New Blood Specimen Collection Checklist.

The Table of Cases, Bibliography, and Index are also updated to reflect all changes to the text.

10/04

For questions concerning this shipment, billing, or other customer service matters, call our Customer Service Department at 1-800-234-1660.

For toll-free ordering, please call 1-800-638-8437.

A WoltersKluwer Company

DRUNK DRIVING DEFENSE
2004 Cumulative Supplement

This supplement supersedes all previous supplements.

DRUNK DRIVING DEFENSE
Fifth Edition

LAWRENCE TAYLOR, J.D.
Long Beach, California

Member, California and Washington Bars
Former Deputy Public Defender, Los Angeles
Former Deputy District Attorney, Los Angeles
Former Fulbright Professor of Law, Osaka University

2004 Cumulative Supplement prepared by
Steven Oberman, J.D.
Knoxville, Tennessee

Member, Tennessee Bar
Adjunct Professor, University of Tennessee Law School

ΛSPEN
PUBLISHERS

1185 Avenue of the Americas, New York, NY 10036
www.aspenpublishers.com

This publication is designed to provide accurate and authoritative information in regard to the subject matter covered. It is sold with the understanding that the publisher is not engaged in rendering legal, accounting, or other professional services. If legal advice or other professional assistance is required, the services of a competent professional person should be sought.

© 2005 Lawrence E. Taylor
Published by Aspen Publishers, A Wolters Kluwer Company

Printed in the United States of America

1 2 3 4 5 6 7 8 9 0

Library of Congress Cataloging-in-Publication Data

Taylor, Lawrence, 1942-
    Drunk driving defense / Lawrence Taylor. — 5th ed.
        p.   cm.
    Includes bibliographical references and index.
    ISBN 0-7355-1146-2
    ISBN 0-7355-4722-X (supplement)
    1. Drunk driving defense — United States. 2. Defense (Criminal procedure) —
United States. I. Title.
KF2231.T39   1999   99-41726
345.73′0247 — dc21   CIP

Fifth Edition

About Aspen Publishers

Aspen Publishers, headquartered in New York City, is a leading information provider for attorneys, business professionals, and law students. Written by preeminent authorities, our products consist of analytical and practical information covering both U.S. and international topics. We publish in the full range of formats, including updated manuals, books, periodicals, CDs, and online products.

Our proprietary content is complemented by 2,500 legal databases, containing over 11 million documents, available through our Loislaw division. Aspen Publishers also offers a wide range of topical legal and business databases linked to Loislaw's primary material. Our mission is to provide accurate, timely, and authoritative content in easily accessible formats, supported by unmatched customer care.

To order any Aspen Publishers title, go to *www.aspenpublishers.com* or call 1-800-638-8437.

To reinstate your manual update service, call 1-800-638-8437.

For more information on Loislaw products, go to *www.loislaw.com* or call 1-800-364-2512.

For Customer Care issues, e-mail CustomerCare@aspenpublishers.com; call 1-800-234-1660; or fax 1-800-901-9075.

Aspen Publishers
A Wolters Kluwer Company

SUBSCRIPTION NOTICE

This Aspen Publishers product is updated on a periodic basis with supplements to reflect important changes in the subject matter. If you purchased this product directly from Aspen Publishers, we have already recorded your subscription for the update service.

If, however, you purchased this product from a bookstore and wish to receive future updates and revised or related volumes billed separately with a 30-day examination review, please contact our Customer Service Department at 1-800-234-1660, or send your name, company name (if applicable), address, and the title of the product to:

ASPEN PUBLISHERS
7201 McKinney Circle
Frederick, MD 21704

To my parents, Albert and Marian,
   to whom I owe my character,
To my wife, Evelyn, and my children, Rachael and Benjamin,
   to whom I owe my happiness,
To my siblings, David and Karen,
   to whom I owe my advocacy skills, and
To my clients,
   to whom I owe the gratification I receive from my profession.

Steven Oberman

CONTENTS

2.

THE SENTENCE

3.

THE ADMINISTRATIVE LICENSE SUSPENSION

Contents

IV

TRIAL

13.

CROSS-EXAMINATION

ABOUT THE SUPPLEMENT AUTHOR

Steven Oberman is nationally recognized as an authority on the intricacies of DUI defense. An adjunct professor at the University of Tennessee Law School since 1993, he has received prestigious awards for his faculty contributions. He is the author of *DUI: The Crime and Consequences in Tennessee* (West 2003) and has written numerous articles on the subject for several state and national publications. Mr. Oberman has been chair or co-chair of the National Association of Criminal Defense Lawyers' DUI Advocacy Committee since 1995 and has served on the Board of Regents for the National College of DUI Defense since 1999.

Board-certified by the College and a graduate of the National Highway Traffic Safety Administration DUI and Traffic Safety Faculty Development Workshop, Mr. Oberman is a popular speaker at seminars throughout the United States, educating defense lawyers, the judiciary, and the prosecution on the many issues that arise in DUI cases.

ACKNOWLEDGMENTS

I would like to express my heartfelt thanks to Lawrence Taylor for allowing me the opportunity to perpetuate his acclaimed work. I will strive to maintain the standard of excellence he has established in writing this essential text.

I would also like to thank Troy McKinney, Esq., and Mary C. McMurray, who have generously permitted the use of their materials and information in this supplement, as well as James A.H. Bell, Esq., who continually provides me with valuable ideas and inspiration.

Finally, I would like to express my deep appreciation to Sara Compher-Rice, Esq., Richard Burnette, Esq., and my assistant, Kim Davis, for their invaluable assistance in researching, editing, and proofreading the contents of this supplement.

Steven Oberman

DRUNK DRIVING DEFENSE
2004 Cumulative Supplement

I

CRIME AND PUNISHMENT

1

THE OFFENSE

§1.1 The Corpus

Page 12. Add at end of carryover paragraph:

Many states have passed legislation making certain multiple drunk driving offenses a felony.

§1.2 What Constitutes "Driving"?

Page 17. Add after carryover paragraph:

On similar facts, other appellate courts have reached a different conclusion. For example, in *State v. Lawrence,* 849 S.W.2d 761 (Tenn. 1993), the Tennessee Supreme Court held that a defendant who was asleep on the driver's side of the vehicle parked on a public road with the keys to the vehicle in his pants pocket had "physical control" of the vehicle for purposes of Tennessee's DUI statute. Similarly, in *State v. Peterson,* 769 P.2d 1221 (Mont. 1989), the Montana Supreme Court held that the defendant was in "actual physical control" of the vehicle when he was found in the driver's seat with the keys to the vehicle in his pocket, even though the vehicle was off the roadway and the defendant was slumped to his right onto the middle of the front seat of the vehicle.

Page 17. In last paragraph, replace citation for State **Department of Public Safety v. Juncewski** *with:*

308 N.W.2d 316 (Minn. 1981)

Page 19. Add after second sentence of first full paragraph:

"Subsequently, the Colorado Supreme Court reversed the intermediate appellate court, holding that a motorist in the driver's seat of an automobile that had its motor running and its parking lights on in a private parking lot was in actual physical control of the automobile, and thus was driving for purposes of the "express consent" statute. *Motor Vehicles Div., Dept. of Revenue v. Warman,* 763 P.2d 558 (Colo. 1988).

Page 21. Add after first full paragraph:

Subsequently, in *Cagle v. City of Gadsden,* 495 So. 2d 1144 (Ala. 1986), the Alabama Supreme Court abandoned the test applied in *Key v. Town of Kinsey,* 424 So. 2d 701 (Ala. 1982), holding that a totality of the circumstances test, through circumstantial evidence, applies in determining whether a motorist who was not seen driving the vehicle had actual physical control over the vehicle while under the influence. In *Cagle,* the Alabama Supreme Court found that there was insufficient evidence to support a conviction for driving under the influence of alcohol based on the totality of the circumstances in that case.

Page 22. Add after first carryover paragraph:

The Tennessee Court of Criminal Appeals reached a different conclusion in *State v. Turner,* 952 S.W.2d 213 (Tenn. Crim. App. 1997). In that case, the defendant was arrested outside a bar while he was sitting in the driver's seat of his vehicle with the headlights on and the engine running. The arresting officer had watched the defendant enter the vehicle, and the proof at trial was that the vehicle had remained stationary. At trial, the defendant testified that he had no intent to drive, and that he was merely seated in his vehicle waiting for his nephew to arrive and give him a ride home. In affirming the conviction, the Tennessee Court of Criminal Appeals held that the offense of driving under the influence did not require intent to operate a vehicle; rather, it was sufficient that the defendant voluntarily placed himself in physical control of his vehicle while under the influence of an intoxicant.

§1.2.1 Putting the Defendant Behind the Wheel

Page 24. Delete second sentence of second paragraph.

§1.2.2 "Vehicle"

Page 25. Add after first sentence of second paragraph:

See also State v. Saiz, 24 P.3d 365 (N.M. App. 2001) (moped is a vehicle under DWI statute).

Page 25. Add after second paragraph:

Similarly, the Utah Supreme Court has held that a horse is not a vehicle as the term is used in Utah's driving while intoxicated statutes. *Utah v. Blowers,* 717 P.2d 1321 (Utah 1986).

Page 25. Add after third paragraph:

Courts have differed as to whether a snowmobile is a vehicle as defined in the state's drunk driving statute. The Michigan Supreme Court has held that it is a vehicle within the meaning of the statute prohibiting the operation of a vehicle while under the influence of intoxicating liquors. *People v. Rogers,* 475 N.W.2d 717 (Mich. 1991). Conversely, an Illinois appellate court has held that a snowmobile is not a vehicle under the state's DUI statute. *People v. Staton,* 619 N.E.2d 777 (Ill. App. 1993).

§1.2.3 "Highway"

Page 27. In first full sentence of carryover paragraph, replace **State v. Ball** *citation with:*

264 S.E.2d 844 (W. Va. 1980)

Page 27. Delete last sentence of carryover paragraph.

§1.3   Under the Influence of Alcohol

§1.3.1   Presumption of Intoxication from Blood-Alcohol Analysis

Page 42. Add at end of subsection:

Counsel may encounter the increasingly prevalent situation where the prosecutor has filed drunk driving charges when the blood-alcohol level tested *below* the statutory level. The reasoning may be that, for example, the BAC was falling and that although tested an hour or two after the stop at .07 percent, retrograde extrapolation (see §5.2) indicates a probable level of .10 percent at the time of driving. This is, of course, speculation and quite susceptible to cross-examination. In addition, counsel may wish to consider an argument to the jury that, absent other compelling evidence, reasonable doubt *automatically* exists.

The logic is this: It appears that a rebuttable presumption exists when defendants are under the influence of alcohol at levels above, say, .08 percent — but not below that level. When the alcohol level is below .08 percent we can no longer predict with any confidence that the individual *is* impaired. However, there is not even a *rebuttable* presumption: The legislature in its infinite wisdom was not willing to give that edge to impairment versus nonimpairment. Quite simply, the law makes the .05 to .08 percent zone a toss-up. Stated another way, absent other compelling evidence, it is just as possible that the person was not impaired as it is that he was ... and 50–50 does not amount to proof "beyond a reasonable doubt."

This approach can be used in conjunction with an opening statement, suggested by attorney Paul Ahern of Minnetonka, Minnesota, in which he tells the jury that "Today, you will meet someone who knew when to say when — a person who tested under our state's legal limit, a person who knew when to stop drinking."

§1.4   Over .08 or .10 Percent Blood Alcohol

Page 43. Add after carryover sentence:

(Note: On October 23, 2000, President Clinton signed a new law requiring states to implement a 0.08 percent BAC standard as the legal level by 2004. Failure to do so would result in the loss of millions of dollars in federal highway funds.)

§1.4.5   Admissibility of Non-Impairment Evidence

Page 51. Add new subsection after subsection 1.4.5:

§1.4.6   "Direct Breath" Statutes

§1.4.6.1   Over .08 or .10 Percent Blood Alcohol

Many states have followed California in adopting so-called direct breath statutes in an attempt to avoid the scientific reality of variable partition ratios. (See §6.0.1 of the main volume for a discussion of partition ratio.)

The so-called direct breath-alcohol statute has come under considerable scientific fire. One world-renowned blood-alcohol expert, for example, has shown that implicit in such statutes is an equation that incorrectly describes the relationship between blood- and breath-alcohol concentration in a human subject. Simpson, *The New "Direct Breath" Statutes: Both Bad Law and Bad Science,* 6(4) DWI Journal 1 (1991). In another article, written by Simpson and Professor Dominick Labianca, the scientists concluded that the statutes "thus put into law the relationship, blood-alcohol concentration (BAC) equals breath-alcohol concentration (BrAC), which is incorrect." Labianca and Simpson, *Medicolegal Alcohol Determination: Variability of the Blood- to Breath-Alcohol Ratio and Its Effect on Reported Breath-Alcohol Concentrations,* 33 European Journal of Clinical Chemistry 919 (1995). The direct breath statute "is tantamount to instructing jurors that the defendant's blood/breath ratio was 2100:1 or greater, when he/she was tested, and that the defendant is not permitted to rebut this presumption in any way" — despite the widely accepted fact that partition ratios vary widely. *Supra* at 923.

§1.5   Under the Influence of Drugs

Page 56. Add after carryover paragraph:

Independent of the question of tolerance, does marijuana impair driving at all? A report from the California Department of Justice, Office of the Attorney General, found that marijuana undoubtedly impairs psychomotor abilities that are functionally related to driving and that driving skill itself may be impaired, particularly at high-dose levels or among naïve subjects. A. A. Biasotti, et al., Marijuana and Alcohol: A Driver Performance Study, California Office of Traffic Safety Project No. 087902 (Sept. 1986).

The United States Department of Transportation, however, seems to have reached at least a conclusion more tenuous than, if not contrary to, the California study and popular opinion. As early as 1982, research was performed in a fully interactive driving simulator on the effects of alcohol and marijuana, alone and in combination, on driver-controlled behavior and performance. Based on a large number of measures of driver behavior and performance, alcohol was found consistently and significantly to cause impairment, while marijuana had only an occasional effect. Also, there was little evidence of interaction between alcohol and marijuana. Accidents and speeding tickets reliably increased under alcohol, but no marijuana or combined alcohol-and-marijuana influence was noted. See *The Effects of Alcohol and Marihuana on Driver-Controlled Behavior in a Driving Simulator, Phase I*, DOT-HS-806-414.

Further, a federal report entitled Marijuana and Actual Driving Performance, DOT-HS-808-078 (Nov. 1993), concludes that "THC is not a profoundly impairing drug.... It apparently affects controlled information processing in a variety of laboratory tests, but not to the extent which is beyond the individual's ability to control when he is motivated and permitted to do so in driving."

... An important practical objective of this study was to determine whether degrees of driving impairment can be actually predicted from either measured concentration of THC in plasma or performance measured in potential roadside "sobriety" tests of tracking ability or hand and posture stability. The results, like many reported before, indicated that none of these measures accurately predicts changes in actual performance under the influence of THC. . . .

The researchers found that it "appears not possible to conclude anything about a driver's impairment on the basis of his/her plasma concentrations of THC and THC-COOH detemined in a single sample."

Defense counsel should be aware of the chemical aspects of tetrahydrocannabinol (THC), the active ingredient in marijuana. The following information regarding marijuana is reproduced in part from the article, *Drugs Other Than Alcohol: Marijuana,* 17 For the Defense 3, 5–6 (May-June 2003), with the permission of the author, David T. Stafford, Ph.D., as well as the Tennessee Association of Criminal Defense Lawyers.

> Tetrahydrocannabinol, THC, and its metabolites, result from marijuana use. Marijuana is generally considered the plant material consisting of the dried leaves of the hemp plant, Cannabis sativa. It may contain from traces to 12% or more THC, depending on the strain, growing conditions and harvesting and treatment techniques. Most marijuana available on the streets is 3–5% THC. Sinsemilla is marijuana derived from unpollinated female plants and usually has a high THC content. Dried resin collected from the flower tops is marketed as hashish. It contains higher concentrations of THC, 12–20%, and can be extracted with alcohol or gasoline to produce hash or hemp oil which is even higher in THC content. Seeds, which used to be widely marketed as a bird feed constituent, contain very little THC, and today those commercially available have been sterilized to prevent germination and subsequent growth to plants.
>
> Smoking a marijuana cigarette takes approximately 15 minutes. The maximum blood THC concentration is achieved before smoking is finished, and the concentration decreases rapidly to about 20–25% of maximum in about 30 minutes, reaching nearly zero in about 2–3 more hours. The increase in heart rate associated with THC reaches its maximum 20–30 minutes after start of smoking and returns to normal in about 90–120 minutes. The perceived "high" reaches a maximum about 30–40 minutes after beginning of smoking, levels off, and then declines slowly over the next 1–2 hours. Some effects can be

measured at significant levels for about 3–4 hours after start of smoking. Most of the outward manifestations are essentially gone by about 6 hours. Some of the acute effects of marijuana use are sedation, prolonged reaction time, euphoria, decreased attention to surroundings, and temporal distortion.

Hallucinations are not frequently encountered. One of the effects of long-term marijuana smoking can be impairment of memory.

In the body, THC is the major psychoactive compound. It is metabolized rather rapidly to two hydroxylated metabolites which are active but present in very low concentrations, and one inactive acid metabolite, THC-COOH. There are a large number of other metabolites, but at much lower concentrations.

Both THC and THC-COOH are detectable in blood or serum for about 5–6 hours after use. The Tennessee Bureau of Investigation Laboratory does these analyses on request, but not as a part of their regular blood drug screen. These are usually a screen followed by confirmation by gas chromatography/mass spectrometry, GC/MS. Urine tests are more frequently done, and cannabis analysis is part of their regular drug screen. THC is not generally detected in the urine since very little of it is excreted in the urine. When you get a urine drug screen result, it is reported as THC metabolites, positive. This may be reported as having been done by immunoassay, or EMIT. The cutoff concentration, the concentration at or above which the analyte is reported as positive, will vary from one laboratory to another. If the analysis is done by a Substance Abuse and Mental Health Services Administration, SAMHSA, certified laboratory[,] the cut-off concentration for THC metabolites is 300ng/ml for the immunoassay screen. This is total reacting metabolites. If the screen result is at or above the cut-off concentration the laboratory must do a confirmatory test. This is in almost all cases by GC/MS and is done for only THC-COOH. The confirmation cut-off is 15ng/ml. SAMHSA certified laboratories are required to keep any positive samples, frozen, for a year. These samples can be retested. In addition, the laboratory can supply you with a "litigation" package, which contains everything about that sample and chain of custody from collection to report.

So what does a positive result tell you about your case? Nothing, except that the individual was exposed to marijuana prior to sample collection. How long before? Without concentration data no definitive estimate is possible. With concentration data any estimates should be done with caution. If the analysis was positive for THC in the blood and you know the cut-off concentration you might estimate that the exposure was probably within 3–5 hours prior to collection. If concentration data are available, then a better estimate may be possible.

The acid metabolite THC-COOH may be detected in urine for days to weeks after exposure. If concentration data are available, then it may be possible to estimate a time frame of use, and perhaps whether marijuana use may have been a significant factor in the case. Of course, as with all cases, the perceived actions of the individual as derived from creditable observances are an important factor.

I have had a number of cases where the individual said he was not smoking, but he was in the vicinity of others who were; therefore, he had a positive test because of passive inhalation. The highest concentration of the THC-COOH I have seen reported in the literature was about 30nl/ml. This was achieved under conditions which were so severe that the participants had to wear goggles because of atmospheric irritation. This of course is 1/10 of the screening cut-off concentration and should have been reported as negative.

Page 57. Add at end of section:

Any law enforcement officer who testifies to recognition of symptoms of specific drugs must, of course, be qualified to do so — and the simple fact is that very few are. Many have received no formal training of any kind; others rely on reading materials or field experience. The credentials of any officer claiming to be a drug recognition expert (DRE) should be investigated, and his expertise challenged in a foundational motion *in limine* or on voir dire of the witness.

In *State v. Baity*, 991 P.2d 1151 (2000), for example, the Washington Supreme Court held that under the *Frye* test a DRE must follow a complete 12-step protocol, as originally developed by the Los Angeles Police Department (see *supra*) and later refined into a standardized curriculum by the National Highway Traffic Safety Administration:

> To be certified as a DRE, an officer must complete a three-phase program of instruction. First, the officer must attend a 16-hour 'preschool,' which involves an overview of the DRE program, and instruction on the seven drug categories and basic

drug terminology. Second, the officer must complete a 56-hour DRE school program. The program consists of 30 modules of instruction, including an overview of the development and validation of the drug evaluation process, and sessions on each drug category. Additionally, the officer must pass a written examination before beginning the next phase of training. Finally, the officer begins certification training. Certification requires the officer participate in a minimum of 12 complete examinations under the supervision of a trained DRE instructor. Of those 12 evaluations, the officer must identify a minimum 75 percent toxicological corroboration rate. The officer must then pass another written examination and a separate skills demonstration examination performed in front of two DRE instructors before he or she becomes certified as a DRE. Finally, the officer must maintain an up-to-date resume or curriculum vitae.

Additionally, a DRE must be recertified every two years. During that time period, the DRE is required to conduct four hands-on evaluations and to attend eight hours of in-service training.

§1.6 Felony Drunk Driving: DUI with Injury

§1.6.2 Manslaughter

Page 62. Add at end of second complete paragraph:

See also *State v. Pomykala,* No. 3-99-0715 (Ill. App., Oct. 11, 2001), where an instruction that driving under the influence of alcohol "shall be presumed evidence of a reckless act" in a reckless homicide trial was held to have "compelled the jury to presume that the defendant was acting recklessly when the incident occurred, thus effectively removing the burden of proving that element from the State."

§1.6.3 Murder: DUI with Inferred Malice

Page 67. Add at end of second paragraph:

See also *People v. Murray,* 275 Cal. Rptr. 498 (1990), where the prosecution offered evidence that the defendant had attended a drinking driver education program and had stated that he had learned a lot from it. This was held properly admitted to show awareness of the life-threatening risk of drunk driving — and therefore the existence of implied malice.

§1.7   Civil Liability

Page 71, add new subsection:

§1.7.1   The Fifth Amendment Right to Remain Silent in Civil Litigation

The DUI practitioner often encounters cases where another party is injured as a result of the client's driving and a civil lawsuit either has been filed or potentially will be. In these cases, there are several reasons a defendant should consider invoking his Fifth Amendment right to remain silent in the civil litigation, as it could greatly affect a parallel criminal case. Citing *Kastigar v. United States,* 406 U.S. 441, 444–45 (1972), in an article entitled, "Staring Down Both Barrels in a Corporate Fraud Case: Can a Civil Stay Help the Defense?," 8 No. 22 Andrews' Bank & Lender Liab. Litig. Rep. 15 (Apr. 3, 2003), authors John J. Falvey, Jr., Matthew A. Wolfman, and Nancy E. Maroney list three reasons for not testifying in a civil matter. The first and most obvious is the need to avoid providing testimony or other evidence that may furnish a link in the chain to criminal investigators. The *Kastigar* court held that the Fifth Amendment "can be asserted in any proceeding, civil or criminal … and it protects against any disclosures that the witness reasonably believes could be used in a criminal prosecution or could lead to other evidence that might be so used." As the authors point out, even seemingly benign information can lead to incriminating evidence against a DUI defendant. In a DUI case, for instance, the history and facts of the defendant driver's driving history, his or her drinking habits, and most certainly the facts leading up until the time of the accident can all be used to convict the defendant in the criminal case.

The second reason to plead the Fifth Amendment in a civil action is that not all of the facts may be known at the time of discovery in the civil case. As any experienced lawyer knows, discovery often takes place through the conclusion of the prosecution's proof at trial. Therefore, the defendant may be unaware of facts to which he would otherwise need to testify. In addition, the defendant would be required to reveal exculpatory information that would otherwise not be discoverable by the prosecution, but which would most likely be relayed from the plaintiff's counsel in the civil case to the prosecutor in the criminal case. Further, if a defendant is found guilty by either plea agreement or trial, the testimony obtained during the civil discovery may provide sufficient grounds for related charges, or even unrelated charges such as perjury or obstruction of justice.

The third reason is the very real risk that even limited testimony in a civil case — an assertion or denial in an answer or interrogatory response, for example — may cause the defendant to waive his or her Fifth Amendment privilege. Testimonial waivers are not lightly inferred, however, and courts accordingly indulge every reasonable presumption against finding a testimonial waiver, and even then only where the partial disclosure may mislead the finder of fact. See *In Re Vitamins Antitrust Litigation,* 120 F. Supp. 2d 58, 66 (D.D.C. 2000); *Klein v. Harris,* 667 F.2d 274, 287 (2d Cir. 1981).

In addition to these three reasons, a fourth should be added. When the defendant invokes the privilege to remain silent, it is likely that the civil case will be stayed, at least for a short time. Then, possibly, (1) the plaintiff settles for less money than the case would otherwise be worth; (2) the plaintiff waits until the criminal case is concluded; or (3) in the best-case scenario for the defense, the DUI defense counsel coordinates the cases so that the civil plaintiff, in the role of victim, recommends to the prosecutor a plea agreement to a lesser offense. This allows the civil case to be concluded sooner rather than later; thus, the plaintiff receives for damages funds which would otherwise be necessary to pursue the criminal defense.

The DUI practitioner should recognize that the Fifth Amendment applies to every phase of the civil proceeding. This means that it may be advisable to move for a stay, or to refuse to respond to complaints, requests to admit, interrogatories, or deposition questions, if the witness might *reasonably* believe such disclosures would be used in a criminal prosecution or could lead to other evidence that might be so used. See *Richardson v. Tennessee Board of Dentistry,* 913 S.W.2d 446, 461 (Tenn. 1995) (emphasis in original), citing *Murphy v. Waterfront Commission,* 378 U.S. 52, 94, 84 S.

Ct. 1594, 1611, 12 L. Ed. 2d 678 (1964); *State ex rel. Shriver v. Leech,* 612 S.W.2d 454, 459 (Tenn.), *cert. denied,* 454 U.S. 836, 102 S. Ct. 139, 70 L. Ed. 2d 116 (1981). "The Fifth Amendment privilege can be claimed in any proceeding, civil or criminal, administrative or judicial, investigatory or adjudicatory." *Murphy v. Waterfront Commission,* 378 U.S. 52, 94, 84 S. Ct. 1594, 1611, 12 L. Ed. 2d 678 (1964). Although the privilege is available to the criminal defendant in a civil suit, it does not protect witnesses in circumstances in which the answer may subject them only to civil liabilities. See *Richardson v. Tennessee Board of Dentistry,* 913 S.W.2d 446, 462 (Tenn. 1995).

The authors of the article *Taking the Fifth in Civil Litigation,* emphasize that

> [w]hen properly claiming the privilege, a party may not simply ignore its discovery obligations. For example, an individual who intends to assert the Fifth Amendment may not refuse to attend the deposition, and a notice of deposition will not be vacated on a claim that the privilege will be asserted. Instead, the party must attend the deposition, answer those questions that are not properly within the scope of the privilege, and claim the privilege as to the specific questions that create a risk of self-incrimination. Similarly, a party facing interrogatories that might address protected matters must claim the Fifth Amendment only in response to those particular questions. In short, there is no such thing, at least not legally, as a blanket claim of the Fifth Amendment.

Richard L. Scheff, Scott A. Coffina, & Jill Baisinger, *Taking the Fifth in Civil Litigation,* 29 Litig. 34, 36 (Fall 2002).

While there is no prohibition against parallel civil and criminal proceedings, many times the defendant may request a stay of the civil action until the criminal litigation has concluded. While the defendant does not enjoy a constitutional right to a stay, the U.S. Supreme Court has stated in a footnote that, "[f]ederal courts have deferred civil proceedings pending the completion of parallel criminal prosecutions when the interests of justice seemed to require such action, sometimes at the request of the prosecution, and sometimes at the request of the defense. *United States v. Kordel,* 397 U.S. 1, 90 S. Ct. 763, 770 n.27 (1970) (citations omitted).

"Following *Kordel,* the federal courts have employed a balancing test in addressing motions for stays, typically considering some variant of these factors: The plaintiff's interest in continuing the litigation and potential prejudice to the plaintiff incurred by a stay, the burden on the defendant of having to defend his or her interests in two forums, the burden on the court of granting a stay, the burden on any non-parties, and the public interest." Richard L. Scheff et al., 29 Litig. at 39, citing *Keating v. Office of Thrift Supervision*, 45 F.3d 322, 324–25 (9th Cir. 1995); *S.E.C. v. Dresser Indus.*, 628 F.2d 1368, 1375 (D.C. Cir. 1980); *Golden Quality Ice Cream Co., Inc. v. Deerfield Specialty Papers, Inc.*, 87 F.R.D. 53, 56–57 (E.D. Pa. 1980).

Only after all of these factors are considered should counsel discuss with his or her client whether or when to invoke the Fifth Amendment right to remain silent.

§1.8   *Inchoate and Accomplice Liability*

§1.8.1   Attempted Drunk Driving

Page 72. Add at end of subsection:

Other courts have reached a different conclusion, holding that attempted DWI is not a legally cognizable criminal offense. See *Strong v. State*, 87 S.W.3d 206 (Tex. App. 2002); *People v. Prescott*, 745 N.E.2d 1000 (N.Y. App. 2001).

§1.8.2   Accomplice to Drunk Driving

Page 73. Replace last paragraph of subsection with:

The majority rule, in fact, is that any passenger of a vehicle, including the owner, may be held criminally liable as an aider or abettor in the commission of the offenses of driving while intoxicated and vehicular homicide. See, e.g., *Eager v. State*, 325 S.W. 2d 815, 821 (Tenn. 1959), citing *Story v. United States*, 16 F.2d 342 (D.C. Cir. 1926). There is no requirement that the accomplice be a passenger or owner of the vehicle. In *Guzman v. State*, 586 S.E. 2d 59 (Ga. Ct. App. 2003), the defendant was convicted of two counts of vehicular homicide when he allowed a 14-year-old to drive his brother and a friend in Guzman's vehicle after having given beer to the boys. Mr. Guzman's criminal intent was inferred by his conduct in giving the driver alcohol and the car keys, and standing silently by as the 14-year-old got behind the wheel and drove away, knowing the alcohol would make him a less safe driver in light of his age and lack of driving experience. The element of showing Mr. Guzman was the legal or proximate cause of the deaths was satisfied when the state showed he played a substantial part in setting in motion the combination of an intoxicated minor driving after consuming alcohol. In this case, the court found that the acts of the driver and a passenger were not intervening causes of the accident when the defendant could have reasonably anticipated or foreseen that an intoxicated minor might drive recklessly, and that other minors who had been drinking might contribute to the general reckless nature of the outing.

§1.9 Affirmative Defenses

§1.9.1 Necessity

Page 74. Add after first paragraph:

This defense is available in a number of states, including California, Maine, Vermont, and New Jersey. New Jersey Supreme Court Justice Stein, in a dissenting opinion, has characterized the court's obligation by stating that, " . . . once in a great while a DWI case comes along that presents facts so bizarre and remote from the public policy underlying the law that even a court . . . committed . . . to the strict enforcement of the drunk-driving statutes can pause to make certain that no injustice has been done." *State v. Fogarty,* 607 A.2d 624, 632 (N.J. 1992). This same justice, in another dissenting opinion, recognized that

> cases may occasionally turn up [a] freakish factual context in which the rigid, mechanistic application of a sound, well-established, respected principle of law will produce a result that is plainly at odds with substantial justice. . . . When, as here, there is a collision between law and common sense, this court should exert its best effort to vindicate good sense. Our institutional legitimacy depends on our succeeding in that endeavor."

Id. at 637, citing *State v. Vick,* 566 A.2d 531, 294–95 (N.J. 1989).

Page 75. Add at end of second full paragraph:

Likewise, the defendant was entitled to a jury instruction on the necessity defense when his driving was required to escape a brutal and possibly deadly attack from three unknown assailants, when he did not create the circumstances which he then had to avoid. See *State v. Romano*, 809 A.2d 158 (N.J. 2002), citing *State v. Tate*, 477 A.2d 462 (N.J. Sup. Ct. 1984).

Page 75. Add at end of subsection:

In *State v. Romano*, 809 A.2d 158 (N.J. 2002), the Superior Court of New Jersey, Appellate Division, held that a defendant in a DUI prosecution may assert the common law defense of necessity.

§1.9.2   Duress

Page 76. Add at end of subsection:

A California court has held that duress is not applicable to an administrative license suspension hearing — impliedly recognizing its application in a criminal prosecution. Appellant in that case testified that a guest at a party threatened him with a knife; when he tried to leave the party, the knife-wielding guest followed him outside and it became necessary to get in his car and flee. The argument was that the defenses of necessity and duress applied, as driving under the circumstances was necessary to avoid serious injury or death. The suspension was upheld by the hearing officer, but this was reversed by the superior court. The court of appeals reversed, apparently reasoning that duress is a defense that negates *intent,* and state of mind was not relevant to the administrative proceeding. In also dismissing necessity as a defense, the court apparently ruled that equitable principles simply do not apply to DMV hearings:

> Even in the absence of considerations involving duress as negating the element of intent, the relevant statutes and their clear public policy preclude the application of the necessity defense to administrative per se hearings. The relevant provisions plainly

and fully involve a remedial scheme that does not leave room for the discretionary application of equitable defenses....

In contrast to a criminal prosecution for drunk driving, the administrative remedy involving the suspension of driver's licenses was designed to be a "swift and certain" method of deterring such conduct.... It would be inconsistent with the purpose of this fact-finding procedure, and with the intent to suspend the driving privilege of those who are thus found to have been driving under the influence, to rescind the suspension for reasons that have nothing to do with whether the person was in fact driving while intoxicated. *Foster v. Reed*, — Cal. App. 4th — (1999).

But see *Curtin v. DMV*, 123 Cal. App. 3d 481 (1981), where another California court applied equitable principles to the administrative hearing:

It is undeniably true that under any reasonable concept, right and justice would be defeated by the erroneous suspension of [plaintiff's] driver's license. And it is a basic principle of jurisprudence, at least in the absence of some transcendent public interest, that *equity* will assert itself in those situations where right and justice would be defeated but for its intervention.

§1.9.5 Involuntary Intoxication

Page 80. Add at end of section:

Many of the other jurisdictions that permit an accused to be completely relieved of criminal responsibility based on involuntary intoxication do so premised upon the notion that he or she was temporarily rendered legally insane at the time of the offense. (*Author's Note:* This legal insanity defense should be distinguished from the defense used with clients suffering from acute alcoholism as discussed in more detail in §1.9.6.)

The defense of involuntary intoxication has been recognized in other jurisdictions in four types of situations: (1) where the intoxication was caused by the fault of another (i.e., through force, duress, fraud, or contrivance); (2) where the intoxication was caused by an innocent mistake on the part of the defendant (i.e., defendant took hallucinogenic pill in reasonable belief it was aspirin or lawful tranquilizer); (3) where a defendant unknowingly suffers from a physiological or psychological condition that renders him abnormally susceptible to a legal intoxicant (sometimes referred to as pathological intoxication); and (4) where unexpected intoxication results from a medically prescribed drug.

Commonwealth of Pennsylvania v. Smith, 831 A.2d 636 (Pa. Super. Ct. 2003), citing Phillip E. Hassman, Annotation, *When Intoxication Deemed Involuntary so as to Constitute a Defense to Criminal Charge*, 73 A.L.R.3d 195 at §2[a] (1976) (footnotes omitted); W. Lafave & A. Scott, *Handbook on Crim. Law*, §45 at 342 (1972).

In *Smith*, the court recognized that varying circumstances make it difficult to formulate a comprehensive definition of the defense; nonetheless, it would appear that a key component is lack of culpability on the part of the defendant in causing the intoxication. Like the insanity defense, the defendant is excused from criminality because intoxication affects the ability to distinguish between right and wrong. Thus, the mental state of an involuntarily intoxicated defendant is measured by the test of legal insanity. See *Commonwealth of Pennsylvania v. Smith*, 831 A.2d 636 (Pa. Super. Ct. 2003); *State v. Gardner*, 601 N.W.2d 670 (Wis. Ct. App. 1999); *State v. Lucas*, 368 N.W.2d 124 (Iowa 1985); *City of Minneapolis v. Altimus*, 238 N.W.2d 851 (Minn. 1976) (*en banc*); *State v. Mriglot*, 550 P.2d 17 (Wash. 1976), *aff'd*, 564 P.2d 784 (Wis. 1977) (*en banc*). It should be noted that the Model Penal Code uses the term "self-induced" intoxication, rather than "voluntary" intoxication, and defines that term to mean intoxication caused by substances which the actor knowingly introduces into his body, the tendency of which to cause intoxication he knows or ought to know, unless he introduces them pursuant to medical advice or under such circumstances as would afford a defense to a charge of crime. Model Penal Code §2.08(5)(b).

This defense may not be available, however, in cases where a defendant knowingly takes more than the prescribed dosage, mixes a prescription medication with alcohol or other controlled substances, or voluntarily undertakes an activity incompatible with the drug's side effects. See *State v. Gardner*, 601 N.W.2d 670 (Wis. Ct. App. 1999).

If such a defense is to be cognizable under this theory, the defendant should establish a necessary factual foundation to support such a claim. The defendant normally has the burden to show such intoxication by a preponderance of the evidence. See *Commonwealth v. Collins,* 810 A.2d 698 (Pa. Super. Ct. 2002). Because the trial court cannot take judicial notice of the facts necessary to support this defense, the defendant should, at a minimum, present expert testimony to establish that the medication, or combination of medication and alcohol, caused the intoxication necessary to establish the inebriating effect. See *Commonwealth of Pennsylvania v. Smith,* 831 A.2d 636 (Pa. Super. Ct. 2003).

2

THE SENTENCE

§2.0 Sentencing in the DUI Case

Page 84. Add after carryover sentence:

Subsequently, the Illinois Supreme Court reversed, holding that a professional alcohol evaluation of defendant convicted of driving while under the influence would not violate a defendant's Fifth Amendment privilege against self-incrimination, as the court could sentence a defendant to the maximum penalty unless the evaluation revealed reasons to impose less than the maximum sentence. *People v. Baker,* 526 N.E.2d 157 (Ill. 1988).

§2.0.1 Ignition-Interlock Devices

Page 85. Add after first full paragraph:

In *Cole v. Faulkner,* 573 S.E.2d 614 (N.C. Ct. App. 2002), a North Carolina court determined that the Division of Motor Vehicles did not have sufficient evidence to show a driver had operated a motor vehicle after consuming alcohol. This decision was rendered in spite of the fact that the ignition interlock showed positive alcohol readings on three different occasions, ranging from 0.02 to 0.11 percent. The driver in this case was resourceful enough to call a police officer to administer an Alco-Sensor test on one occasion to rebut the ignition interlock. The Alco-Sensor registered 0.00 percent. The inconsistency was explained by a technician for the manufacturer of the device as being "consistent with a fast-dissipating mouth contaminant." *Faulkner* at 618.

§2.0.2   Vehicle Impound or Forfeiture

Pages 85–87. Delete this section in its entirety and replace with:

§2.0.2   Vehicle Confiscation and Forfeiture

A number of states have enacted legislation permitting the confiscation and forfeiture of the vehicle used in the commission of a drunk driving offense. In particular, such legislation often pertains to multiple-offense drunk driving cases and related driving offenses committed by a defendant who has previously been convicted of one or more drunk driving offenses.

For example, in Florida, a motor vehicle driven by a person under the influence of alcohol or drugs in violation of Florida's DUI statute is subject to seizure and forfeiture if, at the time of the offense, the person's driver's license is suspended, revoked, or canceled as a result of a prior conviction for driving under the influence. Fla. Stat. Ann. §322.34 (9)(a).

In Tennessee, the vehicle operated by a defendant in the commission of a second or subsequent DUI offense is subject to seizure and forfeiture by the Tennessee Department of Safety. Tenn. Code Ann. §55-10-403(k). Similarly, the vehicle operated by a defendant who is driving with a suspended, revoked, or cancelled license is also subject to confiscation and forfeiture, provided that at the time of the offense the defendant's license was suspended or revoked as a result of a prior DUI conviction. Tenn. Code Ann. §55-50-504(h)(1).

In most jurisdictions, vehicle forfeiture legislation creates a civil administrative process that allows police agencies to confiscate and seek forfeiture of a defendant's vehicle in accordance with rules and procedures promulgated by the state's department of safety or its equivalent. As such, vehicle forfeiture is generally not a penalty that may be imposed by the sentencing court presiding over the DUI or other criminal proceedings.

Since vehicle forfeiture procedures often involve a separate administrative proceeding, a defendant may succeed in the DUI prosecution but lose his or her vehicle in the separate administrative proceeding. However, the DUI practitioner who also represents the client in a vehicle forfeiture action should not lose sight of the fact that often the same defenses may be raised in both proceedings. In addition, certain defenses may be available in the vehicle forfeiture action if the state failed to follow statutory requirements and/or department of safety rules and procedures relating to vehicle forfeiture actions. Counsel should consider requesting a stay of the administrative proceedings or advising the client to remain silent as discussed in more detail in §1.7.1.

What if the defendant is not the owner of the confiscated vehicle? This situation presents a common defense, but only when the "innocent" owner or co-owner was unaware the vehicle was being operated by an intoxicated driver. In this circumstance, the unknowing owner, such as a spouse or lending institution, may apply to have the vehicle returned, following the proper procedures. The owner should be aware, however, that this good-faith defense is rarely successful on a second or subsequent occasion.

In *United States v. Ursery*, 518 U.S. 267 (1996), the U.S. Supreme Court held that property forfeiture actions are generally civil in rem proceedings and do not impose punishment for the underlying criminal acts. Thus, the Court reasoned, the separate forfeiture proceeding of a house and other personal property under the federal drug forfeiture laws raised no double jeopardy concerns. In making this determination, the *Ursery* Court established a two-part test to determine whether a specific forfeiture statute amounts to punishment for double jeopardy purposes. First, a court must determine whether or not the legislative body intended the forfeiture proceedings to be criminal/punitive or civil/remedial. Next, the reviewing court must consider whether the party challenging the statute has shown by "the clearest proof" that the forfeiture is so punitive that it "may not legitimately be viewed as civil in nature." The *Ursery* Court further explained that a civil in rem forfeiture that has some punitive aspects will not necessarily violate double jeopardy protections if the forfeiture serves important non-punitive goals.

State appellate courts have generally followed *Ursery* in finding no double jeopardy violations under the reviewing state's own constitution, or the U.S. Constitution, as applied to that state's forfeiture laws. For example, in *Stuart v. State Dept. of Safety*, 963 S.W.2d 28 (Tenn. 1998), the Tennessee Supreme Court held Tennessee's forfeiture laws to be remedial civil in rem proceedings, and not punishment for criminal acts. Therefore, the court found no double jeopardy violations under the Tennessee state constitution or federal Constitution.

In *Davis v. Municipality of Anchorage*, 945 P.2d 307 (Alaska App. 1997), the Alaska Court of Appeals held that a municipal statute that permitted confiscation and forfeiture in a separate proceeding of a vehicle operated by an intoxicated driver, or any vehicle operated by a driver who refused to submit to a breath test, did not violate the double jeopardy clause of the Alaska state constitution, or the federal Constitution.

Although double jeopardy challenges have been foreclosed by the appellate courts, other constitutional challenges may prove successful in a forfeiture action. For instance, in *Austin v. United States*, 509 U.S. 602 (1993), the U.S. Supreme Court recognized that the Eighth Amendment prohibition against excessive fines is applicable to civil forfeiture proceedings, provided that the specific forfeiture is, at least in part, punitive. The *Austin* Court, however, did not announce an applicable test to determine whether a specific forfeiture action violates the excessive fines clause. In declining to do so, the majority opinion commented that prudence dictated that the Supreme Court allow the lower courts to first consider the issue.

In *Stuart v. Department of Safety*, the Tennessee Supreme Court found that while the subject forfeiture statute is not a criminal action for purposes of the double jeopardy clause, it is, at least in part, a punitive measure. As such, the court held, the excessive fines clause is applicable to these types of civil in rem forfeiture proceedings. Thus, the forfeiture may be defended on the grounds that the forfeiture action violates the excessive fines clause of the Eighth Amendment of the U.S. Constitution. In so holding, the Tennessee Supreme Court adopted a test that that includes a proportionality analysis that utilizes the following factors: (1) harshness of penalty compared with gravity of underlying offense; (2) harshness of penalty compared with culpability of claimant; and (3) relationship between property and offense, including whether use of property was (a) important to success of crime, (b) deliberate and planned or merely incidental and fortuitous, and (c) extensive in terms of time and spatial use.

The *Stuart* court explained that some jurisdictions might choose to apply an instrumentality test, while others may choose a stricter application of a proportionality test. An instrumentality test considers how closely related the property is to the under-lying offense. A strict proportionality test would compare the value of the forfeited property with the gravity of the criminal conduct. The *Stuart* court noted that the majority of jurisdictions reviewing the issue have adopted some form of a hybrid test incorporating aspects of both approaches.

On two occasions, the Tennessee Court of Criminal Appeals has found a forfeiture of a vehicle to be an excessive fine in viola-tion of the excessive fines clause of the U.S Constitution and the Tennessee constitution. See *Taylor v. Greene,* No. M1999-00594-COA-R3-CV (Tenn. Ct. App., Jan. 22, 2002) and *Hawks v. Greene,* No. M1999-02785-COA-R3-CV (Tenn. Ct. App., Dec. 18, 2001).

Applying a similar test adopted in Minnesota, in *Miller v. One 2001 Pontiac Aztek,* 669 N.W.2d 893 (Minn. 2003), the Minnesota Supreme Court held that the forfeiture of a vehicle worth approximately $16,000 from its owner, who had been twice con-victed of driving while impaired, did not amount to an excessive fine under either the federal or state constitution. In *Hawes v. 1997 Jeep Wrangler,* 602 N.W.2d 874 (Minn. App. 1999), in addi-tion to finding no double jeopardy or excessive fines violations, the Minnesota Court of Appeals held that the forfeiture of a vehi-cle owned by a DUI offender did not violate the equal protection clause of the state or federal constitutions.

This area of law continues to evolve as the constitutionality of these statutes is questioned. The DUI defense practitioner must be ever mindful of these laws and at the very least use these pro-ceedings as an additional discovery tool.

§2.0.3 Deportation Consequences

Page 87. Add after fourth full paragraph:

Not all courts have characterized DUI as a "crime of violence" or an aggravated felony under the United States sentencing guidelines. In *United States v. Lucio-Lucio,* 347 F.3d 1202, 1203 (10th Cir. 2003), the court noted that 18 U.S.C. §16 defines "crime of violence" as:

(a) an offense that has as an element the use, attempted use, or threatened use of physical force against the person or property of

another, or (b) any other offense that is a felony and that, by its
nature, involves a substantial risk that physical force against the
person or property of another may be used in the course of
committing the offense.

The *Lucio-Lucio* court found that a DUI offense clearly does
not satisfy §16(a). In considering whether a DUI offense satisfies
§16(b), the court recognized that a drunk driver typically does
not mean to cause an accident at all, and can hardly be said to
"commit" the resulting violence in the same way that a burglar does.

Although the drunk driver recklessly risks harming others, the risk
is not that this will happen intentionally (as in burglary). Rather, it
is that the impairment of the driver's faculties will result in
negligent driving, which in turn will result in an accident. Thus,
while burglary and DWI are similar in that they both recklessly
risk harm, they differ greatly in the character of the act that
immediately causes the harm. A burglar is reckless of the risk of
committing an intentional act of violence; a drunk driver is
reckless of the risk that he will accidentally cause harm. Whatever
the precise degree of intent necessary to separate violent conduct
from conduct that leads to harmful consequences, it seems plain
that DWI resulting in an accident — which, when it happens, is a
purely unintended result — falls into the latter category. Hence,
DWI is not within the ambit of §16(b).

Lucio-Lucio at 1206.

The *Lucio-Lucio* decision is confined to cases where the statutory offense does not involve actual injury to others. Further,
there is a distinction between §16(b) and U.S.S.G. §4.B.1.2(a)(2),
which in one respect more broadly defines the term "crime of
violence." Finally, the court also rejected the government's argument that repeat offenders, because they have special reason to
know of the dangers of DUI, are particularly reckless when they
commit the offense and therefore their conduct would be
included in the definition of a "crime of violence." In rejecting
the government's argument, the courts stated, "Whatever
increased awareness of risk accompanies prior convictions, it is
not so great that the risked injury becomes more in the nature of
intentional conduct than an unintended consequence." *Lucio-
Lucio* at 1208.

§2.1   Statutory Enhancements: Refusal, Speed, and Other Factors

Page 90. Add at end of section:

Of course, such judicial findings can only be made with the defendant's waiver of a jury determination of the sentence enhancing factors.

Most practitioners in the field of criminal defense are familiar with the case of *Apprendi v. New Jersey,* where the U.S. Supreme Court mandated that any fact, other than a prior conviction, which increases the penalty for a crime beyond the statutory maximum must be submitted to a jury and proved beyond a reasonable doubt. See *Apprendi v. New Jersey,* 530 U.S. 466, 488. In *Blakely v. Washington,* an extremely important case, the Supreme Court interpreted the phrase, "statutory maximum" for *Apprendi* purposes as the maximum sentence a judge may impose *"solely on the basis of the facts reflected in the jury verdict or admitted by the defendant." Blakely v. Washington,* No. 02-1632, *4, citing *Ring v. Arizona,* 536 U.S. 584, 602, (2002) (emphasis in original).

> In other words, the relevant "statutory maximum" is not the maximum sentence a judge may impose after finding additional facts, but the maximum he may impose *without* any additional findings. When a judge inflicts punishment that the jury's verdict alone does not allow, the jury has not found all the facts "which the law makes essential to the punishment," and the judge exceeds his proper authority.

Blakely at *4, citing J. Bishop, 1 Criminal Procedure §87, at 55 (2d ed. 1872).

As noted by Justice Scalia:

> This rule reflects two longstanding tenets of common-law criminal jurisprudence: that the "truth of every accusation" against a defendant "should afterwards be confirmed by the unanimous suffrage of twelve of his equals and neighbours," 4 W. Blackstone, Commentaries on the Laws of England 343 (1769), and that "an accusation which lacks any particular fact which the law makes essential to the punishment is . . . no

accusation within the requirements of the common law, and it is no accusation in reason."

Blakely at *4, quoting 4 W. Blackstone, Commentaries on the Laws of England 343 (1769).

In the *Blakely* case, the defendant was sentenced to more than three years above the 53-month statutory maximum of the standard range set forth by the State of Washington Sentencing Grid because he had acted with "deliberate cruelty." The facts supporting that finding were neither admitted by the defendant nor found by a jury. The prosecution argued no *Apprendi* violation occurred because the "statutory maximum" was not 53 months, but the ten-year maximum for a Class B felony. The Supreme Court held that a judge exceeds his proper authority when inflicting punishment that the jury's verdict alone does not allow, because the jury has not found all the facts "which the law makes essential to the punishment."*Blakely* at *4, citing J. Bishop, 1 Criminal Procedure §87, p. 55 (2d ed. 1872).

Justice Scalia characterized as unfair a judicial system in which a defendant, with no warning in either his indictment or plea, would routinely see his maximum potential sentence balloon based on facts extracted after trial from a probation officer's report. See *Blakely* at *8. In recognizing the fear of prosecutors that determinate sentencing schemes would be declared unconstitutional, the court acknowledged the *Blakely* decision was not about whether determinate sentencing is constitutional, but only about how it can be implemented in a way that respects the Sixth Amendment right to a jury trial. See *Blakely* at *7. The *Blakely* court further noted that in implementing plea agreements, nothing prevents a defendant from waiving his *Apprendi* rights. See *Blakely* at *8. In that circumstance, the prosecution is free to seek judicial sentence enhancements so long as the defendant either stipulates to the relevant facts or consents to judicial fact-finding. See *Blakely* at *8, citing *Apprendi*, 530 U.S. at 488; *Duncan v. Louisiana*, 391 U.S. 145, 158, (1968). Accordingly, if appropriate waivers are procured, the state may continue to offer judicial fact-finding as a matter of course to all defendants who plead guilty. See *Blakely* at *8. Even a defendant who stands trial may consent to judicial fact-finding as to sentence enhancements, which may be in the defendant's interest if relevant evidence would prejudice him at trial. See *Blakely* at *8.

The *Blakely* decision will apply to all criminal cases still pending on direct review. See *Blakely* at *16, citing *Schriro v. Summerlin*, No. 03-526 (2004)(holding analogous the decision in *Ring v. Arizona*, 536 U.S. 584 (2002), that a sentencing judge, sitting without a jury, may not find aggravating circumstance necessary for imposition of death penalty). A case released the same date as *Blakely*, *Schriro v. Summerlin*, No. 03-526 (2004), holds that when a decision of the Supreme Court results in a "new rule," that rule applies to all criminal cases still pending on direct review. See *Schriro* at *3, citing *Griffith v. Kentucky*, 479 U.S. 314, 328 (1987). As to convictions that are already final, however, the rule applies only in limited circumstances. See *Schriro* at *3. Thus, these new procedural rules are distinguished from new substantive rules, which generally apply retroactively. See *Schriro* at *3 (2004).

Of course, only time will allow the courts the opportunity to determine the full effect of this decision upon the criminal justice system. It is clear, though, that this decision will have an impact on the sentencing of defendants in both state and federal courts. See e.g. *United States v. Gonzalez*, No. 03 CR. 41(DAB) (S.D.N.Y. 2004); *United States v. Shamblin*, No. CRIM.A. 2:03-00217 (S.D. W. Va. 2004). In particular, it will be of great interest to observe how the courts provide for the sentencing of DUI defendants who have been sentenced to more than the mandatory minimum period of incarceration after the trial judge, without the intervention of a jury, finds enhancing factors to increase the defendant's sentence. At present, however, it appears a sentencing judge may commit error by sentencing any DUI defendant, misdemeanor or felony, to more than a mandatory minimum sentence without the intervention, or waiver, of a jury to determine any sentencing enhancement factors.

§2.1.0   Prior Convictions

Page 91. Add after carryover paragraph:

In states such as Alabama and Tennessee, where the trial is bifurcated so that the jury will not learn of a prior conviction until after a decision has been made on guilt or innocence in the case before them, counsel must be alert to any attempt by the prosecution to introduce otherwise inadmissible evidence of the defendant's prior offense. As was so colorfully summarized by the Alabama Supreme Court in *Ex parte Sparks*, 730 So. 2d 113, 115–16 (Ala. 1998):

> "[D]espite a corrective instruction, once such statements are made, the damage is hard to undo: "Otherwise stated, one 'cannot unring a bell'; 'after the thrust of the saber it is difficult to say forget the wound'; and finally, 'if you throw a skunk into the jury box, you can't instruct the jury not to smell it.'" *Dunn v. United States*, 307 F.2d 883, 886 (5th Cir.1962).'" *Quinlivan v. State*, 579 So. 2d 1386, 1389 (Ala. Crim. App.), *writ quashed*, 596 So. 2d 658 (Ala. 1991) (quoting *United States v. Garza*, 608 F.2d 659, 666 (5th Cir. 1979)).

Page 91. Replace first sentence of first full paragraph with:

In the states where the prior conviction will be presented to the jury, counsel will have to make a difficult decision.

§2.3 Multiple Punishment

Page 98. In second paragraph, replace citation for **Pennsylvania v. Hernandez** *with:*

488 A.2d 293 (Pa. 1985)

Page 98. Add at end of third paragraph:

Subsequently, the Alaska Supreme Court reversed, holding that a defendant could receive multiple sentences for injuring or killing more than one person while driving under the influence of alcohol. *Dunlop v. Alaska*, 721 P.2d 604 (Alaska 1986).

However, the Tennessee Court of Criminal Appeals has determined that a single course of conduct underlying reckless endangerment charges could support but one conviction. *State v. Ramsey*, 903 S.W.2d 709 (Tenn. Crim. App. 1995). In that case, the defendant had been convicted of three counts of reckless endangerment and one count of criminally negligent homicide, involving an automobile accident in which the defendant was speeding. The three reckless endangerment charges involved passengers in another vehicle that was close by but not physically involved in the collision. In reversing the multiple convictions, the court held that one act of reckless driving, however many people it may victimize, does not transform the single act into separate or multiple offenses. *State v. Ramsey,* 903 S.W.2d 709 (Tenn. Crim. App. 1995); see also *State v. Gilboy,* 857 S.W.2d 884 (Tenn. Crim. App. 1993) (holding that defendant could not be convicted of three separate offenses of reckless driving for one act of driving his truck into path of oncoming train, even though three train conductors were killed); but see *State v. Irvin,* 603 S.W.2d 121 (Tenn. 1980) (holding that multiple convictions for homicide could stand where more than one death resulted from single automobile accident).

3

THE ADMINISTRATIVE
LICENSE SUSPENSION

§3.0 *Implied Consent*

Page 106. Add after first full paragraph:

One constitutional requirement which still must be met before requiring a suspect to be subjected to a chemical test is probable cause to arrest or reasonable suspicion to believe the suspect was driving under the influence. The legislature cannot abrogate a person's right to be free from unreasonable searches and seizures as defined by the U.S. Supreme Court. See *Ybarra v. Illinois,* 444 U.S. 85, 96 (1979) (invalidating state statute authorizing searches without probable cause or warrant and noting that Supreme Court will not hesitate to hold such statutes unconstitutional). As the Indiana Court of Appeals noted, "[t]o hold that the legislature could nonetheless pass laws stating that a person 'again impliedly' consents to searches under certain circumstances where a search would otherwise be unlawful would be to condone an unconstitutional bypassing of the Fourth Amendment. *Hannoy v. State,* 789 N.E.2d 977, 987 (Ind. Ct. App. 2003)."

This situation often occurs in automobile accidents where officers require a blood sample to be taken even though they have never seen the suspect operating a motor vehicle or subjected the suspect to field sobriety tests. As the Georgia Supreme Court has stated, "[t]o the extent that [the implied consent statute] requires chemical testing of the operator of a motor vehicle involved in a traffic accident resulting in serious injuries or fatalities regardless of any determination of probable cause, it authorizes unreasonable searches and seizures in violation of the state and federal constitutions." *Cooper v. State,* 587 S.E.2d 605, 612 (Ga. 2003).

Page 113. Add new subsection before first paragraph:

§3.0.1 Double Jeopardy: Criminal and Administrative Punishment

The Ninth Circuit of the U.S. Court of Appeals has applied the reasoning in *Hudson* to an Alaskan drunk driving case. In holding that a driver's license suspension did not bar subsequent criminal charges arising out of the same incident, the court listed the following reasons for finding that an administrative suspension was only a civil rather than a criminal sanction:

1. License suspensions do not involve an affirmative disability or restraint. A driver's license is a privilege granted by the state, so license revocation is the loss of a privilege. It is immaterial that loss of the ability to drive may severely impact some individuals.
2. License suspensions have not historically been regarded as punishment.
3. A side effect of the suspension scheme may be deterrence, but that does not make the scheme criminal rather than civil.
4. The remedial purpose of license revocation is to protect the public and, in the case of chemical tests, to obtain reliable evidence of intoxication.
5. The length of the suspension in this case (90 days) was not excessive in relation to the remedial purpose.

Rivera v. Pugh, 194 F.3d 1064 (9th Cir. 1999).

Page 113. Add after first paragraph:

In any event, it appears that the argument that a forfeiture action in separate administrative proceedings from a criminal prosecution has been eliminated by the United States Supreme Court's decision in *United States v. Ursery,* 518 U.S. 267 (1996). In *Ursery,* the Supreme Court held that such proceedings are generally civil in rem proceedings and do not constitute punishment within the protections of the Double Jeopardy Clause. Nevertheless, the defense practitioner should carefully review the circumstances of a particular forfeiture to determine if the forfeiture violates the constitutional protection against excessive fines.

Page 113. Add new subsection after first paragraph:

§3.0.2 Due Process and the Administrative License Suspension

As any experienced DUI attorney knows, the administrative license suspension represents all that is wrong with a legal system that increasingly chooses to ignore constitutional safeguards. Aside from the issue of double jeopardy (see §3.0.1), the rules and procedures established for contesting an ALS represent a steadily deteriorating standard of due process generally. This is certainly due in large measure to legislators anxious to please voters and to such pressure groups as Mothers Against Drunk Driving, but it is also caused by legally ignorant bureaucrats staffing the state's department of motor vehicles. It is counsel's job to educate these officials and, where they will not be educated, to seek redress in court for denial of due process at the administrative level.

The following material was presented by attorney Les Hulnick of Wichita, Kansas, at the National College for DUI Defense's 1999 Summer Session at Harvard Law School.* It should provide counsel with an excellent overview of due process issues commonly encountered in the course of representing a client in a license suspension hearing.

I. Introduction

One unifying characteristic of the civil component of DUI charge—the administrative hearing or implied consent hearing—across the country is that it is an unusual, hybrid procedure in which constitutional safeguards often seem to be cast aside in the name of political expediency, efficiency, and public safety. For example, the hearing officer routinely functions as both the judge and prosecutor, time deadlines (for the

*Reprinted with permission.

Government) often seem to be fluid and unenforced, and the notion of discovery for the citizen frequently seems to be regarded as a mere annoyance. Constitutional protections, however, do apply to these proceedings and, as a result, challenges based on due process, fundamental fairness, and other constitutional concepts may be successfully lodged. This is not to suggest that successful challenges to the procedures are frequent or common, but they are possible and can have a tremendous impact on a large number of accused persons.

This outline will set forth some of the basic concepts which may support a constitutional challenge to the proceedings and detail some of the areas in which the constitutionality of the administrative proceedings recently has been challenged. This is not intended to be an exhaustive review of all possible constitutional issues inherent in administrative suspension proceedings, but rather is intended to spark some ideas which may lead to a challenge of the proceedings in your jurisdiction.

II.   Guiding Principle: constitutional guarantees apply

No state shall make or enforce any law which shall abridge the privilege or immunities of citizens of the United States; nor shall any State deprive any person of life, liberty, or property without due process of law; nor deny to any person within its jurisdiction the equal protection of the laws.
— FOURTEENTH AMENDMENT OF THE UNITED STATES CONSTITUTION

There can be no doubt that the suspension of a driver's license constitutes the deprivation of a constitutionally protected property interest, thus invoking the requirements of due process. In *Bell v. Burson*, 402 U.S. 535, 539, 91 S. Ct. 1586, 29 L. Ed. 2d 90 (1971), a motorist challenged Georgia's requirement that uninsured motorists involved in an accident pay a security deposit in the amount of the damages claimed or have their driver's licenses suspended. The motorist, who happened to be a minister, argued that his due process rights were violated under the statute because he had no opportunity for a hearing on the issue of liability prior to the suspension of his license.

The United States Supreme Court held that once driver's licenses are issued "their continued possession may become essential in the pursuit of a livelihood." Because of their value, the Court held they "are not to be taken away without that procedural due process required by the Fourteenth Amendment." *Bell,* 29 L. Ed. 2d at 94.

In determining what process was due, the Court noted that different situations require different levels of due process. Due process, it held, does not automatically require a full adjudicatory hearing. The Court addressed the due process requirements under the statutory scheme being challenged, but left the particulars of meeting the limited hearing requirements to the individual states. This, then, becomes the focus of Fourteenth Amendment challenges to administrative suspension proceedings.

A few years later, the United States Supreme Court was faced with the issue of whether a statute that required suspension of a driver's license for refusal to submit to a breath test violated the due process clause of the Fourteenth Amendment. *Mackey v. Montrym,* 443 U.S. 1, 99 S. Ct. 2612, 61 L. Ed. 2d 321 (1979). Under the law, the driver could have received an immediate hearing after surrendering his license, though none was requested. The Supreme Court noted that because a driver's license was a "protectable property interest," the only issue left was to decide how much process was due.

In so doing, the Court looked back to the test established in *Mathews v. Eldridge,* 424 U.S. 319, 96 S. Ct. 893, 47 L. Ed. 2d 18 (1976). Those factors are: (1) the private interest that will be affected by the official action; (2) the risk of an erroneous deprivation of such interest through the procedures used; and (3) the Government's interest, including the function involved and the fiscal and administrative burdens, that the additional or substitute procedural requirement would entail." *Mathews,* 47 L. Ed. 2d at 33.

The court examined these factors through a balancing test and found that although the motorist's interest in his driver's license was substantial, the State's interest in highway safety justified the summary suspension of privileges, pending the result of a post-supension hearing. It emphasized that under this statutory scheme, motorists had a right to a "same day" hearing on the matter. After balancing the factors, the Court upheld the constitutionality of the implied consent statute.

In these types of cases, the private interest is the license to operate the vehicle. "[T]hat interest is a substantial one, for the Commonwealth will not be able to make a driver whole for any personal inconvenience and any economic hardship suffered by reason of any delay in redressing an erroneous suspension through post-suspension review procedures." *Mackey*, 433 U.S. at 11. The Court, however, found that the risk is not so great so as to automatically render an automatic suspension proceeding, which is followed by a fair hearing, unconstitutional.

The factor involving the risk or erroneous deprivation is analyzed depending on whether a full hearing, after automatic suspension, is available. If so, the Court has found that the risk of error inherent in the suspension procedure is not so substantial to require an evidentiary hearing. "[E]ven though our legal tradition regards the adversary process as the best means of ascertaining truth and minimizing the risk of error, the 'ordinary principle' established by our prior decisions is that 'something less than an evidentiary hearing is sufficient prior to adverse administrative action.'" *Mackey*, 443 U.S. at 13.

Finally, the Government's interest is viewed in terms of highway safety. The Court found that the summary suspension procedure in Massachusetts served substantial public interests because it acted as a deterrent to drunk driving, it provided an inducement to take the breath analysis test, and it summarily removed from the road licensees arrested for drunk driving who refused to submit to the test. "A state has the right to offer incentives for taking the breath-analysis test and, in exercising its police powers, is not required by the Due Process Clause to adopt an all or nothing approach to the acute safety hazard posed by drunk drivers." *Mackey*, 99 S. Ct. at 2620–21.

Following these Supreme Court decisions, most state challenges to the administrative hearings regarding suspension of driving privileges have focused on whether the challenged procedure was similar enough to the procedures previously examined by the Supreme Court to warrant upholding the statutory scheme. The key elements that have emerged necessary for administrative proceedings to be upheld are: (1) an arrest; (2) a sworn report of the officer who requested the chemical test; (3) a hearing if requested by the motorist; and (4) a temporary license until the hearing is provided.

To effectively challenge an implied consent hearing procedure, counsel should examine the state statutory procedures to determine whether motorists are provided these elements, as well as provided a meaningful, fair suspension hearing.

III. Applications

A. DELAYED HEARING AS DENIAL OF DUE PROCESS

Most of the suspension statutes contain time limitations during which the suspension hearing, if requested, is to be held. Although the language of these statutes often sounds mandatory — and jurisdictional — courts often find that they are directory and that the State's failure to hold the hearing in a timely manner does not violate the motorist's rights.

For example, in *Texas Dept. of Public Safety v. Vela,* 980 S.W.2d 672 (Tex. App. 1998), the court held that although the legislature probably intended for the suspension hearing to be held within 40 days, this time requirement was directory rather than mandatory. The court noted that every effort should be made to hold the hearing within the statutory 40 days, but that the time could be extended, for good cause shown.

When a "good cause" loophole exists for the State, however, defense counsel should be diligent in making sure that the State meets this standard of excuse. For example, under a statutory scheme where a hearing must be held within a specified number of days unless "good cause" is shown for a continuance, the licensee may be entitled to cross-examine the person claiming that "good cause" existed.

This was the situation in *Miller v. Tanaka,* 80 Hawaii 358, 910 P.2d 129 (Hawaii App. 1995), *cert. denied,* 80 Hawaii 357, 910 P.2d 128 (1996). The hearing was supposed to be held within 25 days of the mailing of the suspension notice. It was scheduled for day 23 but the hearing officer continued the hearing until day 43. In so doing, he marked on a pre-printed continuance form that the "good cause" was the unavailability of the hearing officer because of illnesss/family emergency. The licensee sought to subpoena the person granting the continuance in order to challenge whether other hearing officers were available, what the other schedules were like for the rest of the day and the rest of the week, etc. The appellate court found that the refusal to issue this subpoena — in order to determine whether the hearing was held in a timely manner — deprived the licensee of his due process rights.

Another example of holding the State to its time deadlines is *Higgins v. Motor Vehicles Division,* 139 Or. App. 314, 911 P.2d 950 (1996). In *Higgins,* the hearing was continued beyond the specified time because the officer certified that he had an official duty conflict. This type of conflict was statutorily defined as arising when, for example, an officer had "priority training." The officer in this case had only certified that he was in training — not in "priority training" and so, the court held, there was not an adequate basis for delaying the hearing past the statutory 30 days.

Another key to increasing the chances of success in arguments based on delay of proceedings is to be able to demonstrate how the licensee was harmed by the delay in the hearing. Creativity (and the facts) are the only limits on this argument. Here are some ways in which drivers are sometimes prejudiced by the seizure of that little plastic rectangle, even if they have temporary driving privileges:

- Unable to rent a car
- Unable to satisfy photo ID requirements needed to board an airplane
- Unable to enter any federal enclave
- Unable to cash a check
- Unable to satisfy document requirements for some employment
- Unable to obtain auto insurance
- Unable to apply for bank loan

B.   LIMITATION OF ISSUES AT HEARING

Most state administrative suspension statutes limit the issues which may be raised or addressed at the administrative hearing. These limitations may provide the basis for a challenge based on due process. In *Javed v. Department of Public Safety,* 921 P.2d 620 (Alaska 1996), the motorist challenged the ruling of the hearing officer that prohibited him from presenting evidence that he had not been driving the vehicle. The hearing officer barred this evidence because it did not fall within one of the issues set forth in the statute: whether the officer had reasonable grounds to believe that the accused was operating the vehicle.

The Alaska court held that the limiting language in the statute denied the driver of a meaningful hearing because the issue of whether he was driving is of central importance. In arriving at this decision, the court noted that in determining whether there has been a meaningful hearing, the court must be guided by considerations of fundamental fairness. *Id.* at 266. "It is hard to imagine an issue of more 'central importance' to a driver's license revocation hearing than whether the person accused of DWI was driving a vehicle in the first place." *Id.* at 623. "Due process requires that an arrestee who fails a breath test must be afforded the opportunity at an administrative revocation hearing to present evidence that he was not driving in order to make that hearing meaningful and fundamentally fair." *Id.* at 624. The court ultimately held that because of the limiting language, the statute was unconstitutional.

C.   RIGHT OF CROSS-EXAMINATION

Many states have administrative proceedings at which the arresting officer is not required to appear and the hearing officer simply relies on his written — sworn or unsworn — report. This has been an area in which due process challenges have been frequent and have had a measure of success — particularly when cross-examination has been limited. The courts still tend to find that hearsay statements — particularly in sworn statements — are sufficient and not violative of due process, so long as the accused has the right to subpoena the law enforcement officers involved.

For example, in *Department of Revenue and Taxation v. Hull*, 751 P.2d 351 (Wyo. 1988), the court found that although the arresting officer's implied consent form may be admitted as an exception to the hearsay rule and can be used as dispositive evidence, due process is satisfied if the hearing officer affords the driver an opportunity to secure the attendance of the police officer.

Similarly, in *Carson v. Division of Vehicles, Kansas Department of Revenue*, 237 Kan. 166, 699 P.2d 447 (1985), the Kansas Supreme

Court held that the challenged license suspensions were void as violations of due process because the affidavits relied upon contained only the officer's conclusions, but did not contain facts showing the arresting officer had reasonable grounds under the Fourth Amendment to believe that prior to arrest, the drivers were operating the vehicles under the influence of alcohol. The court held that although the State could proceed on the sworn affidavits, it had to include sufficient facts for the hearing officer to make a determination of whether the facts supported a finding of reasonable grounds.

Further, the court emphasized that the accused had a right to request that subpoenas be issued for the officers. "We recognize that to require the officer's presence at every hearing would not only be an unreasonable expense to the taxpayers, but, in many cases, would be totally unnecessary and an unreasonable burden upon both law enforcement officials and the KDR. . . . Of course, if the licensee requests the presence of the officer, or any other relevant witness, subpoenas are required to be issued for them." *Id.* at 454–455.

Some courts have found, however, that reliance on even sworn reports does not comport with due process. For example in *Thomas v. Fiedler*, 700 F. Supp. 1527 (E.D. Wis. 1988), the hearing officer relied on the sworn report of the arresting officer. The hearing officer would review the reports for the presence of evidence on each of six statutory factors that could be raised and then would accept the police report "as the true recitation of events and continue the suspension." *Fiedler,* 700 F. Supp. at 1538. This, along with other procedural irregularities, led to a finding of a denial of due process.

Despite the seemingly obvious denial of due process attendant with proceeding on written reports, some jurisdictions have found this to be acceptable. See, e.g., *Brouillette v. Department of Public Safety,* 589 So. 2d 529 (La. App. 1991) (hearsay evidence is acceptable so long as it possesses probative value commonly accepted by reasonably prudent men in the conduct of their affairs); *Gray v. Adduci,* 73 N.Y.2d 741, 532 N.E.2d 1268 (N.Y. 1988) (hearsay evidence may be basis of an administrative license revocation); *Department of Revenue and Taxation v. Hull,* 751 P.2d 351 (Wyo. 1988) (police implied consent form is an exception to the hearsay rule because it is a public record and thus may be introduced in evidence at administrative hearing).

Even in jurisdictions in which it is acceptable to proceed on written documents, however, care should be taken to be certain that the reports strictly comply with any and all statutory or regulatory requirements. Any failure to comply should be vigorously challenged. This was done with great success in *Shea v. Department of Motor Vehicles*, 62 Cal. App. 4th 1057, 72 Cal. Rptr. 2d 896 (Cal. App. 4 Dist. 1998). There, forensic alcohol reports were allowed into evidence, as official records of the DMV. These reports fell within a hearsay exception for reports prepared by public employees within the scope of their employment duties. The forensic reports in question were signed by forensic alcohol analyst trainees. The court found that trainees, who were required to be supervised, could not conduct the tests in scope of their employment. In addition, the court found it to be a material misrepresentation, that these trainees signed the reports as analysts, when in fact they were trainees. This was an additional reason to not allow the reports to be admitted. "[A]s Lord Light, the fictional English judge created by A.P. Herbert put it in *Rex v. Haddock*, 'it is like the thirteenth stroke of a crazy clock, which not only is itself discredited but casts a shade of doubt over all previous assertions.'" *Id.* at 898, quoting Herbert, *Uncommon Law* (Eyre Methuen Ltd. 1978, p.28).

In addition to the issue of reliance on reports, the accused should also be allowed to cross-examine the officer on any relevant issue. Failure to allow vigorous cross-examination results in a denial of due process. For example, in *Coracci v. Commissioner of Motor Vehicles*, 42 Conn. Super. 599, 634 A.2d 924 (Conn. Super. 1993), the court found that the hearing officer's failure to allow the motorist's attorney to question an officer about the repair and certification records of the Intoximeter 3000 used to test his client denied the defendant due process. The court noted that the condition of the testing device was highly relevant to the issues at hand and that to deny counsel the chance to question the reliability of the tests performed on him was a denial of due process.

Likewise, in *Barcott v. State Department of Public Safety*, 741 P.2d 226 (Alaska 1987), the motorist was prohibited, at the suspension hearing, from offering any evidence concerning the margin of error inherent in the breath testing procedure. The court held that the accused in a license revocation proceeding has the constitutionally guaranteed right to challenge the accuracy of the breath test independently. "We have thus concluded that due process will not allow the results of a chemical test . . . to be conclusively presumed accurate." *Id.* at 230.

D.   Right to issue subpoenas/discovery

As noted above, courts have "expanded" what type of evidence is allowed in the administrative hearing by consoling the accused with assurances that he can subpoena the officer if he wished to contest the contents of the report. It is critical, then, for counsel to fully exercise this right — as it is one of the few positions of power available during the administrative process. Being able to cross-examine the officer at the administrative hearing — which most generally occurs before the officer has "consulted" with the prosecuting attorney — can produce a wealth of information and should not be a missed opportunity.

The courts have generally found that the right to cross-examine witnesses — and thus subpoena them — exists even in the administrative forum. For example, in *Thomas v. Fielder*, 700 F. Supp. 1527 (E.D. Wis. 1988), the court discussed a number of challenges to the administrative hearings under an implied consent statute. One of the factors noted by the court was that the agency's regulation prohibited the arresting officer from being subpoenaed. The court found that not allowing such a subpoena to issue — along with other problems in the statutory scheme — violated due process.

In addition, if a licensee has a regulatory or statutory right to request that subpoenas be issued, and attempts to do so, but none is issued, this violates his due process rights. In *Nye v. Department of Revenue*, 902 P.2d 959 (Colo. App. 1995), the court held that because the department had ignored the motorist's request for subpoenas, his due process rights had been violated. The court noted that cross-examination is a fundamental right, even in administrative proceedings, and found that regardless of the driver's likelihood of success at the hearing, he was entitled to have the witnesses subpoenaed to the hearing. *Id.* at 961–62.

Similarly, in *Miller v. Tanaka*, 80 Hawaii 358, 910 P.2d 129 (Hawaii App. 1995), *cert. denied*, 80 Hawaii 357, 910 P.2d 128 (Hawaii 1996), the court held that the failure of the department to issue the subpoenas requested by the licensee was an abuse of discretion, denying the licensee of his due process rights. But, it is important to exercise this right — or it is lost. For example, in *People v. Johnson*, 186 Ill. App. 3d 951, 542 N.E.2d 1226 (1989), the court held that because the accused had failed to exercise his right to subpoena the officers, the case could proceed on only the sworn reports of the officers, when the officers did not voluntarily appear at the hearing.

Discovery of "things" — reports, videotapes, etc. — are also an important function of the administrative hearing that should be covered by due process concepts. For example, the Alaska Supreme Court found that the State had the duty to preserve a videotape of the accused performing field sobriety tests so that the licensee could contest, at the revocation hearing, whether the officer had reasonable grounds to believe he was under the influence of alcohol. *Thorne v. Department of Public Safety*, 774 P.2d 1326, 1329 (Alaska 1989). The court noted that the accused at a revocation hearing "must be granted the opportunity to fully contest issues of central importance of the revocation decision." *Id.* at 1331.

Even if other discovery methods are blocked in the administrative hearing proceedings, counsel may try to obtain useful information through the State's Open Records Act or the Freedom of Information Act (FOIA)....

E.   RIGHT TO COUNSEL

Generally, there is no right to counsel, appointed or retained, in a civil proceeding. Because revocation proceedings are based on the same set of facts as criminal proceedings, however, the two proceedings are closely linked; therefore, arguably, the criminal right to appointed counsel should attach to the civil administrative proceedings. Because the United States Supreme Court has held that the criminal right to counsel attaches only in criminal proceedings that can lead to actual imprisonment, any claim to counsel must be framed in terms of the argument that the proceeding is sufficiently analogous to, and intertwined with, the criminal DUI charge, that the appointment of counsel is warranted.

In *Friedman v. Commissioner of Public Safety*, 473 N.W.2d 828 (Minn. 1991), the court recognized a motorist's limited state constitutional right to counsel before chemical testing. The driver's license was revoked for refusal to submit to testing, and on appeal she challenged the revocation on the theory that she was denied her right to counsel prior to the testing. The court interpreted the Minnesota constitution as providing a limited right to counsel that attaches once an officer asks a motorist to submit to testing.

Most courts have rejected right to counsel arguments and have applied the rule that there is no right to counsel, appointed or otherwise, in civil proceedings. For example, in *People v. Golden*, 117 Ill. App. 3d 150, 453 N.E.2d 15 (Ill. App. 1983), the motorist argued that the administrative suspension hearing was a critical stage in the drinking/driving proceedings because the issues and evidence in both the civil and criminal proceedings were sufficiently similar to make the implied consent hearing a critical stage. The motorist further complained that an unrepresented motorist could make incriminating statements at the administrative hearing that might later be introduced at the criminal proceeding.

All of these arguments were rejected by the court. It held that the implied consent hearing is independent from the criminal prosecution and noted the differences in the two proceedings, including the issues addressed and the burdens of proof. It also rejected the claim that the motorist could be prejudiced in the criminal proceedings by findings in the civil proceedings. The court also dismissed the argument that counsel should be appointed because incriminating statements might be made, finding that acceptance of this argument would result in the necessity of appointing counsel in any matter concerning an indigent person. Although these challenges have not met with great success, the argument still exists. Noted DUI defense experts and authors Flem Whited and Donald Nichols include the following points to consider, raise, and argue, in their treatise, *Drinking/Driving Litigation Criminal and*

Civil (2d ed. §11.6):

(1) Can a public defender protect a defendant's rights if the implied consent proceedings are held prior to the final adjudication of the criminal case?

(2) In states that have recognized the right to counsel prior to the election of a test, does a person have the right to a public defender before making the election?

(3) Does the "civil" label attached to the implied consent proceedings realistically reflect the quasi-criminal nature of the implied consent statute?

(4) Does effective assistance of counsel require a public defender to use the implied consent procedure to prepare the drinking/driving case?

(5) Can a public defender advise a defendant with regard to the defendant's rights in the implied consent hearing? Furthermore, does the public defender have a duty to explain the complex interrelationship between the implied consent law and the drinking/driving law?

F. FAIRNESS OF HEARING OFFICER

A possible challenge to the administrative implied consent proceedings may be based on the separations of functions argument. Routinely, hearing officers work for the same agency which is seeking to suspend the accused's driver's license. Clearly established law requires that an impartial decisionmaker is essential to an administrative adjudication that comports with due process, even if *de novo* review is available. See, e.g., *Withrow v. Larkin,* 421 U.S. 35, 95 S. Ct. 1456, 43 L. Ed. 2d 712 (1975); *Gibson v. Berryhill,* 411 U.S. 564, 93 S. Ct. 1689, 36 L. Ed. 2d 488 (1973); *Butler v. Department of Public Safety & Corr.,* 609 So. 2d 790 (La. 1992).

The Louisiana Supreme Court rejected such a challenge in *Butler,* but it should be noted that under that statutory scheme, the State Administrative Procedures Act attempted to prevent partiality or bias in adjudicative settings by prohibiting *ex parte* consultations and requiring recusal of subordinate deciding officers or agency members from proceedings in which they could not afford a fair and impartial hearing. In so doing, the Louisiana court noted that the United States Supreme Court has placed the burden on the party challenging the constitutionally of an administrative adjudication for bias to overcome the strong presumption of honesty and integrity in those serving as hearing officers. "That party must present convincing evidence that the combination of functions in the same individuals poses such a risk of actual and substantial bias or prejudgment that the practice must be forbidden if the guarantee of due process is to be preserved." *Id.* at 793.

The Louisiana court identified five possible kinds of "bias" calling the decisionmaker's impartiality into question: (1) a prejudgment or point of view about a question of law or policy; (2) a prejudgment about legislative facts that help answer a question of law or policy; (3) advance knowledge of adjudicative facts that are in issue; (4) a personal bias or personal prejudice — an attitude towards a person, as distinguished from an attitude about an issue; and (5) one who stands to gain or lose by a decison either way or a conflict of interest. *Id.* at 794–795. See also, *Department of Highway Safety v. Stewart*, 625 So. 2d 123 (Fla. App. 5 Dist. 1933) (fact that hearing offices are fellow employees of highway patrol troopers does not result in an inherently unfair or unconstitutional hearing).

Thus, although a combination of functions is not a due process violation, per se, this argument still does exist when there is evidence — perhaps statistical or anecdotal — to overcome the presumption of propriety. Be creative when looking for evidence of bias: Has the hearing officer received an award from a local MADD chapter as a champion of victims' rights? Does he attend training sessions put on by law enforcement agencies? Consider using your state's Open Records Act or FOIA to obtain copies of attendance lists of those participating in law enforcement sponsored seminars. . . .

G. Non-Attorney as Hearing Officer

In some jurisdictions, the hearing officer is not required to be a licensed attorney. Does it deny the motorist of his due process rights if the person adjudicating the merits of legal motions and arguments has not been trained in the law?

In *Tremain v. State*, 343 So. 2d 819 (Fla. 1977), the court addressed the issue of whether it violated due process protections to have a non-lawyer judge presiding in a misdemeanor case. The motorist argued that the expertise of the professional attorney is wasted if his forensic challenges are directed toward a judge "who has no more educational background to absorb and apppreciate such arguments than any spectators in the courtroom gallery." The court agreed, in theory, saying: "[I]t is clear that a judge who is ignorant of the law cannot afford due process of law to an individual facing imprisonment upon conviction." *Id.* at 823. It went on, however, to find that if the hearing officer successfully completed the state's system for training non-lawyer judges, that would be sufficient to satisfy due process.

IV. Conclusion

There can be no doubt of the devastating impact that a suspension of driving privileges can have on a client's family, financial situation, community involvement, and recreation. As Justice Stewart said in his dissent in *Mackey,* "Even a day's loss of a driver's license can inflict grave injury upon a person who depends upon an automobile for continued employment in his job." 443 U.S. at 30. Although constitutional challenges to the administrative suspension proceedings are an uphill battle, because of the dire consequences of suspension hearings, they are worth considering, evaluating, and developing.

---

§3.1.2 Collateral Estoppel

Page 122. Add at end of second paragraph:

In denying review, the California Supreme Court ordered that the *Gonzalez* opinion not be officially published.

Pages 124–125. Delete last (carryover) paragraph.

Page 125. Replace first full paragraph with:

In *State v. Summers,* 528 S.E.2d 17 (2000), an administrative finding that there was no refusal to submit to chemical testing was held to be binding upon the trial court. The district attorney prosecuting the criminal matter was found to have an interest in common with the attorney general prosecuting at the license suspension hearing—and was therefore estopped from relitigating the issue.

§3.2 The "Per Se" Suspension (.08 or .10 percent)

Page 127. Add at end of first full paragraph:

Subsequently, the Oregon Supreme Court overruled the intermediate appellate court, holding that the accuracy of the chemical breath test results may not be challenged or impeached if the person who administered the test was qualified to administer it, and if the methods, procedures, and equipment used during the test complied with applicable statutory requirements. *Owens v. Motor Vehicles Division*, 875 P.2d 463 (Or. 1994).

§3.2.2 Proof of Driving

Page 129. Add at end of first full paragraph:

However, the appellate court's holding was later rejected in *State v. Wright*, 527 A.2d 379 (N.J. 1987). In that case, the New Jersey Supreme Court held that proof of actual operation is not required to convict a defendant for refusing to submit to a breathalyzer test.

§3.3 The Refusal Suspension

§3.3.1 What Constitutes a "Refusal"

Page 137. Add at end of first full paragraph:

In denying review, the California Supreme Court ordered that the *Hart* opinion not be officially published.

§3.3.2 The Defective Implied Consent Advisement

Page 141. Replace second and third full paragraphs with:

Counsel should carefully consider the exact language used by the officer in his advisement of the state's implied consent provisions, particularly the language that warns the suspect what the ramifications will be for refusal to comply with testing. As an example of an incomplete advisement, see *Buchanan v. Registrar,* 619 N.E.2d 523 (Ohio App. 1993). In that case, the motorist signed a written form advising him under the state's implied consent provisions that his license would be suspended if he refused to submit to blood-alcohol testing; he afterwards refused. On appeal from the resulting suspension, he contended that the form was not complete: It omitted the fact that in order to obtain the return of the license after the suspension period was over, it was necessary to pay a license reinstatement fee and file proof of financial responsibility. The appellate court agreed and ordered the suspension reversed.

Page 142. Replace second sentence of second paragraph with:

The Supreme Court of Washington was confronted with the question of whether warnings stating that evidence of a refusal "shall" or "may" be used against them were so misleading that the suspects were deprived of an opportunity to make an intelligent choice.

§3.3.3   Confusion: Implied Consent, *Miranda,* and the Right to Counsel

Page 148. In first sentence of second paragraph, replace citation for Write v. State *with:*

703 S.W.2d 850 (Ark. 1986)

§3.3.4   Inability to Provide Sample or Understand Advisement

Page 152. Add at end of third full paragraph:

Another important factor to consider is the device's required flow rate of breath over time. Comparing this ratio with other devices may reveal a substantial difference, which would provide the necessary objective proof to the court to dismiss the refusal charge.

Page 152. Add after fourth full paragraph:

Some states provide by statute that if the person is physically unable to submit to the breath test, a blood test must be given. See, e.g., Va. Code Ann. §18.2-268.2(B). At least in Virginia, if the accused sufficiently carries the burden of establishing a physical inability to blow into a breath test device, and further that a blood test is not offered, then the charge must be dismissed. *Lamay v. Commonwealth,* 513 S.E.2d, 411, 418 (Va. Ct. App. 1999).

§3.3.5   Attempts to "Cure" a Refusal

Page 158. Add new section after end of subsection 3.3.5:

§3.4   The FAA and Pilot License Suspensions

Counsel may well encounter the client who is a pilot and for whom the loss of his pilot's license presents greater concern than the loss of his driver's license and/or criminal conviction. For a commercial pilot, it may well represent the end of a rewarding career — at least, if improperly handled by an attorney not familiar with Federal Aviation Administration regulations and procedures. It may also represent potential grounds for a legal malpractice action. The following material will give the DUI practitioner sufficient information to at least be aware of some of the pitfalls in advising or representing a pilot who has been arrested for drunk driving.

The following information regarding the ramifications of pilots charged with DUI related offenses is reproduced in part from the article, *Alcohol Prohibitions for Pilots and Flight Instructors,* Air Line Pilot 26 (Apr. 2003), with the permission of the author, Suzanne Kalfus, Esq., and the publisher, Air Line Pilots Association.

Airline pilots must know and abide by the current regulations governing alcohol use. As a result of certain high-profile cases, *the*

FAA is now taking emergency revocation action against pilots' airman certificates when alcohol test results are reported above the legal limits or when pilots are believed to have violated other alcohol prohibitions. Clearly, this is the most serious penalty the FAA can impose and one with grave ramifications for the affected pilot. Revocation of an airman certificate remains a permanent part of the pilot's FAA file.

A pilot whose airman certificate has been revoked may not reapply for one for a full year. The FAA requires the pilot to re-take and pass all of the tests required for each certificate and rating.

Given the gravity of the sanction a pilot may face if the FAA finds an alcohol (or drug-related) violation, understanding and complying with the applicable regulations is vital.

FAR addressing *driving a motor vehicle while impaired* Section 61:15 requires pilots who have a "motor vehicle action" to report it to the FAA's Security Division within 60 days of the date of the action.

A "motor vehicle action" includes a conviction for operating a motor vehicle while intoxicated, impaired, or under the influence of either alcohol or a drug. A "motor vehicle action" also includes an action in which a pilot's license to operate a motor vehicle is cancelled, suspended, or revoked (or his or her application for such a license is denied) for a cause related to operating the motor vehicle while intoxicated, impaired, or under the influence.

This means that a pilot may have a reportable incident *even if never charged or convicted* if his or her driver's license or driving privileges have been adversely affected. In some states, an individual who is asked to submit to alcohol testing but refuses is subject to automatic suspension of driving privileges. The suspension may be contained in the paperwork the person is given. At times, an individual who is stopped in a state other than the one in which his or her driver's license is issued may not even be aware that the state in which he or she was stopped suspended driving privileges and *reported that suspension to the National Drivers' Registry (NDR).*

The FAA monitors pilots' compliance with their reporting obligations by searching the NDR.

Motor vehicle actions, also, are more broadly defined for purposes of answering the questions on the medical application (Form 8500) and include actions that resulted in a course of counseling or educational program even if no conviction occurred.

The failure to properly report a motor vehicle action, either by not writing to the FAA's Security Branch or by not answering the applicable question correctly on the medical application, can result in FAA investigation and certificate action. A single motor vehicle action (i.e., a DUI) that is properly reported — without more — is not the basis for certificate action by the FAA. However, two such actions within a 3-year period can result in certificate action.

You should also be aware that a pilot who has a *second instance* of using alcohol (or any other substance) in a situation in which that use was physically hazardous, such as in connection with a potentially dangerous instrument like a car — no matter how far apart the two incidents were — may no longer be authorized to exercise the privileges of his medical certificate. The FAA has considered DUIs and DWIs to evidence alcohol use in a physically hazardous situation for purposes of the medical standards.

Accordingly, if you get a single DUI or DWI, consider it a warning, and reexamine your drinking habits. Your HIMS and Aeromedical Committee representatives and the ALPA Aeromedical Office doctors are available to help you.

The authors are grateful to J. Gary Trichter (a Houston DUI attorney with a pilot's license and the owner of three airplanes) and Christian Samuelson for their following contribution.*

Captain Lucky Lindy, a 15-year major-airline pilot with 15,000 flight hours and who is also a United States Air Force Reserve Flight Officer of 19 years, tells you that 16 days ago he was not so lucky as he was arrested for drunk driving by a member of the local constabulary. He apologizes for not coming in sooner, but he had been on a weeklong round-trip flight out of the country and had to immediately report for military reserve duty upon his return. Unlucky Lindy then informs you that he refused the Intoxiliar breath test and he is very concerned that this incident might cause him to be forced into early retirement. The client's high level of stress is clearly manifested in his voice and by the fact that he continually asks for assurances that he is not going to lose his lifetime investment in his aviation career. Reassuring him that

* Reprinted with permission.

he will be all right and that he is in the best of hands, you schedule an afternoon appointment for him.

Not being a pilot or a person with any real aviation experience, you call a local flight school to ask what is the Federal Aviation Adminstration (FAA) reporting requirement for DWI/DUI. A young certified flight instructor (CFI) first tells you that there are three types of pilot medical certificates, i.e., a first class that is good for six months, a second class that is good for 12 months, and a third class that is good for 24 months. He further explains that all pilots must have a current medical certificate in order to be legal to fly. The CFI then said the only requirement that he knew about concerning a DWI/DUI conviction was that it be admitted in the space provided for it on the medical certificate application form. Feeling somewhat better informed, you thank the youngster, say good-bye and wait for your new client to arrive.

At your office interview later that day, Lindy tells you that his FAA First Class Medical Certificate will expire in two weeks and then requests your advice as to whether or not he needs to report his arrest to the feds. Not knowing about the Federal Aviation Regulations (FARS), you tell him not to worry, that you will do some research into the matter, and have an answer for him soon.

During the interview, you properly and thoroughly explain that his case is very defendable, that a DWI/DUI first offense, if there is a conviction, could theoretically result in a sentence of jail, a fine, both jail and a fine, and a driver's license suspension of up to one year. You further inform him that as a consequence of his breath-test refusal and because he missed the 15-day period after his arrest to request an administrative hearing, he will lose his driver's license for 90 days. The good news, however, is that he is eligible for an occupational license and that it is almost a sure thing the court will grant him one during the three month suspension period.

Unlucky Lindy again revisits the questions with you as to "how will all this affect my flying?" and "do I have to report this to the FAA at this time or later?" Exactly how you answer this question will make a big difference to your legal malpractice carrier, if you have one, and to your retirement account if you do not have coverage. More importantly, it will make all the professional and emotional difference in the world to your pilot client.

Remembering the CFI's quick tutorial, you inform the client that it is your opinion the medical certificate form only requires the reporting of "convictions" so there is no need to make reference of the arrest on the form when he applies for a new medical certificate. Fortunately, for you, that information is correct. You then say that it is your opinion that the FAA need not be notified at all unless there is a conviction. Oops! This advice just caused a "disturbance in the Force," as it is incorrect. Section 61.15 of the FARS is what caused the disturbance. It provides:

Offenses involving alcohol or drugs ...

(c) For the purposes of ... this section, a motor vehicle action means:
(1) A conviction after November 29, 1990, for the violation of any Federal or State statute relating to the operation of a motor vehicle while intoxicated by alcohol or a drug; while impaired by alcohol or a drug, or while under the influence of alcohol or a drug;
(2) The cancellation, suspension or revocation of a license to operate a motor vehicle after November 29, 1990, for a *cause related* to the operation of a motor vehicle while intoxicated by alcohol or a drug, or while under the influence of alcohol or a drug, [emphasis added]; ...

(d) Except for a motor vehicle action that results from the same incident or arises out of the same factual circumstances, a motor vehicle action occurring within three years of a previous motor vehicle action is grounds for: ...
(2) Suspension or revocation of any certificate, rating, or authorization issued under this part....

(e) Each person holding a certificate issued under this part shall provide a written report of each motor vehicle action to the FAA, Civil Action Security Division (AMC-700), P.O. Box 25810, Oklahoma City, OK 73125, not later than 60 days after the motor vehicle action. The report must include:
(1) The person's name, address, date of birth, and airman certificate number;
(2) The type violation that resulted in the conviction or the administrative action;
(3) The date of the conviction or administrative action;

(4) The State that holds the record of the conviction or administrative action; and

(5) A statement of whether the motor vehicle action resulted from the same incident or arose out of the same factual circumstances related to a previously reported motor vehicle action ...

(f) Failure to comply with paragraph (e) of this section is grounds for ...

(2) Suspension or revocation of any certificate, rating, or authorization issued under this part.

Your incorrect advice could cause client Lindy to have his pilot's license suspended or revoked if he does not notify the FAA Civil Aviation Security Division not later than 60 days after his driver's license goes into suspension for refusing to submit to the Intoxiliar test. Of course, should Lindy lose his pilot's license then he most likely would lose his job, too, and you will inevitably get sued! Ouch!

Let's change the facts a bit so that Unlucky Lindy comes to you and says he simply wants to plead guilty, get probation, and get this unfortunate episode behind him. He then asks, "Will it be sufficient to report my plea and conviction by affirmatively noting them on my medical certificate application?" If you are inclined to think that it is logical to assume the answer is "yes" because your client is actually notifying the FAA of his conviction by admitting it on the form, then you should be happy to know it is indeed a logical conclusion. Regrettably, however, like the rest of the government, the FAA does not always think, act, or promulgate its rules logically, and again you should feel a "disturbance in the Force."

If you don't like that answer or you do not believe in the "Force," then consider the bureaucratic nightmare that befell a major-airline captain in 1991. In May the pilot was arrested for drunk driving. Days after his arrest, feeling very concerned about his career and about following the rules, he actually called the local FAA office (Flight Standards District Office a/k/a "FSDO") to ask about the effect the DUI/DWI would have on his pilot's license. The FSDO, being helpful, only reminded him that it would be necessary to report the conviction, if one happened, on his medical application form when he reapplied for it the next month in June.

Not wishing to contest the DUI/DWI, the captain pled guilty on June 10. Within two weeks, during the completion of his medical application form, the captain in answer to question "21v" checked "yes" and self-disclosed the conviction. Notwithstanding the fact that he did not make further reference to the conviction on the form, he did explain and further disclose the events giving rise to the conviction to the FAA Medical Examiner Physician. The doctor, ostensibly believing the captain fit for flying, issued him a new medical certificate.

On the first of October, the FAA's Aeromedical Branch, following routine procedures, requested the captain to furnish further details of the conviction. The information was promptly furnished to the satisfaction of the branch.

Then comes the "disturbance in the Force." The FAA popped the captain for a 20-day suspension for violating FAR 61.15 because he did not specifically notify the Civil Aviation Security Division in Oklahoma City within the 60 days, as called for by the rule. "Wow!" you say? Well, so said the captain too! "Unreasonable!" you say? Well, you must be clairvoyant because that is exactly what the dumbfounded captain also said.

Does the word "appeal" come to mind? It did to the captain and he appealed to the National Transportation Safety Board (NTSB) saying in effect that because he had no intent to deceive and that he had in fact reported his conviction to the FAA, although not to the security division because he was unaware of the rule, it was unreasonable to find a violation and suspend him. "Wow!" said the judge agreeing with the pilot. "Unreasonable!" said the judge again agreeing with the pilot. Indeed, after hearing the evidence the judge not only found that there was "substantial compliance" with the rule, but also, he dismissed the case against the pilot.

Does the word "appeal" come to mind again? It did to the FAA and it appealed to the full five-member NTSB. "Wow!" said the Board. "Reversed" said the Board, and they reinstated the record of the conviction albeit without the suspension. The Board went on to say that, *"[a]s a general rule, airmen are expected and obliged to know the regulations to which they are subject, and ignorance of them is no defense. The reporting requirement regulation was in effect at the time of the [captain's conviction] and its language is absolutely clear"* [emphasis added]. "Ouch!" said the captain. His lawyer probably said, "HOLY S–T!!!!!!!!!"

The above examples ought to make you very careful in representing pilots in drunk driving prosecutions and/or administrative driver's license proceedings that are collateral to the drunk driving case. Clearly, the effect of either a failure to report or even a properly filed report are quite consequential for the pilot. Clearly, too, if that effect was brought about by ignorance and improper advice of counsel then, it too, has serious consequences for the lawyer.

Unquestionably, FAR 61.15 is a landmine just waiting to get stepped on by the innocent pilot/client and the unwary lawyer. One would think if the self-disclosure requirement were that important to the FAA that it would have created a form for reporting the required information just as it did on the medical certificate application. That, however, is not the case because there is no preprinted form.

To summarize, the pilot/client who is convicted of DUI/DWI must report that conviction on his medical application. He must also notify the FAA Civil Security Division in Oklahoma City within 60 days of the conviction. Contacting the local FAA FSDO is not compliance under the rule. The pilot/client must also report any action taken on his driver's license that emanated from the drunk driving arrest, i.e., a suspension for either failing the breath/blood test or for refusing a breath/blood test. This report, too, is made to the FAA Oklahoma Office Civil Security Division and must be made within 60 days of the suspension. In cases where the pilot/client suffers both a DUI/DWI conviction as well as an administrative license suspension that arose out of the same factual circumstances, he must timely report both of them to the Security Division or face a non-reporting violation. Note, however, that only one of the two reports can be used for suspension/revocation purposes under FAR 61.15 (d), i.e., the FAA needs two separate incidents within a three-year period to deny an application or suspend/revoke a pilot license.

Playing lawyers for the moment, arguably the reporting requirement for both a conviction and/or a suspension for refusing and/or failing a breath/blood test is in our opinion stayed for as long as the conviction and/or suspension are on appeal. There is no law on this question as of yet, but the 60-day clock on appeals we have handled has been treated by the FAA as starting when the appellate process was over and there were actual final court orders in effect.

Playing lawyers again, from a strategy viewpoint, in many jurisdictions it may be advantageous in defendable DUI/DWI prosecutions where the pilot/client plans on contesting the charge to always appeal the loss of an administrative driver's license revocation/suspension hearing. This is true because in many jurisdictions, the license suspension is rescinded as a matter of law where the criminal case ends with a verdict of "not guilty." Clearly, this strategy will prevent you and your client from having to deal with the FAA on the issue of record correction and/or expungement. Said another way, it is a lot easier not to ring the bell in the first instance than it would be to un-ring it after the fact.

Let's stroll through the minefield with two more examples before we put this topic to rest. Example 1: How about where the pilot/client is arrested for drunk driving, he refuses the Intoxiliar test, DUI/DWI charges are filed but subsequently dismissed for insufficient evidence; however, he still suffers a driver's license suspension for the breath test refusal. Looking at FAR 61.15(c)(2), the quesion becomes: does the not so clear language: " ... for a cause related to the operation of a motor vehicle *while intoxicated* ... " excuse such a pilot from the self-reporting requirement because there was not sufficient evidence of "while intoxicated" to warrant a continued drunk driving prosecution [emphasis added]?

Applying the NTSB logic about "language [that] is absolutely clear" from our first example, a reasonable pilot and/or reader should clearly interpret the "while intoxicated" language of FAR 61.15(c)(2) to mean what it says, i.e., that there must be sufficient evidence that the driver *was intoxicated* to require him to notify the Civil Aviation Security Division. Requiring that a statute, rule, regulation, or law be interpreted in light of the clear meaning of its words makes good sense to us. Indeed, that has been a judicial and legislative rule of construction for quite some time now. Moreover, one would also think that a reasonable pilot and/or reader could rely on the doctrine of *"stare decisis."* Remember, this is the doctrine that requires consistency so that "we the people" can rely on precedent in order for us to be "expected and obliged to know the regulations to which [we] are subject. . . . "

Regrettably, there is no guarantee in life that either the FAA or the NTSB will act logically, reasonably, sensibly, on the clear meaning of a FAR, or on precedent. Such was the hard 120-day pilot's license suspension lesson learned by an Ohio commercial pilot who had been stopped for erratic driving and subsequently refused to submit to a breath test. In that case the pilot was neither arrested nor charged with drunk driving but did suffer a one-year driver's license suspension.

This case turned on the FAA's and NTSB's interpretation of FAR 61.15(d)'s language "motor vehicle action." On the rationale side of the controversy was the pilot who argued that a breath test refusal is not proof of alcohol or drug involvement. Indeed, the definition of "motor vehicle action" requires that the suspension be "for a cause related to the operation of a motor vehicle *while* intoxicated by alcohol or a drug, *while* impaired by alcohol or a drug, or *while* under the influence of alcohol or a drug [emphasis added]." In this regard, it is of import to note that the suspension was not for being intoxicated, but, rather, only for refusing the requested test. Of course on the flip side of the controversy was the FAA, which claimed in a conclusory and wholesale fashion that a breath test refusal fit within the broad meaning of "motor vehicle action" under section 61.15. In a decision that runs afoul with reason and plain language, the NTSB simply deferred to the FAA and rubber-stamped its definition. So much for fairness, uniformity, and *"stare decisis."*

Example 2: Our final example involves the scenario where the pilot/client, although originally charged with DUI/DWI, is allowed to plead to a lesser or new nonintoxication/nonimpairment/noninfluence charge, such as reckless driving, and the original charge is dismissed, or where the DUI/DWI prosecution resolves itself with a pre-trial diversion, deferred adjudication, or probation before judgment, i.e., there is no final conviction. The question here is "whether or not FAR 61.15 requires self-reporting of cases that are resolved without alcohol, drugs, intoxication, impairment, influence or that do not involve a final conviction." The short answer, at least for now, is "no!"

So what does all this mean to the lawyer who represents the client/pilot who is accused of DUI/DWI? It means you need to be really careful to protect your pilot and yourself from collateral dangers that abound to the client because he is subject to a different and additional set of rules than the non-client/pilot due to his winged status. It means that not only do you need to go out and get a copy of the current FARS, but, also, that you need to read and understand them. Review of NTSB decisions is also a must! Don't get trapped! Read and don't hesistate to ask others more knowledgeable for help or advice. A great place to start is the Aircraft Owners and Pilots Association (AOPA). It has a pilot assistance hotline for members at 1-800-USA-AOPA (1-800-872-2572) and a Web site at www.aopa.org.

In closing, those of us who have been lucky enough to represent pilots know that they are some of the greatest clients and nicest friends around. Remember, protecting a pilot's license is protecting your own law license. Avoid the FAA pitfalls. Don't crash and burn.

II

EVIDENCE

4

FIELD EVIDENCE

§4.1   Driving Symptoms

Page 175.   *Add the following new subsections:*

§4.1.2   The Distracted Driver

On many occasions, the erratic driving observed by the officer giving him legal grounds to stop the vehicle is nothing more than a manifestation of other innocent behavior. Driver distractions such as the use of cellular phones, changing compact discs, smoking cigarettes, or consuming food and beverages may all lead to an officer's incorrect conclusion that the driver is intoxicated.

For years, various government agencies, both domestic and abroad, have warned against the use of cell phones while driving. Distractions caused by cell phones have been reported to significantly increase the number of accidents and are often cited to be as dangerous as drunk driving. The United States National Safety Council, the UK-based Transport Research Laboratory, and even the American Automobile Association (AAA) have either used driving simulators to test reaction times and driving performance, or in the case of the study released by AAA in May 2001, gathered statistics based on drivers involved in serious motor vehicle crashes. Recognition of this problem provides DUI defense counsel with objective information upon which to base a viable and often-encountered defense, for an experienced DUI defense practitioner often hears from their clients that the accident in which they were involved resulted from the use of their cell phones. See Jane C. Stutts, Ph.D., et al., *The Role of Driver Distraction in Traffic Crashes*, AAA Foundation for Traffic Safety (2001), http://www.aaafoundation.org/pdf/distraction.pdf.

Perhaps the most detailed study was by David L. Strayer, Frank A. Drews, and Dennis J. Crouch of the University of Utah in Salt Lake City in a paper presented in July 2003 at the Second International Driving Symposium on Human Factors in Driver Assessment, Training and Vehicle Design. In their paper, *Fatal Distraction? A Comparison of the Cell-phone Driver and the Drunk Driver*, the authors report their research performed on a high-fidelity Patrol-Sim driving simulator manufactured by GE I-Sim. The researchers measured a number of real-time performance variables to determine how participants reacted to vehicles braking in front of them. Both the cell-phone and alcohol conditions differed from the baseline. Drivers conversing on a cell phone were involved in more rear-end collisions, and their reactions to vehicles braking in front of them were 8 percent slower relative to baseline. In addition, it took participants 15 percent longer to return to their initial driving speed after braking, compared to their baseline, when they were talking on the cell phone. Cell-phone–using drivers attempted to compensate for their behavior by driving 3 percent move slowly than baseline. Interestingly, the study did not find any difference in impairment between hand-held and hands-free cell phones.

By contrast, when participants were legally drunk (at or above a .08 percent blood alcohol level) neither accident rates, nor reaction time to vehicles braking in front of the participant, nor recovery to initial driving speeds after braking, differed significantly from baseline.

In summary, the researchers found that both drivers with a blood alcohol level at 0.08 percent and drivers using cell phones performed differently from the baseline. However, the driving profiles of the two conditions differed. When controlling for driving difficulty and time on task, this study showed that drivers on cell phones exhibited greater impairment, and less responsive driving behavior, and had more accidents, than drunk drivers.

§4.1.3   The Drowsy Driver

In 2003, the New Jersey State Senate passed a bill, known as "Maggie's Law," establishing fatigued driving as recklessness under the existing vehicular homicide statute. See N.J. Stat. Ann. §2C: 11-5. This was the first law in the nation to specifically address the issue of drowsy driving. The law provides that being without sleep for a period in excess of 24 consecutive hours may give rise to an inference that the defendant was driving recklessly. This law was passed as a result of a 1997 automobile accident where 20-year-old college student Maggie McDonnell was killed when a driver crossed three lanes of traffic to strike her vehicle head-on. The driver admitted to being awake for 30 consecutive hours.

The following information on drowsy driving is taken in part from an article authored by Steve Oberman, *Drunk or Drowsy? How Fatigue Can Be Mistaken for Intoxication*, The Champion 56 (Jan.-Feb. 2001). Those portions reproduced herein are done so with the express permission of the National Association of Criminal Defense Lawyers. Readers interested in a more extensive discussion of this issue should refer to the original article, which can be obtained from NACDL at www.nacdl.org.

Vehicular crashes caused by drowsiness are a common event on our highways. In the 1996 appropriations bill for the U.S. Department of Transportation, it was noted that there have been approximately 56,000 crashes per year in which driver fatigue was cited as the cause, and of those crashes, 1,550 were fatal. National Center on Sleep Disorders Research (hereinafter referred to as NCSDR)/National Highway Traffic Safety Administration (hereinafter referred to as NHTSA) Expert Panel on Driver Fatigue and Sleepiness, Report: Drowsy Driving and Automobile Crashes 1 (1999). By comparison, a 1998 National Highway Traffic Safety Administration report stated that there were 41,171 traffic fatalities in the U.S. during 1998 and of those, 15,935 (38%) were alcohol-related. NHTSA Traffic Safety Facts 1998, DOT HS 808 950. The drowsy driving numbers, while sizeable, are widely believed to be underreported. NCSDR/NHTSA Expert Panel on Driver Fatigue and Sleepiness, Report: Drowsy Driving and Automobile Crashes 1 (1999). This is primarily because there is no standardized, objective method by which law enforcement officers can assess and report crashes resulting from drowsy driving. For one reason, hyperarousal, in part caused by the adrenaline rush following the accident, usually eliminates all residual traces of impairment due to fatigue that might have otherwise been detected, adding an element of uncertainty to the reporting of these incidents.

SYMPTOMS OF DROWSY DRIVING

The symptoms of drowsy driving are primarily performance impairing, and are quite similar to the symptoms of drunk driving. According to studies, sleepiness leads to crashes because it impairs elements of performance that are critical to safe driving. D. Dinges & N. Kribbs, *Performing While Sleepy: Effects of Experimentally Induced Sleepiness, in* Sleep, Sleepiness, and Performance 98–128 (T. Monk ed., 1991). Three major impairments caused by sleepiness have been identified.

1. Slower reaction time. Optimum reaction times are reduced by sleepiness, and even moderately sleepy people can have an increased reaction time that hinders stopping to avoid an accident. Even small increases in reaction time can greatly increase the risk of a crash, especially at high speed. D. Dinges, *An Overview of Sleepiness and Accidents*, J. Sleep Res. 4(2), 4–14 (1995). (Figure 4-1)

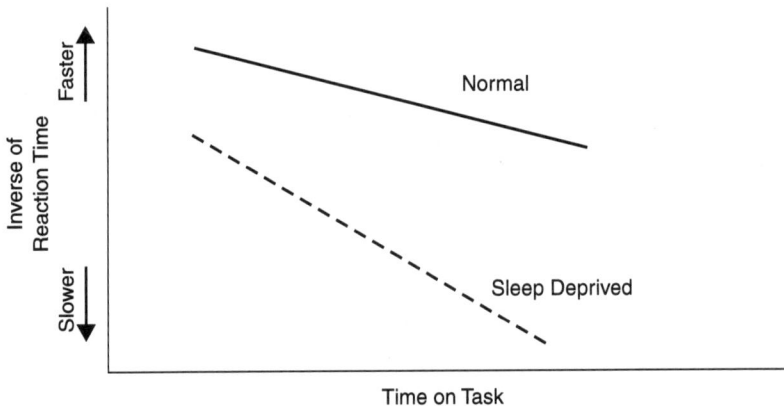

Figure 4-1. A summary of data on reaction to an event marker presented to a subject approximately once every 4 seconds over a 10-minute time period. N. Kribbs & D. Dinges, *Vigilance Decrement and Sleepiness, in* Sleep Onset Mechanisms 113–125 (J. Harsh & R. Ogilvie eds., 1994).

NCSDR/NHTSA, Drowsy Driving and Automobile Crashes, (1999)

2. Reduced vigilance while driving. Sleepiness causes impaired performance in attention-based tasks, including increased periods of non-response and delayed response. N. Kribbs & D. Dinges, *Vigilance Decrement and Sleepiness, in* Sleep Onset Mechanisms 113–125 (J. Harsh & R. Ogilvie eds., 1994).

3. Deficits in information processing. Processing and integrating information takes longer, short-term memory is impaired, and general performance declines. D. Dinges, *An Overview of Sleepiness and Accidents*, J. Sleep Res. 4(2), 4–14 (1995).

People try to counter their symptoms of drowsiness with physical activity, dietary supplements, and/or drugs, all of which mask their level of sleepiness. However, when they sit and perform repetitive and passive tasks such as driving long distances, these defenses usually fail, and sleep comes rapidly. M. Mitler et al., *Catastrophes, Sleep, and Public Policy: Consensus Report*, Sleep 11(1), 100–109 (1988).

CHARACTERISTICS OF DROWSY-DRIVING CRASHES

In contrast to alcohol-related crashes, no blood, breath, or other objective test for sleepiness currently exists that can be administered to a driver at the scene of a crash or after a traffic stop for abnormal or illegal driving. Furthermore, there are few definitive criteria for judging how sleepy a driver is, or establishing a "bright line" test to show a person's driving is adversely affected by sleepiness. As a result, an analysis of drowsy-driving crashes must be based largely on subjective evidence, such as police reports and driver statements following the event. However, a 1999 joint report by the National Center for Sleep Disorder Research (NCSDR) and the National Highway Traffic Safety Administration (NHTSA) identified six general characteristics of drowsy-driving crashes. NCSDR/NHTSA Expert Panel on Driver Fatigue and Sleepiness, Report: Drowsy Driving and Automobile Crashes 9–10 (1999).

1. Drowsy-driving crashes usually occur after midnight. Driver drowsiness is considerably greater for most drivers during night driving than during daytime driving, peaking from late evening until dawn. NCSDR/NHTSA Expert Panel on Driver Fatigue and Sleepiness, Report: Drowsy Driving and Automobile Crashes 9 (1999) (citing A. Pack et al., *Characteristics of Crashes Attributed to the Driver Having Fallen Asleep*, Accid. Anal. Prev. 27(6), 769–75 (1995); R. Knipling & J. Wang, *Crashes and Fatalities Related to Driver Drowsiness/Fatigue*, Research Note from the Office of Crash Avoidance Research 1–8 (NHTSA, 1994); New York GTSC Sleep Task Force, Public Information and Education Subcommittee, *Drowsy Driving Focus Group Study: Final Report* (Aug. 1994); New York State Task Force on Drowsy Driving, *Status*

Report, Institute for Traffic Safety Management and Research (May 1996); P. Langlois et al., *Temporal Patterns of Reported Single Vehicle Car and Truck Accidents in Texas, USA During 1980–83*, Chronobiol. Int. 2, 131–40 (1985); P. Lavie et al., *Frequency of Sleep Related Traffic Accidents and Hour of the Day*, Sleep Res. 15, 175 (1986); M. Mitler et al., *Catastrophes, Sleep, and Public Policy: Consensus Report*, Sleep 11(1), 100–9 (1988); J. Horne & L. Reyner, *Sleep Related Vehicle Accidents*, BMJ 310, 565–67 (Mar. 4, 1995); G. Maycock, *Sleepiness and Driving: The Experience of UK Car Drivers*, J. Sleep. Res. 5(220), 220–37 (1996); A. McCartt et al., *The Scope and Nature of the Drowsy Driving Problem in New York State*, Accident Analysis and Prevention 28(4), 511–17 (1996)). (Figure 4-2)

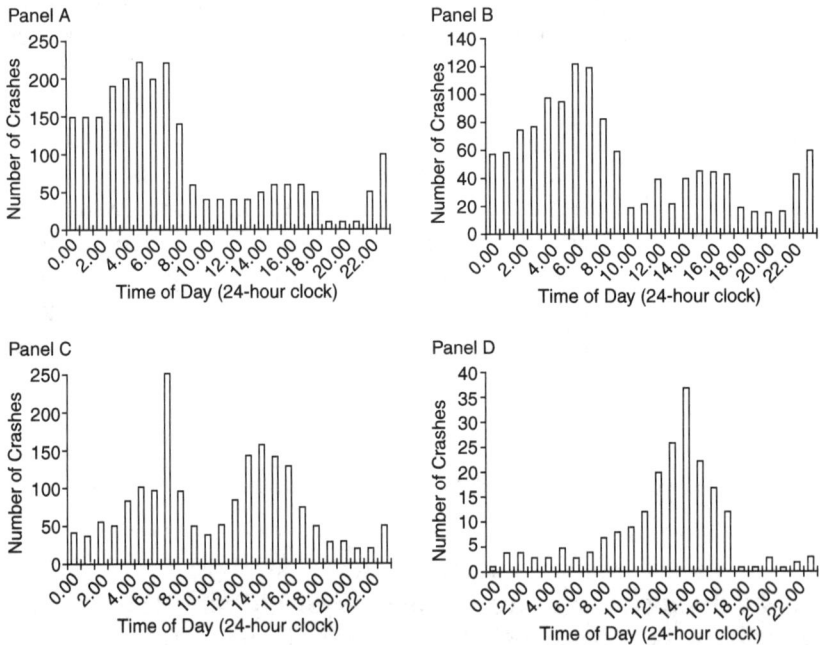

Figure 4-2. Time of occurrence of crashes in drivers of different ages where driver was reported as falling asleep, but alcohol was not involved. The panels show statistics for the following ages: (A) drivers 25 or younger, (B) drivers between 26 and 45, (C) drivers between 46 and 65, and (D) drivers older than 65. The data are for 1990 to 1992, inclusive. NCSDR/NHTSA Expert Panel on Driver Fatigue and Sleepiness, Report: Drowsy Driving and Automobile Crashes 10 (1999).

NCSDR/NHTSA, Drowsy Driving and Automobile Crashes (1999)

2. *Drowsy-driving crashes are likely to be serious.* The higher speeds involved in drowsy-driving crashes, combined with delayed reaction times, increase the danger of fatalities in such crashes. NCSDR/NHTSA Expert Panel on Driver Fatigue and Sleepiness, Report: Drowsy Driving and Automobile Crashes 9 (1999) (citing J. Horne & L. Reyner, *Sleep Related Vehicle Accidents*, BMJ 310, 565–67 (Mar. 4, 1995)).

3. *Usually, a single vehicle leaves the roadway.* NHTSA General Estimates data show a trend of single-vehicle roadway departure resulting from driver fatigue. However, the data suggest that drowsiness also is a factor in rear-end crashes and head-on crashes. NCSDR/NHTSA Expert Panel on Driver Fatigue and Sleepiness, Report: Drowsy Driving and Automobile Crashes 11 (1999) (citing R. Knipling & J. Wang, *Crashes and Fatalities Related to Driver Drowsiness/Fatigue*, Research Note from the Office of Crash Avoidance Research 1–8 (NHTSA, 1994)).

4. *Drowsy-driving crashes usually occur on high-speed roads.* Compared to other types of crashes, drowsy-driving crashes usually take place on highways and other roadways with speed limits of 55 to 65 mph. It is likely that this is because more long-distance night driving occurs on highways. NCSDR/NHTSA Expert Panel on Driver Fatigue and Sleepiness, Report: Drowsy Driving and Automobile Crashes 11 (1999).

5. *Drowsy drivers usually do NOT attempt to avoid crashing.* Sleepy drivers are less likely than alert drivers to take corrective action before crashing. Furthermore, reports of drowsy-driving crashes show an absence of physical evidence, such as skid marks or brake lights, that would indicate corrective maneuvers. NCSDR/NHTSA Expert Panel on Driver Fatigue and Sleepiness, Report: Drowsy Driving and Automobile Crashes 11 (1999) (citing J. Wang, R. Knipling, & M. Goodman, *The Role of Driver Inattention in Crashes: New Statistics from the 1995 Crashworthiness Data System*, Fortieth Annual Proceedings of the Association for the Advancement of Automotive Medicine 377–92 (Oct. 7–9, 1996)).

6.   Drowsy drivers are usually alone in the vehicle.   A New York State survey of lifetime incidents revealed that 82 percent of drowsy-driving crashes occurred with a single occupant in the vehicle. NCSDR/NHTSA Expert Panel on Driver Fatigue and Sleepiness, Report: Drowsy Driving and Automobile Crashes 11 (1999) (citing A. McCartt et al., *The Scope and Nature of the Drowsy Driving Problem in New York State*, Accident Analysis and Prevention 28(4), 511–517 (1996)). By contrast, drivers who reported falling asleep without crashing were more likely to have had passengers in the vehicle with them.

Drowsy-driving crashes also have other common characteristics regarding driver age, time of the crash, crash type, and severity. One must note, however, that when intoxication is combined with drowsiness, the patterns become even more pronounced. For example, crashes involving drowsiness *and* alcohol involve a higher percentage of young males than drowsy-driving crashes without the additional influence of an intoxicant. J. Wilkins et al., *Sleep- and Fatigue-Related Motor Vehicle Crashes, With and Without Alcohol Involvement*, presented at the 11th annual meeting of the Association of Professional Sleep Societies (June, 1997).

FACTORS INCREASING THE RISK OF A DROWSY-DRIVING CRASH

As with studying the characteristics of drowsy-driving crashes, the identification of factors that increase the risk of these crashes is based on limited evidence. However, the NCSDR/NHTSA panel of researchers was able to identify five factors that increase the risk of drowsy-driving crashes.

1.   Sleep   loss.   Insufficient sleep is perhaps the most common factor increasing the risk of a drowsy-driving crash. A 1995 Gallup poll showed that nearly 50 percent of adults reported experiencing some sort of difficulty sleeping, while about 10 percent reported frequent difficulty sleeping. National Sleep Foundation, Survey: Sleep in America (1995). Even the loss of one night's sleep can cause acute sleepiness that increases the risk of drowsy-driving crashes. And sleep-restrictive work patterns, such as working late shifts, can also restrict sleep to the point where the risk of a crash is increased.

2. Driving patterns. Driving patterns that interfere with the natural sleep-wake cycle of the body can also increase the risk of a drowsy-driving crash. Such driving patterns can include the time of day when driving occurs and the length of time spent behind the wheel. NCSDR/NHTSA Expert Panel on Driver Fatigue and Sleepiness, Report: Drowsy Driving and Automobile Crashes 13 (1999). For example, the greatest number of drowsy-driving crashes occur during late-night hours, which is the point of highest sleepiness in the sleep-wake cycle.

3. Use of sleep-inducing medications. The NHTSA report cites several studies which conclude that the use of certain sedating medications increases drowsiness, thereby increasing the risk of a drowsy-driving crash. NCSDR/NHTSA Expert Panel on Driver Fatigue and Sleepiness, Report: Drowsy Driving and Automobile Crashes 13 (1999) (citing L. Kozena et al., *Vigilance Impairment After a Single Dose of Benzodiazepines*, Psychopharmacology 119(1), 39–45 (1995); M. Van Laar et al., *Acute and Subchronic Effects of Nefazodone and Imipramine on Highway Driving, Cognitive Functions, and Daytime Sleepiness in Healthy Adult and Elderly Subjects*, J. Clin. Psychopharmacol. 15(1), 30–40 (1995); W. Ray et al., *Psychoactive Drugs and the Risk of Injurious Motor Vehicle Crashes in Elderly Drivers*, Am. J. Epidemiol. 136, 873–83 (1992); S. Leveille et al., *Psychoactive Medications and Injurious Motor Vehicle Collisions Involving Older Drivers*, Epidemiology 5, 591–98 (1994); C. Ceutel, *Risk of Traffic Accident Injury After a Prescription for a Benzodiazepine*, Ann. Epidemiol. 5(3), 239–44 (1995); F. Gengo & C. Manning, *A Review of the Effects of Antihistamines on Mental Processes Related to Automobile Driving*, J. Allergy Clin. Immunol. 86, 1034–39 (1990)). These include benzodiazepine anxiolytics, long-acting hypnotics, sedating antihistamines, and tricyclic antidepressants. The risk of drowsy-driving crashes increases with higher doses of such medications and also when these medications are taken in combination with each other.

4. Untreated sleep disorders. The NHTSA panel of researchers identified two sleep disorders that can increase the risk of a drowsy-driving crash: sleep apnea syndrome and narcolepsy. Sleep apnea syndrome, associated with chronic snoring, disrupts the flow of oxygen during sleep, which fragments natural sleep and often leads to drowsiness while awake. NCSDR/NHTSA Expert Panel on Driver Fatigue and Sleepiness, Report: Drowsy Driving and Automobile Crashes 13 (1999). Narcolepsy is a disorder of the natural sleep-wake mechanism that can also lead to drowsiness while awake, often causing involuntary naps throughout the day. NCSDR/NHTSA Expert Panel on Driver Fatigue and Sleepiness, Report: Drowsy Driving and Automobile Crashes 13 (1999). Narcolepsy also has a symptom termed cataplexy, which is a sudden loss of muscle tone that can range from weakness to a total body collapse. If these sleep disorders remain untreated, the risk of drowsy-driving crashes is greatly increased.

5. Consumption of alcohol. Although fatigue and alcohol intoxication are separate causes of crashes, research has shown that sleep restrictions can increase the drowsiness caused by alcohol consumption alone. The resulting decline in psychomotor performance is greater than the decline caused by either drowsiness or alcohol alone. NCSDR/NHTSA Expert Panel on Driver Fatigue and Sleepiness, Report: Drowsy Driving and Automobile Crashes 14 (1999) (citing T. Roehrs et al., *Sleepiness and Ethanol Effects on Simulated Driving*, Alcohol Clin. Exp. Res. 18(1), 154–8 (1994); S. Peeke et al., *Combined Effects of Alcohol and Sleep Deprivation in Normal Young Adults*, Psychopharmacology 67, 279–87 (1980); M. Huntley & T. Centybear, *Alcohol, Sleep Deprivation and Driving Speed Effects Upon Control Use During Driving*, Human Factors 16, 19–28 (1974)). A 1994 study showed that test subjects who consumed small amounts of alcohol on four hours of sleep had 15 times as many off-road deviations as subjects who consumed the same amount of alcohol on eight hours of sleep. NCSDR/NHTSA Expert Panel on Driver Fatigue and Sleepiness, Report: Drowsy Driving and Automobile Crashes 14 (1999) (citing T. Roehrs et al., *Sleepiness and Ethanol Effects on Simulated Driving*, Alcohol Clin. Exp. Res. 18(1), 154–8 (1994)). (Figure 4-3)

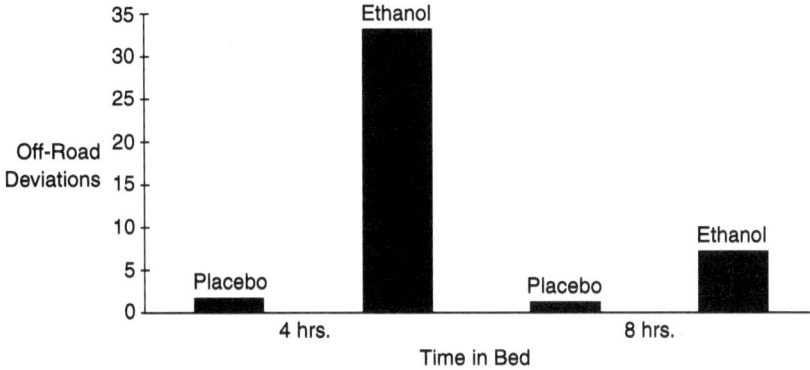

Figure 4-3. NCSDR/NHTSA Expert Panel on Driver Fatigue and Sleepiness, Report: Drowsy Driving and Automobile Crashes 14 (1999) (citing T. Roehrs et al., *Sleepiness and Ethanol Effects on Simulated Driving*, Alcohol Clin. Exp. Res. 18(1), 154–8 (1994)).

NCSDR/NHTSA, Drowsy Driving and Automobile Crashes (1999)

The NHTSA panel could not make a determination as to which of these factors showed the greatest increase in the risk of a crash. NCSDR/NHTSA Expert Panel on Driver Fatigue and Sleepiness, Report: Drowsy Driving and Automobile Crashes 15 (1999). However, the panel emphasized the fact that these factors are *cumulative*, and that combinations of these factors will substantially increase the chance of a crash. NCSDR/NHTSA Expert Panel on Driver Fatigue and Sleepiness, Report: Drowsy Driving and Automobile Crashes 15 (1999). This is a potential trap for attorneys who wish to argue that their client's impairment was caused by fatigue rather than intoxication. When a fatigued person consumes alcohol, the alcohol *increases* the impairment already present due to fatigue. It is important to keep this fact in mind when arguing that a client's ability to drive was impaired by drowsiness, since alcohol has been shown to be a causal factor increasing levels of fatigue in drowsy drivers.

POPULATION GROUPS AT RISK

Considering the factors that increase the risk of a drowsy-driving crash, research reveals three general population groups that appear to be at greater risk for a drowsy-driving crash.

1. Young people. According to NHTSA research, young people between the ages of 16 and 29 are at the highest risk of a drowsy-driving crash. NCSDR/NHTSA Expert Panel on Driver Fatigue and Sleepiness, Report: Drowsy Driving and Automobile Crashes 16 (1999) (citing A. Pack et al., *Characteristics of Crashes Attributed to the Driver Having Fallen Asleep*, Accid. Anal. Prev. 27(6), 769–75 (1995); J. Horne & L. Reyner, *Sleep Related Vehicle Accidents*, BMJ 310, 565–57 (Mar. 4, 1995); G. Maycock, *Sleepiness and Driving: The Experience of UK Car Drivers*, J. Sleep Res. 5(220), 220–37 (1996); R. Knipling & J. Wang, *Revised Estimates of the U.S. Drowsy Driver Crash Problem Based on General Estimates System Case Reviews*, Association for the Advancement of Automotive Medicine, 39th Annual Proceedings (Oct. 16–18, 1995)). Factors increasing the risk for this age group include maturational changes, irregular or disrupted sleep patterns, and lifestyle patterns such as combining schoolwork with employment and extracurricular or social activities. NCSDR/NHTSA Expert Panel on Driver Fatigue and Sleepiness, Report: Drowsy Driving and Automobile Crashes 16 (1999) (citing M. Carskadon, *Adolescent Sleepiness: Increased Risk in a High-Risk Population*, Alcohol, Drugs and Driving 5(4)/6(1), 317–28 (1990)). Strangely, young males are involved in more crashes statistically than young females; however, the reasons for this are unclear at this time.

2. Shift workers.   Research shows that the sleep disruptions caused by shift work is associated with attention lapses, impaired reaction time and overall decreased performance. NCSDR/NHTSA Expert Panel on Driver Fatigue and Sleepiness, Report: Drowsy Driving and Automobile Crashes 17 (1999) (citing D. Dinges et al., *Temporal Placement of a Nap for Alertness: Contributions of Circadian Phase and Prior Wakefulness*, Sleep 10, 313–29 (1987); P. Hamilton et al., *A Study of Four Days Partial Sleep Deprivation, in* Aspects of Human Efficiency, 101–13 (W. Colquhoun ed., 1972); H. Williams et al., *Impaired Performance With Acute Sleep Loss*, Psychol. Monogr. 73, 1–26 (1959)). The NHTSA researchers state that while the evidence does not point to a conclusive link between shift work and drowsy-driving crashes, the increased risks of drowsiness are likely to translate into a corresponding risk of crashes. NCSDR/NHTSA Expert Panel on Driver Fatigue and Sleepiness, Report: Drowsy Driving and Automobile Crashes 17 (1999). This population group also faces increased risk because the number of shift workers is increasing at a rate of approximately 3 percent per year.

NCSDR/NHTSA Expert Panel on Driver Fatigue and Sleepiness, Report: Drowsy Driving and Automobile Crashes 17 (1999).

3. People with untreated sleep disorders. While the number of reported drowsy-driving crashes due to untreated sleep apnea syndrome and narcolepsy is relatively low, the risk for both of these groups is increased due to the performance-impairing symptoms of these disorders. NCSDR/NHTSA Expert Panel on Driver Fatigue and Sleepiness, Report: Drowsy Driving and Automobile Crashes 17 (1999).

COMPARISON OF DROWSINESS TO INTOXICATION

Sleep loss and reduced sleep quality clearly impair driver performance to some degree. Experiments show that sleeping less than four solid hours per night impairs performance on vigilance tasks. P. Naitoh, *Minimal Sleep to Maintain Performance: the Search for Sleep Quantum in Sustained Operations, in* Why We Nap: Evolution, Chronobiology, and Functions of Polyphasic and Ultrashort Sleep 199–216 (C. Stampi ed., 1992). Furthermore, the effects of sleep loss are cumulative, and regularly losing one to two hours of sleep each night creates a "sleep debt." Subjects whose sleep was restricted to four to five hours per night for one week required two full nights of sleep to regain vigilance, performance, and normal mood. D. Dinges et al., *Cumulative Sleepiness, Mood Disturbance, and Psychomotor Vigilance Performance Decrements During a Week of Sleep Restricted to 4–5 hours Per Night,* Sleep 20(4), 267–277 (1997). While identification of performance impairment due to fatigue is clear, objective quantification of the exact degree of impairment caused by drowsiness has only recently been achieved. In 1997, Australian researchers Drew Dawson and Kathryn Reid reported the results of their attempt to equate performance impairment caused by sleepiness with that caused by alcohol intoxication. D. Dawson & K. Reid, *Fatigue, Alcohol and Performance Impairment,* Nature 388, 235 (July 17, 1997). Their study showed that moderate levels of sleepiness produce higher levels of impairment than the proscribed level of alcohol intoxication.

Forty subjects participated in two experiments. In the first, the subjects were kept awake for 28 hours, and in the other they consumed approximately 15 g of alcohol at 30-minute intervals until their mean blood alcohol concentration (BLAC) reached

0.10 percent. In both experiments, cognitive psychomotor performance was measured in 30-minute intervals using a computer-administered test of hand-eye coordination.

In both experiments, subject performance decreased significantly. After 10 hours of wakefulness, subject performance declined by 0.74 percent per hour, up to 26 hours of wakefulness. In the alcohol test, for each 0.01 percent increase in the subject's BLAC, performance on the tracking test decreased by 1.16 percent. When mean BLAC reached 0.10 percent, mean relative performance on the tracking test decreased by an average of 11.6 percent. (Figure 4-4)

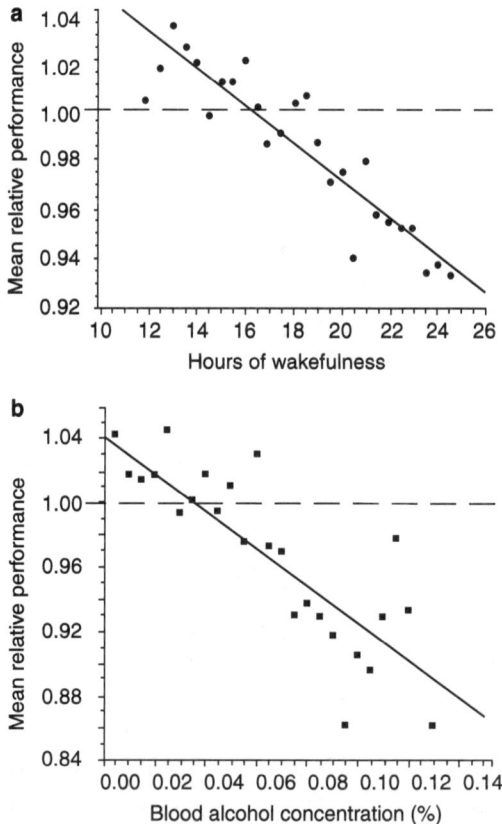

Reprinted by permission from Nature 388:235 (July 17, 1997), copyright 1997 Macmillan Magazines Ltd.

Figure 4-4. D. Dawson & K. Reid, *Fatigue, Alcohol and Performance Impairment*, Nature 388, 235 (July 17, 1997).

Dawson and Reid equated the rates of performance decline in both experiments (percentage decline per hour of wakefulness and percentage decline with change in BLAC). They found that the performance decline for every hour of wakefulness between 10 and 26 hours was equivalent to the performance decline observed with a 0.004 percent rise in BLAC. Therefore, after 17 hours of wakefulness, psychomotor performance decreased in their subjects to a level equivalent to the impairment observed in subjects with a BLAC of 0.05 percent. After 24 hours of wakefulness, performance decreased to a level equivalent to the impairment observed at 0.10 percent BLAC. (Figure 4-5)

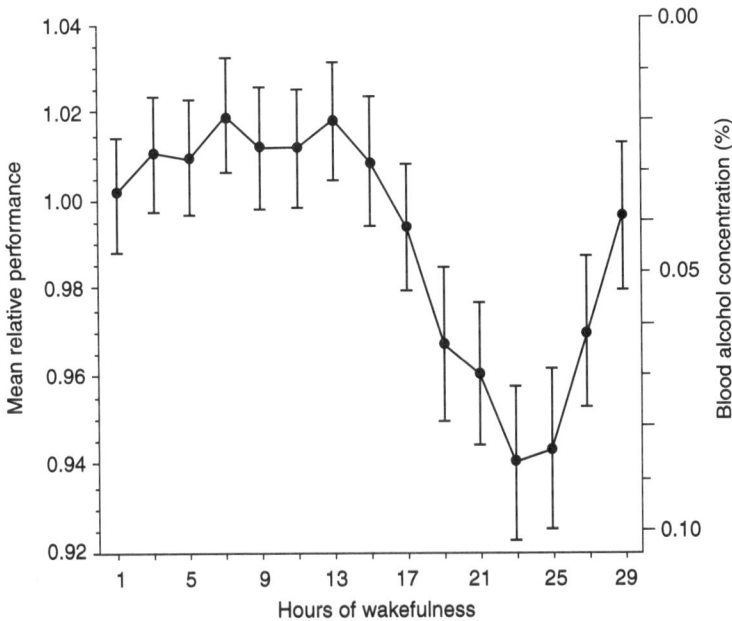

Reprinted by permission from Nature 388:235 (July 17, 1997), copyright 1997 Macmillan Magazines Ltd.

Figure 4-5. D. Dawson & K. Reid, *Fatigue, Alcohol and Performance Impairment*, Nature 388, 235 (July 17, 1997).

The report concluded that the effects of even moderate sleep loss on performance are similar to moderate alcohol intoxication. Dawson and Reid also noted that for drivers who regularly operate under greater fatigue, such as shift-workers, performance impairment could be even greater than was observed in their study. D. Dawson & K. Reid, *Fatigue, Alcohol and Performance Impairment*, Nature 388, 235 (July 17, 1997). The report emphasized that what many consider are moderate levels of fatigue can actually impair driving performance to an extent equivalent to, or even greater than impairment associated with alcohol intoxication. D. Dawson & K. Reid, *Fatigue, Alcohol and Performance Impairment*, Nature 388, 235 (July 17, 1997).

SAMPLE CROSS-EXAMINATION QUESTIONS RELATING TO A DEFENSE OF FATIGUE

The following questions are intended to provide a good start in establishing this defense. Obviously, the facts of each case will necessitate asking questions specific to the case.

Q. Officer, you'd agree that automobile accidents can occur without anybody having consumed alcohol, wouldn't you?

A. Yes.

Q. In fact, you've probably investigated hundreds of automobile accidents, haven't you?

A. Yes.

Q. Out of all those accidents you've investigated, only a small percentage have involved alcohol, isn't that right?

A. Yes.

Q. Automobile accidents can be caused because the driver was distracted, can't they?

A. Yes.

Q. They can be caused simply because the driver is just a poor driver, can't they?

A. Yes.

Q. They can be caused because of fatigue or sleepiness, can't they?

A. Yes.

Q. In fact, from time to time you have to change shifts on the job, don't you?

A. Yes.

Q. And whether it is from shift changes, or other reasons, you know that when you don't get enough sleep, you become irritable and don't perform as well.

A. Yes.

Q. In fact, that is why long-distance truck drivers and airplane pilots have limits on how long they can work without rest, isn't that right?

A. Yes.

Q. This is because people who are deprived of sleep have a slower reaction time, isn't it?

A. Yes.

Q. People who are deprived of sleep don't perform well on attention-based tasks, do they?

A. No, they don't.

Q. You would agree that driving is a very attention-based task, wouldn't you officer?

A. Yes.

Q. People who are deprived of sleep are slower in processing information, aren't they?

A. Yes.

CONCLUSION

Now that more research has been conducted to show how fatigue affects a person's ability to drive and to correlate fatigue with alcohol impairment, an attorney defending the accused drunk driver may use these studies in his or her arsenal to win the applicable case. Use of a human factors expert may be helpful, although counsel should prepare the expert for cross-examination questions relating to the history obtained from the client by the expert.

Obviously, however, counsel should be wary of an argument by the prosecution that alcohol consumption, however slight, increased the sleepiness of the defendant. Responses to this line of questioning would be either that the defendant did not consume a sufficient amount of alcohol to affect the ability to drive, or that there was not sufficient elapsed time between the consumption of alcohol and the accident for the alcohol to have been absorbed into the bloodstream.

---

§4.2 Appearance and Behavior of Defendant

§4.2.5 Odor of Alcohol on Breath

Page 185. Add after third full paragraph:

Recently, the scientists whose studies became the basis for the "standardized" field sobriety tests conducted another study on the effectiveness of alcohol odor in detecting intoxication. Moskowitz, Burns & Ferguson, Police Officers' Detection of Breath Odors from Alcohol Ingestion, 31(3) Accident Analysis and Prevention 175

(May 1999). These researchers used 20 experienced officers working with 14 subjects who were tested at blood-alcohol concentrations ranging from zero to .13 percent. Over a four-hour period, the officers smelled the subject's breath odor under optimal conditions, with the subjects hidden from view. The conclusions of the study: Odor strength estimates were unrelated to BAC levels; estimates of BAC levels failed to rise above random guesses. Officers were unable to recognize whether the alcohol beverage was beer, wine, bourbon, or vodka. According to the scientists, these results demonstrate that even under optimum clinical conditions, breath odor detection is unreliable.

§4.2.6 Slurred Speech

Page 187. Add after first full paragraph:

In fact, even assuming the honesty of the officer that the defendant's speech *was* slurred, there is little evidence that this is symptomatic of intoxication. Impairment of speech is, for example, a common — and sober — reaction to the stress, fear, and nervousness that a police investigation would be expected to engender; fatigue is another well-known cause. However, consider the following excerpt from a recent issue of *Discover* magazine:

> Bartenders, police officers, and hospital workers routinely identify drunks by their slurred speech. Several investigative groups judged the captain of the grounded Exxon Valdez oil tanker to be intoxicated based solely on the sound of his voice in his radio transmissions. But a team led by Harry Hollien, a phonetician at the University of Florida, has found that even self-proclaimed experts are pretty bad at estimating people's alcohol levels by the way they talk.
>
> Hollien asked clinicians who treat chemical dependency, along with a group of everyday people, to listen to recordings made by volunteers when they were sober, then mildly intoxicated, legally impaired, and finally, completely smashed. Listeners consistently overestimated the drunkeness of mildly intoxicated subjects. Conversely, they underestimated the alcohol levels of those who were most inebriated. Professionals were little better at perceiving the truth than the ordinary joes. . . .

He thinks his research could encourage police to be more wary of snap judgments: Mild drinkers might come under needless suspicion. . . .

Saunders, News of Science, Medicine and Technology: Straight Talk, 21(10) Discover (Oct. 2000).

§4.2.8 False Symptoms from Abnormal Blood Sugar Level

Page 191. Add after second full paragraph:

The following information about hypoglycemia is reprinted in part from an article by John Arnold, Ph.D., *Hypoglycemia: Driving Under the Influence*, 8 Medical & Toxicological Information (MTI) Review 1 (Sept. 2003), with permission from both the author and the publisher.

———————————

Hypoglycemia (abnormally low levels of blood glucose) is frequently seen in connection with driving error on this nation's roads and highways, including accidents with personal and material damage. Even more frequent are unjustified DUIs or DWIs, stemming from hypoglycemic symptoms that can closely mimic those of a drunk driver. In this newsletter article we will examine the medical condition of hypoglycemia, its causes, including roles played by disease, alcohol and drugs, and give examples of actual cases in which hypoglycemia proved to be a decisive factor.

In an individual with normal metabolism, blood glucose levels are regulated precisely and kept within a narrow range. This range can vary by individual and in most cases, by laboratory definition, hypoglycemia is defined as a blood sugar level below 60 mg/dl. However, most of the diabetes associations suggest that, in general, action should be taken to restore blood sugar levels to a normative range when the reading falls below 70 mg/dl. Diabetes patients and individuals who have certain kinds of tumors or possess other errors of metabolism, however, are unable to precisely regulate their glucose levels, which can range extremely high or plunge to dangerous lows. The body, through the process of metabolism, breaks down the natural sugars (carbohydrates) that are eaten and converts them to glucose, which can then be absorbed from the intestines into the blood. At any given time during the day blood glucose reflects a balance of the amount of glucose absorbed from the intestine, the glucose converted and released by the liver into the blood, and that going from the blood directly into the cells of the body. Only glucose can be utilized by the cells of the body and glucose needs insulin, which is produced by the pancreas, to get into the cells. Although insulin is the only hormone that directly helps the uptake of blood glucose into the cells, there are several key hormones that work in the opposite fashion — glucagon, epinephrine (also known as adrenaline), cortisol, and growth hormone.

- **Glucagon** — stimulates glycogenolysis and gluconeogenesis (new glucose formation) in the liver and works to raise glucose levels and, like insulin, is manufactured in the pancreas. Works quickly.
- **Epinephrine** (adrenaline) — stimulates glycogenolysis and glucoconeogenesis and is manufactured by the adrenal glands. Works quickly.
- **Cortisol** — stimulates gluconeogenesis and causes the cells to respond less efficiently to insulin and is manufactured in the adrenal glands. Works slowly.
- **Growth hormone** — works to raise blood glucose levels by causing the cells to respond less efficiently to insulin and is released by the pituitary gland. Works slowly.
- **Insulin** — lowers blood glucose levels by allowing glucose to move into the cells and is manufactured in the pancreas.

The table below illustrates how glucose enters the blood and is taken up by the cells of the body:

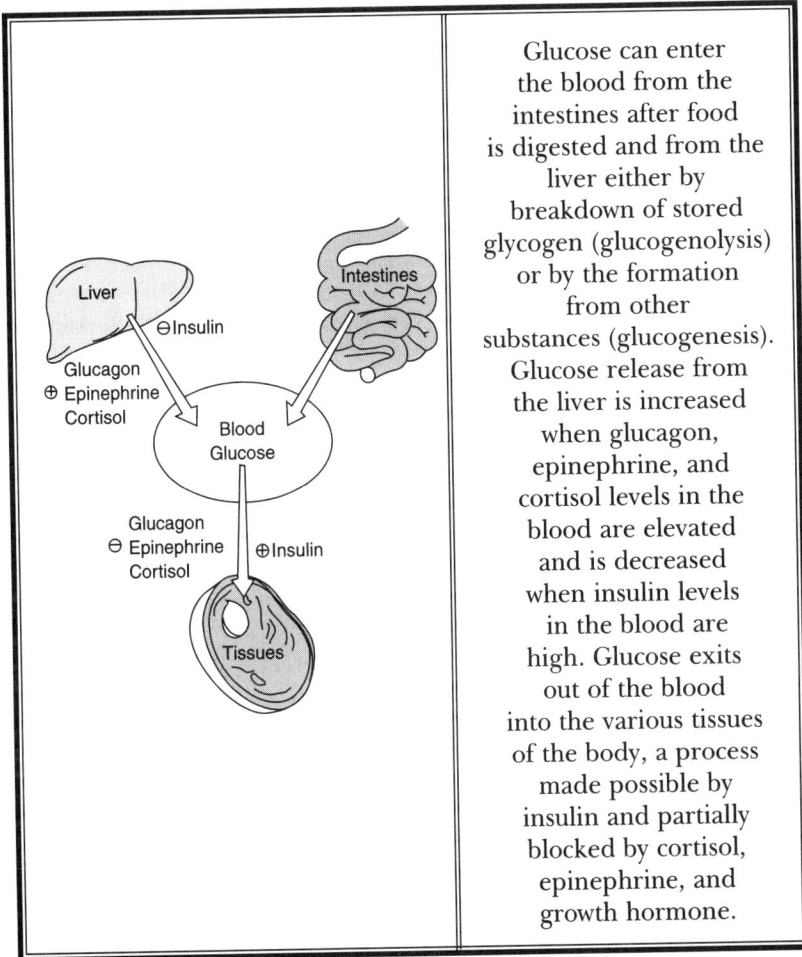

Glucose can enter the blood from the intestines after food is digested and from the liver either by breakdown of stored glycogen (glucogenolysis) or by the formation from other substances (glucogenesis). Glucose release from the liver is increased when glucagon, epinephrine, and cortisol levels in the blood are elevated and is decreased when insulin levels in the blood are high. Glucose exits out of the blood into the various tissues of the body, a process made possible by insulin and partially blocked by cortisol, epinephrine, and growth hormone.

When the cells of the body are deprived of nourishment via glucose, a condition called low blood sugar (hypoglycemia) can develop. Symptoms are usually divided into those affecting the body and those affecting the brain or central nervous system (CNS). Bodily symptoms may include rapid heartbeat, sweating, tremors, anxiety, hunger, and nausea. Those affecting the CNS are light-headedness, confusion, headache, loss of consciousness, seizures, delayed reflexes, and slurred speech. These symptoms are directly related to the brain or body not receiving enough glucose for use as an energy source. Often people who have frequent hypoglycemic episodes are unaware of how serious their symptoms are and may just feel a bit different when, in reality, they may be in a potentially dangerous state of confusion while engaged in activities such as driving which require a high degree of concentration. It is also possible for blood sugar to plunge quite suddenly, causing the individual to lose consciousness completely. This is such a serious problem for those with endocrine problems that numerous studies of hypoglycemia's impact on driving ability and other activities that require a high degree of concentration have been carried out and reported on extensively in the medical literature.

CAUSES OF HYPOGLYCEMIA

Disease. Diabetics are unable to produce enough insulin and must supplement their bodily needs with daily injections or medication. This makes them particularly susceptible to adverse effects of hypoglycemia. The most common prerequisite for hypoglycemia is an overdose of insulin with too little carbohydrate intake or by taking other medications that decrease the blood glucose levels. Although not as common, other errors of metabolism, including insulin-producing tumors or non-islet cell tumors, can also cause hypoglycemia and account for driving errors that call attention to themselves, including, but not limited to, moving in wavy lines, driving in the opposite direction, or running off the road, and subsequently can lead to a driver being charged with a DUI when there may be a negligible amount of alcohol actually involved. Other disease states have also been implicated in hypoglycemia, including, but not limited to, cardiac problems, renal failure, and diseases of the liver.

Alcohol.   Alcohol (ethanol) can lead to hypoglycemia when the liver is depleted of glycogen and will typically develop 6–24 hours after a moderate to heavy intake of ethanol in a person that has had an insufficient intake of food for one or two days. This can have a compounding effect and make the individual appear intoxicated when in fact the person's actual blood alcohol concentration (BAC) may be well below the legal limit. Ethanol can also potentiate the hypoglycemic action of certain classes of drugs like sulfonylurea and insulin.

Drugs.   Insulin and sulfonylureas diabetes medications that stimulate insulin release are the two leading causes of drug-related hypoglycemia; however, many prescription drugs, including some over-the-counter (OTC) medications can directly or indirectly cause hypoglycemia in an unsuspecting user. Examples include salicylates, including aspirin, when taken in large doses; sulfa medicines, used to treat infections; pentamidine, used to treat pneumonia; and quinine, for treating malaria. Pseudoephedrine is found in many over-the-counter cold medications and is one of several drugs that is a close structural analogue of the true amphetamines and has actions and side effects similar to the hormone epinephrine (adrenaline). This OTC can have the effect of speeding up the metabolism to use glucose more rapidly and thereby enhance a hypoglycemic condition. There are also a wide range of drug combinations that can lead to hypoglycemia or enhance an already existing condition.

Overexertion.   Too much or prolonged exercise is another way the body can speed up metabolism and rapidly deplete stored glucose. Sometimes exercise can have a prolonged effect in lowering blood glucose levels — up to 24 hours. Fright or anxiety can also cause the body to overreact and, as with overexertion, can expedite the release of adrenaline speeding up the metabolism and lowering glucose levels.

Diet soda.   One of the most common sweeteners used in diet drinks is Aspartame, which contains the amino acid phenylanine, a chemical known to produce a higher insulin response. This response can be extremely pronounced in endocrine-compromised individuals. Studies in the medical literature have shown this response to be 101–103 percent greater than with a similar beverage containing a carbohydrate sweetener. Drinking diet soda alone or in combination with ethanol could only serve to enhance a state of low blood sugar.

CONCLUSION

As briefly outlined, hypoglycemia is a serious problem for many individuals with faulty metabolism. The ramifications of the condition can sometimes go far beyond the surface medical and scientific issues regarding the physical health of the patient. The problems range from maintaining blood sugar levels in order to live a "normal" life, to life-threatening risks due to sudden spikes or plummets of blood sugar levels, to being falsely accused of driving in an intoxicated condition during periods of unstable metabolism, a charge which can have long-term consequences for a person's life and career. And, if anything, the problem is only going to get worse. The National Health and Nutrition Examination Survey, released in September 2003 and published by the Center for Disease Control and Prevention in the September 5, 2003 edition of its *Morbidity and Mortality Weekly Report,* indicates that one in seven Americans have diabetes or blood sugar problems that are leading toward diabetes. In fact, world health officials meeting in August, 2003 in Paris at the International Diabetes Federation Conference proclaimed that the world is facing a "diabetes catastrophe" with more than 300 million people worldwide facing a serious risk of developing diabetes. With the numbers of people with blood sugar problems and other errors of metabolism rising, it is becoming more important than ever for individuals, medical professionals, and law enforcement personnel to recognize both the danger signals of hypoglycemia and to understand that although the condition mimics closely those who irresponsibly abuse alcohol, judicious use of sound science principles can ensure that a health compromised individual is not unjustly punished for a pre-existing physical condition.

§4.3 *Field Sobriety Tests*

Page 194. Add after first carryover paragraph:

Defense counsel should always remind the court that field sobriety tests are designed and administered to avoid the shortcomings of casual observation. Since field sobriety tests consist of precise body movements, a greater degree of coordination is required than for routine standing or walking. Most courts agree with the Supreme Court of New Hampshire when they admit that the results of field sobriety tests do not possess the scientific reliability or the same degree of certitude attributed to the chemical analysis of the alcoholic blood content by a Breathalyzer or other such methods. See *State v. Arsenault*, 336 A.2d 244, 246 (N.H. 1975), citing 1 Am. J. Crim. L. 96 (1967).

§4.3.2 "Standardized" Field Sobriety Tests

Page 206. Add at end of third full paragraph:

Newer versions of NHTSA's DWI Detection & Standardized Field Sobriety Testing: Student Manual were released in 2000 as DOT-HS-178-R2/00 and in 2002 as DOT-HS-178-R1/02.

Page 207. Replace first sentence of second full paragraph with:

The following subsections (§§4.3.3–4.3.7) set forth the correct procedures to be used by officers in administering the three standardized field sobriety tests, as described in the NHTSA DWI Detection & Standardized Field Sobriety Testing Student Manual, DOT-HS-178-R10/95. The supplement author has taken the liberty of noting material differences from the 1995 student manual in both the 2000 student manual, DOT-HS-178-R2/00, and the 2002 student manual, DOT-HS-178-R1/02. Unless indicated otherwise, all references to a "manual" are to the student version of the Field Sobriety Test manual.

Page 207. Replace first sentence of last paragraph with:

The following "scoring sheet," taken from the NHTSA pamphlet Improved Sobriety Testing (DOT-HS-806–512), and eliminated from the subsequent versions of the student manual, illustrates the scoring system and serves as an overview of the tests:

Pages 208–227. In their entirety, replace §§4.3.3 (Walk-and-Turn), 4.3.4 (One-Leg-Stand), 4.3.5 (Horizontal Gaze Nystagmus), and Checklists 3 (Nystagmus) and 4 (Field Sobriety Tests) with the following:

§4.3.3   The History and Development of the Field Sobriety Tests

The following material setting forth an overview of standardized field sobriety test research and development is taken from the NHTSA DWI Detection and Standardized Field Sobriety Testing Student Manual, which was released in 1995 as DOT-HS-178-R10/95. It offers a discussion of the extensive research conducted by federal authorities and used to standardize the field sobriety tests. The material can be used effectively in cross-examination to compare the arresting officer's methods with those recommended after this research.

[Editor's Note: The Manual's official pagination has been preserved to allow for accurate citation. The notes are the supplement author's commentary and are not in the original.]

OVERVIEW OF SFST
RESEARCH AND DEVELOPMENT[1]

1. First Phase: The Developmental Research

    A. The research objectives

        o   To evaluate currently used physical coordination tests to determine their relationship to intoxication and driving impairment.

        o   To develop more sensitive tests that would provide more reliable evidence of impairment.

        o   To standardize the tests and observations.

    B. Who conducted the research?

        Southern California Research Institute (SCRI)

        The final report:

            Burns, Marcelline and Moskowitz, Herbert
            Psychophysical Tests for DWI; June, 1977
            NHTSA Report Number DOT HS-802 424
            (available from National Technical Information
            Service, Springfield, Virginia 22161)

    C. Who were the test subjects?

        They were 238 volunteers, participating in one testing session.

        The volunteers were interviewed by SCRI staff, and on the basis of the interview they were classified as either light, moderate or heavy drinkers. They were randomly assigned to "target BAC" levels appropriate to their classifications. The following shows the distribution of BACs achieved by volunteers:

---

[1] The explanation of the research and development of the standardized field sobriety tests are substantially edited in the 2000 and 2002 versions. In particular, the latest versions eliminate the detailed discussion of the phases of the research and the results of the studies. NHTSA does not refer to blood alcohol levels in percentage form in any of its versions.

	Light Drinkers	Moderate Drinkers	Heavy Drinkers	Totals
No Alcohol (0.00)	26	27	26	79
Approximately 0.05	36	16	3	55
Approximately 0.075	--	6	7	13
Approximately 0.10	--	37	13	50
Approximately 0.15	--	--	41	41

D. Who tested the subjects?

Ten police officers, representing four agencies in the vicinity of Los Angeles, did all of the testing. Each officer examined an average of 23-24 volunteers. While the officer was conducting the examinations, a member of the SCRI staff observed the examinations.

NOTE: Neither the volunteer nor the officer nor the observer knew the volunteer's BAC. Separate members of the SCRI staff handled the dosing and breath testing of volunteers.

E. What tests were administered?

Each volunteer was subjected to six tests:

o   One-Leg Stand
o   Finger-To-Nose
o   Finger Count
o   Walk-and-Turn
o   Tracing (a paper-and-pencil exercise)
o   Nystagmus (called "alcohol gaze nystagmus" in the final report)

Each officer was given one day's training in the administration and scoring of these tests prior to conducting the experiment. NOTE: Only two of the ten officers had any prior experience with nystagmus.

F. What did the researchers learn?

The researchers analyzed their data and found that, using the scores from all six tests, they could correctly classify a volunteer's BAC as being either above or below 0.10 about 83 percent of the time.

Further, the researchers found that this same level of reliability could be achieved just by considering the scores on nystagmus, Walk-and-Turn, and one-leg stand.

What about the 17% of volunteers whose BACs were misclassified? How did the researchers account for them?

First, half of the volunteers who were misclassified had BACs between 0.08 and 0.12, a "borderline" range in which it can be difficult to distinguish slight differences in impairment. Secondly, almost all of the remaining misclassified volunteers were either light drinkers with BACs of at least 0.05 (who may well have appeared and been very impaired at that level), or heavy drinkers with BACs below 0.15 (whose experience with alcohol may have helped them mask the signs of impairment).

G. What was the overall conclusion?

The three-test battery made up of Horizontal Gaze Nystagmus, Walk-and-Turn, and one-leg stand clearly appeared to offer a very reliable field sobriety testing procedure. But these tests were not yet standardized in their final form. Standardization was achieved in the next phase of research.

H. What were the research objectives?

o   To complete the development and validation of the sobriety test battery.

o   To assess in the field the battery's feasibility, and its effectiveness for estimating BAC and facilitating identification of persons with BACs above 0.10.

Note: Southern California Research Institute (SCRI) conducted the test validation research.

The final report:
Tharp, V., Burns, M. and Moskowitz, H.
Development and Field Test of Psychophysical
Tests for DWI Arrest, March, 1981, NHTSA
Report Number DOT HS-805 864 (available from
NTIS, Springfield, Virginia 22161)

I. Who were the test subjects?

During the first (laboratory) portion of this research effort, the test subjects
were 296 volunteers. The 296 laboratory subjects each participated in at
least one testing session. And, 145 of them returned for a second session,
for a total of 441 subject-days of testing. The following table shows the
distribution of these subjects by drinker classification and "target BAC"; the
numbers in parenthesis refer to the subjects who returned for a second
session.

	Light Drinkers	Moderate Drinkers	Heavy Drinkers	Totals
No Alcohol (0.00)	30 (18)	32 (16)	35 (16)	97 (50)
Approximately (0.05)	33 (15)	33 (16)	36 (17)	102 (48)
Approximately (0.11)	--	30 (15)	34 (14)	64 (29)
Approximately (0.15)	--	--	33 (18)	33 (18)

J. Who tested the subjects?

For the laboratory portion of the study, ten police officers from three
agencies in the metropolitan Los Angeles area did the testing. Each officer
examined an average of 44 subjects (including returnees). While the officer
conducted the examinations, a member of the SCRI staff observed. Neither
the volunteer, nor the officer nor the observer knew the volunteer's BAC.

For the field portion of the study, participating officers were drawn from
four stations of the Los Angeles County Sheriff's Office. They included a
group called the "experimentals" (who received training in the SFSTs), and
a group of "controls" (who were not trained until the final stage of the
study). Both groups were instructed to complete data forms for all of their
traffic stops during the study period. In addition, SCRI researchers
periodically rode with every officer to monitor their performance.

K. What tests were administered?

In both the laboratory and field portion of the study, participating officers
(except the "controls") administered Horizontal Gaze Nystagmus, Walk-and-
Turn, and One-Leg Stand. Some of the officers had some prior experience
with these tests, but all received one-half day's training in test
administration and scoring.

In both the laboratory and field portions of this study, officers were instructed to record the following nystagmus data, for each eye:

o   Whether onset occurred within 45 degrees, with at least 10% of the white of the eye showing;

o   The estimated angle of onset;

o   Whether the eye was unable to follow smoothly;

o   Whether the nystagmus at maximum deviation was absent, minimal, moderate or heavy.

One "point" was "scored" for each eye if onset occurred within 45 degrees; if the eye was unable to follow smoothly; and, if the nystagmus at maximum deviation was moderate or heavy.

L.   What did the researchers learn?

(1) The Laboratory Phase

Results of the laboratory study demonstrated that the battery of three tests could be used reliably to distinguish subjects with BACs of 0.10 or more from those with lower BACs. Collectively, the ten officers and two observers were correct in classifying subjects' BACs (above or below 0.10) about 82% of the time. Subsequent to publication of the SCRI report, NHTSA re-analyzed the laboratory test data and found that the nystagmus test, by itself, could have produced 77% accurate classifications. Similarly, Walk-and-Turn was capable of 68% unaided accuracy, and One-Leg Stand of 65%. NHTSA also found that it would be possible to combine the results of nystagmus and Walk-and-Turn in a "decision matrix", and achieve 80% accuracy.

(2) The Field Phase

SCRI reported a number of problems that plagued the field study, chief among which was a lack of consistency by participating officers in submitting data forms. SCRI concluded that the field test data would not support in-depth statistical analysis, but nevertheless disclosed some favorable trends:

o   after training on the test battery, officers tended to make more DWI arrests; and,

o   trained officers were more accurate in identifying suspects whose
    BACs are above 0.10.

The overall conclusion of this study was that the test battery works
well. But it remained necessary to conduct a rigorous field test.

M. The Field Validation and Standardization of the Tests

(1) What were the research objectives?

o   To develop standardized, practical and effective procedures for
    police officers to use in reaching arrest/no arrest decisions;

o   To test the feasibility of the procedures in operational conditions;
    and,

o   To secure data to determine if the tests will discriminate as well in
    the field as in the laboratory.

In support of the first of the objectives, the NHTSA research staff began
by re-analyzing the SCRI data with a view toward systematizing the
administrative and "scoring" procedures for the three tests. The intent
was to ensure that the tests would be quick and easy to use; that they
could each be used independently of one another, i.e., if the officer
elected to use only one or two of the tests; and, that they would
maximize the detection of drivers with BACs above 0.10 while
minimizing the continued investigation of persons below that level.

Essentially, the current administrative and "scoring" procedures, and
"scoring" criteria, for the three tests emerged from this re-analysis.

(2) Who conducted the research?

SCRI sponsored by The National Highway Traffic Safety
Administration (NHTSA)

The final report:

Anderson, T., Schweitz, R., and Snyder, M.
Field Evaluation of a Behavioral Test Battery for DWI
September, 1983, NHTSA Report Number DOT HS-806 475
(available from NTIS, Springfield, Virginia 22161)

(3) Who were the test subjects?

They were 1,506 drivers stopped for suspicion of DWI during a three-month period during late 1982/early 1983. Of these, approximately 80% were examined using all three tests.

(4) Who tested the subjects?

Police officers representing four large agencies in the eastern portion of the country did the testing. All participating officers completed a one day training session prior to the beginning of the study. The training included practice in administering the tests to volunteer drinkers.

(5) What tests were administered?

The officers used the three tests that make up the Standardized Field Sobriety Testing battery. As previously noted, not all subjects were exposed to all three tests, primarily because circumstances of the stop location and/or the subject sometimes precluded use of one or two of the tests. But 89% of subjects were examined using the horizontal gaze nystagmus test, 84% on Walk-and-Turn and 82% on One-Leg Stand.

(6) What were the test administrative and "scoring" procedures?

The procedures followed in using and interpreting the tests were essentially those spelled out in the current NHTSA training program DWI Detection and Standardized Field Sobriety Testing (1987 Update). The tests are "standardized" in the sense that:

o   they are always administered in the same way;

o   the officer administering the tests always looks for a specific set of clues on each test; and,

o   the officer always assesses a suspect's performance relative to a specific criterion for each test.

N.   The "standardized" elements of the Horizontal Gaze Nystagmus test

(1) Standardized Administrative Procedures

o   Hold the stimulus 12-15 inches in front of the suspect's nose.
o   Keep the tip of the stimulus slightly above the suspect's eyes.

o Always move the stimulus smoothly.
o Always check for all three clues in both eyes, starting with suspect's left eye.
o Check the clues in this sequence: lack of smooth pursuit; distinct nystagmus at maximum deviation; onset of nystagmus prior to 45 degrees.
o Always check for each clue at least twice in each eye.

(2) Standardized Clues

o Lack of smooth pursuit.
o Distinct nystagmus at maximum deviation.
o Onset of nystagmus prior to 45 degrees.

No other "clues" are recognized by NHTSA as valid indicators of horizontal gaze nystagmus. In particular, NHTSA does not support the allegation that onset angle can reliably be used to estimate BAC, and considers any such estimation to be misuse of the horizontal gaze nystagmus test.

(3) Standardized Criterion

The maximum number of clues of horizontal gaze nystagmus that a suspect can exhibit is six. That would occur when all three clues are observed in both eyes. If a suspect exhibits four or more clues, it should be considered evidence that the suspect's BAC is above 0.10. (New information indicates that HGN may be present in suspects under the influence of certain other drugs.)

O. The "standardized" elements of Walk-and-Turn

(1) Standardized Administrative Procedures

o Always begin by having the suspect assume the heel-toe stance, right foot in front of left.

o Verify that the suspect understands that the stance is to be maintained while the instructions are given.

o If the suspect breaks away from the stance as the instructions are given, cease giving instructions until the stance is resumed.

o   Tell the suspect that they will be required to take 9 heel-to-toe steps down the line, to turn around, and to take 9 heel-to-toe steps up the line.

o   Demonstrate several heel-toe steps.

o   Demonstrate the turn.

o   Tell the suspect to keep the arms at the sides, to watch the feet, to count the steps aloud, and not to stop walking until the test is completed.

o   Ask the suspect whether they understand; if not, re-explain whatever is not understood.

o   Tell the suspect to begin.

o   If the suspect staggers or stops, allow them to resume from the point of interruption; do not require the suspect to start over from the beginning.

(2) Standardized Clues

o   Loses balance during the instruction stage (feet must break away from the heel-toe stance).

o   Starts walking too soon.

o   Stops while walking.

o   Misses heel-to-toe while walking (misses by at least one-half inch).

o   Raises arms from side while walking (six inches or more).

o   Steps off the line.

o   Turns improperly.

o   Takes the wrong number of steps.

These eight are the only validated clues of Walk-and-Turn. However, officers may see or hear other noteworthy evidence while the suspect is performing this test, and officers should include any such observations in their reports.

Officers should note in their reports how many times each clue appears. However, for purposes of applying the standardized criterion (discussed below), a clue should be "counted" only once. Except if the suspect steps off the line three or more times, then the test is terminated and scored as if all eight clues were observed.

Also, if the suspect cannot perform or complete the test, it should be considered that they have exhibited all eight clues.

(3) Standardized Criterion

If a suspect exhibits at least two clues on Walk-and-Turn, it should be considered evidence that the suspect's BAC is above 0.10.

P. The "standardized" elements of One-Leg Stand

(1) Standardized Administration Procedures

o   Tell the suspect to stand with feet together, and arms at sides.

o   Tell the suspect not to start the test until told to do so.

o   Ask the suspect if they understand.

o   Tell the suspect to stand on one foot, with the other foot held straight about six inches off the ground, toes pointed out.

o   Demonstrate the stance.

o   Tell the suspect to count for 30 seconds in the following manner: "one thousand and one," "one thousand and two," until told to stop.

o   Demonstrate the count, for several seconds.

o   Ask the suspect whether they understand; if not, re-explain whatever is not understood.

o   Tell the suspect to begin.

o   If the suspect stops or puts the foot down, allow them to resume at the point of interruption; do not require the count to begin again at "one thousand and one".

(2) Standardized Clues

o   Sways
o   Puts foot down
o   Hops
o   Raises arms from side (six inches or more)

These are the only four validated clues of One-Leg Stand. However, officers may see or hear other noteworthy evidence while this test is being performed, and should include any such evidence in their reports.

If the suspect cannot perform or complete the test, it should be considered that they have exhibited all four clues. One event that would warrant this is if the suspect puts the foot down three or more times.

(3) Standardized Criterion

If the suspect exhibits two or more clues on One-Leg Stand, it should be considered evidence that the suspect's BAC is above 0.10. As with Walk-and-Turn, clues should be counted only once in applying this criterion.

Q.   <u>What did the researchers learn?</u> [2]

The three standardized tests were found to be highly reliable in identifying subjects whose BACs were 0.10 or more.[3]   Considered independently, the nystagmus test was 77% accurate, the Walk-and-Turn, 68% accurate, and the One-Leg Stand, 65% accurate. However, Horizontal Gaze Nystagmus used in combination with Walk-and-Turn was 80% accurate.

The importance of this large scale field validation study deserves to be emphasized. It was the first significant assessment of the "workability" of the standardized field sobriety tests under actual enforcement conditions, and it was the first time that completely objective clues and scoring criteria had been defined for the tests. The results of the study validated the SFSTs.

HS 178 R10/95   VIII-11

[2] The 2000 and 2002 versions of the manual provide a brief discussion of additional SFST validation studies, which were undertaken between 1995 and 1998 (Colorado — 1995, Florida — 1997, San Diego — 1998).

[3] Relying on the 1998 San Diego study, the 2002 manual indicates that the SFSTs may accurately discriminate BACs at 0.04 and above. It is important to note, however, that the 2000 manual suggests that only the HGN test may be indicative of BACs at 0.04 and above.

But it is also necessary to emphasize one final and major point. This validation applies ONLY WHEN THE TESTS ARE ADMINISTERED IN THE PRESCRIBED, STANDARDIZED MANNER; AND ONLY WHEN THE STANDARDIZED CLUES ARE USED TO ASSESS THE SUSPECT'S PERFORMANCE; AND, ONLY WHEN THE STANDARDIZED CRITERIA ARE EMPLOYED TO INTERPRET THAT PERFORMANCE.

IF ANY ONE OF THE STANDARDIZED FIELD SOBRIETY TEST ELEMENTS IS CHANGED, THE VALIDITY IS COMPROMISED.

* * *

§4.3.4 Horizontal Gaze Nystagmus

The following material is taken from the student manual (DOT-HS-178-R10/95) published by NHTSA for the purpose of training officers in the correct procedures for administering the standardized field sobriety tests. Any deviation from these procedures (and counsel will encounter few if any officers who follow the protocol correctly) should provide good material for cross-examination.

* * *

OVERVIEW OF HORIZONTAL GAZE NYSTAGMUS

Definition

Nystagmus is the involuntary jerking of the eyes, occurring as the eyes gaze toward the side.[1] Also, nystagmus is natural, normal phenomenon. Alcohol and certain other drugs do not cause this phenomenon, they merely exaggerate or magnify it.[2]

Categories of Nystagmus

Nystagmus of several different origins may be seen. There are three general categories of nystagmus:

1. Vestibular Nystagmus is caused by movement or action to the vestibular system.

    A. Types of vestibular nystagmus:

        o   Rotational Nystagmus occurs when the person is spun around or rotated rapidly, causing the fluid in the inner ear to be disturbed. If it were possible to observe the eyes of a rotating person, they would be seen to jerk noticeably.

        o   Post Rotational Nystagmus is closely related to rotational nystagmus: when the person stops spinning, the fluid in the inner ear remains disturbed for a period of time, and the eyes continue to jerk.

        o   Caloric Nystagmus occurs when fluid motion in the canals of the vestibular system is stimulated by temperature as by putting warm water in one ear and cold in the other.

HS 178 R10/95   VIII-12

---

[1] The subsequent versions of the manual do not state that Nystagmus occurs as the eyes gaze toward the side.

[2] The 2002 manual states that "Alcohol and certain other drugs *cause* horizontal gaze nystagmus." (Emphasis added.)

o   Positional Alcohol Nystagmus (PAN) occurs when a foreign fluid, such as alcohol, that alters the specific gravity of the blood is in unequal concentrations in the blood and the vestibular system. This causes the vestibular system to respond to gravity in certain positions, resulting in nystagmus.

PAN I occurs when the alcohol concentration in the blood is greater than in the inner ear fluid. PAN I occurs while BAC is increasing.

PAN II occurs when the alcohol concentration in the inner ear fluid is greater than in the blood stream. This occurs while BAC is decreasing.[3]

2.   Nystagmus can also result directly from neural activity:

o   Optokinetic Nystagmus occurs when the eyes fixate on an object that suddenly moves out of sight, or when the eyes watch sharply contrasting moving images.

Examples of optokinetic nystagmus include watching scenery while looking out the window of a moving train or watching a rapidly spinning wheel that has alternating white and black spokes. The horizontal gaze nystagmus test will not be influenced by optokinetic nystagmus if administered properly.

o   Physiological Nystagmus is a natural nystagmus that keeps the sensory cells of the eye from tiring. It is the most common type of nystagmus. It happens to all of us, all the time. This type of nystagmus produces extremely minor tremors or jerks of the eyes. These tremors are generally too small to be seen with the naked eye. Physiological nystagmus will have no impact on our standardized field sobriety tests, because its tremors are generally invisible.

o   Gaze Nystagmus occurs as the eyes move from the center position. Gaze nystagmus is separated into three types:

(1)   Horizontal Gaze Nystagmus occurs as the eyes move to the side. It is the observation of the eyes for horizontal gaze nystagmus that provides the first and most valid test in the standardized field sobriety testing battery. Although this type of nystagmus is most accurate for determining alcohol influence, its presence may also indicate use of PCP, certain inhalants and other central nervous system depressants.

[3] The descriptions of PAN I and PAN II are omitted from the 2002 manual.

(2) Vertical Gaze Nystagmus occurs as the eyes are held in their upmost position. The presence of this type of nystagmus is associated with PCP. High doses for the individual of CNS depressants (including alcohol) and inhalants may also cause this to occur. The drugs that produce vertical nystagmus are the same ones that produce horizontal gaze nystagmus.

Note: All drugs that induce horizontal gaze nystagmus may also induce vertical nystagmus, if enough of the drug is taken. There is no drug that will cause vertical nystagmus that does not cause horizontal nystagmus. If vertical nystagmus is present and horizontal nystagmus is not, it could be a medical condition.

(3) Resting Nystagmus is referred to as jerking as the eyes look straight ahead. This condition is not frequently seen. Its presence usually indicates high doses of PCP. If detected, take precautions. (OFFICER SAFETY.)

3. Nystagmus may also be caused by certain pathological disorders. They include brain tumors and other brain damage or some diseases of the inner ear. These pathological disorders occur in very few people and in even fewer drivers.

4. Medical Impairment.

A. The examinations that you can conduct to assess possible medical impairment include:[4]

o   Tracking ability
o   Pupil size
Note: If suspect has an obvious abnormal eye disorder or an artificial eye, HGN should not be administered.[5]

Procedures of Horizontal Gaze Nystagmus Testing: The Three Clues

As explained earlier, nystagmus means a jerking of the eyes. There are a number of different kinds of nystagmus. The test you will use at roadside is a test of "horizontal gaze nystagmus" -- the nystagmus that occurs when the eyes move to the side. Many eyes will show some jerking if moved far enough to the side. Under the influence of alcohol and certain other drugs, three signs often will be observed:

1. The suspect cannot follow a slowly moving stimulus smoothly with the eyes;[6] instead, the eyes can be observed to jerk or "bounce" as they move left and right in pursuit of a smoothly moving object, such as a pencil or penlight.

HS 178 R10/95   VIII-14

---

[4] The 2002 manual includes resting nystagmus as a third examination that can be conducted.

[5] The 2002 manual omits this notation.

[6] In the subsequent versions, this clue is referred to as the Lack of Smooth Pursuit.

2. When you have the suspect move their eyes as far to the side as possible, distinct nystagmus will be evident when the eye is held at maximum deviation for approximately[7] four seconds;[8] some people exhibit slight jerking of the eye at maximum deviation, even when sober, but when under the influence of alcohol, the jerking is likely to be very pronounced, and easily observable.[9]

3. The more intoxicated a person becomes, the less the eyes have to move toward the side before jerking begins.[10] Usually when a person's BAC is above 0.10, the jerking will begin before the eye has moved 45 degrees to the side.[11]

Estimating a 45-Degree Angle

Because the 45-degree angle is a key factor in assessing a suspect's degree of alcohol influence, it is important to know how to estimate that angle.

For practice, a 45-degree template can be prepared by making a 15"-square cardboard and connecting its opposite corners with a diagonal line.

To use this device, hold it up so that the person's nose is above the diagonal line. Be certain that one edge of the template is centered on the nose and perpendicular to (or, at right angles to) the face. Have the person you are examining follow a penlight or some other object until suspect is looking down the 45-degree diagonal. Note the position of the eye. With practice, you should be able to recognize this angle without using the template.

Specific Procedures

Begin by asking "are you wearing contact lenses", make a note whether or not the suspect wears contacts before starting the test.[12]

If the suspect is wearing eyeglasses, have them removed.

Give the suspect the following instructions from a position of interrogation (FOR OFFICER SAFETY KEEP YOUR WEAPON AWAY FROM THE SUSPECT):

o   "I am going to check your eyes."
o   "Keep your head still and follow this stimulus with your eyes only."
o   "Keep focusing on this stimulus until I tell you to stop."

[7] Both the 2000 and 2002 manuals specify that distinct Nystagmus will be evident when the eye is held at maximum deviation for a *minimum* of four seconds.
[8] This clue is referred to in the subsequent versions as Distinct Nystagmus at Maximum Deviation.

---

[9] The 2002 manual further adds that Nystagmus exhibited in persons who are not impaired will "not be evident or sustained for more than a few seconds. When impaired by alcohol, the jerking will be larger, more pronounced, sustained for more than four seconds, and easily observable."

[10] This clue is referred to in the subsequent versions as Onset of Nystagmus Prior to 45 Degrees.

[11] The 2000 and 2002 manuals state that the onset of Nystagmus prior to 45 degrees is evidence that the person has a BAC of above 0.08, "as shown by recent research."

[12] Both the 2000 and 2002 manuals omit the requirement to inquire as to whether the defendant is wearing contact lenses.

Position the stimulus approximately 12-15 inches from the suspect's nose and slightly above eye level.[13] Check the suspect's eyes for the ability to track together. Move the stimulus smoothly across the suspect's entire field of vision. Check to see if the eyes track the stimulus together or one lags behind the other. If the eyes don't track together it could indicate a possible medical disorder, injury, or blindness.

Next, check to see that both pupils are equal in size. If they are not, this may indicate a head injury.

Check the suspect's left eye by moving the stimulus to your right. Move the stimulus smoothly, at a speed that requires about two seconds to bring the suspect's eye as far to the side as it can go. While moving the stimulus, look at the suspect's eye and determine whether it is able to pursue smoothly. Now, move the stimulus all the way to the left, back across suspect's face checking if the right eye pursues smoothly. Movement of the stimulus should take approximately two seconds out and two seconds back for each eye. Repeat the procedure.

After you have checked both eyes for lack of smooth pursuit, check the eyes for distinct nystagmus at maximum deviation beginning with the suspect's left eye. Simply move the object to the suspect's left side until the eye has gone as far to the side as possible. Usually, no white will be showing in the corner of the eye at maximum deviation. Hold the eye at that position for approximately four seconds, and observe the eye for distinct nystagmus.[14] Move the stimulus all the way across the suspect's face to check the right eye holding that position for approximately four seconds. Repeat the procedure.[15]

After checking the eyes at maximum deviation, check for onset of nystagmus prior to 45 degrees. Start moving the stimulus towards the right (suspect's left eye) at a speed that would take about four seconds for the stimulus to reach the edge of the suspect's shoulder. Watch the eye carefully for any sign of jerking. When you see it, stop and verify that the jerking continues. Now, move the stimulus to the left (suspect's right eye) at a speed that would take about four seconds for the stimulus to reach the edge of the suspect's shoulder. Watch the eye carefully for

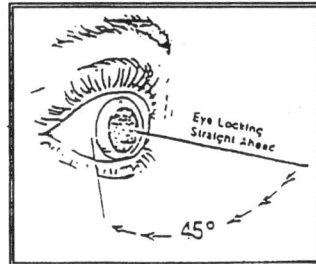

any sign of jerking. When you see it, stop and verify that the jerking continues. Repeat the procedure. NOTE: It is important to use the full four seconds when checking for onset of nystagmus. If you move the stimulus too fast, you may go past the point of onset or miss it altogether.

HS 178 R10/95   VIII-16

[13] The 2002 manual also indicates that resting nystagmus may be observed at this time.
[14] The 2002 manual specifies that the officer must observe the eye for distinct *and sustained* Nystagmus (emphasis in original).
[15] The 2000 and 2002 manuals add the following notation: "*Fatigue Nystagmus.* This type of nystagmus may begin if a suspect's eyes are held at maximum deviation for more than 30 seconds."

If the suspect's eyes start jerking before they reach 45 degrees, check to see that some white of the eye is still showing on the side closest to the ear. If no white of the eye is showing, you either have taken the eye too far to the side (that is more than 45 degrees) or the person has unusual eyes that will not deviate very far to the side.

```
ADMINISTRATIVE PROCEDURES

 1. EYEGLASSES/CONTACTS
 2. VERBAL INSTRUCTIONS
 3. POSITION OBJECT (12-15 INCHES)
 4. TRACKING
 5. PUPIL SIZE
 6. CHECK FOR LACK OF SMOOTH PURSUIT
 7. CHECK FOR DIST. NYSTAGMUS @ MAX. DEV
 8. CHECK ONSET OF NYSTAGMUS PRIOR TO 45°
 9. TOTAL THE CLUES
10. CHECK FOR VERTICAL NYSTAGMUS
```

NOTE: Nystagmus may be due to causes other than alcohol. These other causes include seizure medications, PCP, inhalants, barbiturates and other depressants. A large disparity between the performance of the right and left eye may indicate a medical condition.

Test Interpretation

You should look for three clues of nystagmus in each eye.

1. The eye cannot follow a moving object smoothly.
2. Nystagmus is distinct when the eye is at maximum deviation.[16]
3. The angle of onset of nystagmus is prior to 45 degrees.

If you observe four or more clues, it is likely that the suspect's BAC is above 0.10. Using this criterion you will be able to classify correctly about 77% of your suspects with respect to whether they are above 0.10. That probability was determined during laboratory and field testing and helps you weigh the various field sobriety tests in this battery as you make your arrest decision.

Vertical Nystagmus

The Vertical Nystagmus test is very simple to administer. During the Vertical Nystagmus test, look for distinct jerking when the eyes are held for four seconds in the upmost position.

1. Position the stimulus horizontally, about 12-15 inches in front of the suspect's nose.

2. Instruct the suspect to hold the head still, and follow the object with the eyes only.

3. Raise the object until the suspect's eyes are elevated as far as possible.

HS 178 R10/95   VIII-17

---

[16] The 2002 manual indicates that this clue is present when Nystagmus is both distinct *and sustained* when the eye is held at maximum deviation for a minimum of four seconds.

112

4. Hold for approximately four seconds.

5. Watch closely for evidence of jerking.

Horizontal and Vertical Gaze Nystagmus can be observed directly and does not require special equipment. You will need something for the suspect to follow with the eyes, but this can be as simple as the tip of your index finger, penlight, or pen. The stimulus used should be held slightly above eye level, so that the eyes are wide open when they look directly at it. It should be held about 12-15 inches in front of the nose for ease of focus. Remain aware of your position in relation to the suspect at all times. OFFICER SAFETY IS THE NUMBER ONE PRIORITY ON ANY TRAFFIC STOP.

* * *

§4.3.4.1   Discussion of Horizontal Gaze Nystagmus

A new type of field sobriety test, the "Horizontal Gaze Nystagmus" (HGN) test, arose in the early 1980s in the western states. Used initially only on an experimental basis, the test quickly spread and is now being used by police agencies in almost all jurisdictions. Although administered by the officer at the scene of the traffic stop as a field sobriety test, it is really a superficial test to determine blood-alcohol content. It should also be recognized that evidence of the test can have devastating effects in a drunk driving trial. Properly handled by the defense, however, this test may never be admitted into evidence; if admitted, the test can be discredited.

Dr. L. F. Dell'Osso, Professor of Neurology at Case Western Reserve University School of Medicine and Director of the Ocular Motor Neurophysiology Laboratory at the Veteran's Administration Medical Center in Cleveland, is a noted expert in the area of nystagmus. In his article "Nystagmus, Saccadic Intrusions/Oscillations and Oscillopsia," 3 Current Neuro-Ophthalmology 147 (1989), listing 47 different kinds of nystagmus, he commented:

> Using nystagmus as an indicator of alcohol intoxication is an unfortunate choice, since many normal individuals have physiologic end-point nystagmus; small doses of tranquilizers that would not interfere with driving can produce nystagmus; nystagmus may be congenital or consequent to neurologic disease; and without a neuro-ophthalmologist or someone knowledgeable about sophisticated methods of eye movement recordings, it is difficult to determine whether the nystagmus is pathologic. It is unreasonable that such difficult judgments have been placed in the hands of minimally trained officers.

Further, the Court of Special Appeals of Maryland has judicially recognized 38 non–alcohol-related causes of Horizontal Gaze Nystagmus. They include:

(1) problems with the inner ear labyrinth;
(2) irrigating the ears with warm or cold water under peculiar weather conditions;
(3) influenza;

(4) streptococcus infection;

(5) vertigo;

(6) measles;

(7) syphilis;

(8) arteriosclerosis;

(9) muscular dystrophy;

(10) multiple sclerosis;

(11) Korchaff's syndrome;

(12) brain hemorrhage;

(13) epilepsy;

(14) hypertension;

(15) motion sickness;

(16) sunstroke;

(17) eyestrain;

(18) eye muscle fatigue;

(19) glaucoma;

(20) changes in atmospheric pressure;

(21) consumption of excessive amounts of caffeine;

(22) excessive exposure to nicotine;

(23) aspirin;

(24) circadian rhythms;

(25) acute trauma to the head;

(26) chronic trauma to the head;

(27) some prescription drugs, tranquilizers, pain medications, anti-convulsants;

(28) barbiturates;

(29) disorders of the vestibular apparatus and brain stem;

(30) cerebellum dysfunction;

(31) heredity;

(32) diet;

(33) toxins;

(34) exposure to solvents, PCBs, dry-cleaning fumes, carbon monoxide;

(35) extreme chilling;

(36) eye muscle imbalance;

(37) lesions;

(38) continuous movement of the visual field past the eyes, *i.e.*, looking from a moving train; and

(39) antihistamine use.

Schultz v. State, 664 A.2d 60, 77(Md. App. 1995) (citations omitted).

There are three basic types of physiologic "end-point" nystagmus that are regarded as normal physiologic phenomena. These are described in *Duane's Clinical Ophthalmology*, 20 (William Tasman, M.D. & Edward A. Jager, M.D. eds., vol. 2 2004). *Fatigue nystagmus* has been found in up to 60 percent of normal patients when horizontal gaze is maximally deviated for a time exceeding 30 seconds. *Unsustained end-point nystagmus* is described as the most frequently encountered physiologic nystagmus. All experienced clinicians recognize that a few beats of nystagmus are within perfectly normal limits at gaze deviations of 30 degrees or more. *Sustained end-point nystagmus* begins immediately or within several seconds after reaching an eccentric lateral-gaze position. It has been found in over 60 percent of normal subjects with horizontal-gaze maintenance greater than 40 degrees.

One other common non-alcohol related cause of nystagmus is *optokinetic nystagmus*. Optokinetic nystagmus is a normal type of nystagmus. A common example occurs when a passenger in a vehicle looks out the window at utility poles. The passenger's eyes will fix on one pole, and then follow it until at some point the eyes will quickly move forward to target the next pole. Optokinetic nystagmus can also be simulated in an office setting with the patient looking at a drum of alternating colors which rotates. This test is commonly used in clinical neuro-ophthalmology to provide evidence of visual function in infants or to verify lack of vision in patients who claim to be blind.

The authors of *Duane's Clinical Ophthalmology* also describe drug-induced nystagmus as a common effect of barbiturate, tranquilizer, phenothiazine, and anticonvulsant therapy.

The editors of this leading ophthalmologic treatise recognize the problems associated with allowing law enforcement officers to base opinions of intoxication on their assessment of whether a suspect exhibits horizontal gaze nystagmus. This text states in part,

> Unfortunately, the fact that alcohol can produce horizontal gaze-evoked nystagmus has led to a "roadside sobriety" test conducted by law-enforcement officers. Nystagmus as an indicator of alcohol

intoxication is fraught with extraordinary pitfalls: many normal individuals have physiologic end-point nystagmus; small doses of tranquilizers that wouldn't interfere with driving ability can produce nystagmus; nystagmus may be congenital or consequent to structural neurologic disease; and often a sophisticated neuro-ophthalmologist or oculographer is required to determine whether nystagmus is pathologic. It seems unreasonable that such judgments should be the domain of cursorally trained law officers, no matter how intelligent, perceptive, and well meaning they might be. As noted, meticulous history-taking and drug-screening blood studies are often essential in evaluating patients with nystagmus.

Duane's Clinical Ophthalmology at 20.

Legal authority seems to follow the medical authority in concluding that HGN evidence should be limited to those experts trained in the scientific field rather than those with a modicum of knowledge concerning this medical condition. See generally *United States v. Horn*, 185 F. Supp. 2d 530 (D. Md. 2002); *People v. Williams*, 3 Cal. App. 4th 1326, 5 Cal. Rptr. 2d 130 (5th Dist. 1992). The concurring opinion of Justice Starcher of the Supreme Court of Appeals of West Virginia in *State v. Dilliner*, 569 S.E.2d 211 (W. Va. 2002), provides an excellent legal summary of the manner in which various jurisdictions have treated the admissibility of the horizontal gaze nystagmus test.

In *State v. Murphy*, 953 S.W.2d 200 (Tenn.1997), the court stated that testimony linking HGN to intoxication is "scientific, technical, or other specialized knowledge" and therefore must be offered through an expert witness. See also *State v. Duffy*, 146 N.H. 648, 778 A.2d 415 (2001); *State v. Doriguzzi*, 334 N.J. Super. 530, 760 A.2d 336 (2000); *State v. Torres*, 127 N.M. 20, 976 P.2d 20 (1999); *Duffy v. Director of Revenue*, 966 S.W.2d 372 (Mo. Ct. App. 1998); *State v. Helms*, 348 N.C. 578, 504 S.E.2d 293 (1998); *Young v. City of Brookhaven*, 693 So. 2d 1355 (Miss.1997); *Com. v. Sands*, 424 Mass. 184, 675 N.E.2d 370 (1997); *Com. v. Apollo*, 412 Pa. Super. 453, 603 A.2d 1023 (1992); *People v. Erickson*, 156 A.D.2d 760, 549 N.Y.S.2d 182 (1989).

* * *

In *State v. Witte*, 836 P.2d 1110, 1119–1120 (Kan. 1992), the
court discussed the mixed state of scientific opinion regarding
the reliability of HGN evidence. The court stated:

> Our research indicates that the reaction within the scientific com-
> munity is mixed. [citations omitted] Some articles endorse the HGN
> testing and its accuracy. [citations omitted] Other articles discuss
> concerns with the HGN test.... In addition to intoxication, many
> other factors can cause nystagmus. Nystagmus can be caused by
> problems in an individual's inner ear labyrinth. In fact, irrigating
> the ears with warm or cold water, not a farfetched scenario under
> particular weather conditions, is a source of error. Physiological
> problems such as certain kinds of diseases may also result in gaze
> nystagmus. Influenza, streptococcus infections, vertigo, measles,
> syphilis, arteriosclerosis, muscular dystrophy, multiple sclerosis,
> Korsakof's Syndrome, brain hemorrhage, epilepsy, and other psy-
> chogenic disorders all have been shown to cause nystagmus.
> Furthermore, conditions such as hypertension, motion sickness,
> sunstroke, eyestrain, eye muscle fatigue, glaucoma, and changes in
> atmospheric pressure may result in gaze nystagmus. The consump-
> tion of common substances such as caffeine, nicotine, or aspirin also
> lead to nystagmus almost identical to that caused by alcohol con-
> sumption. [citations omitted]
>
> Temporary nystagmus can occur when lighting conditions are
> poor. [citations omitted] An individual's circadian rhythms (bio-
> rhythms) can affect nystagmus readings — the body reacts differently
> to alcohol at different times of the day. One researcher has suggested
> that because of this, the angle of onset should be decreased five
> degrees between midnight and 5 a.m. [citations omitted] A number
> of driving under the influence arrests occur after midnight, which
> "would seem to indicate that sensitivity of HGN to alcohol is
> enhanced during the hours of the day when the greatest number of
> drunk driving arrests occur." [citations omitted]...
>
> A prosecution-oriented group in California conducted its
> own research: The study measured the correlation of police officer
> estimations of the angle of onset of nystagmus against chemical tests
> involving breath and blood samples. The data in the study revealed
> that there was virtually no correlation between the actual value of
> blood alcohol concentration and the predicted value based upon the
> angle of onset of nystagmus.... This study points out the fact that
> horizontal gaze nystagmus tests should never be intended as a
> substitute for actual blood or breath alcohol testing. The purpose
> of the procedure, if any is strictly a field screening function, like
> other presumptive tests. 836 P.2d at 1119–1120 (citations omitted).

The court concluded in *State v. Witte* that the State had not established the scientific reliability of the HGN evidence, and that the

police officer's testimony about his observations could not establish that reliability. *Accord, State v. Chastain*, 265 Kan. 16, 22, 960 P.2d 756, 761 (1992).

State v. Dilliner, 569 S.E.2d 211, 220–21 (W. Va. 2002).

THE TEST ITSELF

The test is essentially a measurement of the movement of the eye. Simply stated, *nystagmus* means a jerking of the eyes. Although there are different types of Nystagmus, the type involved in field sobriety testing is Horizontal Gaze Nystagmus, that is, the involuntary pendular (back and forth) movement of the eye. This type of Nystagmus is commonly measured by the officer in any or all of three different ways. *Vertical* Nystagmus, it should be noted, is a different phenomenon with different causes. Although often testified to by police officers on the issue of alcohol intoxication, the relevance of Vertical Nystagmus is primarily to indicate the presence of *drugs* in the body.

The first is to determine the *angle of onset* of the Nystagmus. By measuring the angle at which the eye begins jerking, the officer can, theoretically, come to a rough approximation of the blood-alcohol concentration (*see infra*). The second method is to notice whether the jerking becomes more *distinct* when the eye is moved to the lateral extreme — that is, when there is no longer any white of the eye visible at the outside of the eye. The third technique is to notice the lack of *smooth pursuit*: rather than following a moving object smoothly, the eye jumps or "tugs."

To administer the test, the officer instructs the suspect, "keep your head straight ahead and follow this object with your eyes." The officer then moves a finger or pencil, or a penlight at night, from the center of the head steadily toward one side. The object is held 12 to 15 inches directly in front, 2 to 3 inches above the eye being tested. The object is moved slowly (three to four seconds to complete the arc) in a level, even arc, maintaining the 12- to 15-inch distance. At the onset of Nystagmus, the object is held for one to two seconds at the point and the officer notes the angle of onset. The jerking should continue as long as the individual stares at the object, even though it is no longer being moved. The officer then repeats the test with the other eye.

The eyes of a person under the influence of alcohol will begin to jerk sooner than those of a sober person, and the more intoxicated the individual, the sooner the onset of jerking. Thus, blood-alcohol content can be roughly estimated by the angle on the device; i.e., by that point at which jerking begins. In a study for the National Highway Traffic and Safety Administration, researchers concluded that the onset of Nystagmus (jerking) at about 40 degrees would correlate with a blood-alcohol level of .10 percent; at about 35 degrees, with a level of .15 percent; and at 30 degrees, with a level of about .20 percent. Individuals with blood-alcohol levels above .20 percent often cannot even follow a moving object with their eyes. Thus, theoretically, a rough formula may be used to arrive at blood-alcohol content: Simply subtract the angle from 50 and convert to percent; for example, an angle of 37 degrees would convert to .13 percent blood alcohol. See V. Tharp, et al., Psychophysical Tests for DUI Arrest, DOT-HS-8-01970, 1981.

An alternative and increasingly common means of administering the test is to simply determine if jerking begins before the eye reaches a 45-degree angle. This is usually observed by the officer without the aid of any angle-measuring device, and obviously would be subject to question during cross-examination. If the jerking began at about 45 degrees, of course, this would indicate a blood-alcohol level of only .05 percent — and defense counsel may *want* the Nystagmus evidence admitted.

As is discussed in §11.5.3, counsel should attack the Nystagmus field sobriety test before trial. This motion *in limine* should present a two-pronged approach:

1. suppression
2. limitation

For a discussion of cross-examination on Nystagmus, see §13.2.1 and the sample cross-exam following that section.

In addition to the material in §4.3.4, counsel should also consider the research on which NHTSA relied in determining that Nystagmus was a relatively reliable field sobriety test. One of those studies is found in a NHTSA brochure authored by V. Tharp, Psychophysical Tests for DUI Arrests (DOT-HS-8-01970). Although recommending the test, the author mentions the following additional procedures (emphasis added to indicate potential sources for cross-examination):

> The person being tested should *remove all corrective lenses*; glasses may impede an officer's view of the eyes and hard contact lenses tend to limit the lateral movement of the eyes (which might prohibit the recognition of the borderline cases). The occurrence of nystagmus is not affected by visual acuity. The stimulus should be positioned *above the eyes*, in order to elevate them and reduce squinting, and about 15 inches away from the eyes. At night if the street lighting is not adequate, *a penlight should be used* to illuminate the face and eyes. The officer should move the stimulus *at least twice in each direction*, looking at the eye on the side of the head to which he is moving the stimulus. The suspect must keep his/her head still. The officer's flashlight makes a good chinrest for suspects who persist with head movements. The first movement in each direction should be slow (i.e., at about *10 degrees per second*), while the second movement should be somewhat faster (i.e., at about *20 degrees per second*).
>
> During the first movement of the stimulus in each direction, the officer should look for the onset of nystagmus. When he first detects a slight jerking, he should *stop moving the stimulus* to make sure that the jerking continues. If the nystagmus stops, then the officer has not found the point of onset and he should continue his examination.
>
> When the officer finds the onset point, he should determine whether or not it occurs *before* 45 degrees with some of the conjunctiva (i.e., the white of the eye) showing. The 45 degree angle was chosen as a criterion because it is *close* to the expected onset point for a BAC of 0.10% and *because it is easy to estimate*. The 45 degree angle splits the right angle that runs from the tip of the nose to the center of the head to the middle of the ear. Since some individuals cannot deviate their eyes more than 45 degrees, *some white of the eye must show* to ascertain that nystagmus is not occurring at the most extreme deviation for that individual.
>
> Smooth pursuit eye movements should also be examined by a police officer at roadside, although this is *the least reliable of the three signs*. We recommend that the second movement of the stimulus in each direction be at about *20 degrees per second*, while the officer looks for impaired smooth pursuit. The officer must be careful to move the stimulus smoothly to be sure that impaired pursuit is not *due to his manner of moving the stimulus*. What a police officer will see as the BAC increases is: (1) at a BAC of 0.08%–0.10% impaired

smooth movements interrupted by small jerks or saccades; (2) at a BAC in the range of 0.15% to 0.20% the eye movements will be characterized by much bigger saccades; (3) at high BACs (e.g., above 0.25%) most people cannot track at all.

Also, counsel should be aware that the technology now exists for videotaping nystagmus tests. This would, of course, provide an objective and verifiable record of the defendant's performance on the test. The EM/1 is an instrument developed by Eye Dynamics, Inc. of Torrance, California. Designed to be operated by a drug recognition expert (DRE), it has a separate video camera for each eye and records on videotape smooth pursuit, Nystagmus, pupil reaction, and eyelid tremor. It has already been successfully used in court. See *State v. Rosasco*, No. TD 92-02-006 (County of Yavapai, Ariz. 1992). Another instrument, the EPS-100, is a computerized version of the EM/1; it evaluates the defendant's performance on a pass/fail basis. (In view of this technology, counsel may wish to ask the officer if his police agency has the instrument to corroborate his testimony — and why not.)

W. Troy McKinney, a regent for the National College for DUI Defense, has compiled a summary of the NHTSA requirements for administering the HGN test. This summary is part of his article, Challenging and Excluding HGN Tests, published at page 50 in the April edition of *The Champion*, copyright 2002 by the National Association of Criminal Defense Lawyers.*

1. **Pretest.** The subject should be asked to remove their glasses. The presence of contacts should be noted but contacts need not be removed.[1]
2. **Instructions.** The officer should verbally instruct the person to place their feet together and their hands by their side. The officer should verbally instruct the person that they will be asked to follow a stimulus with their eyes and that while they are doing so, they should follow it only

*Reprinted with permission.

[1] Some versions of the NHTSA manuals have also required or suggested that the examiner should inquire into whether the person has previously suffered a head or neurological injury that might affect the HGN. However, the current version of the NHTSA SFST manual contains no such requirement.

with their eyes and should not move their head. The officer should ask the person if they understand the instructions and should not continue with the administration of the test unless and until they have obtained an acknowledgment of understanding from the person.

3. **Positioning the Stimulus.** The officer should position the stimulus between 12 and 15 inches away from the person's nose, slightly above eye level. The stimulus is positioned slightly above eye level in order to cause the person's eyes to open more widely and thus make viewing the eyes easier.[2]

4. **Passes — General.** The movement of the stimulus consists of a total of at least 14 passes of the stimulus. These 14 passes are divided into four stages or segments[3] and each eye must have two passes for each segment except for the initial equal tracking passes, which require only one for each eye. One pass of the stimulus for the left eye, as viewed from the perspective of the person administering it, is the movement of the stimulus from the center position to the right-hand limit of the pass and back to center. One pass of the stimulus for the right eye is the movement of the stimulus from the center position to the left-hand limit of the pass and back to center.

5. **Passes — Equal Tracking.** The first set of passes is designed to confirm equal tracking and equal pupil size. The officer is required to rapidly move the object from the center to the person's far left, to the person's far right, then back to the center position. This portion of the test should take at least two seconds. While looking for equal tracking, the officer is also required to look for and confirm that the pupils are of equal size. This set of passes is designed to alert the officer to the blatant presence of neurological symptoms that may require immediate medical attention. A person whose eyes do not track equally or who exhibits unequal pupil size should be immediately

[2] By raising the stimulus above normal horizontal eye level, the NHTSA-designed HGN may not actually be testing the muscles in the eye controlling only horizontal movement. Logically, it seems that if the stimulus is raised, eye muscles involved in vertical and diagonal movement of the eye become involved.

[3] Only the final three sets of passes are graded as part of the testing process.

referred for medical evaluation and treatment and the HGN should be terminated.[4]

6. **Passes — Smooth Pursuit.** The second set of four passes is designed to determine whether the person has or lacks smooth pursuit of the stimulus. In this phase, the stimulus is moved from the center position to the person's far left and back to the center position twice for each eye. The stimulus should be moved at a speed that takes at least two seconds from the center position to the side position.[5] At a rate of at least four seconds per eye per pass (two second out to the side and two seconds back to center), this phase of the HGN should take at least 16 seconds. In this phase, the officer is looking for a lack of smooth pursuit. If a lack of smooth pursuit is detected, a "clue" is scored for the eye in which the officer observed a lack of smooth pursuit.

7. **Passes — Maximum Deviation.** The third set of four passes is designed to determine whether the person has distinct nystagmus at maximum deviation. Maximum deviation is the point at which the eye has moved fully to one side and cannot move any further. In this phase, the stimulus is moved from the center position to the person's far left at a rate taking at least two seconds, held for at least four seconds, and then moved back to the center position at the same two-second rate.[6] In this phase, each pass for each eye must take at least eight seconds and the four passes together must take at least 32 seconds. When the stimulus is at maximum deviation, the officer must observe "distinct" nystagmus in order to score a clue for

---

[4] While the NHTSA protocol for the HGN only provides for one pass across each eye, many officers will make at least two passes for equal tracking. There is nothing wrong with making additional passes for equal tracking. It does, however, increase the number of passes that must be present for a complete HGN test. Thus, if the officer testifies that he made two passes across each eye for equal tracing, then the required number of passes for a complete HGN will increase to 16.

[5] The stimulus should be moved at a constant rate so as not to induce a lack of smooth pursuit. Speeding up and slowing down through the passes can create the appearance of lack of smooth pursuit because the examiner is varying the speed of the stimulus.

[6] As with the other passes, the stimulus should be moved at a constant, slow pace. Varying the speed can induce an appearance of what the examiner is looking for during the test.

that eye. It is insufficient to simply observe nystagmus at maximum deviation since most people will exhibit some visible nystagmus when the eye is held at maximum deviation. The nystagmus that must be observed in this phase must be distinct: that is, greater than the natural nystagmus that will occur from holding the eye at maximum deviation.[7]

8. **Passes—Onset Angle of Nystagmus.** The fourth and final set of four passes is designed to determine whether the onset of nystagmus occurs prior to the eye's movement to a 45-degree deviation. In this phase, the stimulus is moved very slowly—at a rate that would take at least four seconds to move the stimulus to the person's shoulder or at a rate of no more than 10 degrees per second. Once the officer thinks that he sees nystagmus he is required to stop moving the stimulus and hold it steady to confirm the presence of nystagmus. The stimulus must be held sufficiently long to confirm the onset of nystagmus, sufficiently long for the officer to examine the alignment between the stimulus and the edge of the shoulder (approximately 45 degrees) so that he can estimate the angle of onset, and sufficiently long for the officer to confirm the presence of some white remaining in the corner of the eye. Assuming an onset angle of 30 degrees and the stimulus being held for two seconds to confirm the continuation of nystagmus, each of the four passes in this phase must take at least eight seconds (three seconds out, two second hold, three seconds back) and the four passes together must take at least 32 seconds.[8]

9. **Vertical Nystagmus.** Although there is also a protocol for two passes for vertical nystagmus (VGN) upon completion of the HGN, VGN was not examined in the NHTSA validation research of the SFSTs and it was not included in the SFST battery during the original research.

---

[7] Of course, if the officer is not able to explain what normal Nystagmus looks like, it is doubtful that he will be able to tell that the alleged Nystagmus at maximum deviation is truly distinct.

[8] As a practical matter, it takes at least two seconds, and frequently longer, to make the confirming observations once the stimulus is stopped. Any examiner holding the stimulus steady for less than two seconds will not have made all of the necessary observations.

14 × 82 Litmus Test

When the four phases and 14 passes of the HGN are combined, administration of the HGN from the time the stimulus first begins moving must take **NOT LESS THAN** 82 seconds. Any HGN test that does not contain at least 14 passes and take at least 82 seconds from the time the stimulus first begins moving is improperly administered because it was not administered in accordance with NHTSA protocol and requirements. As a practical matter, most HGN administrations should take at least 90 seconds. Since very few people are 100 percent proficient all of the time, since some pauses during the administration are natural, and since some passes, such as the onset passes may actually take longer than the theoretical minimum, when for instance, the onset is at 40 degrees instead of 30 degrees, any HGN that takes less than 90 seconds is suspect and should be more closely examined for compliance with each individual phase of the test.

Other Common Mistakes

Other common mistakes in the administration of the HGN include moving the stimulus too quickly — or less commonly too slowly — on individual passes, holding the stimulus closer than 12 inches or further away than 15 inches, not holding the stimulus for at least four seconds at maximum deviation, and curving the stimulus upward, downward, or around (also called looping) as it is being moved through the passes. If any of these mistakes are present in the administration of the HGN, the test and its results are not reliable because the officer did not administer the test in accordance with NHTSA protocol and requirements.[9]

According to the NHTSA material, the presence of four clues indicates a likely blood alcohol level of at least .10. In most states, however, it is improper for any witness or officer to testify to any

---

[9] Interestingly, in order to have a correctly administered HGN, the person must have held his head still during the administration. Viewed objectively, this means that when the person was told to hold his head still (and not sway), he was able to do so. Of course, this can be compared to the Romberg or one-leg-stand where clues are given for swaying even though the person is not told not to sway. It can be argued that, like the HGN, if the person had been told not to sway, he would not have done so.

correlation or relationship between any number of clues and any quantifiable blood or breath alcohol level. Rather, what is admissible from the presence of at least four clues is testimony that the administration of the HGN indicated "intoxication." In reality, all that the presence of gaze nystagmus indicates is the presence of a central nervous system (CNS) depressant in the person's system. While alcohol is a CNS depressant, the HGN is not specific for alcohol. Indeed, alcohol does not even cause nystagmus. Rather, its presence in a person's system simply exaggerates the presence of the nystagmus present in all people.

In a publication entitled *End Position Nystagmus as an Indicator of Ethanol Intoxication*, the author, J.L. Booker, ran an independent study comparing volunteers who had been dosed with alcohol against those who had been sleep-deprived, with results that raise serious issues about the validity of the HGN test for identifying blood alcohol content at or above 0.10 percent. According to Booker, the accuracy of the HGN test is inflated and erroneous for at least three reasons:

1. The baseline error (up to 55 percent false positives for fatigued, non-drinking subjects) for end-position nystagmus component of the HGN test is high, especially considering that the result of the test is often used without a confirming chemical assay as the primary evidence that alcohol is present at a concentration greater than 0.10 w/v% (100 milligrams per 100 millilitres).
2. The dose-response relationship of alcohol and distinct end-position nystagmus varies widely (37 percent to 68 percent in the very low BAC subjects) according to whether the subject is absorbing or eliminating alcohol — a factor impossible to determine in field situations.
3. Distinct end-position nystagmus is exhibited by more than half the test subjects an hour or more after the subject's BAC returned to 0.00 percent (zero milligrams per 100 millilitres).

J.L. Booker, *End Position Nystagmus as an Indicator of Ethanol Intoxication*, 40(2) Sci. & Just. 113–116.

§4.3.5 Walk-and-Turn

The following material setting forth the proper procedures to follow in administering the walk-and-turn (also called the "heel-to-toe" or "walk-the-line") portion of the "standardized" field sobriety test is taken from the DWI Detection and Standardized Field Sobriety Testing Student Manual distributed to law enforcement agencies by the National Highway Traffic Safety Administration (DOT-HS-178-R10/95). It can be used effectively in cross-examination to compare the arresting officer's methods with those recommended after extensive research by federal authorities. The material is also helpful for showing that the test can be scored objectively.

* * *

Procedures for Walk-and-Turn Testing

1. Instructions Stage: Initial Positioning and Verbal Instructions

   For standardization in the performance of this test, have the suspect assume the heel-to-toe stance by giving the following verbal instructions, accompanied by demonstrations:

   o "Place your left foot on the line."[1] (Place your own left foot on the line to demonstrate.)

   o "Place your right foot on the line ahead of the left foot, with heel of right foot against toe of left foot." (Demonstrate).

   o "Place your arms down at your side."[2]

   o "Keep this position until I tell you to begin. Do not start to walk until I tell you to do so."

   o "Do you understand the instructions so far?" (Make sure suspect indicates understanding.)

2. Demonstrations and Instructions for the Walking Stage

   Explain the test requirements, using the following verbal instructions, accompanied by demonstrations:

HS 178 R10/95   VIII-18

---

[1] The 2000 and 2002 manuals indicate that the line can be real or imaginary.
[2] The 2000 and 2002 manuals instruct the officer to demonstrate this instruction.

o   "When I tell you to start, take nine heel-to-toe steps down the line, turn
     around, and take nine heel-to-toe steps back up the line."[3] (Demonstrate 2
     or 3 heel-to-toe steps.)

o   "When you turn, keep the front foot on the line, and turn by taking a series
     of small steps with the other foot, like this." (Demonstrate).

o   "While you are walking, keep your arms at your sides, watch your feet at all
     times, and count your steps out loud."

o   "Once you start walking, don't stop until you have completed the test."

o   "Do you understand the instructions?" (Make sure suspect understands.)

o   "Begin, and count your first step from the heel-to-toe position as 'One.'"

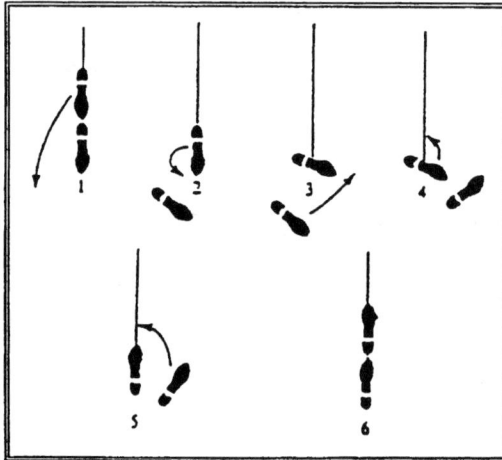

3. Test Interpretation

You may observe a number of different behaviors when a suspect performs this
test. Research, however, has demonstrated that the behaviors listed below are
the most likely to be observed in someone with a BAC above 0.10. Look for the
following clues each time this test is given:

[3] The 2000 and 2002 versions omit the specification to take the steps
"down the line" and then "back up the line."

4. Field Evidence

A. <u>Cannot keep balance while listening to the instructions</u>. Two tasks are required at the beginning of this test. The suspect must balance heel-to-toe on the line, and at the same time, listen carefully to the instructions. Typically, the person who is intoxicated can do only one of these things. The suspect may listen to the instructions, but not keep balance. Record this clue if the <u>suspect does not maintain the heel-to-toe position throughout the instructions</u>. (Feet must actually break apart.) <u>Do not</u> record this clue if the suspect sways or uses the arms to balance but maintains the heel-to-toe position.

B. <u>Starts before the instructions are finished</u>. The impaired person may also keep balance, but not listen to the instructions. Since you specifically instructed the suspect not to start walking "until I tell you to begin," record this clue if the suspect does not wait.

C. <u>Stops while walking to steady self</u>.[4] The suspect pauses for several seconds after one step. <u>Do not</u> record this clue if the suspect is merely walking slowly.

D. <u>Does not touch heel-to-toe</u>. The suspect leaves a space of one-half inch or more between the heel and toe on any step.

E. <u>Steps off the line</u>. The suspect steps so that one foot is entirely off the line.

F. <u>Uses arms to balance</u>. The suspect raises one or both arms more than 6 inches from the sides in order to maintain balance.

G. <u>Improper turn</u>. The suspect removes the front foot from the line while turning. Record this clue if both feet are removed from the line. Also record this clue if the suspect clearly has not followed directions as demonstrated.

H. <u>Incorrect number of steps</u>. Record this clue if the suspect takes more or fewer than nine steps in either direction.

Note: If suspect cannot do test, record as if all eight clues were observed. Consideration should be given to terminating the test if the suspect cannot safely complete it.

Should the suspect have difficulty with this test (for example, steps off the line), repeat the test from the point of difficulty, not from the beginning. This test tends to lose its sensitivity if it is repeated several times.

[4] The 2000 and 2002 manuals omit the "to steady self" portion of this clue.

Observe the suspect from 3 or 4 feet away and remain motionless while suspect performs the test. Being too close or excessive motion on your part will make it more difficult for the suspect to perform, even if sober.[5]

If the suspect exhibits two or more distinct clues on this test or fails to complete it, classify the suspect's BAC as above 0.10. Using this criterion, you will be able to correctly classify about 68% of your suspects.

4. Test Conditions

Walk-and-Turn test requires a designated straight line, and should be conducted on a dry, hard, level, nonslippery surface, under relatively safe conditions.[6] There should be sufficient room for suspects to complete nine heel-to-toe steps. If these conditions do not exist, suspects should be asked to perform this test elsewhere or only HGN should be used.[7] SUSPECT'S AND OFFICER'S SAFETY SHOULD BE CONSIDERED AT ALL TIMES.[8]

NOTE: In the research study, suspects were only asked to "assume a heel-to-toe position on a designated line". Therefore, a suspect could start with either the right or left foot on the line and not violate the procedures used in the research study. However, for standardization of the administrative procedures for this test, have suspect place left foot on line first, right foot in front, heel-to-toe.[9]

Some people have difficulty with balance even when sober. The test criteria for Walk-and-Turn is not necessarily valid for suspects 65 years of age or older, persons with injuries to their legs, or persons with inner ear disorders. Individuals wearing heels more than 2 inches high should be given the opportunity to remove their shoes. Individuals who cannot see out of one eye may also have trouble with this test because of poor depth perception.[10]

5. Combined Interpretation of Horizontal Gaze Nystagmus and Walk-and-Turn Tests

The Decision Table below is designed to help you classify those suspects with a potential BAC above 0.10. You will recall that the decision point on the Gaze Nystagmus Test was four clues, while on the Walk-and-Turn Test it was two.

---

[5] The 2000 and 2002 manuals omit this paragraph and replace it with the following: "Observe the suspect from a safe distance and limit your movement which may distract the suspect during the test. *Always consider officer safety.*" (Emphasis in original.)

[6] The "under relatively safe conditions" criterion has been omitted from the 2000 and 2002 manuals.

⁷ This sentence has been omitted from the 2000 and 2002 manuals. It has been replaced with the following notation: "Recent field validation studies have indicated that varying environmental conditions have not affected a suspect's ability to perform this test."

⁸ This sentence has been omitted from the 2000 and 2002 manuals.

⁹ This paragraph has been omitted from the 2000 and 2002 manuals.

¹⁰ This paragraph has been altered in the 2000 and 2002 manuals to read as follows: "The original research indicated that individuals over 65 years of age, [with] *back*, leg, or middle ear problems had difficulty performing this test. Individuals wearing heels more than 2 inches high should be given the opportunity to remove their shoes." (Emphasis added.)

However, a suspect may score higher on one test and lower on the other. How do you make your decision? Find the box on the Decision Table where the two test results intersect and see if it falls in the shaded area. (For example, suppose a suspect produced only three clues on the Horizontal Gaze Nystagmus but two clues on the Walk-and-Turn. Is suspect intoxicated? The Decision Table says yes. But if suspect scored three on the Horizontal Gaze Nystagmus and only one on the Walk-and-Turn, the Table indicates the suspect's BAC is probably below 0.10.)

Using this method, you will correctly classify about 80% of your suspects as to whether their BAC's are above or below 0.10.[11]

DECISION TABLE

Nystagmus Gaze Test Clues

* * *

[11] The decision table has been omitted from the 2000 and 2002 manuals. The manuals now indicate that "based on the original research, combining four or more clues of HGN and two or more clues of the Walk-and-Turn, suspects can be classified as above 0.10 BAC 80% of the time."

§4.3.6   One-Leg-Stand

The following material describes the proper procedures to follow in administering the one-leg-stand portion of the "standardized" field sobriety test. As with the preceding subsection, it is taken from the manual distributed to law enforcement agencies by the National Highway Traffic Safety Administration (DOT-HS-178-R10/95) and can be used effectively in cross-examination to compare the arresting officer's methods with those recommended after extensive research by federal authorities. The material is also helpful for showing that the test can be scored objectively.

* * *

Procedures for One-Leg Stand Testing

1. Instructions Stage: Initial Positioning and Verbal Instructions

    Initiate the test by giving the following verbal instructions, accompanied by demonstrations.

    o "Please stand with your feet together and your arms down at the sides, like this." (Demonstrate)

HS 178 R10/95   VIII-22

o   "Do not start to perform the test until I tell you to do so."

o   "Do you understand the instructions so far?" (Make sure suspect indicates understanding.)

2. Demonstrations and Instructions for the Balancing and Counting Stage

Explain the test requirements, using the following verbal instructions, accompanied by demonstrations:

o   "When I tell you to start, raise one leg, either leg, approximately six inches off the ground, toes pointed out."[1] (Demonstrate one leg stance.)

o   "You must keep both legs straight, arms at your side."

o   "While holding that position, count out loud for thirty seconds in the following manner: "one thousand and one, one thousand and two, until told to stop." (Demonstrate a count, as follows: "one thousand and one, one thousand and two, etc." Officer should not look at his foot when conducting the demonstration - OFFICER SAFETY.)

ó   "Keep your arms at your sides at all times and keep watching the raised foot."

o   "Do you understand?" (Make sure suspect indicates understanding.)

o   "Go ahead and perform the test." (Officer should always time the 30 seconds. Test should be discontinued after 30 seconds.)

Observe the suspect from at least 3 feet away. If the suspect puts the foot down, give instructions to pick the foot up again and continue counting from the point at which the foot touched the ground. If the suspect counts very slowly, terminate the test after 30 seconds. If the suspect is counting quickly, have the suspect continue counting until told to stop.[2]

3. Test Interpretation

You may observe a number of different behaviors when a suspect performs this test. Researchers, however, have found that behaviors listed below are the most likely to be observed in someone with a BAC above 0.10. Look for the following clues each time the One-Leg Stand test is administered.

---

[1] The 2000 and 2002 manuals instruct the suspect to point his or her *foot* out rather than toes.

[2] This sentence has been omitted from the 2000 and 2002 manuals.

A. The suspect sways while balancing. This refers to side-to-side or back-and-forth motion while the suspect maintains the one-leg stand position.

B. Uses arms for balance. Suspect moves arms 6 or more inches from the side of the body in order to keep balance.

C. Hopping. Suspect is able to keep one foot off the ground, but resorts to hopping in order to maintain balance.

D. Puts foot down. The suspect is not able to maintain the one-leg stand position, putting the foot down one or more times during the 30-second count.

Note: If suspect cannot do test or puts foot down three or more times, record as if all four clues were observed. Consideration should be given to terminating the test if the suspect cannot safely complete it.

Remember that time is critical in this test. Research has shown that a person with a BAC above 0.10 can maintain balance for up to 25 seconds, but seldom as long as 30.

If an individual shows two or more clues or fails to complete the One-Leg Stand, there is a good chance the BAC is above 0.10. Using that criterion, you will correctly classify about 65% of the people you test as to whether their BAC's are above or below 0.10.

Observe the suspect from at least 3 feet away, and remain as motionless as possible during the test so as not to interfere. If the suspect puts the foot down, give instructions to pick the foot up again and continue counting from the point at which the foot touched the ground. If the suspect counts very slowly, terminate the test after 30 seconds. If the suspect is counting quickly, have the suspect continue counting until 30 seconds have elapsed. [3]

Test Conditions

One-Leg Stand requires a reasonably level, and smooth surface. There should be adequate lighting for the suspect to have some visual frame of reference. [4] Suspect's safety should be considered at all times.

[3] This sentence has been omitted from the 2000 and 2002 manuals.
[4] This sentence has been omitted from the 2000 and 2002 manuals.

Some people have difficulty with the One-Leg Stand even when sober. The test criteria for the One-Leg Stand is not necessarily valid for suspects 65 years of age or older, or 50 pounds or more overweight. Persons with injuries to their legs, or inner ear disorders, may have difficulty with the test.[5] Individuals wearing heels more than 2 inches high should be given the opportunity to remove shoes.

* * *

[5] The 2000 and 2002 manuals also indicate that persons with back injuries may also have difficulty with the test.

§4.3.7 Field Notes on the Field Sobriety Tests

The following material describes how an officer should record field notes on a suspect's performance on field sobriety tests. This material is also taken from the 1995 version of NHTSA's DWI Detection and Standardized Field Sobriety Testing Student Manual (DOT-HS-178-R10/95). It details how an officer should record the results of a defendant's performance on the SFSTs in his report and also for purposes of courtroom testimony. Counsel can use this material effectively in cross-examination to compare the arresting officer's recordation methods with those recommended after extensive research by federal authorities.

* * *

5. Taking Field Notes on Suspects' Performance of Field Sobriety Tests

For purposes of the arrest report and courtroom testimony, it is simply not enough to record the total number of clues on the three tests. The number of clues is important to the police officer in the field because it helps determine whether there is probable cause to arrest. But to secure a conviction, much more descriptive evidence is needed.

The officer must be able to describe <u>how</u> the suspect performed on the tests, and exactly <u>what</u> the suspect did.

The standard note taking guide provided in this Manual is designed to help you develop a clear description of the suspect's performance on the tests.

6. Taking Field Notes on Horizontal Gaze Nystagmus Testing

The section on the horizontal gaze nystagmus test appears on the bottom of the guide's front side.

First, make sure that you inquire whether the suspect is wearing contact lenses. Check the "No" or "Yes" box to record the suspect's response.[1]

Complete the entire test for both eyes, writing "yes" or "no" for each nystagmus clue.

o   Write "yes" if the clue is present;
o   Write "no" if the clue is not present.

HORIZONTAL GAZE NYSTAGMUS

note: suspect wearing contact lenses?[2]   ☐   ☐
                                         NO   YES

                                    LEFT   RIGHT
• EYE DOES NOT PURSUE
  SMOOTHLY

• DISTINCT NYSTAGMUS
  AT MAX. DEVIATION

• NYSTAGMUS ONSET
  BEFORE 45 DEGREES

OTHER:

---

[1] This paragraph has been omitted from the 2000 and 2002 manuals.

[2] The 2002 manual indicates that there is a "section for Medical Assessment [which] appears at the bottom of the guide's front page." The manual then notes that the boxes should be checked "yes" or "no" for equal tracking and for equal pupil size, and that in the section labeled "other" any facts, circumstances, conditions, or observations that may be relevant to this procedure (i.e., Resting Nystagmus) should be recorded.

In the section labeled "other," record any facts, circumstances, conditions or observations that may be relevant to this test.

o   Examples of additional evidence of alcohol impairment emerging during nystagmus test:

   -   suspect unable to keep head still;
   -   suspect swaying noticeably;
   -   suspect utters incriminating statements.

o   Examples of conditions that may interfere with suspect's performance of the horizontal gaze nystagmus test:

   -   wind, dust, etc. irritating suspect's eyes;
   -   numerous visual or other distractions impeding the test (always face suspect away from flashing or strobe lights).[3]

7. .Taking Field Notes on Walk-and-Turn Testing

The section on the Walk-and-Turn test appears at the top of the guide's back side.

The first two clues, "cannot keep balance" and "starts too soon" apply only during the instructions stage of the test. Record the number of times each of those clues appear.

For example, if the suspect's feet "break apart" from the heel-to-toe stance twice during the instructions stage, write "2" in the box alongside the "cannot keep balance" clue. Similarly, if the suspect never "starts too soon," write "0" in that box. Note: Actual steps taken is for scoring purposes only. Wrong number of steps is the validated clue.

---

[3] The 2000 and 2002 manuals note that the officer should "always face suspect away from *rotating* lights, strobe lights *and traffic passing in close proximity*." (Emphasis added.)

Don't leave boxes blank. If a particular clue never shows up, write "0" in the corresponding box.

Record the next five clues <u>separately</u> for the walk <u>down</u> the line, and then up the line.

A. If a suspect <u>stops walking</u>, record how many times in the following manner: Draw a vertical line across the toe of the step at which the stop occurred. Do this for the first as well as the second nine steps. Place the letter "S" at top of the vertical line to indicate stops walking.

WALK AND TURN TEST	Cannot keep balance _____		
	Starts too soon _____	1st Nine	2nd Nine
	Stops Walking		
	Misses Heel-Toe		
	Steps off Line		
	Raises Arms		
	Actual Steps Taken		
Improper Turn (Describe)	Cannot do Test (explain)		

B. If suspect <u>fails to touch heel-to-toe</u>, record how many times this happens. Draw a vertical line across the toe of the step at which the miss occurred. Place the letter "M" at the top of the vertical line to indicate missed heel to toe.

C. If suspect <u>steps off the line</u> while walking, record how many times this happens in the following manner.   Draw a line from the appropriate foot print at an angle in the direction in which the foot stepped. Do this for the first as well as the second nine steps.

D. If suspect <u>uses arms to balance</u>, give some indication of how often or how long this happens.

    o   <u>Example</u>: suspect raised arms from sides three times; place a check for each occurrence in appropriate box.

    o   <u>Example</u>: suspect held arms away from sides during 3 through 7; place a check for each occurrence in appropriate box.

    o   <u>Example</u>: suspect "flapped" arms continuously; make a note.

E. Record the actual number of steps taken by suspect in each direction.

For the next point, "improper turn," record a description of the turn.

If you note that the suspect "cannot perform test." indicate explicitly why you did so.

o Example: "off line three times;"
o Example: "staggered six steps to right, nearly fell;"
o Example: "fear of injury."

At end of the test, examine each factor and determine how many distinct clues have been recorded. Remember, each clue may appear several times, but still only constitutes one distinct clue. Failure to perform test should be recorded as "eight" clues observed.

In the section labeled "other," record any facts, circumstances, conditions or observations that may be relevant to this test.

o Examples of additional evidence of impairment during Walk-and-Turn test:

    - suspect verbally miscounts steps;
    - suspect utters incriminating statements.

o Examples of conditions that may interfere with suspect's performance of the Walk-and-Turn test:

    - wind/weather conditions;
    - suspect's age, weight;
    - suspect's footwear.

8. Taking Field Notes on the Combined Interpretation of Nystagmus and Walk-and-Turn

The decision table for combining nystagmus and Walk-and-Turn scores appears on the upper right of the page.[4]

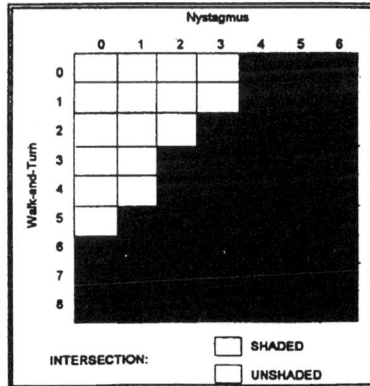

---

[4] The 2000 and 2002 manuals omit this chart. Instead, they note that "by combining four or more clues of HGN with two or more clues of the WAT test, suspects can be correctly classified as above 0.10 BAC 80% of the time."

Along the top of the table, circle the number corresponding to the suspect's nystagmus clues. Along the left side of the table, circle the number corresponding to the suspect's Walk-and-Turn clues.

On the "intersection" line immediately below the table, check either "shaded" or "unshaded."

o   Check "shaded" if the intersection of the two test results falls in the black or shaded area of the table;

o   Check "unshaded" if the intersection falls in the white or unshaded area.

Remember: Combined interpretation of nystagmus and Walk-and-Turn is more reliable than either test, separately. By using the decision table, you can correctly classify about 80% of your suspects in terms of whether their BAC's are above or below 0.10.

9.   Taking Field Notes on One-Leg Stand Testing

The section on the One-Leg Stand test appears midway down the page.

By recording when things happen as well as what happens, you will be able to prepare a more descriptive arrest report.

You will place check marks in or near the small boxes to indicate how many times you observed each of the clues. You will do this separately for the test on the left leg (L) or on the right leg (R). In addition, if the suspect puts the foot down during the test, you will record when it happened (write the count on new note guide). For example, when standing on the left leg the suspect lowered the right foot at a count of "one thousand and thirteen", and again at "one thousand and twenty". Your diagram should look like the sketch to the right. You must also pay attention to the suspect's general appearance and behavior while the test is being performed.

At end of the test, examine each factor and determine how many distinct clues have appeared.

Remember: A clue may appear several times, but will constitute only one distinct clue, except if suspect puts foot down three or more times.

At end of the test, examine each factor and determine how many distinct clues have been recorded. Remember, each clue may appear several times, but still only constitutes one distinct clue. Failure to perform test should be recorded as "four" clues observed, as should putting foot down three or more times.

§4.3.8   Field Sobriety Test Checklists

All citations in the following checklists refer to the DWI Detection and Standardized Field Sobriety Testing Student Manual distributed to law enforcement agencies by the National Highway Traffic Safety Administration (DOT-HS-178-R10/95).

Checklist 3   Field Sobriety Test

Initial Considerations

☐ Did the tests consist of the federally recommended "standardized" battery: walk-and-turn, one-leg stand, and nystagmus?
    ☐ If so, were they administered and scored as recommended?
    ☐ If not, why were tests that have been proven invalid used by the officer?
☐ Should a foundational motion *in limine* be made to exclude the tests?
☐ Should the officer and prosecutor be instructed to refrain from using such terms as "test" or "fail"?

Defendant's Condition

☐ Was the defendant 50 pounds or more overweight? (VIII-25)
☐ Was the defendant 65 years of age or older? (VIII-25)
☐ Was the defendant suffering from any illness affecting his balance or coordination?
☐ Was the defendant taking any drugs or medication that might affect his balance?
☐ Did the defendant have any physical disabilities affecting his ability to take the tests?
☐ Was the defendant upset by or injured in a traffic collision?
☐ Was the defendant suffering from any emotional reactions to the procedure—fear, embarrassment, anger, nervousness?
☐ Was the defendant wearing shoes with high heels while performing the tests?

Administration of Field Sobriety Tests

☐ Were the tests given on a smooth and level area?
    ☐ Was the area covered with gravel, loose dirt, or other possible obstructions?
    ☐ Were the tests administered near passing vehicles, creating nose and wind waves?
    ☐ Did the lighting conditions impede the defendant's successful performance?
    ☐ Did the weather conditions make the tests more difficult to perform?
    ☐ Did the police vehicle have flashing lights creating a strobe effect?
☐ Could unclear instructions by the officer have contributed to test results?
    ☐ Was the defendant given the opportunity to practice each of the tests once before attempting them? Why not?
    ☐ What was the physical line used in the walk-the-line test?
    ☐ Did he demonstrate to the defendant by first performing each test?
☐ Does "passing" involve a subjective opinion by the officer?
    ☐ Had the officer already formed an opinion that the defendant was intoxicated?
    ☐ Are there any objective criteria?
    ☐ Did the officer use negative scoring?
    ☐ Did the officer take into consideration the "impaired learning curve" (fear, nervousness) in assessing pass/fail?

Corroboration

☐ Were any videotapes or photographs taken of the defendant performing the tests?
    ☐ Were any audio or video devices available to the officer — and why weren't they used?
☐ Are there any defense witnesses who observed the tests being given?
    ☐ Were any potential witnesses prevented by the police from viewing the tests?
☐ Did the officer diagram the walk-the-line and/or finger-to-nose tests as they were performed?

☐   Was he capable of recalling all details when he later drafted his report?

☐ Can a comparison of the defendant's signature and/or handwriting be effectively made?

Checklist 4   Nystagmus

Admissibility

☐ Is evidence of the nystagmus test admissible in trial?
  ☐   Is the officer qualified as an expert?
  ☐   Does the test pass the state and/or *Frye* standards?

☐ Does the evidence consist of testimony as to the indicated blood-alcohol level — or as to whether the defendant passed or failed?
  ☐   If nystagmus is being used as a test for blood-alcohol concentration, is it subject to the state's requirements for regulation of blood-alcohol analysis?
  ☐   If the jury is told that "passed" or "failed" means above or below a given blood-alcohol level, does this constitute a blood-alcohol analysis in fact?

☐ If the evidence is limited to the issue of probable cause, has counsel already litigated the issue out of the presence of the jury?

☐ Has testimony concerning nystagmus been limited to excluding reference to specific blood-alcohol levels or "failing?"

Foundation

☐ Was the officer qualified to administer the horizontal gaze nystagmus test?
  ☐   Has he had sufficient training and experience?
  ☐   Is he familiar with the physiological theory behind the test?
  ☐   Is the officer aware of the many sources for error inherent in the test?
  ☐   Should the officer be examined on voir dire to determine his expertise?

Administration

☐ Was the test administered according to the standardized pro-
    cedures? (VIII-12)
   ☐ Did the officer ask the defendant if he or she was wearing
       contacts and note the answer? (VIII-15)
   ☐ Did the officer have the defendant remove glasses before
       testing? (VIII-15)
   ☐ Did the officer tell the defendant, "I am going to check
       your eyes?" (VIII-15)
   ☐ Did the officer instruct the defendant: "Keep your head
       still and follow this stimulus with your eyes only?"
       (VIII-15)
   ☐ Was the defendant told: "Keep focusing on this stimulus
       until I tell you to stop?" (VIII-15)
   ☐ Did the officer hold stimulus 12 to 15 inches from the
       suspect's nose and slightly above eye level? (VIII-16)
   ☐ Pupils not equal in size may indicate a head injury; did
       the officer check to see if pupils are equal in size? (VIII-
       14, 16)
   ☐ Eyes that don't track together could indicate a possible
       medical disorder, injury, or blindness; did the officer
       check the defendant's eyes for the ability to track
       together? (VIII-14, 16)
   ☐ Did the officer move stimulus smoothly? (VIII-16)
   ☐ Did the officer move stimulus two seconds out, two sec-
       onds back for each eye? (VIII-16)
   ☐ Was stimulus moved to maximum deviation, and held
       four seconds for each eye? (VIII-16)
   ☐ Did the officer check to see if the onset of nystagmus was
       before 45 degrees? (VIII-16)
   ☐ Was the sclera visible? (VIII-16)
   ☐ Did the officer check for each clue at least twice in each
       eye? (VIII-8)
   ☐ Was the subject facing away from flashing lights? (VIII-26)
☐ Did the defendant exhibit the standardized clues?
   ☐ Lack of smooth pursuit (VIII-17)
   ☐ Distinct nystagmus at maximum deviation (VIII-17)
   ☐ Onset of nystagmus prior to 45 degrees (VIII-17)
☐ Did the defendant exhibit other clues?

☐ Did the defendant sway noticeably during the test? (VIII-26)

☐ Did the defendant keep his head still during the test? (VIII-26)

☐ Does this testimony conflict with the officer's earlier or later testimony that the defendant was staggering, weaving, or unstable on his feet?

Sources of Error

☐ Was the angle of onset measured accurately and honestly?
    ☐ Was the angle of onset measured with a template — or by estimate? (VIII-15)
        ☐ Has the officer received training in estimating angles?
        ☐ Has the officer undergone recent verification of his ability to estimate angles?
        ☐ Did the officer simply use the defendant's shoulders to measure 45 degrees?
    ☐ Was the jerking of the eye observed by the officer due to his moving the focal object in a jerking manner?
    ☐ Is there any evidence corroborative of the officer's testimony concerning the angle?
    ☐ Did the officer use the objective scoring system recommended by NHTSA?

☐ Are there any sources of possible error in the test?
    ☐ Is the officer aware of physiological grounds for error?
        ☐ As an "expert," is he aware of specific studies indicating inaccuracies in the test?
    ☐ Did the officer consider the possible presence of drugs such as antihistamine or phencyclidine?
    ☐ Had the defendant consumed coffee, smoked a cigarette, or taken an aspirin?
    ☐ Did the defendant suffer from any physiological problems that would affect nystagmus, such as influenza, streptococcus, vertigo, or epilepsy?
    ☐ Is the defendant hypertensive or hypotensive?
    ☐ Was the defendant carsick?
    ☐ Were there any inner ear problems?
    ☐ Was the defendant suffering from eyestrain or eye muscle fatigue?

☐   Is the officer aware of the effects of circadian rhythm on the onset of nystagmus?

☐   Is the officer/expert aware of Umeda's and Sakata's study indicating that nystagmus is one of the least sensitive methods of measuring intoxication by eye measurement? See Y. Umeda and E. Sakata, Alcohol and the Ocular System, 87 Annals of Otology Rhinology 69 (1978), further discussed in §13.0.5.

Checklist 4.1   Walk-and-Turn

☐   Was the test administered in accordance with the standardized procedures? (VIII-12)

☐   Were the required conditions for the administration of this test met? (VIII-21)

    ☐   Was the test conducted on a dry, hard, level nonslippery surface? (VIII-21)

    ☐   Was there a designated straight line? (VIII-21)

    ☐   Was the test administered under relatively safe conditions? (VIII-21)

☐   Were the proper instructions given?

    ☐   Did the officer tell the defendant: "Place your left foot on the line?" (VIII-18)

    ☐   Did the officer further explain: "Place your right foot on the line ahead of the left foot, with the heel of your right foot against the toe of your left foot?" (VIII-18)

    ☐   Was the defendant told: "Place your arms down at your side?" (VIII-18)

    ☐   Was the defendant instructed: "Keep this position until I tell you to begin; *Do not start* to walk until I tell you to do so?" (VIII-18)

    ☐   Did the officer verify that the subject understands the stance is to be maintained while instructions are given? (VIII-8)

    ☐   If the defendant broke away from the stance during the instructions, did the officer cease instructions until the stance was resumed? (VIII-8)

    ☐   Did the officer tell the subject that he or she would be required to do nine heel-to-toe steps down the line, turn around, and take nine heel-to-toe steps up the line? (VIII-9)

☐ Did the officer demonstrate several heel-to-toe steps? (VIII-9)

☐ Did the officer demonstrate the turn? (VIII-9)

☐ Did the officer tell the subject to look at his or her feet, keep arms at sides, count steps aloud, and not to stop walking until the test is completed? (VIII-9)

☐ Did the officer ask the subject whether he or she understood and re-explain what was not understood? (VIII-9)

☐ Were the proper procedures followed while the defendant performed the test?

☐ Was the defendant told to begin? (VIII-9)

☐ If the defendant staggered or stopped, did the officer allow him or her to resume from the point of interruption rather than go back to the beginning? (VIII-9)

☐ Officer should not follow alongside suspect. (VIII-21)

☐ Officer should not be within three or four feet of the suspect during the test. (VIII-21)

☐ Did the defendant exhibit any of the standardized clues?

☐ Lose balance during instructions (feet must break away from the heel-to-toe stance) (VIII-9)

☐ Start walking too soon (VIII-9)

☐ Stop while walking to steady self (VIII-9)

☐ Miss heel-to-toe while walking (by ½ inch or more) (VIII-9)

☐ Raise arms from side while walking (6" or more) (VIII-9)

☐ Step off the line (VIII-9)

☐ Turn improperly (VIII-9)

☐ Take wrong number of steps (VIII-9)

Checklist 4.2   One-Leg-Stand

☐ Was the test administered according to the standardized procedures? (VIII-12)

☐ Were the required conditions for the administration of the test met?

☐ Was the test administered on a smooth, level surface? (VIII-24)

☐ Was the lighting adequate? (VIII-24)

☐ Were the proper instructions given?

    ☐ Was the defendant told to stand with feet together and arms at sides? (VIII-10)

    ☐ Did the officer tell the subject not to start until told to do so? (VIII-10)

    ☐ Did the officer ask the subject if he or she understood? (VIII-10)

    ☐ Was the defendant told to stand on either foot with the other foot held straight and about six inches off the ground, toes pointed out? (VIII-10)

    ☐ Did the officer demonstrate the proper stance? (VIII-10)

    ☐ Did the officer instruct the subject to count from 1-30 by thousands until told to stop? (VIII-10)

    ☐ Did the officer demonstrate the count for several seconds? (VIII-10)

    ☐ Did the officer ask the subject if he or she understood, and if not, did the officer re-explain? (VIII-10)

    ☐ Were the proper procedures followed while the defendant performed the test?

    ☐ Did the officer tell the subject to begin? (VIII-11)

    ☐ If subject stopped or put his or her foot down, did the officer allow him or her to begin at the point of interruption? (VIII-11)

    ☐ Was the defendant permitted to remove his or her shoes? The officer should not stand within three feet of the suspect during the test. (VIII-24)

    ☐ The officer should not move around during the test. (VIII-24)

☐ Did the defendant exhibit any of the standardized clues?

    ☐ Sway in trying to balance (VIII-11)

    ☐ Put foot down (VIII-11)

    ☐ Hop (VIII-11)

    ☐ Raise arm from side six inches or more (VIII-11)

§4.4   Preliminary Breath Tests

Page 231. Add at end of section:

Practitioners across the country should be aware of recent developments in California concerning the use of preliminary breath devices — a development that, in the opinion of this author, will rapidly spread nationwide. That state is apparently making plans to use hand-held breath testing devices *as evidential breath test instruments*. In other words, steps have been taken to phase out current PBT devices as well as the evidential machines currently found in police stations and replace them with a single new handheld unit, which accomplishes the functions of both.

The following is excerpted from a letter forwarded by a member of the California Department of Justice to the *California Association of Toxicologists Newsletter* and printed in its February 1999 edition:

> On September 16, 1996, the California Department of Justice sent a letter to manufacturers of breath analyzers outlining a new law enforcement concept that utilizes hand-held breath analyzers as EBTs....
>
> ...The Alcotest 7410 Plus hand-held breath analyzer with "Smart Cal" and PC software, is the result. The Alcotest 7410^{Plus} is the smartest, most powerful, and flexible hand-held breath analyzer ever created....
>
> The Department will purchase 20 initially with the OTS grant and be placed in one county to demonstrate Title 17 compliance and will then add them to the License of the DOJ, Bureau of Forensic Services. Then another 100 units will replace Bureau Intoxilyzer 5000 complement. Steve Scott, the BFS Blood Alcohol Coordinator, has applied for a $2.5 million OTS grant in the second phase of this continuing grant to place 800 Alcotest Plus units in patrol cars throughout the state.

This California version of the Draeger 7410, the "7410 Plus," varies from the standard model primarily in using a special software — "Smart Cal." With the capacity to give the tests in the field, of course, retrograde extrapolation (see §5.2) will cease to be a significant problem.

There appear, however, to be defects that will render it susceptible to attack. First, it appears that the new device is not currently designed to incorporate a mouth alcohol detector (see §6.2.5). Thus, mouth alcohol (see §6.2) will become an even greater issue. Second, there is also, apparently, only a very primitive RFI detector planned for the device (see §6.3.10). This will be a particular problem in view of the close proximity of the police car's radio transmitter and the officers' walkie-talkies. And, of course, all the usual infirmities of the relatively primitive RBTs apply.

The new units may also provide counsel with a new strategy in trial. Generally, it has been the author's experience that juries are not impressed with small, mobile, hand-held PAS devices — certainly not as impressed as with the large, more complex stationary machines. This is particularly true now that there is little reason for the officer not to bring the Draeger Alcotest in to trial to show the jury — unlike in the existing situation where the jury never sees the evidential machine. Can the hand-held "gizmo" do what a big, complex machine could do? Can this little unit carried around in the officer's pocket — appearing similar to commercially available units selling for only $100–200 — be trusted to analyze blood-alcohol from breath samples? Beyond a reasonable doubt?

§4.4.1   The Alco-Sensor

Page 232. Replace all material from first complete paragraph on page 232 ("The Alco-Sensor model IV is . . .") to end of the section on page 238 with the following:

The Alco-Sensor IV model, along with Draeger's Alcotest 7410, is seeing widespread use nationwide. As with any fuel cell device, its attractions are portability, cost, ease of use — and relative specificity (see §6.1) for ethyl alcohol (Intoximeters, Inc., claims that it "does not read acetone or hydrocarbons which might be found on the breath," although it will apparently still read other compounds — including alcohols other than ethanol). Further, an RFI detector is built into the device's circuitry; however, as discussed in §6.3.10, these "negative slope" circuits for detecting radio frequency interference are generally ineffective; in the case of any PBT device, it is unlikely that they are calibrated or tested in the working environment.

The handheld device is powered by a nine-volt alkaline battery, good for about 300 tests, and uses a disposable mouthpiece. It contains a fuel cell sensor—a porous disk coated with a thin layer of gold and platinum and saturated with an electrolyte. Using a disposable mouthpiece, a one-cubic-centimeter breath sample is drawn into the machine and across the top of the fuel cell by a piston sampling pump, where any alcohol is absorbed and converted into acetic acid plus electrons. This results in an electric current which is amplified and then converted into an output curve of the fuel cell response; this is then analyzed by a microprocessor and in turn converted into a three-digit reading on the Alco-Sensor digital display. The reading is kept in the computer's memory and can be recalled before the mouthpiece is ejected. A printer is also available for use with the Alco-Sensor IV.

There are several versions of the Alco-Sensor IV, varying primarily in the internal computer programming. The particular version can be identified by the color of a dot on the face plate of the unit; Red, Green, Blue and Black Dot versions appear to be the most common.

The manufacturer claims that the Alco-Sensor IV has a life of two to five years, though its warranty in the manual only "warrants all new Alco-Sensor IVs to be free from defects in material and worksmanship, under normal use and service, for a period of 12 months from original invoice date." Concerning the software which operates the machine, Intiximeters, Inc., "does not warrant that it will be error free or operate without interruption." Further, "repaired components are warranted for a period of 90 days."

Some possible sources of error noted by the manufacturer: (1) The manual warns that "a recent drink of an alcoholic beverage or regurgitation could introduce 'mouth alcohol' to the breath, causing an exaggerated reading. A 15-minute waiting period prior to testing will insure the elimination of 'mouth alcohol.'" (2) Any cigarette smoke blown into the device "will permanently damage the fuel cell." (3) "Sufficient time after each test must be allowed for all traces of alcohol on the cell surface to be eliminated.... Even when exposed to breath samples with high alcohol levels, a cell should clear within 2 minutes." (4) New mouthpieces must be inserted with each new test, or alcohol from the previous user can elevate the reading. (5) Monthly calibration checks are recommended.

Note: The Alco-Sensor IV captures a very tiny amount of breath, but the device captures it only after "the subject … has just about run out of breath." In other words, it is designed to analyze only the very last part of an exhalation — i.e., the deepest alveolar air of the lungs. And as discussed in §6.0, the deepest alveolar air will contain an unrepresentative higher blood-alcohol concentration than the average of air in the lungs.

It is extremely important for the officer to obtain a complete air blank when using this device. The National Highway Traffic Safety Administration has recognized possible false-positive results may occur with this device when the test is conducted in low temperatures. See §6.3.9 for a complete discussion of this issue.

The following operator's checklist is provided in the manufacturer's manual. Any failure to follow it — and, perhaps, to produce an executed copy used in the client's test — should be pointed out in cross-examination.

SAMPLE

ALCO-SENSOR IV BREATH TEST CHECK LIST

Date of Test _____/_____/_____

Ship: _____   Location of Test: _____

Operator: _____   Subject: _____

Witness: _____   Alco-Sensor IV Serial No. _____

Test #1*	Accuracy Check If Necessary*	Test #2	(Check as completed)
_____		_____	Time Test Began. (Do not begin test#2 until at least 5 minutes after the end of test #1 or 15 minutes after the ingestion of any substance.)
1. _____	Reading Received	_____	Mount mouthpiece to turn unit on.
	Reading Expected		
2. _____		_____	Observe temperature reading & record.
3. _____		_____	Depress SET BUTTON—if display shows SET.
4. _____		_____	When display shows BLNK, unit runs a Blank automatically and display shows .000.
5. _____		_____	If display shows SET, depress SET BUTTON —display shows TEST.
6. _____		_____	Instruct subject how to give a proper breath sample.
7. _____		_____	Record final 3 digit reading.
8. _____		_____	When display changes to SET, depress SET BUTTON.
9. _____		_____	Remove mouthpiece using the mouthpiece release button on side of unit—unit turns off. Discard mouthpiece.
10. _____		_____	Note if sample was taken automatically (A) or Manually (M).

Reason for Manual Sample_____

_____

Time Test Ended: Test #_____   Test #2 _____

*IF TEST #1 IS POSITIVE, RUN AN ACCURACY CHECK BETWEEN TEST #1 AND #2 OR AFTER TEST #2.

The diagram below represents the back plate of an Alco-Sensor IV, setting forth the instructions for administering a test to a subject.

ALCO-SENSOR IV BACK PLATE

OPERATING INSTRUCTIONS
1. MOUNT MOUTHPIECE.
   Unit turns on.

2. NOTE TEMPERATURE.

If unit displays Set,
3. DEPRESS *SET* BUTTON.

When unit displays Blnk,
Unit runs BLANK auto-matically & displays .000 (*)

If unit displays Set,
4. DEPRESS *SET* BUTTON.

When unit displays Test,
5. COLLECT A BREATH SAMPLE.

6. RECORD 3 DIGIT READING.

7. DEPRESS *SET* BUTTON AND REMOVE MOUTHPIECE.

If unit displays a message not mentioned above, consult manual.

U.S. Patent No.   4,487,055
                   4,770,026
U.K. Patent No.   2201245
Other patents pending

SERIAL NUMBER

(*) The type of software in your unit requires specific information at this point. Each unit has different wording here. Complete information on what to expect for the Red, Green and Blue Dot **ALCO-SENSOR IV** follows.

The following material is excerpted from Intoximeter's operaors's manual for the Alco-Sensor IV, and sets forth the procedures for administering a test. Note that slight variations exist for the different versions ("Red Dot," "Black Dot," etc.) of the device.

EXPLANATION OF BACKPLATE OPERATING INSTRUCTIONS
Your ALCO-SENSOR IV must not be attached to an RBT IV printer at this time.

1. MOUNT MOUTHPIECE.
Unit turns on.

Remove ALCO-SENSOR IV from its case and mount a **NEW** mouthpiece as described previously. This will power up the unit and within 1 second the display will be active. If the battery is too low, the first display will be "**Bat**". Replace the battery as soon as the test is concluded.

2. NOTE TEMPERATURE.

The temperature in °C will be displayed for 3 seconds after turn-on. ALCO-SENSOR IV is designed to provide maximum accuracy when the unit temperature is between 10°C and 40°C. Below 10°C, the FUEL CELL process becomes progressively slower, measurement times become longer and some information begins to be lost, so that accuracy begins to decline. Clearing time for the cell increases and, consequently, the required interval between tests is increased. On the other hand, temperatures above 40°C tend to degrade FUEL CELL performance and shorten the useful life of the cell. All ALCO-SENSOR IV's with a serial number higher than 002343 will not allow a test if the unit, i.e. fuel cell, is out of the proper operating temperature range. If the temperature is outside of the proper operating range, take appropriate corrective action by removing the mouthpiece and placing the instrument in a cooler or warmer environment.

3. *If unit displays SET*
DEPRESS SET BUTTON.

If the previous test has been properly concluded, the pump mechanism should already be cocked and "**Set**" will not appear. If this was not correctly done, or if by impact or rough handling the mechanism has been sprung, this instruction requires the pump to be restored to its cocked position. The test cannot proceed until it is done.

18

IMPORTANT:

The type of unit you purchased determines what will be the next step that you will observe. Following is an explanation for each type of unit. Depending upon the operating instructions as laid out on the back of your unit, you will notice a difference in the numeric sequencing.

During the initial phase of this step, the computer is monitoring the FUEL CELL output to be sure that the system is essentially zero so that a measurement may start. During the first ten seconds, a *BUSY* display consisting of alternating "√" and ">" characters appears. If, at the end of this time, the output is still not low enough, "**Wait**" or "**Void**" appears. Generally, if a minute or more has elapsed since the last test, the wait will only be a few seconds. If "**Wait**" persists more than 3 or 4 seconds, it is suggested, in the interest of battery life, that the mouthpiece be removed and the test be started again from Step 1 30 seconds later. When the FUEL CELL output is zero and stable, your unit will proceed in one of the following manners:

On Red Dot ALCO-SENSOR IV (Air Blank) unit, you will see:

4. *When unit displays Bink,*
Unit runs Blank and displays .000

"**Blink**" appears on the ALCO-SENSOR IV display while the unit draws a blank sample and checks for alcohol residue in both the manifold and the fuel cell. The busy signal ">√" displays while the sample is analyzed. If both the manifold and the fuel cell are clean, ".000" appears followed by "**Set**".

19

If the manifold and/or the fuel cell are not clean, ".XXX" (a numeric value) appears followed by "**Void**". Eject the mouthpiece and wait 15 seconds to 1 minute (depending upon the magnitude of the reading) before attempting to reinitiate the test with a new, clean mouthpiece. DO NOT BLOW BY MOUTH THROUGH THE MANIFOLD AS THIS CAN RETARD THE CLEARING.

161

5. *When unit displays Set,* **DEPRESS THE SET BUTTON.**

On Green Dot **ALCO-SENSOR IV** (Sensor Blank) unit, you will see:

When unit displays Blnk, Unit runs Blank automatically & displays .000

Depress the **SET BUTTON** to cock the breath pump and the unit is ready for a breath sample.

"**Blnk**" appears on the **ALCO-SENSOR IV** display while the unit draws a blank sample and checks for alcohol residue on the fuel cell only. The busy signal "**>:<**" displays while the sample is analyzed. If the fuel cell is clean, ".000" appears.

If the fuel cell is not clean, "**XXX**" (a numeric value) appears followed by "**Wait**". Eject the mouthpiece and wait 15 seconds to 1 minute (depending upon the magnitude of the reading) before attempting to re-initiate the test with a new, clean mouthpiece. DO NOT BLOW BY MOUTH THROUGH THE MANIFOLD AS THIS CAN RETARD THE CLEARING.

6. *If the unit displays Set,* **DEPRESS SET BUTTON.**

On Blue Dot **ALCO-SENSOR IV** (Omnibus) unit, there is no outward indication of the internal operation at this point:

If "**Set**" appears, depress the **SET BUTTON** to cock the breath pump and the unit is ready for a breath sample.

After the unit displays the temperature, the busy signal "**>:<**" flashes while the unit automatically draws a blank sample and checks for alcohol residue on the fuel cell. The busy signal "**>:<**" continues to display while the sample is analyzed. If the fuel cell is clean, the unit displays "**Test**". The Blue Dot **ALCO-SENSOR IV** unit is ready for a breath sample.

If the fuel cell is not clean, "**Wait**" appears. Eject the mouthpiece and wait 15 seconds to 1 minute (depending upon the magnitude of the reading) before attempting to re-initiate the test with a new, clean mouthpiece. DO NOT BLOW BY MOUTH THROUGH THE MANIFOLD AS THIS CAN RETARD THE CLEARING.

20

CHECK THE BACK PLATE OF YOUR UNIT FOR THE CORRECT NUMERIC SEQUENCE OF THE NEXT STEP.

5. COLLECT A BREATH SAMPLE.

BREATH PROFILE

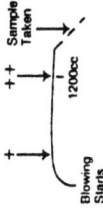

+ +　Sample Taken

+

1200cc

Blowing Starts

At the beginning of this step, the busy symbol "**>:<**" previously described is displayed while the computer monitors the breath flow sensor for stability. (A display of "**Man**" at this point indicates that the breath flow sensor is disabled and that ONLY a manual sample is possible.) When the display shows "**Test**", instruct the subject to take a deep breath, hold it and then blow steadily through the mouthpiece for as long as he can. A (+) sign appears to indicate that the subject is blowing hard enough to complete an automatic sample. (If (+) does not appear, tell subject to blow harder.) When subject has blown a minimum volume of approximately 1.2 liters, a second (++) sign appears. The sample will be taken ONLY when this condition has been met AND the flow diminishes indicating that the end of the exhalation is approaching. If BOTH conditions are met in 10 seconds or less, the unit will automatically sample. If more than 10 seconds elapses or if blowing is interrupted before the second (+) sign appears, the unit will display "**NoGo**" and return to the beginning of Step 5 to start another sample attempt.

If subject has obviously impaired breathing, it is recommended that the sample be taken manually as close to the end of exhalation as possible by pressing the **MANUAL BUTTON.** The same technique can be used with an uncooperative subject to get the best possible reading under the circumstances.

21

7. DEPRESS SET BUTTON AND REMOVE MOUTHPIECE.

After the 3 digit display disappears, "Set" appears. Depress the SET BUTTON and eject the mouthpiece unless you need to recall the test result. When the pump is cocked with the SET BUTTON, an intermittent BEEP signals that the mouthpiece should be removed to turn the unit off. At any time during this BEEPING period and before the mouthpiece is ejected, depressing the RECALL BUTTON will display the 3 digit result of the test just completed.

RECALLING THE CURRENT TEST RESULT
Until the SET BUTTON is depressed after a test, the RECALL function is not available. Once the SET BUTTON has been engaged, depressing the RECALL BUTTON will display the final reading of the current test. After the mouthpiece is ejected, the test result cannot be recalled.

23

A total of 3 minutes is allocated to achieve a successful sample either automatically or manually. At the end of 3 minutes "Void" appears and the test must be started again at Step 1 with a NEW mouthpiece.

Any time the sampling pump does not successfully draw a sample on either the manual or automatic command, the display will show "Void". After 3 seconds an intermittent BEEP indicates that the mouthpiece should be removed to turn power off. The cause of this failure should be investigated by a technician.

THE BACKPLATE STATES:

**6. RECORD 3 DIGIT READING.
OR RECORD INITIAL OR FINAL READING.**

As soon as a successful breath sample has been taken, the busy signal ">:<" is displayed *(BUSY)* to indicate the computer is analyzing the breath sample.

On some units:
After a few seconds a 2 digit display will appear for 3 seconds in addition to the busy symbol ">:<". This is an approximation of the final reading to better than 10%. If this value is too low to be of interest, or is adequate for screening purposes, the test may be terminated at this point by depressing the SET BUTTON and removing the mouthpiece. If not terminated, the display will continue to indicate *BUSY* until the final 3 digit display appears in 20-30 seconds. It is accompanied by a 3 second series of BEEPS.

On the Blue Dot ALCO-SENSOR IV:

The final 3 digit display appears in 20-30 seconds, accompanied by a 3 second series of BEEPS.

22

163

QUICK REFERENCE GUIDE TO DISPLAY LEGENDS

DISPLAY	MEANING
< and > alternating	The symbol ">:<" has been used in the previous text to denote this display. The computer is busy and the unit is functioning—wait for the next message.
Wait	A waiting period is necessary to ready the system for another test. Generally, if "Wait" persists more than 3 or 4 seconds, the unit should be turned off for a period of time before another test is attempted.
Blnk	After the display shows "Blnk", the instrument automatically reads a blank to be sure the system is free of alcohol residue.
Set	SET BUTTON should be depressed to cock sampling pump.
Void Followed by intermittent beep	An improper condition exists that requires the unit to be turned off and restarted from Step 1.
Man	The breath flow sensor is inoperative and ONLY a manual sample may be taken. Proceed with breath sample, but depress the MANUAL BUTTON near the end of exhalation.
Test	A breath sample should be collected from the subject or an ACCURACY CHECK sample should be delivered.
RBT	Appears when ALCO-SENSOR IV is connected to an RBT printer in place of "Test".
NoGo	The proper conditions for an automatic sample have not been achieved. When "Test" appears again, start a new sample.
+	A sufficient minimum breath flow is being provided for automatic sampling.
+ +	A minimum sample volume of at least 1.2 liters (1200cc) has been delivered.
> XXX	A sample has been introduced that exceeds the measuring range of the instrument. This may be seen during testing, Cal, Cal1 or Cal2. Example: >400.
Bat	The 9-volt alkaline battery should be changed. If this display is followed by normal operation, the battery is capable of completing the current test. If "Bat" is followed by "Void", the test must be terminated and a new battery must be installed. Good practice demands that the battery be changed at the end of the first test where "Bat" appears.
RFI	Followed by "Void" indicates that an RFI signal was detected which is sufficiently strong that the results of a test might be affected. Test must be started over by removing mouthpiece to turn unit off.
Cal or Cal1 or Cal2	Appears during the CALIBRATION PROCEDURE and indicates that a sample of the test gas should be delivered following instructions in the ACCURACY CHECK section.
XX°C	Temperature is displayed in Celsius.
XX°C (Repeatedly)	A high resistance or loose battery is indicated and should be replaced.
Tmp>	Temperature greater than allowed.(*)
Tmp<	Temperature less than allowed.(*)
>>>>	There are improper conditions during a calibration procedure that prevent proper calibration of the unit (requires servicing by a technician). (*) Seen only during Cal, Cal1, or Cal2.

24

25

§4.4.2   Defense Use of Favorable PBT Evidence

Page 239. Add new subsection after end of subsection 4.4.2:

§4.4.3   The Alcotest 7410

The Alcotest 7410 is a small battery-powered device, which employs fuel-cell technology to measure blood-alcohol concentration from a breath sample. It is produced in Lubeck, Germany, by Draeger Safety, Inc., manufacturers of the Alcotest 7110 evidentiary breath machine (see §11.5.4); Draeger got into the business by taking over Smith and Wesson's Breathalyzer Division (185 Suttle Street, Suite 105, Durango, CO 81301-7911; 970-385-5555). The device is a recent development that is seeing rapid acceptance nationwide. The California version is planned for statewide distribution within the next three years — and, notably, since it has been certified as an evidentiary machine, it will be admissible in court as evidence of the defendant's actual blood-alcohol concentration.

As was briefly discussed in §4.4, this handheld unit measures ethyl alcohol in the breath by oxidizing it in the fuel cell, thus generating a small electrical current, which is measured over a given time period; the more ethyl alcohol in the breath sample, the greater the oxidation, the more current generated, the higher the reading. A separate printer is available to record the results of tests. Being a fuel-cell device, it is susceptible to numerous problems, including a lack of specificity (see §6.1). Although the unit theoretically will not react with some compounds that register as alcohol on infrared machines (hydrocarbons, organic acids, ketones, common anorganic gases), it will oxidize and thus read as alcohol such compounds as:

1. Aldehydes, such as acetaldehyde, present to varying degrees on the human breath (see §6.1.1);
2. Ethers;
3. Esters; and
4. Alcohols (methanol, propanol, I-propanol).

In fact, many organic substances with oxygen in the functional compound group may react with fuel cells.

Although the 7410 has a mechanism for detecting radio frequency interference (see §6.3.10), it is a fairly primitive system, which appears to be sensitive only to RFI sources within one to two feet of the device. Most notably, however, the device *does not have a "mouth alcohol" detector* — a significant shortcoming in any breath-testing device and one that should provide material for cross-examination (particularly if the officer's 15-minute pretest observation period is suspect, which is likely to be the case if the test is administered in the field).

The device will decrease in accuracy due to contamination of surface sites, causing decreased conductivity. For this and other reasons, it has an expected life of three years, and must be calibrated according to manufacturer's specifications at least every six months by a certified technician using a NHTSA-approved wet bath simulator.

In attempting to get states to accept the device for evidentiary purposes as in California, the advantages of the new unit have been set forth in promotional literature:

1. There is no delay in obtaining a test result, thus it "eliminates the 'rising BA' defense";
2. It "keeps the officer on the street";
3. It permits more remote areas to be served;
4. It costs about 1/3 as much as stand alone evidentiary units; and
5. It replaces units such as the Intoxilyzer 5000 that are 10–15 years old.

Note that none of the advantages relate to the accuracy of the device.

Although retrograde extrapolation will become less of an issue with this device, defense counsel should find it an easier machine to attack in trial — if for no other reason than its diminutive size and unimposing appearance (note: unlike the larger evidentiary instruments, there is no reason the device cannot be brought into court and shown to the jury).

The following material from the California Department of Justice presents excerpts from Draeger's manual for technical specifications, evidential operation, maintenance, and troubleshooting. The author is grateful to forensic toxicologist Anne

ImObersteg (302 Toyon Avenue, Suite F266, San Jose, CA 95127; 408-272-5696) for providing and discussing these materials.

TECHNICAL SPECIFICATIONS

Measurement range
Accurate between 0.000 gm/210L to 0.400 gm/210L

Ambient conditions for operation
23° to 104° F (–5° to +40° C)
or –4° (–20° C), if in use for less than 30 minutes and if 600 to 1300 mbar
10 to 98% relative humidity

Ambient conditions for storage
–40° to +149° F (–40° tp +65°C)
600 to 1300 mbar
10 to 98% relative humidity

Minimum Sample Requirements
Blowing time   4 to 12 seconds (depending on intensity)
Flow rate   >6 liters/minute
Volume   >1.2 liters

Measurement accuracy
Reproducible with an ethanol standard:
0 to 0.100%   +/– 0.005% gm/210L
   >0.100%   +/– 5% of measured value

Dimensions
9.0 x 2.8 x 1.3 in (230 x 70 x 34 mm)

Weight
1.1 lb (0.5 kg)

Electrical power supply options:
1. Battery pack which holds three (3) rechargeable NiCd batteries

Notes:
   NiCd or rechargeable battery packs will provide approximately 300 tests between charges.
   Charging time takes 24 hours for full charge.
   LO BAT warning is displayed when there is approximately 5 minutes of operating time remaining.

Printer

Environmental conditions for operation
32° to 122°F (0° to 50°c)
600 to 1300 mbar
10 to 98% relative humidity

Environmental conditions for storage
–40° to 158°F (–40° to 70°C)
600 to 1300 mbar
10 to 98% relative humidity

Dimensions
5.6 x 5.3 x 1.9 in (140 x 133 x 48 mm)

Weight
1.0 lb (0.5 kg)

Power supply

Operating voltage:	9.5V to 17V / 1A
Consumption:	10 W for log printout, 200 mW in standby mode
Fuse:	M 1.0 A DIN 41571 91x)
Batteries:	LR6 DIN IEC 86 (AA) (2ea) (Usage period at 25°C is approximately 2 years)

STRUCTURAL DIAGRAM

1. Electronics compartment
2. ON/OFF switch
3. Calibration sticker
4. Mouthpiece holder
5. Yellow ON light/Red warning light
6. Green READY light
7. LCD display
8. Electrical contacts for battery pack connection
9. Battery pack
10. Wrist strap
11. Electrical contacts for NiCd charger
12. Battery pack release button
13. Safety lock tab
14. PC interface

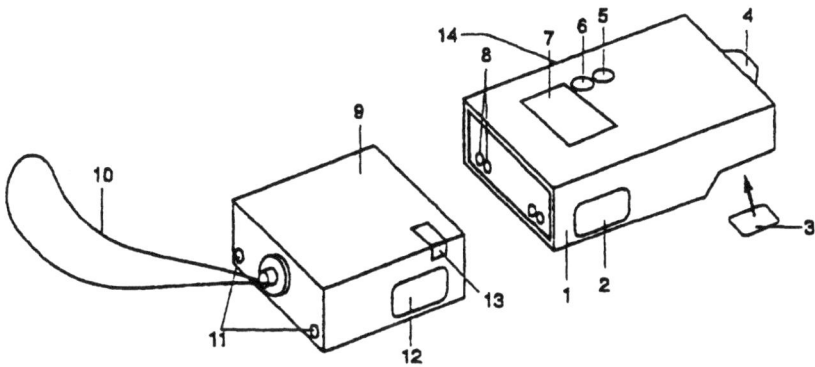

Printer

1. Top cover
2. Paper feed slot
3. Paper roll
4. Red button
5. White button

6. Printing mechanism
7. Batteries
8. Power receptacle
9. PC interface

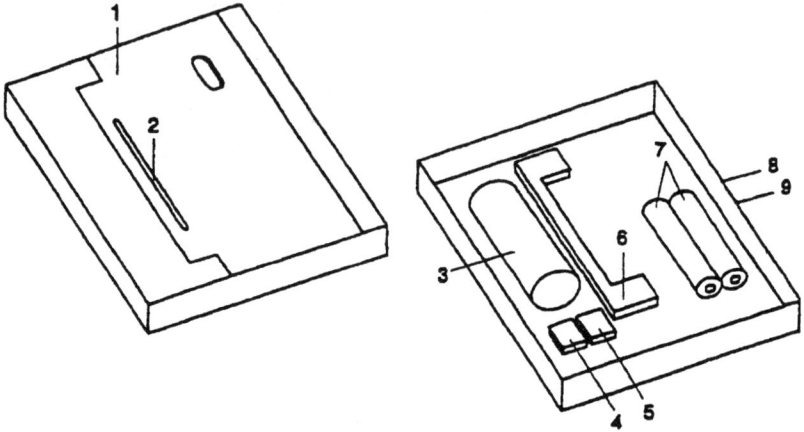

OPERATION

This section explains the operation of the various components of the Draeger *EPAS*. The basic preparation and operation of all components is explained in detail, although the operator will usually not need to do any special preparation to use a properly charged Draeger *EPAS*.

To prepare the Draeger EPAS, simply plug the case into a power source to charge the system batteries. The first time you charge the EPAS, it is recommended to leave it charging for a full 24 hours.

Alcotest® 7410^{Plus} Operation

This section details the preparation required to use the Alcotest® 7410^{Plus}, and the steps for performing a breath test.

Before using the Alcotest® 7410^{Plus}, the battery pack must be connected and fully charged.

Connecting the battery pack

The Alcotest® 7410^{Plus} is powered by a rechargeable NiCd battery pack.

To connect the battery pack:

1. Pull up the safety lock on the battery pack unit.
2. Position the battery pack unit into the base of the instrument and depress the safety lock.

To remove the battery pack:

1. Pull up the safety lock on the battery pack unit.
2. Depress the release button.

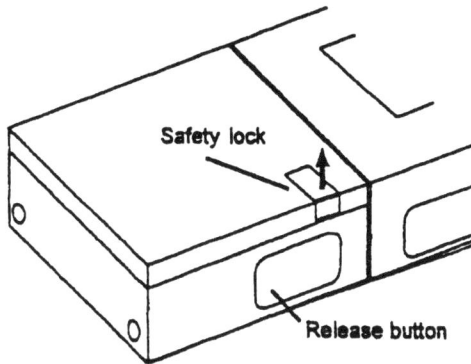

Safety lock

Release button

The Alcotest® 7410^{Plus} must be charged in the case or charger station whenever LO BAT appears at the bottom of the display, or when the NiCd battery is completely exhausted. Below is the procedure to charge the Alcotest® 7410^{Plus} using the NiCd charger station of the *EPAS* case.

To use the NiCd charger station:

1. Plug in NiCd charger station to power source.
2. Put the rechargeable NiCd battery pack into the charger with the "Power Supply Unit" to the front.
3. When the yellow light in the charger is on, the battery pack unit is being charged.
4. Store the NiCd battery pack in the charger so that it is ready for immediate use.

Operating the EPAS:

NOTE: **The Alcotest® 7410^{Plus}** is always charging while it is in the case. The below instructions are intended for routine maintenance and special situations where the EPAS has been in the field for extended periods of time.

1. Leave the battery pack attached to the Alcotest® 7410^{Plus}.
2. Place the Alcotest® 7410^{Plus} in the special holster inside the *EPAS* case.
3. Plug in the case to a power source, utilizing the correct power cord (110V or 12V).

Turning the 7410 on and off
ON (for screening tests)

1. Pick up the Alcotest® 7410^{Plus} from the *EPAS* case.
2. Press the ON/OFF button once.

The yellow ON light comes on and a self-test is carried out by the microprocessor. The LCD displays date and time data.

Evidential Test Procedure

There are two ways to enter data into the Alcotest®7410^{Plus} for an evidential test; with a valid California Driver's License and Operator's Card, or via the Cassiopeia® palm device's virtual keyboard and Jot® system.

Activating Magnetic Card Data Entry with Cassiopeia®

1. Press the program button on the Cassiopeia® to activate the Data Entry Sequence.
2. Swipe the subject's driver's license through the magnetic card reader as indicated on page 6.
3. Verify that the subject's data has been accepted (The corresponding boxes on the Cassiopeia will turn green).
4. Swipe the Operator's Card through the magnetic card reader.
5. Verify that the operator's data has been accepted (The corresponding boxes on the Cassiopeia will turn green).
6. Select "Upload" from the Cassiopeia's touch screen.

The data is transfered to the Alcotest® 7410^{Plus}, which beeps to indicate a successful transfer. The Alcotest® 7410^{Plus} is automatically powered on and ready to accept an evidential breath test. The Cassiopeia® will automatically power off after a successful data upload.

POWER-OFF for the Alcotest® 7410^{Plus}

Press the ON/OFF button twice in the Screening mode or Evidential mode.

Note: The Alcotest® 7410*Plus* will automatically shut off after four(4) minutes if the unit is in the READY mode and no test has been performed.

Activating Manual Data Entry with the Cassiopeia®

1. Press the program button on the Cassiopeia® to activate the Data Entry Sequence.
2. On the Cassiopeia® touch screen, tap each box for the subject's data and enter the data with the virtual keyboard or the Jot® system.
3. To enter the operator's data, repeat step 2, tapping the appropriate boxes on the Cassiopeia's touch screen.
4. When all of the data boxes are green, the data is ready to be sent to the Alcotest® 7410*Plus*.
5. Select "Upload" from the Cassiopeia's touch screen.

The data is transferred to the Alcotest® 7410*Plus*, which beeps to indicate a successful transfer. The Alcotest® 7410*Plus* is automatically powered on and ready to accept an evidential breath test. The Cassiopeia® will automatically power off after a successful data upload.

POWER-OFF for the Alcotest® 7410*Plus*

Press the ON/OFF button twice in the Screening mode or Evidential mode.

Note: The Alcotest® 7410*Plus* will automatically shut off after four (4) minutes if the unit is in the READY mode and no test has been performed.

Performing a Breath Test
Conditions for test subject (*follow State requirements*)
Performing a Screening Test

Press and release the ON/OFF button once. The 7410 will go through the date sequence,

month   day   year

| nn | 08 | dd | 06 | 'yy | '99 |

followed by the time sequence . . .

hour   minute

| hh | 15 | nn | 45 |

followed by . . .

---	ABL	T	000	---	Scr
	Airblank	Measuring	Result		

--- , indicates that the unit is warming up. Once the Alcotest®
7410^{Plus} is ready for a Screening Test, the display shows:

Scr and the green "ready" light is on.

A Screening Test can be performed at this point:

Instruct the subject to take a deep breath and blow evenly as long
as the horn sounds. If the test was successful the result will automatically be displayed.

> (Note: Display time of the results will vary due to the
> alcohol concentration measured).

If the subject does not fulfill the volume and flow rate requirements, EO will be displayed, indicating an insufficient breath
sample. The test can be repeated when the green "Ready" comes on.

This will not change the sequential test number.

All valid test results are stored in the 7410^{Plus} memory, including
date, time, and sequential test number.

The test results can be printed at this time.

The Alcotest® 7410^{Plus} is turned off by pressing the ON/OFF
button twice, or it will automatically shut off after four minutes.

Evidential Testing

An evidential test can be conducted in the field using the magnetic card reader or the Cassiopeia® for data entry. However,
there are situations when an evidential breath test will need to
be conducted in a laboratory or station house; for these situations
it is also possible to use a PC for data entry. The PC, Card Reader,
and Manual Entry protocols are detailed below.

Performing an Evidential Breath Test with a PC

Start the Alcotest® 7410^{Plus} Upload program on the PC. Enter an
access code or swipe the Operator/Supervisor access card through

the mag card reader when prompted. The operator will now have the option to "Conduct Evidential Test" or, "Down-load 7410 Data."

Connect the 7410 to the PC by plugging the RS232 cable into the 7410's PC Interface data port. The 7410 must be turned off.

Swipe the subject's driver's license through the mag card reader, or type in subject data in the appropriate fields.

Next, select violation and press enter.

Then choose City/County and press enter.

If the subject and operator data is correct, select "Upload Data" to send the data to the 7410.

If the Upload was successful, the following messages will be displayed:

"Connection Successful," followed by "Data Upload Successful" and "Continue Evidential Test By Pressing OK."

The 7410 will start the evidential test sequence by displaying the date:

$$\boxed{nn}, \boxed{08}, \boxed{dd}, \boxed{06}, \boxed{'44}, \boxed{'99}$$

followed by the time:

$$\boxed{hh}, \boxed{15}, \boxed{nn}, \boxed{45}$$

followed by: $\boxed{- - -}$, $\boxed{RBL}$ (Air Blank),

followed by: $\boxed{T} \ \boxed{.000}$ (Result).

Note: If alcohol is detected by the 7410 in the ambient air or the 7410 has not reached .000 from the previous breath test, the 7410 will automatically perform additional Air Blanks until .000 is displayed.

After a successful Air Blank, the 7410 will display $\boxed{- - -}$, then

$\boxed{br1}$ (Breath Test Number 1) followed simultaneously by the horn, green "Ready" light.

Instruct the subject to take a deep beath and blow evenly as long as the horn sounds. If the test was successful the result will automatically be displayed. After 5 seconds the result will be cleared

and the following is displayed: $\boxed{-\ -\ -}$. The unit will proceed to the second test.

> Note: If the test was not successful, EO will be displayed and the test repeated when the green "Ready" light comes on.

For the second breath test ($\boxed{\mathsf{br2}}$), the above steps will be repeated.

Evidential Testing with the *EPAS*

There are two ways to conduct an evidential breath test in the field with the EPAS, via the Cassiopeia® and the magnetic card reader, or via the virtual keyboard and Jot® system on the Cassiopeia®.

Evidential Testing with the Magnetic Card Reader

Open the *EPAS* case and press the program button on the Cassiopeia®. Next, swipe the subject's driver's license through the magnetic card reader. Verify that all of the data boxes for the subject's information are green.

Next, swipe the operator's card through the magnetic card reader. Verify that all of the operator's data boxes are green.

Enter a violation code, and verify that all of the data boxes are now green.

Tap the "Upload" option on the touch screen, and the data is automatically uploaded to the Alcotest® 7410^{Plus}.

The Alcotest® 7410^{Plus} powers up and is now ready to conduct an evidential breath test.

The 7410 will start the evidential test sequence by displaying the date:

$\boxed{nn}$, $\boxed{08}$ $\boxed{dd}$, $\boxed{06}$ $\boxed{'44}$, $\boxed{'99}$

followed by the time:

$\boxed{hh}$, $\boxed{15}$ $\boxed{nn}$, $\boxed{45}$

followed by: $\boxed{- - -}$, $\boxed{ABL}$ (Air Blank),

followed by: $\boxed{\Uparrow}$ $\boxed{0.00}$ (Result).

> Note: If alcohol is detected by the 7410 in the ambient air or the 7410 has not reached .000 from the previous breath test, the 7410 will automatically perform additional Air Blanks until .000 is displayed.

After a successful Air Blank, the 7410 will display $\boxed{- - -}$,

then $\boxed{br\,1}$ (Breath Test Number 1) followed simultaneously by the horn, green "Ready" light.

Instruct the subject to take a deep breath and blow evenly as long as the horn sounds. If the test was successful the result will automatically be displayed: $\boxed{- - -}$. The unit will proceed to the second test.

> Note: If the test was not successful, EO will be displayed and the test repeated when the green "Ready" light comes on.

For the second breath test $\boxed{br\,2}$, the above steps will be repeated.

Evidential Testing with the Virtual Keyboard and Jot®

To conduct an evidential breath test using the virtual keyboard or Jot®, open the case and press the program button on the Cassiopeia®.

Next, tap the first data box for the subject's data, and enter the data using the virtual keyboard or the Jot® system.

Enter all subject and operator data, including a violation code. All of the data boxes should now be green, indicating that data has been successfully entered.

When all subject and operator data has been entered, tap the "Upload" option from the Cassiopeia® touch screen. The data is automatically entered into the Alcotest® 7410^{Plus}, which is now ready to conduct an evidential test.

The 7410 will start the evidential test sequence by displaying the date:

$$\boxed{nn}, \quad \boxed{08} \quad \boxed{dd}, \quad \boxed{06} \quad \boxed{'44}, \quad \boxed{'99}$$

followed by the time:

$$\boxed{hh}, \quad \boxed{15} \quad \boxed{nn}, \quad \boxed{45}$$

followed by: $\boxed{- - -}$, $\boxed{ABL}$ (Air Blank),
followed by: $\boxed{\uparrow}$ $\boxed{0.00}$ (Result).

> Note: If alcohol is detected by the 7410 in the ambient air or the 7410 has not reached .000 from the previous breath test, the 7410 will automatically perform additional Air Blanks until .000 is displayed.

After a successful Air Blank, the 7410 will display $\boxed{- - -}$,

then $\boxed{br\,1}$ (Breath Test Number 1) followed simultaneously by the horn, green "Ready" light.

Instruct the subject to take a deep breath and blow evenly as long as the horn sounds. If the test was successful the result will automatically be displayed. After 5 seconds the result will be cleared and the following is displayed: $\boxed{- - -}$. The unit will proceed to the second test.

> Note: If the test was not successful, EO will be displayed and the test repeated when the green "Ready" light comes on.

For the second breath test ($\boxed{br2}$), the above steps will be repeated.

Aborting Test or Subject Refusal

If the operator wants to abort the test or the subject does not deliver a breath sample within a preset time frame, approx. 45 seconds, after $\boxed{br1}$ or $\boxed{br2}$ is displayed, $\boxed{End}$ will be displayed along with a series of short beeps.

The operator can select by pressing the ON/OFF button once while the beeping continues. An arrow will appear on the display to indicate that END TEST was selected ($\boxed{End}$).

The results of the $\boxed{End}$ can be printed by following the printing procedures.

If the ON/OFF button is not pressed, the $\boxed{End}$ will disappear after 5 seconds and the breath test can be administered.

> Note: the 7410 will continue to go through the above "time out" sequence until a breath test is conducted or $\boxed{End}$ is selected.

> Important: If the two Evidential Breath Tests are not within 0.02 gm/210L of each other, the decimal point will flash, and $\boxed{br3}$ will be displayed, indicating that a third test is required.

Once the test is completed, the 7410 will store the data in its memory.

The test results can be printed at this time by aligning the LCD's (On and Ready lights of the 7410) with the window on the printer.

Press the ON/OFF button of the 7410 two times to turn the unit off, or once to clear the results and get ready for another test.

EXAMPLES OF PRINTOUT

```
YOUR LOCATION HERE
ALCOTEST 7410 PLUS
SERIAL NUMBER:  ARMD-0253

ALCOTEST 7410 PRINTER
SERIAL NUMBER:  AREE-0141

MM.DD.YY.  HH:MM
 02 . 24. 00  18:20   ST
SEQUENTIAL TEST #:  00098
********************************
          SUBJECT:
SURNAME :        KRAPPUR
NAME :           JOHAN
CDL :            55-57891
DOB :            10-07-1970
         OPERATOR:
LAST:            DEETER
FIRST:           STEVEN
ID-NUMBER :  678-907-2543
AGENCY :         CHP
********************************

AIR BLANK       0.000 17:36
BREATH TEST 1   0.09  17:37
BREATH TEST 2   0.09  17:41
BREATH TEST 3  .- - - -  - -:- -
   ALL RESULTS IN gm/210L
********************************

15 MINUTE OBSERVE _____
OPERATOR SIGNATURE:


......................................

————CUT HERE————
```

Example of Evidential
Breath Test printout.

```
YOUR LOCATION HERE
ALCOTEST 7410 PLUS
SERIAL NUMBER:  ARMD-0253

MM.DD.YY.  HH:MM
 10. 14. 97   18:20   ST
SEQUENTIAL TEST # :   00075
********************************
       SCREENING TEST :
AIR BLANK       0.000   09:59
BREATH TEST     0.038   14:37
   ALL RESULTS IN gm/210
********************************

OPERATOR SIGNATURE:


......................................
```

Example of Screening Test
printout.

```
YOUR LOCATION HERE
ALCOTEST 7410 PLUS
SERIAL NUMBER:  ARMD-0253

ALCOTEST 7410 PRINTER
SERIAL NUMBER:  AREE-0141

MM.DD.YY.  HH:MM
 10. 14. 97   18:20   DST
SEQUENTIAL TEST # :   00098
********************************
        ACCURACY TEST
AIR BLANK       0.000   17:36
TEST RESULT     0.090   17:37
   ALL RESULTS IN gm/210L
********************************

OPERATOR SIGNATURE:


......................................
```

Example of Accuracy Check
printout.

TROUBLE SHOOTING

FAULT	CAUSE	REMEDY
Instrument switches off automatically or yellow light is not lit after switching on, or is only faintly lit; the display shows incomplete symbols.	Battery pack is discharged, or battery pack is completely exhausted. Instrument has been left ready for measurement for more than 10 minutes.	Recharge battery pack.
"READY" light is not lit after switching on and 10 minute waiting interval has not elapsed.	Instrument Malfunction.	Contact Draeger Safety Customer Support Department.
No continuous audible tone when blowing into the instrument.	Instrument not yet ready for measurement. Horn needs replacement (very unusual) or intake is blocked by foreign matter.	Wait until green "READY" light is lit. Contact Draeger Safety, Inc. Customer Support Department.

ERROR CODE	CAUSE	REMEDY
E0	Test subject is not blowing hard enough or steadily enough. Intake is blocked by foreign matter. Pressure sensor or flow rate suspect.	Ask subject to blow harder or more steadily. Sensor or flow rate must be checked by Draeger Safety, Inc. Technical Department.
E1	RFI present or sensor fault (unusual).	Switch instrument off, change location, and switch back on. If E1 persists, sensor must be inspected by Draeger Safety, Inc. Technical Department.
E2	Instrument does not recognize calibration clip. Cal switch malfunction.	Attach calibration clip correctly before turning on instrument. Cal switch must be replaced by an authorized Service Technician.
E3	Calibration data invalid. Lifetime of sensor reached or cal data malfunction.	Calibrate instrument. Sensor must be replaced or inspected by Draeger Safety.
E4	Improper value was used for calibration.	Calibrate with proper value.
E5	Fault in sampling system (due, most likely, to motor malfunction).	Repeat measurement. If E5 reappears, contact Draeger Safety, Inc.
E6	Instrument Malfunction.	Contact Draeger Safety, Inc. Customer Support Department.
E7	Sensor signal error.	Contact Draeger Safety, Inc. Customer Support Department.
Err	Breath test or Accuracy Check is out of limits.	Calibrate instrument.

PRINTER

FAULT	CAUSE	REMEDY
Not printing although supply voltage is supplied.	Voltage is too low, too high, or wrong polarity. Defective fuse malfunction.	Detach unit from power supply, provide voltage greater than 9.5V/1A and less than 17V/1A. Detach unit from power supply and replace fuse (1A). Contact Draeger Safety Customer Support Department.
Although supply voltage is available, paper feed is irregular or printer stops.	Faulty power cord. Power supply inadequate or faulty. Mounting Socket broken.	Replace power cord. Provide voltage greater than 9.5V/1A and less than 17V/1A. Contact Draeger Safety, Inc. Customer Support Department.

Message printed	Cause	Remedy
DATA ACCEPTED	Printer received complete new data record.	Normal function message.
DATA AVAILABLE	Printer received known data record.	Normal function message.
TRANSMISSION ERROR	Incorrect log received.	Position Alcotest® 7410^{Plus} again, or clean transparent window or lenses.
BATTERY EMPTY	Memory battery for time and date is empty.	Replace memory batteries (2 x type AA/1.5V).
HARDWARE ERROR	Hardware error.	Contact Draeger Safety, Inc. Customer Support Department.

5

INTRODUCTION TO
BLOOD-ALCOHOL ANALYSIS

§5.2   Retrograde Extrapolation: Projecting Test Levels
Back to Time of Driving

Page 258. Add at end of second full paragraph:

The Michigan Supreme Court has overruled *Schwab*, holding that
for purposes of admitting results of blood alcohol tests performed
on a driver, there is no requirement that such tests be given
within a reasonable time. *People v. Wager*, 594 N.W.2d 487
(Mich. 1999).

Page 258. Add at end of section:

In view of the scientific criticism of the practice (see §5.2.1),
some courts are beginning to question the validity — and hence
admissibility — of retrograde extrapolation. An Alabama appellate court, for example, commented:

> ... careful analysis of these studies indicates that retrograde
> extrapolation is an unreliable method of determining a
> defendant's condition at the time of operation. The inadequacies
> of retrograde extrapolation extend beyond mere technical
> inaccuracies to problems which are inherent in the basic
> premises and calculations of this technique. These inadequacies
> render retrograde extrapolation inherently untrustworthy and
> therefore inappropriate for use as evidence to convict drunk
> drivers. *Smith v. Tuscaloosa*, 601 So. 2d 1136 (Ala. Ct. App. 1992).

The court cited a law review article, Abbott, One for the Road —
The Reliability of Retrograde Extrapolation and the Implications
for Vermont Statutes, 16 Vermont Law Review 395 (1991).

And in *Mata v. State*, 46 S.W.3d 902 (Tex. Crim. App. 2001), a
Texas appellate court held that "the trial court abused its discretion in admitting that part of (the state's expert's) testimony
pertaining to the extrapolation of Mata's BAC" and remanded
the case:

> ...Our study of retrograde extrapolation leads us to several
> conclusions. Initially, we recognize that even those who believe
> retrograde extrapolation is a reliable technique have utilized it
> only if certain factors are known, such as the length of the drinking
> spree, the time of the last drink, and the person's weight....In
> addition, there appears to be general disagreement on some of the
> fundamental aspects of the theory, such as the accuracy of
> Widmark's formulas, whether a standard elimination rate can be
> reliably applied, and the effect that food in the stomach has on
> alcohol absorption....

The court concluded that "retrograde extrapolation can be reliable in a given case," but the testimony presented by the state's
expert was not sufficient to establish reliability "by clear and convincing evidence."

§5.2.1   The Fallacy of Retrograde Extrapolation

Page 260. Add at end of first full paragraph:

In the first cited article, Dubowski also reported variation in
elimination rates of .001 percent to .08 percent per hour. In
another study of subjects who consumed mixed drinks with a
meal, researchers found absorption rates ranging from .02
percent to .08 percent per hour; the average was .05 percent.
Jones & Neri, 24 Canadian Society of Forensic Sciences Journal
165 (1991).

§5.3 General Sources of Error

§5.3.9 Internally Produced Alcohol

Page 292. Add at end of subsection 5.3.9:

If the client was taking antacids such as Tums or Rolaids, he may have created a situation in which his body was manufacturing alcohol internally. Scientific literature indicates that antacids change the gastric acidity in the stomach—which can lead to alcohol production by resident bacteria and elevated blood-alcohol readings. Bode, et al., Effects of Cimetidine Treatment on Ethanol Formation in the Human Stomach, 19(6) Scandinavian Journal of Gastroenterology 853 (1984); Ericson, Effects of Antacids on Alcohol's Reaction, 5(5) Alcoholism 28 (1985).

6

BREATH ANALYSIS

§6.0   The Reliability of Breath-Alcohol Analysis

Page 295.   Add after first full paragraph:

Subsequently, *McGinley* was overruled in *State v. Downie*, 550 A.2d 1313 (1988). In that case, the State had appealed a number of cases in which a municipal court judge had allowed the defendants to advance certain arguments relating to the admissibility of the breathalyzer evidence. In each case, the defendant did not assert error with regard to the operation of the particular breathalyzer involved in his case, but rather challenged whether the breath-alyzer machines in general accurately test the subject's blood-alcohol content. The *Downie* court began by reviewing the New Jersey Supreme Court's decision in *Romano v. Kimmelman*, 474 A.2d 1 (N.J. 1984), wherein the *Romano* Court had ordered:

> The Smith and Wesson Breathalyzer Models 900 and 900A are found to be scientifically reliable and accurate devices for determining the concentration of blood alcohol. Such scientific reliability shall be the subject of judicial notice in the trial of all cases under N.J.S.A.39:4-50 [New Jersey's DWI statute].
> Further, all future cases under N.J.S.A.39:4-50 shall be prosecuted in accordance with the terms of the within Order, which shall remain in effect unless otherwise modified by further order, or final decision of this Court.

The *Downie* court recognized the potential validity of the defen-dants' arguments relating to the accuracy of the breath test results, but found that it was bound by the New Jersey Supreme

Court's order in *Romano*. The *Downie* court explained:

> The Order is definite when it states that it is binding in all future cases. While we recognize the scholarly and persuasive analysis of the court in *McGinley*, we must overrule that decision unless and until the Supreme Court takes some action to relax the *Romano* Order. We can only suggest that this matter be reviewed immediately.

To date, the New Jersey Supreme Court has not withdrawn its Order in *Romano*.

Page 297. *Add after carryover paragraph:*

Many variables can affect the accuracy of a breath-alcohol testing device. Scientists have recognized that in addition to problems inherent with the machine, variables such as temperature, breathing pattern, and the health of the subject can affect the result produced from the breath test device. In an article, The Flawed Nature of the Calibration Factor in Breath-Alcohol Analysis, 79 Journal of Chemical Education, 1237-1240 (Oct. 2002), Dominick A. Labianca of the Department of Chemistry at Brooklyn College, City University of New York, has opined that in addition to the variables of the tested subject, the calibration factor in breath testing devices is flawed.

> Clearly, the claim by users of breath-alcohol analyzers that such instruments are accurate because they produce accurate results within a specified margin of error when calibrated with simulator solutions (or dry gas standards) is a very limited claim. The only acceptable point of accuracy in this situation is that the breath-alcohol analyzer that functions properly at a fixed [blood:breath] ratio is capable of accurately analyzing such a solution (or dry gas standard). However, when the same breath-alcohol analyzer is used to test a human subject, the result cannot automatically be deemed accurate: it must be evaluated within the context of its uncertainty.

§6.0.1   The Blood-Breath Partition Ratio

Page 299. *Add after second full paragraph:*

Later, the Nebraska Supreme Court overruled *Burling*, holding that the reading of the test results from a specific model of breath test machine is not to be automatically adjusted as a matter of law on the basis of the testimony of a witness who does not speak on behalf of the State; whether an adjustment is required is dependent upon the credible evidence present in each case. *State v. Baue,* 607 N.W.2d 191 (Neb. 2000).

Page 301. Add at end of subsection:

Confronted with the reality of a legislative/judicial bar to presenting scientific truth as to the partition ratio, counsel should consider turning the new "breath statute" against itself. This can be done by emphasizing the minute amount of breath measured compared to the amount involved in defining the offense. The new statute's definition clearly requires the breath test to be based upon grams of alcohol per 210 liters of breath—a rather voluminous amount. The simple fact is, however, that the lung capacity of human beings is only about four to six liters of breath; the breath machines can capture only about 50 cubic centimeters of this breath for analysis—about 1/20th of one liter. In other words, the machine is measuring a breath sample that is a tiny fraction of the amount relevant to the charge: The statute's 210 liters is about 4,200 times more than the sample being analyzed by the machine. Assuming a reading on the machine of .08 percent, this 50 cc breath sample would contain about *one-millionth of a fluid ounce of alcohol.* Is the machine capable of reliably and accurately measuring such an infinitesimal amount? Can the amount of alcohol in 210 liters (the size of an oil drum) be determined from measuring a quantity so tiny that it is invisible to the human eye? What would be the impact of even the slightest error if magnified 4,200 times?

§6.1 Non-Specific Analysis

Page 316. Add after second paragraph:

Note: As is discussed in §6.4.6, Draeger's new Alcotest 7110 incoporates dual technology (infrared and fuel cell) and a new 9.5-micron filter, which will improve specificity. Contrary to claims, however, the nonspecificity problem is far from solved. One of the leading figures in breath-alcohol analysis, Professor

Dominick A. Labianca, has conducted studies on 9.5-micron filters and has concluded that the "claim that the most efficient way to avoid the influence of organic compounds in evidential breath testing is the use of the 9.5 micron ethanol absorption band is questionable." 404 Journal of Analytical Toxicology 16 (1992):

> Breath-alcohol analyzers operating in the [3.39- and 3.48-micron] wavelength region have been plagued with problems arising from their lack of specificity.... That lack of specificity is, in part, a consequence of the fact that thousands of organic molecules contain the methyl group, and that the corresponding carbon-hydrogen stretching vibrations of many of these molecules, which can contaminate breath samples, cannot be distinguished from those of ethanol....
>
> While IR [infrared] analyses for breath-alcohol at 9.5-microns would eliminate [some] problems, it would not provide a foolproof solution. Common volatile organic compounds, other than ethanol, which occur, for example, in solvents, perfumes, and food, also contain carbon-oxygen functionality and exhibit IR absorption bands that overlap this wavelength....

Draeger has also produced a hand-held version of the Alcotest 7110, the Alcotest 7410 (sometimes referred to as the Breath-alyzer 7410; §4.4.1). The California Department of Justice is in the process of replacing all PBT (preliminary breath test) devices and evidential breath testing machines with these PBT-type hand-held units—i.e., the hand-held unit will be offered in court as the primary evidence of blood-alcohol concentration. This development can be expected to spread nationwide.

Page 320. Add at end of section:

Practitioners should be aware of a potential interferant in inhalers used by their asthmatic clients. Spanish scientists have found that certain asthma inhalers that do not contain ethanol produce false positive results of ethanol when subjects are given a breath test within 10 minutes of using the inhaler. The *British Medical Journal* reported that 60 volunteers with asthma who attended a Spanish hospital submitted to a breath test on the

Alcotest 7110-E, an infrared breath alcohol testing device manufactured by Draeger, which is widely used in Spain and France. Xavier Bosch, Using Asthma Inhalers Can Give False Positive Results in Breath Tests, 324 British Medical Journal 756 (March 30, 2002) (citing Juan Manuel Ignacio Garcia, et al., Influence of Asthma Inhalers on a Breath Alcohol Test, 118 Medicina Clinica 332 (2002)). These researchers studied the effects of different inhalers containing salbutamol, salmeterol, formoterol, budesonide, and fluticasone.

Dr. Ignacio-Garcia, the lead scientist, stated the only confounding factor that could have led to a false positive result in the study was the propellant gases used in the aerosols, in particular, chlorofluorocarbons. His next challenge is to find out what happens with puffer devices that do not use propellants — for example, dry powder inhalers.

§6.1.1 Interferents on the Breath: Acetone and Acetaldehyde

Page 321. Add after second full paragraph:

Australian scientists have apparently found that the familiar "new car smell" is caused in part by high levels of acetone. In other words, individuals arrested for drunk driving who had been driving a recently purchased new vehicle might be inhaling high levels of acetone — and later exhaling the compound into the breath machine. An excerpt from the Reuters news agency press release (Sydney, Dec. 9, 2001):

Australian Scientists Warn of New Car Illness

Australian scientists have warned that the reassuring smell of a new car actually contains high levels of toxic air emissions which can make drivers ill.

A study by Australia's main scientific body, the Commonwealth Scientific and Industrial Research Organization (CSIRO), found high levels of toxic emissions in cars for up to six months and longer after they leave the showroom.... The toxic emissions include Benzene, a cancer-causing toxin; Acetone, a mucosal irritant; Ethylbenzene, a systemic toxic agent; and Xylene isomers, a foetal development toxic agent....

§6.2   Mouth Alcohol

Page 332. Add after carryover paragraph:

If the client is asthmatic or was having any kind of breathing problems requiring the use of an inhaler, counsel should explore the probability that this elevated the breath machine's reading. These inhalers operate primarily by injecting a mist containing a substantial quantity of alcohol into the lungs; as an example, one of the most commonly used inhalers, Primatene Mist, contains 34 percent alcohol. This alcohol apparently does not pass into the blood stream, but remains in the alveolar lining of the lungs — where it will constantly be exhaled. The machine's partition ratio computations will, of course, greatly magnify its effect on the reading, as it assumes the alcohol has been absorbed into the blood and metabolized. Note: Because the alcohol is being breathed out in relatively uniform quantity, unlike the metabolized alcohol in true alveolar breath, there will be no "negative slope" to be detected by the machine's "mouth alcohol detector" (see §6.2.5).

Page 333. Add after carryover paragraph:

A foreign substance that is becoming more prevalent is that of tongue or lip studs. In *Guy v. State of Indiana,* 805 N.E.2d 835 (Ind. Ct. App. 2004), the breath-testing operator noticed a bar with a ball on top of the defendant's tongue and a fastener underneath. The appellate court ultimately granted the defendant's motion to suppress the breath test because the state failed to establish the foundation for admitting the test. In particular, the state must show that the person to be tested must have had nothing to eat or drink and must not have put any foreign substance in his or her mouth or respiratory tract, and must not smoke within 20 minutes prior to the time a breath sample was taken. While the state argued that the defendant placed the metal stud (foreign substance) in her mouth more than 20 minutes prior to the test, the appellate court rejected that argument, stating that the plain meaning of the rule contemplates that a substance "put" in the mouth must be *removed* more than 20 minutes before the test is administered. *Id.* at 839, citing *State v. Molnar,* 803 N.E.2d 261, 266 (Ind. Ct. App. 2004).

Further, the parties in the *Guy* case disputed whether a tongue stud was a "foreign substance." The state argued that if the metal stud was determined to be a foreign substance, then a variety of dental appliances would necessarily be foreign substances under the rule, as well. The prosecution noted that other states have determined that a test subject was not required to remove dentures or false teeth before a breath test. See *Farr v. State*, 914 S.W.2d 38, 40 (Mo. Ct. App. 1996); *People v. Witt*, 630 N.E.2d 156, 158 (Ill. App. Ct. 1994).

The court pointed out, however, that based on the plain meaning of the statute as defined by both Black's Law Dictionary and the American Heritage Dictionary of the English Language, dental appliances would not necessarily constitute "foreign substances" under the rule since they are not situated in an abnormal, unusual, or irregular place in the body, and such appliances are prevalent throughout the general population. The *Guy* court left the issue of dental appliances to be decided on another date, but held that the metal stud was a "foreign substance" under Indiana law and thus overruled the trial court's denial of the defendant's motion to suppress.

In contrast, a new mouthpiece placed into the suspect's mouth prior to blowing into the breath test device has been determined *not* to be a foreign substance. See *People v. Wilhelm*, 803 N.E.2d 1032 (Ill. App. Ct. 2004). Wilhelm had been observed for 20 minutes before administering the first test, but both the first and second breath test attempts resulted in an insufficient sample. A new mouthpiece was inserted on the breath test tube prior to the second and third attempts, but the officer did not begin a new 20-minute observation period after each unsuccessful blow. The third test, which was successful, occurred approximately four minutes after the first. In overruling the trial court, the appellate court found that interpreting the breath test device's mouthpiece as a foreign substance was a preposterous interpretation and clearly contrary to the drafter's intent. *Id.* at 1035.

§6.2.2 Heartburn, Reflux, and Hiatus Hernias

Page 339. Add after first sentence of first paragraph:

The terms *acid reflux* and *heartburn* are often used interchangeably with the terms *gastroesophogeal reflux disease*, commonly referred to as *GERD*, and *hiatal hernia*. Technically, however, they are not synonymous. GERD is the condition that can cause the acid reflux; GERD is commonly caused by a herniated valve, also called a hiatus hernia or hiatal hernia, separating the stomach from the esophagus; heartburn is the sensation experienced by the person suffering from the condition.

Page 340. Add at end of section:

For a discussion — and scientific corroboration — of the effects of GERD/reflux, see Kechagias, Jonsson, Franzen, Andersson and Jones, Reliability of Breath-Alcohol Analysis in Individuals with Gastroesophageal Reflux Disease, 44(4) Journal of Forensic Sciences 814 (1999); Kechagias, Johnsson, and Jones, Breath Tests for Alcohol in Gastroesophageal Reflux Disease, 130 Annals of Internal Medicine 328 (1999).

§6.3   Additional Sources of Error

§6.3.6   Simulator Calibration

Page 355. Add after second paragraph:

Note: As forensic toxicologist Mary McMurray has pointed out:

> The use of an *internal* "standard" does not serve the same purpose that an external standard does. Internal "standards" are not standards in the true sense of the term. Internals use either the filters themselves or a separate quartz plate as a beam attenuator. This can aid the monitoring or voltages, and indirectly can be considered a monitor of the calibration, however the correlation is very limited. Internal standards do not check or give any insight to the sampling system. Internal standards do not resemble a breath alcohol sample in that there is no moisture or alcohol being measured with an internal standard. Internal standards cannot be used to calibrate a device and are not on the NHTSA Conforming Products List.

§6.3.8 Ambient Air

Page 366. Add at end of subsection:

The necessity for running a true "air blank" to obtain an arguable accurate breath test result is critical. In fact, however, this step is commonly omitted or done incorrectly — often without the operator's knowledge. Yet, errors in this important step are difficult to detect. The following material, provided to the author by noted forensic toxicologist Mary C. McMurray of Minneapolis, should point counsel in the right directions.*

———————————

What is an air blank? It isn't a term that you will find in a dictionary, nor is it a term that you can find in an encyclopedia. The term "air blank" is used in the field of breath-alcohol testing, but the meaning of the term varies depending on the source and the context of usage. So what exactly is an air blank?

In 1968, the National Safety Council Committee on Alcohol and Other Drugs developed recommendations for Testing and Training.[1] Included in the recommendations is the requirement for a blank analysis with every test. Unfortunately there is no definition given for the term "blank analysis."

From a pure science perspective, a blank analysis is the analysis (test) of a sample that contains all of the components as the unknown sample(s) *except* the particular compound of interest for which it is being analyzed. Most importantly, the blank must be treated and analyzed in the same manner as the unknown sample(s). The purpose of conducting a blank is to establish whether the sample matrix or the handling of the sample (i.e., the addition of solvents and/or reagents) has any effect on the detection of the compound in question. A blank analysis is necessary to determine if there is anything in the analytical process that could result in false postive or negative results. A blank analysis is also used for establishing the "background" reading at the time of

———————————

* Reprinted with permission.
[1] Committee Handbook 1992, Recommendations of the Ad Hoc Committee on Testing and Training of the Committee on Alcohol and Other Drugs, National Safety Council.

analysis and is necessary to assure that there is no interference outside of the established parameters.

In blood alcohol analysis a blank would be a blood sample containing no alcohol that is treated in the same manner as the unknown blood samples. The blank-blood samples would have the same preservatives, anticoagulants, internal standards, etc., as the other blood samples and would be handled and analyzed in the same fashion as the blood samples of unknown alcohol concentration. It follows that a blank-breath would be a breath sample that is known to contain no alcohol.

The Federal Register Model Specification for Evidential Breath Alcohol Testers[2] identifies the evaluation process for accuracy and precision for the breath testing devices. One phase of the testing is a blank test, also referred to as testing at 0.0000 BAC. For this testing the analyst is required to abstain from consuming any alcohol for a period of 48 hours prior to the testing and must not smoke for a period of at least 20 minutes prior to testing. The analyst then provides a minimum volume of two liters of his or her own breath into the device being evaluated. The testing parameters require that the systematic error be less than or equal to +/− 0.005 BAC with no single result being greater than 0.005.

In 1971 the Committee on Alcohol and Other Drugs identified the operational standards that should be expected for quantitative breath alcohol analysis and developed guidelines for evaluating evidential breath-alcohol testing devices.[3] Among the recommendations is:

> The instrument must be capable of performing a blank analysis on ambient air, free of alcohol and other interfering substances, that yields an apparent alcohol concentration of less than 0.01% W V.

Today, the use of an air blank is common in breath-alcohol testing, and all evidential breath-alcohol testing devices have a testing mode for blank analysis. From a scientific perspective, it should be safe to assume that an air blank is an analysis of the

[2] Federal Register, Vol. 58, No. 179, Sept. 17, 1993; Model Specifications for Evidential Breath Alcohol Testers, pages 48705–48710.
[3] Committee Handbook 1992, Recommendations of the Ad Hoc Committee on Quantitative Breath Alcohol Instrumentation of the Committee on Alcohol and Other Drugs, National Safety Council.

ambient air and that if the results of such an analysis are less than a 0.01 g/210L there is no reason to believe that the air or sampling system are contaminated. But are these assumptions correct?

A quick review of the various breath-alcohol testing devices reveals that the air blanks are generally explained in the manufacturer's literature as a check of the ambient air, the sample chamber and/or the fuel cell (if present) to assure that there are no contaminants present that would affect the accuracy of the test results. More than one manufacturer includes information in their operational manual indicating that if the air being drawn into the device is contaminated with alcohol or other detectable substances, some type of "ambient fail" error will be generated alerting the operator. Such statements imply that the purpose of an air-blank analysis is to establish what reading the device shows, at the time of the test, when the ambient air is analyzed.

Precautions do need to be taken to assure that during the air blank analysis the sampling system is not being contaminated. Sources for contamination of an air blank have been traced to used mouthpieces, the breath tube inlet being in close proximity to a heavily contaminated or intoxicated subject, or the recent use of solvents or cleaning compounds in the vicinity of the breath test devices. The installation of the devices should allow for ample air circulation around the vents of the unit, especially the breath exhaust port. The proximity of the breath exhaust port to the inlet of the breath tube can in some cases cause contamination of an air-blank, especially if there is inadequate air circulation around the device.[4]

The concept of an air-blank analysis provides a sense of security that if there is contamination of the sampling system or the room air the device will indicate such to the operator. The indication being either an alcohol reading on the blank or an audible and visual display alerting the operator. Interestingly, in evaluating the current evidential instrumentation this hasn't always proven to be the case. For example, the Intoxilyzer© 5000 uses the air blank as a purging system, then, using the analysis of

[4] While working for the State of Wisconsin, this author was advised, by CMI, to attach a segment of tygon tubing to the exit port of the sample chamber that was long enough to extend under the tabletop. This assured that vapors being purged out of the chamber will not be sucked back into the breath tube where they could potentially contaminate the air blank.

the ambient air sample at the end of the purge, arbitrarily sets zero. A system such as this will never print a numeric result for an air blank that is greater than 0.000 g/210L regardless of how much alcohol or other contamination is in the sampling system.[5] The purpose for performing a blank analysis is totally lost with this type of a system as there is no way of determining if there is any contamination of the air or sampling system that would affect the accuracy of the test results.

The setting of a new "zero" with each and every air blank can produce some very interesting results. Obviously the recommendation for a blank analysis with every evidential test cannot be intended to mean the test subject's own breath in an alcohol-free state. So what is the source of the blank analysis that should accompany every evidential breath test? Perhaps the breath test operator could be used as a source for a blank-breath sample — assuming there is no alcohol, or other interfering substances, on his or her breath. Instead it was, somehow and somewhere, decided that room air can serve as the blank. It seems logical to assume that, since room air is inhaled then exhaled as breath, the ambient air can be used as a source for the blank analysis. It also seems logical to assume that, in most cases, room air is alcohol free.

If there is alcohol in the sampling system blank the Intoxilyzer© will "see" that amount of alcohol as zero — and then subtract that amount of alcohol from the next sample. The result is not accurate if it is reading too low. An instrument that cannot detect the very substance that it is supposed to be measuring during an air blank does not assure accuracy.

Some people will argue that the low reading benefits the test subject. So who cares? If the claim is scientifically accurate and the results are reliable, you should care. Poor precision of test results can be masked by the floating zero. The arbitrary setting of zero with each air blank can result in what appears to be a 0.02 correlation between two samples or it can mask a correlation and make it appear that two samples are not in agreement. Unfortunately there is no way that a breath test operator will ever know if this is occurring at any given time.

[5] For more information refer to Law and Science DWI Journal, Vol. 11, No. 6, June 1996 and Vol. 11, No. 7, July 1996.

In the August 1994 update to the Omnibus Rules[6] it was noted in the discussion that the main point of an air blank is to ensure that the testing device is a "clean slate" and is unaffected by any alcohol from previous tests or other sources.[7] The Omnibus Rules require the results of an air blank prior to a test to be 0.00 g/210L or the testing is not to be continued on that device. If an air blank preceding a test is not 0.00 the test is considered invalid. The arbitrary establishment of "zero" on each air blank assures that the requirement for a 0.00 g/210L will always be satisfied.

The Department of Transportation regulations for the Omnibus Employee Testing Act[8] definitions for breath alcohol testing in 49 CFR Part 40 includes:

Air blank: A reading by an EBT of ambient air containing no alcohol. (In EBTs using gas chromatography technology, a reading of the device's internal standard.)[9]

The addition of the use of a device's internal standard in doing a blank check is quite interesting. It is a modification of the concept of an air blank so that an air sample is no longer necessary for the blank analyses. The analysis of blank-breath samples were used to demonstrate that the device does not create false positive or negative results — thus assuring some level of accuracy at the lower limits of detection under laboratory conditions. The air blanks have been used to purge the sampling system followed by an analysis of the ambient air samples — establishing the baseline value for the test device at that point in time. An analysis to assure that there are no contaminants that would affect the accuracy of the test result.

Today a blank analysis means the blank checked itself and is reading 0.00 g/210L. What does such a check show? The blank sample (sometimes referred to as a system blank) is not

[6] Federal Register, Vol. 59, No. 160, Aug. 19, 1994. 49 CFR Part 40 Final Rule, page 42999.

[7] Federal Register, Vol. 59, No. 31, Feb. 15, 1994. 49 CFR Part 40 Rules and Regulations, pages 7340–7366. Federal Register, Vol. 59, No. 160, Aug. 19, 1994. 49 CFR Part 40 Final Rule, pages 42996–43019.

[8] Federal Register, Vol. 59, Feb. 15, 1994. 49 CFR Part 40 Rules and Regulations, 7340–7366.

[9] EBT is an Evidential Breath Test device.

necessarily a sample. It can be a reading generated by the testing device to show what the sampling system registers at the moment. If the system blank is designed to provide a true reading of what is present in the sampling system, then, it can be used to show the baseline or background value. However, if the device simply blanks out the background, a random analytical error is introduced that cannot be measured.

It appears that the air blank can be anything the instrument manufacturer wants it to be without concern for scientific credibility. The air-blank measurement in some cases does not even serve the purpose claimed by the manufacturer. Apparently the efforts of the manufacturer are to placate the breath test governing bodies.

§6.3.9   Incomplete Purging and the "Air Blank"

Page 368. Add at end of section:

The importance of a complete air blank, and in some circumstances a warm air flushing of the airway of the roadside breath testing device, cannot be overstated. The National Highway Traffic Safety Administration (NHTSA) reports that roadside testing at low temperatures presents a potential problem not experienced in the protected environments of law enforcement stations or mobile vans. In its March 2002 report entitled Special Testing for Possible Alcohol Carry-over Effects Using the Intoximeters, Inc. Alco-Sensor IV at 10 degrees C (DOT-HS-809-424), NHTSA recognizes that a subject's breath, as it exits the mouth, is saturated with moisture.

If the ambient air is cold enough, and if the hand-held breath tester is unheated, it is possible for the moisture in the breath to condense onto the airway surface of the tester, and cause alcohol present to condense with it. If this condensation occurs, it is possible for alcohol in one test to carry over to a second test, causing a false positive result. While some hand-held breath testers have a heated airway, many do not, in order to extend their battery life. This carryover is not possible if sufficient time is allowed for condensed alcohol to evaporate, if the breath testing device is heated and flushed prior to a second test, or if an air blank is made prior to the breath test to check for the presence of residual alcohol. NHTSA is considering this potential problem in its next modification of the NHTSA model specifications for both evidential breath testers, as well as alcohol screening devices. Until that time, counsel should refer to the following table when investigating roadside testing at low temperatures.

Table 1
Hand Held Breath Testers on NHTSA Conforming Products
List (CPL)

Table 1 Notes: Devices on the Evidential CPL may also be used as Screening Devices. Presence or absence of features to prevent false positives due to residual alcohol at low temperatures are indicated.

Features: *Heated* sample airway; *Flushing* of previous sample before next test; *Instructions* address possibility of carryover at low-temperature operation.

Screening CPL

Company	Model	Heated	Flushing	Instructions
Alco Check International	Alco Check 3000 DOT Alco Screen Alco Check 9000	yes	yes	no
Guth Laboratories, Inc.	Alco Tector Mark X[1] Mark X Alcohol Checker[1]	no	no	no
PAS Systems International, Inc.	PAS IIIa PAS Vr[2]	no	no	no
Han International Co., Ltd.	A.B.I.	no	no	no
Repco Marketing, Inc.	Alco Tec III	no	no	no
Sound Off, Inc.	Digitox DOT Alco Screen 1000	no	yes	yes

[1] No longer manufactured.
[2] User activated heater.

Evidential CPL

Company	Model	Heated	Flushing	Instructions
Alcohol Countermeasures Systems Corp.	Alert J3AD, PBA 3000C[3,4]	no	no	no
CMI, Inc.	Intoxilyzer 200, 200D, 300,[3] 400,[3] 400PA,[2] SD2, SD5[6]	no	no	no
Draeger Safety, Inc.	AlcoTest 7410, 7410 Plus Breathalyzer 7410, 7410-II	yes	yes	no
Gall's Inc.	ADS 500[1]	yes	yes	no
Intoximeters, Inc.	Alco Sensor III, IV,[5] IV-XL,[5] IV AZ,[5] RBT-AZ,[5] III, III-A, IV[5]	no	no	no
Lifeloc Technologies, Inc.	PBA 3000B,[3,4] 3000-P,[3,4] 3000C,[3,4] Alcohol Data Sensor, Phoenix, FC-10,[6] FC-20[6]	no	no	no
Lion Laboratories, Ltd.	Alco Meter 300,[3] 400,[3] SD-2, Intoxilyzer 200, 200D	no	no	no
National Draeger, Inc.	Alco-Test 7410, 7410 Plus Breathalyzer 4710, 7410 Plus	yes	yes	not available
Seres	Alco Pro[7]	yes	yes	not available
Sound-Off, Inc.	Seres Alco Pro[7] Alco Data[1]	yes	yes	no

[1] No longer manufactured.
[2] User activated heater.
[3] Design of mouthpiece minimized potential for carryover.
[4] Auto air blank.
[5] Carry over not possible in evidential mode. CEM heated flushing accessory available for Alco-Sensor IV, RBT IV models.
[6] Devices have passed testing against the NHTSA model specifications for EBTs, but a new CPL for EBTs has not yet been published.
[7] No longer sold in the United States.

§6.4   The Machines

Page 378. Change the numeral "74" to "126" in last line of first (carryover) paragraph.

Page 379. Add after list of machines in first full paragraph:

As of this writing, the "new wave" of breath machines is well on the way to supplanting existing models. These devices — notably, the Intoximeter EC-IR and Draeger/Breathalyzer 7110 — feature increased specificity (through combining fuel cell and infrared analysis with improved filtering) and, usually, improved calibration and data collection. CMI's Intoxilyzer 5000 continues to be popular in updated series models, but appears slated for replacement in the future by the new, more competitive Intoxilyzer 8000 (equipped with an industry-leading nine filters). In November 2002, Florida approved use of and ordered the Intoxilyzer 8000 for use in that state.

Page 381. Add at end of section:

Counsel confronted with a breath machine — evidential or PBT (see §4.4) — not commonly encountered should check to see whether it is an *approved* device. Most jurisdictions require any breath-testing equipment to be reviewed and approved by appropriate governmental agencies. Such machines are usually included on a list of "conforming" devices maintained by the state's regulatory agency. In most cases, the agency simply adopts the federal National Highway Traffic Safety Administration's "Conforming Products List" — a list that is periodically updated as some instruments are added while others are discontinued. Any breath tests conducted with an unapproved machine should, of course, be subject to a pretrial motion to suppress.

Counsel should be aware that law enforcement agencies in some states *modify* machines that are on the Conforming Products List. The modifications may be made by the manufacturers at the agency's request, or they may be made by the agencies themselves. It is important to understand that *such modifications create a different device* — and thus one no longer on the list of approved instruments.

Of course, the defense practitioner should recognize that "new, enhanced" versions of a device provide excellent opportunities for attacking the results of the previous model. Care should be taken to recognize any improvements in the device and be prepared to cross-examine on the problems they allegedly overcome. For instance, the October 3, 2002 Conforming Products List notes that the new Alco-Sensor III with serial numbers above 1,200,000 is an enhanced version with a new fuel cell and a microprocessor that improves performance. If the improved performance includes improved accuracy or reliability, the results of the predecessor model are now suspect.

The following is the latest available list of conforming breath-testing products, taken from the *Federal Register*, Vol. 67, No. 192, p. 62091 (Oct. 3, 2002):

DEPARTMENT OF TRANSPORTATION: National Highway Traffic Safety Administration. [Docket No. NHTSA-02-13409] Highway Safety Programs; Model Specifications for Devices To Measure Breath Alcohol

AGENCY: National Highway Traffic Safety Administration, DOT.

ACTION: Notice.

SUMMARY: This notice amends the Conforming Products List for instruments that conform to the Model Specifications for Evidential Breath Testing Devices (58 FR 48705).

EFFECTIVE DATE: October 3, 2002.

FOR FURTHER INFORMATION CONTACT: Dr. James F. Frank, Research and Technology Office, Behavioral Research Division (NTI-131), National Highway Traffic Safety Administration, 400 Seventh Street, SW., Washington, DC 20590; Telephone: (202) 366-5593.

SUPPLEMENTARY INFORMATION: On November 5, 1973, the National Highway Traffic Safety Administration (NHTSA) published the Standards for Devices to Measure Breath Alcohol (38 FR 30459). A Qualified Products List of Evidential Breath

Measurement Devices comprised of instruments that met this standard was first issued on November 21, 1974 (39 FR 41399).

On December 14, 1984 (49 FR 48854), NHTSA converted this standard to Model Specifications for Evidential Breath Testing Devices, and published a Conforming Products List (CPL) of instruments that were found to conform to the Model Specifications as Appendix D to that notice (49 FR 48864).

On September 17, 1993, NHTSA published a notice (58 FR 48705) to amend the Model Specifications. The notice changed the alcohol concentration levels at which instruments are evaluated, from 0.000, 0.050, 0.101, and 0.151 BAC, to 0.000, 0.020, 0.040, 0.080, and 0.160 BAC; added a test for the presence of acetone; and expanded the definition of alcohol to include other low molecular weight alcohols including methyl or isopropyl. On July 21, 2000, the most recent amendment to the Conforming Products List (CPL) was published (65 FR 45419), identifying those instruments found to conform with the Model Specifications.

Since the last publication of the CPL, seven (7) instruments have been evaluated and found to meet the model specifications, as amended on September 17, 1993, for mobile and non-mobile use. In alphabetical order by company, they are: (1) Alert J4X.ec manufactured by Alcohol Countermeasure Systems, Inc. of Mississauga, Ontario, Canada. This is a hand held device that uses a fuel cell sensor and is powered by an internal battery. (2) Intoxilyzer 8000 manufactured by CMI, Inc. of Owensboro, KY. This is a non-dispersive infrared device which uses the 3.4 micron and the 9 micron band for measurement of alcohol. It is powered by 120 volts AC power or by 12 volts DC power from a car battery. (3) Intoxilyzer S-D5 manufactured by CMI, Inc. of Owensboro, KY. This device is a hand-held device that uses a fuel cell sensor. (4) The new Alco-Sensor III with serial numbers above 1,200,000. This is an enhanced version of the earlier Alco-Sensor III. The enhanced version has a new fuel cell and a microprocessor that improves performance. It is a hand held device intended for stationary or roadside operations. As indicated, it uses a fuel cell sensor and is powered by an internal battery. (5) The Intox EC/IR 2 manufactured by Intoximeters, Inc. of St. Louis, Missouri. This is a bench top device intended primarily for use in stationary operations. It uses a fuel cell sensor and can be powered by either 110 volts AC or 9 volts DC power sources. (6) The FC 10, manufactured by Lifeloc Technologies, Inc. of Wheat Ridge, CO. This is a handheld device that uses a fuel cell sensor. (7) The FC 20, also manufactured by Lifeloc Technologies, Inc. of Wheat Ridge, CO. This is also a handheld device that uses a fuel cell sensor. The Lifeloc FC 20 is similar to the FC 10 except that it has additional features that are not addressed by the model specifications.

Finally, three devices are being removed from the CPL, because they are no longer manufactured and are no longer in use. They are: (1) Alco.Tector Model 500, manufactured by Decator Electronics of Decatur, Illinois. This device was introduced more than 30 years ago. It has not been manufactured for at least 20 years, and its manufacturer is no longer in existence. It would be impossible to repair because replacement parts are not available. The agency has no knowledge of any such devices in use. (2) The AE-D1 manufactured by Lion Laboratories, Ltd. of Cardiff, Wales, UK. The manufacturer has confirmed in writing that this unit is totally obsolete, no longer in use and no longer in production. (3) The Auto-Alcolmeter manufactured by Lion Laboratories, Ltd. of Cardiff, Wales, UK. The manufacturer has also confirmed in writing that this unit is totally obsolete, no longer in use and no longer in production.

The CPL has been amended to add the seven instruments identified above to the list, and to remove the three instruments also identified above.

In accordance with the foregoing, the CPL is therefore amended, as set forth below.

Conforming Products List of Evidential Breath Measurement Devices

Manufacturer and model	Mobile	Nonmobile
Alcohol Countermeasure Systems Corp., Mississauga, Ontario, Canada:		
Alert J3AD*	X	X
Alert J4X.ec	X	X
PBA3000C	X	X
BAC Systems, Inc., Ontario, Canada:		
Breath Analysis Computer*	X	X
CAMEC Ltd., North Shields, Tyne and Ware, England: IR Breath Analyzer*	X	X
CMI, Inc., Owensboro, KY:		
Intoxilyzer Model:		
200	X	X
200D	X	X
300	X	X
400	X	X
400PA	X	X
1400	X	X
4011*	X	X
4011A*	X	X
4011AS*	X	X
4011AS-A*	X	X
4011AS-AQ*	X	X
4011 AW*	X	X
4011A27-10100*	X	X
4011A27-10100 with filter*	X	X
5000	X	X
5000 (w/Cal. Vapor Re-Circ.)	X	X
5000 (w/3/8" ID Hose option)	X	X
5000CD	X	X
5000CD/FG5	X	X
5000EN	X	X
5000 (CAL DOJ)	X	X
5000VA	X	X

*Instruments marked with an asterisk (*) meet the Model Specifications detailed in 49 FR 48854 (December 14, 1984) (i.e., instruments tested at 0.000, 0.050, 0.101, and 0.151 BAC.) Instruments not marked with an asterisk meet the Model Specifications detailed in 58 FR 48705 (September 17, 1993), and were tested at BACs = 0.000, 0.020, 0.040, 0.080, and 0.160. All instruments that meet the Model Specifications currently in effect (dated September 17, 1993) also meet the Model Specifications for Screening Devices to Measure Alcohol in Bodily Fluids.

Manufacturer and model	Mobile	Nonmobile
8000	X	X
PAC 1200*	X	X
S-D2	X	X
S-D5	X	X
Draeger Safety, Inc., Durango, CO:		
Alcotest Model:		
7010*	X	X
7110*	X	X
7110 MKIII	X	X
7110 MKIII-C	X	X
7410	X	X
7410 Plus	X	X
Breathalyzer Model:		
900*	X	X
900A*	X	X
900BG*	X	X
7410	X	X
7410-II	X	X
Gall's Inc., Lexington, KY: Alcohol Detection		
System-A.D.S. 500	X	X
Intoximeters, Inc., St. Louis, MO:		
Photo Electric Intoximeter*	—	X
GC Intoximeter MK II*	X	X
GC Intoximeter MK IV*	X	X
Auto Intoximeter*	X	X
Intoximeter Model:		
3000*	X	X
3000 (rev B1)*	X	X
3000 (rev B2)*	X	X
3000 (rev B2A)*	X	X
3000 (rev B2A) w/FM option*	X	X
3000 (Fuel Cell)*	X	X
3000 D*	X	X
3000 DFC*	X	X
Alcomonitor	—	X
Alcomonitor CC	X	X
Alco-Sensor III	X	X
Alco-Sensor III (Enhanced with Serial		
Numbers above 1,200,000)	X	X
Alco-Sensor IV	X	X
Alco-Sensor IV-XL	X	X

Manufacturer and model	Mobile	Nonmobile
Alco-Sensor AZ	X	X
RBT-AZ	X	X
RBT III	X	X
RBT III-A	X	X
RBT IV	X	X
RBT IV with CEM (cell enhancement module)	X	X
Intox EC/IR	X	X
Intox EC/IR 2	X	X
Portable Intox EC/IR	X	X
Komyo Kitagawa, Kogyo, K.K.:		
Alcolyzer DPA-2*	X	X
Breath Alcohol Meter PAM 101B*	X	X
Lifeloc Technologies, Inc., (formerly Lifeloc, Inc.), Wheat Ridge, CO:		
PBA 3000B	X	X
PBA 3000-P*	X	X
PBA 3000C	X	X
Alcohol Data Sensor	X	X
Phoenix	X	X
FC 10	X	X
FC 20	X	X
Lion Laboratories, Ltd., Cardiff, Wales, UK:		
Alcolmeter Model:		
300	X	X
400	X	X
SD-2*	X	X
EBA*	X	X
Intoxilyzer Model:		
200	X	X
200D	X	X
1400	X	X
5000 CD/FG5	X	X
5000 EN	X	X
Luckey Laboratories, San Bernadino, CA:		
Alco-Analyzer Model:		
1000*	—	X
2000*	—	X
National Draeger, Inc., Durango, CO:		
Alcotest Model:		
7010*	X	X

Manufacturer and model	Mobile	Nonmobile
7110*	X	X
7110 MKIII	X	X
7110 MKIII-C	X	X
7410	X	X
7410 Plus	X	X
Breathalyzer Model:		
900*	X	X
900A*	X	X
900BG*	X	X
7410	X	X
7410-II	X	X
National Patent Analytical Systems, Inc., Mansfield, OH:		
BAC DataMaster (with or without the Delta-1 accessory)	X	X
BAC Verifier Datamaster (with or without the Delta-1 accessory)	X	X
DataMaster cdm (with or without the Delta-1 accessory)	X	X
Omicron Systems, Palo Alto, CA:		
Intoxilyzer Model:		
4011*	X	X
4011AW*	X	X
Plus 4 Engineering, Minturn, CO: 5000 Plus4*	X	X
Seres, Paris, France:		
Alco Master	X	X
Alcopro	X	X
Siemans-Allis, Cherry Hill, NJ:		
Alcomat*	X	X
Alcomat F*	X	X
Smith and Wesson Electronics, Springfield, MA:		
Breathalyzer Model:		
900*	X	X
900A*	X	X
1000*	X	X
2000*	X	X
2000 (non-Humidity Sensor)*	X	X
Sound-Off, Inc., Hudsonville, MI:		
AlcoData	X	X
Seres Alco Master.	X	X
Seres Alcopro	X	X

Manufacturer and model	Mobile	Nonmobile
Stephenson Corp.:		
Breathalyzer 900*	X	X
U.S. Alcohol Testing, Inc./Protection Devices, Inc., Rancho Cucamonga, CA:		
Alco-Analyzer 1000	—	X
Alco-Analyzer 2000	—	X
Alco-Analyzer 2100	X	X
Verax Systems, Inc., Fairport, NY:		
BAC Verifier*	X	X
BAC Verifier Datamaster	X	X
BAC Verifier Datamaster II*	X	X

23 U.S.C. 402; delegations of authority at 49 CFR 1.50 and 501.1)

Issued on: September 27, 2002.
Marilena Amoni,
Associate Administrator for Program Development and Delivery.
[FR Doc. **02-25185 Filed** 10-2-**02**; 8:45 am]
BILLING CODE 4910-59-P

§6.4.1   Intoxilyzer 5000

Page 383. Add after first full paragraph:

As of this writing, CMI was in the process of developing its newest breath-alcohol machine, the *Intoxilyzer 8000*. In apparent response to the increasing popularity of Draeger's newer Alcotest 7110 (see §6.4.6) and Intoximeter's EC/IR (see §6.4.7.), the model 8000 will have two filter wheels rather than just one, which will be capable of reading nine channels from the 3.0 + to 9.0 + micron range. This should improve — not eliminate — specificity. However, the device will apparently not have the even greater specificity afforded by the addition of a second electro-chemical fuel cell system as is found in the Draeger and in the Intoximeter EC/IR (see §6.4.7).

Page 384. Insert the following material and table after the carryover paragraph:

The table below sets forth the gradual evolution of the Intoxilyzer 5000 through its various model permutations, summarizing the improvements and differences between them. Each of the models can be found in use today in various jurisdictions. The author is grateful to forensic toxicologist Mary Catherine McMurray of Forensic Associates, Inc., (651-784-7721) for permission to reproduce the table.

THE	INTOXILYZER 5000	EVOLUTION	
	64-00 and 66-00	68-00	68-01
	Identified in the Federal Register as: 5000, 5000 w/cal vapor re-circulation, 5000 w/3/8" ID hose option, 5000V/A	Identified in the Federal Register as: 5000CD, 5000CD/FG5	Identified in the Federal Register as: 5000EN
Dimensions	18" x 18" x 6"	18" x 18" x 6"	18.75" x 17.35" x 5.75"
Test card	4" wide multi-ply	4" wide multi-ply, external printer optional	4" wide multi-ply, external printer optional
Detector	Warm, lead selenide	Thermoelectrically-cooled, lead selenide. The detector is electronically cooled to 0°C.	Thermoelectrically-cooled, lead selenide. The detector is electronically cooled to 0°C.
Filters	3 filters	5 filters, state may request 3	5 filters, state may request 3
	3.80, 3.48, 3.39 μm (microns)	3.80, 3.52, 3.47, 3.40, 3.36 μm (microns)	3.80, 3.52, 3.47, 3.40, 3.36 μm (microns) Started using wide band filters in 2000
Sample chamber, vol.	81.4 ml	81.4 ml	82.2 ml
Minimum detection	0.02 g/210L	0.01 g/210L	0.01 g/210L
IR source	Quartz iodide projection lamp with a reflective back coating.	Same as earlier models	Same as earlier models

Created by Mary Catherine McMurray

Photo Interrupter	One interrupter that looks at the complete loop, thus establishing the basic timing for the signals.	Two -- one interrupter looks at the filters, while the other looks at the complete loop. The two interrupters synchronize the separation of the signals for each wavelength.	Two -- one interrupter looks at the filters, while the other looks at the complete loop. Two interrupters synchronize the separation of the signals for each wavelength.
Monitor breath volume	No	Yes, unless opted for pressure switch. A transducer is used to measure the volume in liters. Check valves at the entry to and exit from the sample chamber prevent backward flow, thus preventing a subject from "sucking back" and diluting the sample.	Yes, unless opted for pressure switch. A transducer is used to measure the volume in liters. Check valves at the entry to and exit from the sample chamber prevent backward flow, thus preventing a subject from "sucking back" and diluting the sample.
Internal Tubing	1/4" ID	1/4" ID	3/8" ID used to reduce the opposition to air flow
Microprocessor	Z80	Multiprocessor system with the slave microprocessor dedicated to the instrument's analytical tasks.	Multiprocessor system with the slave microprocessor dedicated to the instrument's analytical tasks.
Sample chamber temperature	45° ±5°C Ghost readings (false positive alcohol readings) have been reported for sample chamber temperatures of less than 47°C.	45° ±5°C Ghost readings (false positive alcohol readings) have been reported for sample chamber temperatures of less than 47°C.	47° ±5°C The sample chamber is constructed of thinner tubing than in earlier models. The thinner mass warms to the 2-degree higher temperature quicker than in earlier models.
Barometric pressure measurement	No	Yes, if dry gas is used as a calibration verification medium, a barometric pressure sensor is included to provide automatic correction for barometric pressure.	Yes, if dry gas is used as a calibration verification medium, a barometric pressure sensor is included to provide automatic correction for barometric pressure.

Created by Mary Catherine McMurray

217

Monitors for alveolar air, aka deep lung air, end-expiratory air	Time, pressure, slope The pressure switch was the only choice with these early models. The minimum pressure needed to activate the tone is 6" water pressure. The tone must be kept on throughout the entire exhalation (minimum time 4-6 seconds) and the alcohol concentrations must be leveling off. A plateau, or leveling off of the slope is defined as no more than a +0.002 or -0.001 on three consecutive pairs of readings.	Volume, time and slope There is a flow sensor, aka a thermistor (a temperature dependant resistor), that, when calibrated, makes it possible to measure the flow of air (in liters per second) as a sample is being provided. The total volume of the expired breath may be measured (liters/sec multiplied by seconds = liters). A minimum breath flow of 0.17 L/sec is required to initiate the tone, 0.15 L/sec must be maintained to keep the tone on. 1.1 liters of air is needed before slope is considered. Slope requirements are the same as for the earlier models. A flow sensor is necessary for using dry gas standards. As an option, a state could request that the device be retrofitted with a pressure switch. No volume measurement is capable with pressure switches. Dry gas is not an option for pressure switch devices.	Volume, time and slope Same as for the 68-00.
Calibration standards	Wet bath simulator	Wet bath simulator or dry gas	Wet bath simulator or dry gas

Created by Mary Catherine McMurray

	Manual, analog	Computerized, digital	Computerized, digital
Calibration process	Variable potentiometers, aka trim pots, are resistors that can be adjusted manually with a small screwdriver to vary the resistance. Each of the channel voltages, the DVM and the $V_{ref}/2$ are manipulated with dedicated trim pots. The calibration information is stored as analog information and periodically the voltages may need to be manually adjusted via the trim pots. Voltage drift is why voltages need to be re-adjusted by the state technicians. Calibration will drift as the voltages drift.	The computerized calibration process stores all of the calibration in a digital manner. The drifting of channel voltages that previously occurred with the earlier models is not as likely to occur with the 68 series.	Same as 68-00
Breath path and calibration path	Shared path and entry into sample chamber	Shared path and entry into sample chamber	Breath path and calibration path are two separate paths that enter the sample chamber at two separate points. By separating the breath and calibration paths there is no 3-way valve in the breath path making it easier to provide a sample into the sample chamber. The separation of the two paths necessitates added quality assurance measures to establish that the sample will read the same on both paths.

Created by Mary Catherine McMurray

INTERNAL DIAGNOSTICS:

EPROM check - erasable programmable read only memory is checked to obtain a checksum that must match that contained in the instructions.

RAM check - random access memory is set to zero and checked to ensure it is zeroed.

TEMP check - sample chamber temperature is checked, must be within 5°C of the set point.

PROCESSOR check - the filter wheel motor, EEPROM programming, serial number, range and stability and auto cal status of the processor board are all checked.

PRINTER check - the printer is checked to verify that it is on and attached.

RTC check - real time clock/calendar is checked.

INTERNAL STANDARD check - the light transmitted thru each of the channel filters is utilized to monitor the electronic stability of the signals. The internals are "set" in the calibration process to read as if they were various alcohol concentrations, thus the name "internal standards".

Sources:
Wisconsin Breath Alcohol Testing Update, 1994;
Minnesota Model Intoxilyzer 5000 series 68, 1998 and updates
CMI sales literature, 2000

Demystfying the Intoxilyzer by MC McMurray

Created by Mary Catherine McMurray

Page 412. Add after first full paragraph:

Adjustments made to the calibration will affect the settings for internal standards. For this reason, whenever calibration adjustments are made the intervals must be reset. Adjustments to the settings for the internal standards may cause changes in the calibration and thus the calibration must be checked after such adjustments.

Page 413. Add after second full paragraph:

In the Intoxilyzer 5000EN (serial numbers that start with 6801), the breath path and the calibration path are separated. Separating the breath path from the calibration path meant the solenoid valve could then be removed from the breath path. Removing the solenoid valve from the breath path reduced the resistance in the breath path, making it easier to provide a sample. The solenoid valves are still necessary for the calibration port control. The valves were subsequently reduced in size and moved to the back of the case between the sample chamber and the case wall. This latter revision made it possible to reconfigure the layout of the analytical bench, thus allowing for a new design enabling much easier and quicker access to the light source. A leak in the sampling or calibration path can cause erroneous sampling messages such as "IMPROPER SAMPLE."

Page 424. Add after last paragraph:

All of the data for every test can, in theory, be collected; however, the data actually collected depends upon the agency collecting the data. Each state tells CMI what data it wants to collect. Some states, such as Minnesota, do not collect or download any tests conducted as part of a servicing at the BCA lab. Only data from tests conducted "in the field" are downloaded. From a scientific perspective, this is not advisable. The purpose of collecting data should be to establish the working history of the device and allow for complete troubleshooting of its operation.

The data actually reported in discovery requests depends on the integrity of the agency handling the data. Wisconsin data is sorted so that only subject tests are reported unless a specific request is made to include all the data. Arizona has written into the software a procedure that allows the results of tests that the technician/operator does not like to be omitted from the database. Minnesota has special funtion keys that allow tests to be conducted that are not stored in the computer memory. When dealing with computer data, always remember that "all tests reported" is not the same as "all tests conducted."

§6.4.2 BAC DataMaster

Page 435. Add at end of fact #6:

Correction: The DataMaster continues to be manufactured by National Patent.

§6.4.6 Alcotest 7110

Page 507. Add after SAFEGUARD 4 paragraph:

ERROR INDICATORS — The Alcotest 7110 is equipped with various error analysis features in the event of a systematic problem. In such a case, the display and printer will indicate the error condition according to the following chart (for example: ERROR [081] INTERFACT-SYS>).

Error Code	Error name:	Potential reason for error:
002	MAIN-SYSTEM, EEPROM memory	Defective memory cell
003	MAIN-SYSTEM, RAM memory	Defective memory cell
004	MAIN-SYSTEM, External RAM memory	Defective memory cell
008	MAIN-SYSTEM, Battery for memory	Discharged battery
009	MAIN-SYSTEM, Power supply	12 VDC insufficient. Turn instrument off and on again.
023	IR-SYSTEM, Source oscillator	Frequency too low

Error Code	Error name:	Potential reason for error:
031	EC-SYSTEM, EC-signal	Incorrect voltage, or early warning that the fuel cell may need to be replaced
032	EC-SYSTEM, Sampling system	Motor, pump, relay
035	EC-SYSTEM, EC-peak signal	Signal peak not found
041	FLOW-SYSTEM, Flow sensor	Short or interrupted circuit
043	FLOW-SYSTEM, Purge	Insufficient flow for air blank. Check to see that back of unit is not obstructed.
051	PRESSURE-SYSTEM, Pressure sensor	Short or interrupted circuit
071	HEATER-SYSTEM, NTC for cuvette	Short or interrupted circuit
072	HEATER-SYSTEM, NTC for breath hose	Short or interrupted circuit
075	HEATER-SYSTEM, Temperature(s)	Cuvette-, breath hose-heater malfunctioning
081	INTERFACE-SYSTEM, Printer	No printer commands
084	INTERFACE-SYSTEM, Function-key	Unacceptable voltage
101	CALIBRATION, IR-system	Unacceptable adjustment
112	CALIBRATION, Calibration data	Lost data in EEPROM
113	CALIBRATION, Configuration	System parameters incorrect

Page 515. Add after chart:

The chart "Selected Compounds with C-O Stretching Vibrations that Absorb in the 9–10 micron Region" was created by Professor Dominick A. Labianca, Ph.D., and may be cited as: Labianca, D.A., How Specific for Ethanol Is Breath-Alcohol Analysis Based on Absorption of IR Radiation at 9.5 microns?, 16 Journal of Analytical Toxicology 404 (1992).

Page 515. Add new subsection:

§6.4.7   Intoximeter EC/IR

Intoximeter, Inc.'s Intoximeter EC/IR (standing for electro-chemical/infrared) is a relatively new breath-alcohol machine, replacing the manufacturer's older model, the Intoximeter 3000. The primary difference between the two devices is that the EC/IR uses fuel cell and infrared analysis, where the 3000 utilized gas chromatography. In this respect it is similar to Drae-ger's Alcotest 7110 (see §6.4.6). The dual technology gives the machine improved specificity as to ethanol (see §6.1), but the device remains prone to most of the other problems inherent in breath-alcohol analysis discussed elsewhere — mouth alcohol, radio frequency interference, retrograde extrapolation, partition ratio variance, etc.

It should be understood that specificity is simply improved; the potential for non-specific analysis still exists. The theory of combining infrared and electrochemical analysis is that different results may indicate the presence of an interferent. Thus, the infra-red component of the EC/IR is the primary method of analysis and fuel cell is the secondary, and any variation over a set amount will trigger an interferent signal. If the infrared reading is, for example, .153 percent, and the fuel cell system reads .132 percent, the machine will give an interferent warning. The variance trigger-ing the warning can be set at any figure, commonly .02 percent. Note: The electrochemical reading is internal, that is, it is not viewed or reported. Thus if a subject tested at .090 percent on the IR part of the Intoximeter and .075 percent on the EC, only the .090 percent will register — and the existence of a non-crim-inal sub-.08 percent reading will never be known. This, of course, certainly suggests a possible area for cross-examination in close EC/IR readings.

Note: The author has received reports from attorneys in some states that have recently adopted the EC/IR as an evidentiary machine. They indicate that the RFI (radio frequency interence) detector and the slope (mouth alcohol) detector have been turned off. One attorney was advised by the state's senior chemist that this was suggested by the manufacturer to facilitate proper use of the machine. To determine whether these critical detectors have been disconnected in a given machine, seek through discovery a print-out of the internal operating standards (easily obtainable with the machine's F11 key).

Note also: As with some other breath testing machines (see §13.3.5), Intoximeter's EC/IR has a limited manufacturer's warranty — for only one year and with no warranty as to software.

The following material taken from the Los Angeles Police Department's "Intox EC/IR Administrator's Manual," is largely reproduced from the manufacturer's manual. Counsel should consider an officer's administration of the test in light of the recommended procedures set forth in the manual. The material also offers possibilities for exploring the officer's lack of knowledge of the machine's theory and operation.

TECHNICAL SPECIFICATIONS

Measurement Range

0.000 to 0.400 grams of ethanol/210 liters of breath

Accuracy and Precision

The Intox EC/IR meets or exceeds all US Department of Transportation specifications for the accuracy and precision of alcohol breath testing instruments. The measurement system is specific to ethyl, methyl, and isopropyl alcohols; it does not respond to other hydrocarbons found naturally in the breath.

The Intox EC/IR is accurate to within 0.003 at 0.100 BrAC.

Internal Clock and Calendar

The internal clock, with or without external power, is accurate to ± 1 minute per month.

Keyboard

101-key, AT-compatible keyboard.

Display

The Intox EC/IR display is two line by twenty character vacuum fluorescent display. The display is:

- highly reliable—rated for a lifetime of 50,000 hours
- very bright—685 cd/m^2 (or 200 f-L)
- has low power consumption
- supports a large international character set

Printer

The Intox EC/IR incorporates a high performance thermal printer that provides:

- Printing speed 7.5 lines per second
- 150 dots/inch resolution
- Integrated paper handling system requires no threading; changing the paper roll takes seconds and there are no paper jams
- Multiple test modes, including compressed, double width and height, bold and reverse image
- Large international character set

Optional External Printer

The Intox EC/IR can print to most IBM PC-compatible printers with a Centronics parallel interface via the 25-pin connector on the instrument's rear panel.

Modem

The Intox EC/IR can communicate via a built-in Hayes-compatible 2400 baud modem. A built-in Hayes-compatible 9600 baud modem is optional.

I/O

2 - RS-232 serial communications ports
1 - parallel port

Electrical

90 to 250 VAC, 47 to 63 Hz, approximaely 65 watts power consumption
12 VDC operation with optional inverter

Mechanical

Desktop model
Height: 7 in. (178 mm)
Width: 17 3/4 in. (451 mm)
Depth: 18 in. (457 mm)
Weight: 22 lb. (10 kg)

Portable model

Height: 7 in. (178 mm)
Width: 14 in. (356 mm)
Depth: 18 in. (457 mm)
Weight (with tank): 30 lb. (14 kg)

SUBJECT TESTS

LOS ANGELES POLICE DEPARTMENT PROTOCOL
The following procedures illustrate testing using the Los Angeles Police Department protocol. The Los Angeles Police Department protocol is a two-test protocol with a conditional third test preceded by a series of questions about the subject and operator.

Conducting a Subject Test Using the Los Angeles Police Department

Once the system has been turned on and the warm-up cycle completed the display will be in the scrolling mode. Follow the steps below noting the display, keyboard entry, and explanation at each step. Note: Always use a new originally packaged mouthpiece for each subject test. Use care when opening the mouthpiece package. Residual pieces of plastic wrap may cling to the mouthpiece which may get blown into the sample assembly causing restriction and possible blockage.

DISPLAY	KEYBOARD ENTRY	EXPLANATION
Normal Scrolling Mode INTOX EC/IR TEST SITE A49 SERIAL NO. 01780 13:59 05/08/95 PRESS ENTER TO START SUBJECT TEST	Press the Enter key.	The Enter key starts the test.
SUBJECT TEST	Information only. No data entry required.	
SUBJECT NAME: JOHN T. SMITH	Enter the test subject's name. John T. Smth.	Entry may be up to 20 characters.
OPERATOR SERIAL #: 153761	Enter the Operator's serial #. 153761	Entry may be up 6 numeric characters.
OPERATOR ASSIGNMENT:	Enter the Operator's assignment.	Entry may be up to 20 characters.
15 MIN OBSERVED BY:	Enter the serial # of the person who observed the subject during the 15 minute waiting period.	Entry may be up to 6 numeric characters.
VERIFY DATA (Y/N)? N	Enter Y to review or edit the previously entered data, or press the Enter key to continue.	Allows the operator to review or edit the previously entered data and correct any errors.
CHECKING SYSTEM	Information only. No data entry required.	The instrument is performing an internal electronic system check.
PURGING	Information only. No data entry required.	The Intox EC/IR is purging the breath path with ambient air.
BLANK CHECK	Information only. No data entry required.	The instrument will flush the breath path with room air for approximately 30 seconds. A sample of this air is analyzed. If the result is .000, the Standard Check is initiated. If the result is >.000 a second purge is done. If a third blank result is >.000 the test is aborted.
BLANK .000	Information only. No data entry required.	The instrument diplays the result of the blank check.

DISPLAY	KEYBOARD ENTRY	EXPLANATION
PLEASE BLOW *************	If the subject refuses to submit a breath sample press the R key. The test will be aborted and the printer will print all of the subject data followed by "TEST REFUSED."	Instruct the subject to take a deep breath and blow into the mouth piece as steadily and as long as possible. Flow and volume will be indicated by the * characters. The test subject is allowed 4 minutes to provide a valid sample. If he/she fails to do so, the test will be treated as a refusal.
EVALUATING SAMPLE	Information only. No data entry required.	The Intox EC/IR is evaluating the sample.
SUBJECT .00	Information only. No data entry required.	The instrument displays the result of the subject test.
PURGING	Information only. No data entry required.	The Intox EC/IR is purging the breath path with ambient air.
BLANK CHECK	Information only. No data entry required.	The instrument will flush the breath path with room air for approximately 30 seconds. A sample of this air is analyzed. If the result is .000, the Standard Check is initiated. If the result is >.000 a second purge is done. If a third blank result is >.000 the test is aborted.
BLANK .000	Information only. No data entry required.	The instrument displays the result of the Blank Check.
PLEASE BLOW *********	If the subject refuses to submit a breath sample press the R key. The test will be aborted and the printer will print all of the subject data followed by "TEST REFUSED."	Instruct the subject to take a deep breath and blow into the mouth piece as steadily and as long as possible. Flow and volume will be indicated by the * characters. The test subject is allowed 4 minutes to provide a valid sample. Failure is treated as a refusal.
EVALUATING SAMPLE	Information only. No data entry required.	The Intox EC/IR is evaluating the sample.

DISPLAY	KEYBOARD ENTRY	EXPLANATION
SUBJECT .00	Information only. No data entry required. If the result of the two subject tests differ by more than .02, a third test will be run and reported in the printout.	The instrument displays the result of the Subject test. Printer now prints the test results as shown below: Intox EC/IR SUBJECT TEST S/N: 01780 Location: TEST SITE A49 Test Date: 01/12/98 Test Time: 12:42 Subject's Name: John T. Smith Operator Serial #: A53242 Operator Assignment: 15 Minimum Observed By: 476432 TEST g/2101 Time Diagnostic Check ok BLK .00 02:41 SUBJ .00 02:42 BLK .00 02:43 SUBJ .00 02:44
PRINT ANOTHER COPY? (Y/N) N	Enter Y to print another copy of the test result or the Enter key to continue.	Multiple copies of the Subject Test printout can be obtained at this point.
PURGING	Information only. No data entry required.	The Intox EC/IR is purging the breath path with ambient air.
Normal Scrolling Mode	Information only. No data entry required.	The instrument returns to the Normal Scrolling Mode.

DOT PROTOCOL

The following procedures illustrate testing using the DOT protocol. The DOT protocol involves a Screening Test followed by a conditional Confirmation Test. The Intox EC/IR will instruct the Operator on the proper sequence of steps needed to perform a DOT protocol alcohol test.

Conducting A Subject Test Using DOT Protocol

Follow the steps below noting the display, keyboard entry, and explanation at each step.

DISPLAY	KEYBOARD ENTRY	EXPLANATION
Normal Scrolling Mode INTOX EC/IR TEST SITE A49 S/N 01780 13:59 05/08/95 PRESS ENTER TO START DOT SUBJECT TEST	Press the Enter key.	The Enter key starts the test.
PASSWORD ****	Enter your password then press the Enter key.	This function requires an Operator level or higher password.
RUN SCHEDULED ACC CHECK (Y/N)? Y	Press the Enter key to initiate the scheduled accuracy check.	This message will only appear before the first test of a given day if a scheduled accuracy check is required. The frequency of scheduled accuracy checks is set under the F10 key.
SUBJECT TEST DISABLED	After displaying this message for approximately 5 seconds, the Intox EC/IR will return to scrolling mode.	If a required accuracy check has not been completed, one must be completed successfully before the Intox EC/IR will allow another test to be run.
SCREEN OR CONFIRM (S/C)? S	Press the Enter key to initiate a Screen Test. Press C and the Enter key for a Confirmation Test.	

THE FOLLOWING SERIES OF STEPS WILL OCCUR IN EITHER A SCREEN TEST OR A CONFIRMATION ONLY TEST.

STEP 1 ON FORM COMPLETED (Y/N)? Y	Complete Step 1 on the DOT test form and then press the Enter key to continue.	

DISPLAY	KEYBOARD ENTRY	EXPLANATION
DATE: MON 12 JUN 95 OK (Y/N)? Y	If the time is correct press the enter key to continue. If the time is incorrect, Type N and the Enter key.	If the Operator answers N to this question the Intox EC/IR exits the test sequence and instructs the Operator that a Key Operator must reset the date.
TIME: 14:43 OK (Y/N)? Y	If the time is correct press the enter key to continue. If the time is incorrect, Type N and the Enter key.	If the Operator answers N to this question the Intox EC/IR exits the test sequence and instructs the Operator that a Key Operator must reset the date.
ENTER BAT NAME/ID: BOB JONES	Enter the BAT's name. Bob Jones	Entry may be up to 20 characters.
EMPLOYEE FIRST NAME: JOHN	Enter the subject's first name. John	Entry may be up to 20 characters.
EMPLOYEE MIDDLE I: T	Enter the subject's middle initial. T	Entry must be 1 character.
EMPLOYEE LAST NAME: SMITH	Enter the subject's last name. Smith	Entry may be up to 20 characters.
EMPLOYEE ID: 453 6125 23	Enter the subject's ID 453 6125 23	Entry may be up to 20 characters.
COMPANY ID: ABC145	Enter the ID of the subject's employer ABC145	Entry may be up to 20 characters.
COMPANY NAME: ABC CORPORATION	Enter the name of the subject's employer. ABC CORPORATION	Entry may be up to 20 characters.
REASON FOR TEST (1-6) PRE-EMPLOYMENT	Type a digit from 1 to 6 to enter the DOT reason for test.	1 Pre-employment 2 Random 3 Suspicion/cause 4 Post-accident 5 Return to duty 6 Follow-up
VERIFY DATA (Y/N)? N	Enter Y or N. N	Entering Y allows the operator to review and/or edit the previous entries and correct any errors.
EXPLAIN TEST PROC. THEN PRESS ENTER	Explain the test procedure to the subject and then press the Enter key to continue.	
STEP 2 ON FORM COMPLETED (Y/N)? Y	Complete Step 2 in the DOT test form and then press the Enter key to continue.	

DISPLAY	KEYBOARD ENTRY	EXPLANATION
INSERT MOUTHPIECE THEN ENTER	Insert the mouthpiece into the breath tube and then press the Enter key.	The Operator should put the mouthpiece into the breath tube at this time so that the Intox EC/IR's purge/blank procedure will insure that the mouthpiece is not contaminated with alcohol.

THE FOLLOWING SERIES OF STEPS WILL OCCUR ONLY IF A SCREEN TEST IS BEING RUN.

DISPLAY	KEYBOARD ENTRY	EXPLANATION
SCREEN #: 950612091 OBSERVED (Y/N)? Y	Note the test number and then press the Enter key to continue.	Display shows the test number until the Enter key is pressed. The format is YYMMDDXXX where XXX is the test number.
CHECKING SYSTEM	Information only. No data entry required.	The instrument is performing self-diagnostic checks.
PURGING	Information only. No data entry required.	The instument is purging the sample path with ambient air.
BLOW UNTIL BEEP ********* TIME LEFT: 02:56	If the subject refuses to submit a breath sample press the R key. The test will be aborted and the printer will print all of the subject data followed by "TEST REFUSED." If the timer expires, the message TEST REFUSED (Y/N)? will be displayed.	Instruct the subject to take a deep breath and blow into the mouthpiece as steadily and as long as possible. Flow and volume will be indicated by the * characters. Typing Shift-M will force a manual sample (See Breath Sample Volume section of Operating Principles).
EVALUATING SAMPLE then RESULT 0.044 14:45	Information only. No data entry required.	The Intox EC/IR is evaluating the sample. Printer now prints the test results as shown below:

DISPLAY	KEYBOARD ENTRY	EXPLANATION
PRINT ANOTHER COPY? (Y/N)? Y	Press Y and the Enter key for another copy or press the Enter key to continue.	Screening Test Intox EC/IR S/N: 01780 Location: TEST SITE A49 Date: Mon 12 Jun 95 Time: 14:45 Test #: 950612091 Employee ID: 453 6125 23

		VALUE (g/2101) TIME
		Result 0.044 14:45

DISPLAY	KEYBOARD ENTRY	EXPLANATION
RESULT 0.044 14:45 OBSERVED (Y/N)? Y	After showing the subject the results, press Enter.	
ATTACH PRINTOUT TO FORM, PRESS ENTER	Attach the printout to the DOT alcohol test form then press enter to continue.	

IF THE RESULT OF THE SCREEN TEST IS LESS THAN .020 THEN THE TEST SEQUENCE WILL TERMINATE WITH THE FOLLOWING STEPS:

COMPLETE FORM STEP 3 THEN PRESS ENTER	Complete Step 3 on the DOT test form and then press the Enter key to continue.	
COMPLETE FORM STEP 4 THEN PRESS ENTER	Complete Step 4 on the DOT test form and then press the Enter key to continue.	
PURGING	Information only. No data entry required.	Instrument is purging the breath path with ambient air.
Normal Scrolling Mode	Information only. No data entry required.	The instrument returns to Normal Scrolling Mode.

IF THE RESULT OF THE SCREEN TEST IS GREATER THAN .020 THEN THE TEST SEQUENCE WILL CONTINUE WITH THE FOLLOWING STEPS:

DISPLAY	KEYBOARD ENTRY	EXPLANATION
DO CONFIRMATION TEST 15 MINUTE WAIT 13:24 REMOVE MOUTHPIECE THEN PRESS ENTER	Remove the mouthpiece from the breath tube and then press the Enter key.	The Intox EC/IR will beep as a reminder to remove the mouthpiece until the Enter key is pressed. After the Enter key is pressed, only the timer portion of the message will appear on the screen.
		When there is less than 1 minute left on the timer the Intox EC/IR will begin beeping.
15 MINUTE WAIT 13:24		After the 15 minute wait the Operator must begin the Confirmation test within 15 minutes.

THE FOLLOWING SERIES OF STEPS WILL OCCUR FOR A CONFIRMATION TEST AS A CONFIRMATION ONLY TEST OR AS A CONFIRMATION TEST FOLLOWING A POSITIVE SCREENING TEST.

DISPLAY	KEYBOARD ENTRY	EXPLANATION
CONFIRMATION TEST INSERT NEW MOUTHPIECE THEN PRESS ENTER	Insert the mouthpiece into the breath tube and then press the Enter key.	The Operator should put the mouthpiece into the breath tube at this time so that the Intox EC/IR's purge/blank procedure will insure that the mouthpiece is not contaminated with alcohol.
CONFIRM #: 950612092 OBSERVED (Y/N)? Y	Note the test number and then press the Enter key to continue.	Display shows the test number until the Enter key is pressed. The format is YYMMDDXXX where XXX is the test number.
CHECKING SYSTEM	Information only. No data entry required.	The instrument is performing self-diagnostic checks.
PURGING	Information only. No data entry required.	Instrument is pruging the breath path with ambient air.

DISPLAY	KEYBOARD ENTRY	EXPLANATION
BLANK CHECK	Information only. No data entry required.	The instrument will flush the breath path with room air for approximately 30 seconds. A sample of this air is analyzed. If the result is .000, the Standard Check is initiated. If the result is >.000 a second purge is done. If a third blank result is >.000 the test is aborted.
BLANK .000 15:03 OBSERVED (Y/N)? Y	After observing the display press the Enter key.	
BLOW UNTIL BEEP ********* TIME LEFT: 13:15	If the subject refuses to submit a breath sample press the R key. The test will be aborted and the printer will print all of the subject data followed by "TEST REFUSED."	Instruct the subject to take a deep breath and blow into the mouthpiece as steadily and as long as possible. Flow and volume will be indicated by the * characters.
EVALUATING SAMPLE RESULT 0.044 15:04	Information only. No data entry required.	The Intox EC/IR evaluates the sample then prints the test results as shown below: Confirmaion Test Intox EC/IR S/N: 01780 Location: TEST SITE A49 Date: Mon 12 Jun 95 Time: 14:45 Test #: 950612092 Employee ID: 453 6125 23

			VALUE (g/2101)	TIME
		Blank	0.000	15:02
		Result	0.044	15:04

DISPLAY	KEYBOARD ENTRY	EXPLANATION
PRINT ANOTHER COPY (Y/N)? N	Press Y and the Enter key for another copy or press the Enter key to continue.	
RESULT 0.044 15:04 OBSERVED (Y/N)? Y	After observing the display press the Enter key.	
ATTACH PRINTOUT TO FORM, PRESS ENTER	Attach the printout to the DOT alcohol test form then press Enter to continue.	

DISPLAY	KEYBOARD ENTRY	EXPLANATION
COMPLETE FORM STEP 3 THEN PRESS ENTER	Complete Step 3 on the DOT test form and then press the Enter key to continue.	
COMPLETE FORM STEP 4 THEN PRESS ENTER	Complete Step 4 on the DOT test form and then press the Enter key to continue.	
PURGING	Information only. No data entry required.	Instrument is purging the breath path with ambient air.

IF THE RESULT OF THE CONFIRMATION TEST IS GREATER THAN THE "POSITIVE VALUE" SET UNDER F10-TANK SETUP, THEN THE DISPLAY WILL ASK THE OPERATOR IF THEY WISH TO RUN AN ACCURACY CHECK. IF THE OPERATOR RESPONDS YES, THEN AN AUTOMATIC ACCURACY CHECK WILL BE INITIATED. THE STEPS DESCRIBING AN AUTOMATIC ACCURACY CHECK CAN BE FOUND IN THE FOLLOWING SECTION UNDER F3-ACCURACY CHECK. IF THE RESULT OF THE CONFIRMATION TEST IS LESS THAN THE "POSITIVE VALUE" OR THE OPERATOR ANSWERS NO TO THE PROMPT FOR AN ACCURACY CHECK THE INSTRUMENT WILL RETURN TO THE NORMAL SCROLLING MODE.

Normal scrolling Mode	Information only. No data entry required.	The instrument returns to the Normal Scrolling Mode.

SUBJECT TESTS—ABORTS, REFUSALS AND ERRORS

Aborting a Test

If you press the Esc key (Shift-Esc key for DOT protocol versions or modes) at any point in this procedure, the instrument aborts the test and indicates that the test has been aborted by the operator on the display and the printout.

Time-outs and Refusals

The instrument waits for a predetermined period after the blow message; "PLEASE BLOW," "BLOW UNTIL IT BEEPS" or "BLOW UNTIL BEEP" appears. If the subject has not provided a breath sample within that period, an appropriate message is displayed and the printer prints a report showing that the test has not been completed. The test number increments by one and the display returns to scrolling mode. You may return to the Subject Test by pressing the Return key and starting again. If you determine that the subject has refused to provide a sample while the blow message is on the screen, press the "R" key and "TEST REFUSED" will be printed in the test result printout.

Insufficient Breath Sample

If the subject does not provide a sufficient amount of breath, the instrument displays "INSUFFICIENT SAMPLE" and goes through another purging or testing cycle. After this cycle, the blow message appears again. At this point you may try another test after instructing the subject to take a deep breath and exhale completely.

If the subject cannot provide enough breath for a valid sample after the number of attempts allowed in the given protocol, the instrument aborts the process. "INSUFFICIENT SAMPLE" or "TEST REFUSED" shows on the display and the printer prints a report similar to the Subject Test report. The report does not show test results, but shows "INSUFFICIENT SAMPLE" or "TEST REFUSED" at the bottom.

Recovery from Internal Printer Errors

If the printer is off line or the door latch has been left open at the end of the test, the display shows "CHECK PRINTER DOOR." Correct the problem by closing the door latch. If the printer is out of paper, "CHECK PRINTER PAPER" is displayed. Install a new roll of paper to correct this. In either case, after correcting the problem, set the printer on line by pressing the LINE/LOCAL push-button. The instrument will print the test results as soon as the problem is corrected and the printer is on line again.

7

BLOOD AND URINE ANALYSIS

§7.0   Blood Analysis

Page 521. Add at end of section:

Aside from scientific error, blood alcohol results may be inadmissible for legal reasons. Counsel should be familiar with the 2004 U.S. Supreme Court case of *Crawford v. Washington,* 124 S. Ct. 1354 (2004), as discussed in detail in §11.3.3. Further, in order to avoid the necessity of having laboratory employees spend their time in court, many hospitals now include language on their laboratory reports that the reports are not to be used for legal purposes. Although the Massachusetts case of *Commonwealth v. Johnson,* 794 N.E.2d 1214 (Mass. App. Ct. 2003), involved the testing of urine rather than blood, it offers helpful analysis when hospital reports include such warnings.

In *Johnson,* the defendant was found in a confused and disoriented state after he ran his vehicle off the roadway. His answers to questions were unintelligible and he seemed to answer questions that were not asked. The trooper found cocaine, Valium, and OxyContin in the vehicle. The defendant was taken to the local hospital for treatment, where medical personnel administered a rapid urine-screening test. The test results, while negative for alcohol, showed positive readings for cocaine, phencyclidine, and benzodiazepine. The record of the test stated prominently: "THIS TEST IS A RAPID SCREENING SYSTEM FOR DRUGS OF ABUSE IN URINE. A SECOND METHOD MUST BE USED TO OBTAIN A CONFIRMED ANALYTICAL RESULT." *Johnson* at 1216. The trial court admitted the record of the urine test over the defendant's objection, relying in part upon the statutory hearsay exception. The appellate court, however, recognized that "the statute relied on a 'pragmatic test of reliability' that permits the introduction of records . . . provided the information in the record is of a nature that is relied upon by medical professionals in administering health care." *Id.* at 1217. The court noted that the statute while creating an exception to the hearsay rule, does not permit the admission of hospital records that are facially unreliable.

The appellate court further found that the disclaimer noted on the laboratory report called the reliability of the test into sufficient question as to create doubt as to whether the record alone can stand competent as proof of the medical facts recited therein. Therefore, the results were inadmissible because the Commonwealth did not provide any testimony to indicate whether the drugs were in the defendant's system at the time of driving, or if the test merely identified residual markers of the drugs that were present in the defendant's system at some indeterminate time in the past. The jury would be left to speculate as to the record's significance upon the important questions of whether, and when, the defendant had ingested a controlled substance, and whether such a controlled substance was in the defendant's system in concentrations sufficient to affect his ability to operate a motor vehicle.

Interestingly, in this same case, the appellate court noted that a second error occurred when the trial judge allowed the prosecution to admit into evidence "The Pill Book," a publication sold at a CVS Pharmacy, purporting to describe the effects of OxyContin and Diazepam. The appellate court found The Pill Book was not an appropriate subject for judicial notice, being neither a matter of common knowledge nor one falling into any of the other categories for which judicial notice is appropriate. See *Johnson* at 1219, citing *Commonwealth v. Hartman*, 534 N.E.2d 1170 (Mass. 1989). Moreover, the book was never established as reliable or authoritative, contained nothing but inadmissible hearsay, and did not satisfy any of the exceptions to the hearsay rule. Furthermore, the court noted that even if the publication had qualified as a learned treatise, it would not be admissible as an exhibit.

§7.0.1 General Sources of Error

Page 540. Add at end of subsection:

If a hospital conducts the blood analysis for alcohol, the enzymatic method of blood analysis may be employed. In such a case, counsel should be aware of a further possible source of error leading to falsely high BAC results: *ringer lactate*.

Dr. Robert Forrest of Sheffield University in England describes the phenomenon:

> Many hospitals use an enzymatic method to measure alcohol in blood... The basis of the test is that the alcohol in the sample reacts with the enzyme alcohol dehydrogenase, present in the reagents used in the test, and is oxidised to acetaldehyde. In the process a linked reaction takes place and nicotinamide adenine nucleotide (NAD) is converted to NADH. The instrument actually measures the amount of alcohol present by following the increase in NADH which is proportional to the amount of alcohol present.
>
> If the enzyme lactate dehydrogenase is present in the sample and if high concentrations of lactate are present, then the lactate dehydrogenase will convert some of the lactate to pyruvate with the concomitant conversion of NAD to NADH. So if you have lactate and a high activity of lactate dehydrogenase present, then you will get a falsely elevated alcohol concentration.
>
> You need both. If the enzymatic alcohol assay involves a stage where a protein precipitant such as perchloric acid is added to the blood, which is then centrifuged, the clear supernatant fluid, which goes into the instruments does not contain any lactate dehydrogenase. Assays that do not include this step are vulnerable to false positive results.
>
> High lactate dehydrogenase activities are found in some blood samples when the red blood cells have broken down or in patients with diseases as diverse as liver failure or pernicious anaemia.
>
> So if you have ringer lactate infusion, plus an assay method for alcohol involving alcohol dehydrogenase which does not include a protein precipitation step, then you may well get a falsely elevated alcohol concentration in the sample. If it is measured by a gas chromatograph assay, however, there is no problem with ringer lactate.

To illustrate, last week I got a postmortem blood sample from another hospital. There was lots of lactate and lactate dehydrogenase in it. The other hospital got a result of 0.23 percent. I got a result of 0.00 percent with a gas chromatograph method.

§7.0.3   Fermentation in the Vial

Page 545. Add after first pararaph:

Ethyl alcohol is generated by fermentation of carbohydrates and proteins in the blood sample. This occurs through the actions of various microorganisms. The simplest and one of the most common processes is the breakdown of enzymes by one of various species of the yeast *Candida*, such as *Candida albicans* (see below).

Page 546. Insert after fourth sentence of third full paragraph.

Dr. Kaye's article concludes that less than 1 percent sodium fluoride (100 mg/10 ml blood) "can allow microorganisms to grow and can also inhibit glycolysis and thus provide glucose for the unkilled microorganisms to ferment into alcohol." Dr. Dubowsky, however, reflects common law enforcement practice in recommending that 15 mg/10 ml blood is sufficient. For a study concluding that 1 percent of sodium fluoride was the only preservative and strength found effective in preventing fermentation, see Plueckhahn and Ballard, Factors Influencing the Significance of Alcohol Concentrations in Autopsy Blood Samples, The Medical Journal of Australia (June 1, 1968). That study also concluded that, despite the presence of preservative, "significant increases in the concentration of ethyl alcohol may occur when blood samples taken at autopsy are left at room temperature for two days." For yet another study concluding that "sodium fluoride at a concentration of not less than 1 percent was needed to maintain sterility of stored blood," see Blackmore, The Bacterial Production of Ethyl Alcohol, 8 Forensic Science Society Journal (1968).

Page 547. Add after carryover (indented) paragraph:

As has been previously indicated, the production of alcohol in blood caused by, among other agencies, yeasts such as *Candida albicans*, is a constant problem. As researchers have observed:

> It has been shown that several microorganisms occasionally found in blood specimens are capable of producing ethyl alcohol. Although (one study) found that sodium fluoride effectively inhibited alcohol production from a variety of microorganisms, one — *Candida albicans* — appeared to be unaffected by the addition of sodium fluoride. *C. albicans* is commonly found in man, usually in the oral cavity and digestive tract, and less commonly in the vaginal tract of women. Though generally harmless, it can manifest itself as a pathogen. The organism has been called the most common and most serious pathogen of man. The legal ramifications of this are obvious. If an organism common to man is capable of producing ethyl alcohol in stored blood, the question arises: Are the results of alcohol analysis reflective of an individual's level of intoxication or of post-testing fermentation?" [Chang and Kollman, The Effect of Temperature on the Formation of Ethanol by *Candida Albicans* in 34(1) Blood, Journal of Forensic Sciences 105 (1989).]

The researchers' conclusion that sodium fluoride was ineffective in preventing ethyl alcohol production by *Candida albicans* has been confirmed by other studies. See, e.g., Blume and Lakatua, The Effect of Microbial Contamination of the Blood Sample on the Determination of Ethanol Levels in Serum, 60 American Journal of Clinical Pathology 700 (1973).

Page 547. Add after first sentence of last full paragraph:

Most blood specimen collection instructions emphasize that immediately following the blood collection, proper mixing of the preservative and anticoagulant must be assured by slowly and completely inverting the blood test tube at least five times. These tubes must not be shaken vigorously because doing so would break the cellular walls and create a further issue regarding the accuracy of the ultimate result.

Page 547. Start new paragraph after original first sentence of last full paragraph.

Page 547. In last full paragraph, replace citation for State v. Schwalk *with:*

430 N.W.2d 317 (N.D. 1988)

§7.0.4   Whole Blood Versus Serum/Plasma

Page 549. Add after second full paragraph:

Similarly, in *People v. Thoman,* 770 N.E.2d 228 (Ill. App. Ct. 2002), the Illinois Appellate Court recognized that blood serum is different from whole blood. In serum blood, the lack of red and white blood cells and other particulate matter serves to increase the relative percentage of water within the serum. Because alcohol has an affinity for water, serum blood results in higher alcohol concentration levels than whole blood. Thus, while the results of a blood serum analysis are admissible at trial, the state must still prove beyond a reasonable doubt that the defendant's whole blood alcohol concentration was above the legal limit. The appellate court went on to recognize that a blood serum alcohol concentration test result can predictably be anywhere from 12 to 20 percent higher than a whole blood alcohol concentration test result. See *Thoman* at 230, citing *People v. Green,* 689 N.E.2d 385 (Ill. App. Ct. 1997). In summary, the court found that allowing a jury to employ a presumptive level on the basis of a defendant's unconverted blood serum alcohol concentration is error.

Conversely, in *People v. Luth,* 780 N.E.2d 740 (Ill. App. Ct. 2002), the jury was confronted with conflicting evidence as to the conversion of the serum alcohol results to whole blood equivalents. The court found the jury was entitled to weigh the testimony of the conflicting experts and could rely on the state expert's opinion of the difference between 10 and 20 percent rather than the defense expert's opinion that the difference can cover a range from 3 to 60 percent. The court held that the jury had the responsibility to resolve conflicts in the evidence and to draw reasonable inferences therefrom.

§7.0.6   Chain of Custody

Page 553. Add the following new checklist before Checklist 11:

Checklist 10.1 Blood Specimen Collection Checklist

The officer or phlebotomist drawing the blood from a suspect should follow the steps noted below in order to ensure the specimen will be accurately analyzed and the chain of custody will be intact. Any significant deviation from these steps may raise questions about the accuracy of the sample analysis.

☐ **Step One**
  Remove all components from the blood alcohol kit box.
☐ **Step Two**
  Assemble needle to holder.
☐ **Step Three**
  Apply tourniquet and prepare venipuncture site using only a non-alcoholic antiseptic.
  Note: Some antiseptics contain alcohol as a solvent.
☐ **Step Four**
  Following normal hospital/clinic procedure, withdraw blood specimen from subject. The arm should be in a downward or lowered position, while the tube should be in a slanted position with the stopper in the highest position.
☐ **Step Five**
  As the tube begins to fill, the tourniquet should be removed. The contents of the tube should not contact the stopper. Special attention should be given to the arm position in order to prevent possible backflow from the tube and the possibility of adverse reaction to the subject.
☐ **Step Six**
  When the tube fill is complete, blood should cease to flow. The tube should be removed from the holder and any additional tubes should be placed into the holder following the same procedure.
☐ **Step Seven**
  When sampling is completed, the needle/holder assembly should be removed in its entirety. A dry, sterile compress

should be applied to he venipuncture site. The arm should be elevated.

☐ **Step Eight**

To assure proper mixing of the chemicals in the tube with the blood, each tube should be slowly and completely inverted at least five times immediately after blood collection. *The tube should not be shaken vigorously.*

☐ **Step Nine**

The subject's name or other identifying information should be placed on the tube.

☐ **Step Ten**

Any paperwork associated with the blood kit must be filled out and signed by the person withdrawing the blood.

☐ **Step Eleven**

The blood tubes should be properly packaged and placed in the blood kit. A liquid-absorbing packet should be included with the test tubes to determine if any leakage occurs during transportation.

☐ **Step Twelve**

A biohazard label should be affixed to the exterior of the blood kit. The kit is now ready for transportation to the laboratory for analysis.

Note: Normally, a complete toxicology screen requires two tubes of blood (20 ml) and 20 ml of urine.

Page 552. Add the following new section:

§7.0.7   Coagulation

As mentioned in §7.0.1 ("General Sources of Error"), a relatively common problem with law enforcement analysis of blood samples occurs when the sample in the vial *clots*. This process, also referred to as *coagulation*, involves solidification of the blood cells of the sample prior to analysis. As a result, the liquid portion separates from the blood cells, or *hematocrit* (see §6.3.2). This will usually be seen in the vial as a red clump at the bottom (cells) with a yellow liquid on top of it. Alcohol, of course, will be suspended only in the liquid portion and thus will be concentrated in the plasma. And it is this liquid portion that is tested, commonly with gas chromatography. Thus, the portion of the sample tested will have a considerably higher blood-alcohol concentration than it would have had if the entire sample of whole blood had been tested.

The standard procedure for preventing coagulation involves both (1) *refrigeration* and (2) inclusion of an *anticoagulant* in the sample; applicable laws or administrative regulations (see §11.6.8) usually require this. This is commonly accomplished in the law enforcement arena by using blood withdrawal kits that contain a preservative, such as sodium fluoride (see §7.0.3 for a discussion of *fermentation*), and an anticoagulant, presumably potassium oxalate, already in the transparent glass vial. This usually appears as a white or pink powder lying in the bottom of the vial. Absent a sufficient amount of preservative of the proper quality, together with adequate refrigeration, clotting is likely to occur. Obviously, counsel should seek through discovery the records establishing law enforcement compliance with these requirements; reanalysis of the blood sample is also an option.

It is common to encounter the officer or technician who produces the proper records showing that the anticoagulant was present in the proper amounts in the vial. The officer or technician may also testify that he saw the powder very clearly in the bottom of the vial. However, this is not sufficient. Counsel should try to establish that the blood was added to the vial, which was then sealed and placed in storage. In other words, commit the witness to a position so that he cannot later say that he *shook* the vial after the blood was added. Quite simply, *if the vial is not adequately shaken, the anticoagulant will not mix with the blood*—and the anticoagulant will be ineffective, with clotting subsequently taking place and a higher BAC the inevitable consequence.

For a discussion of a cross-examination technique for establishing that no preservative or anticoagulant was in the vial, see §13.3.12 ("The Virgin Vial").

§7.1 Urinalysis

Page 556. In second sentence of second full paragraph, replace State v. Donaldson citation with:

452 N.W.2d 531

Page 558. Add at end of second full paragraph:

When the urinalysis is tested at a hospital laboratory for purposes of treatment rather than for legal purposes, counsel should be alert to hospital disclaimers. An example of such a disclaimer is, "THIS TEST IS A RAPID SCREENING SYSTEM FOR DRUGS OF ABUSE IN URINE. A SECOND METHOD MUST BE USED TO OBTAIN A CONFIRMED ANALYTICAL RESULT," which was discussed in *Commonwealth v. Johnson*, 794 N.E.2d 1214, 1216 (Mass. App. Ct. 2003). In *Johnson*, the appellate court found that this disclaimer noted on the laboratory report called the reliability of the test into sufficient question as to create doubt as to whether the record alone could stand competent as proof of the medical facts recited therein. The results of the urinalysis were ultimately determined to be inadmissible because the prosecution did not provide any testimony to indicate whether the drugs were in the defendant's system at the time of driving, or if the test merely identified residual markers of drugs that were present in the defendant's system at some indeterminate time in the past. The court concluded it was not appropriate to allow a jury to speculate as to the record's significance upon the important questions of whether and when the defendant had ingested a controlled substance, and whether such a controlled substance was in the defendant's system in concentrations sufficient to affect his ability to operate a motor vehicle.

Page 565. Add the following new subsection after second full paragraph:

§7.1.4 Inability to Urinate (Paruresis)

The International Paruresis Association (*http://www. paruresis. org*) (800-247-3864), reports that about 7 percent of the public, or

17 million people, may suffer from this social anxiety disorder. This condition is often referred to as Pee-Shy bladder, bashful bladder, etc.

Bavanisha Vythilingum, Dan J. Stein, and Steven Soifer have written an article published in 16 Depression and Anxiety, 84–87 (May 2002), which characterizes paruresis as the fear of not being able to urinate in public bathrooms and further classifies it as a subtype of social anxiety disorder. These scientists report paruresis significantly affects sufferers' lives, with approximately one-third limiting or avoiding parties, sports events, or dating, and just over half of the research sample limiting the job they choose to do. Thepublication concludes that paruresis can be a chronic and disabling condition and is indicated to be associated with other performance anxieties.

Therefore, any DUI suspects who may be unable to urinate in the presence of an officer may, in fact, be suffering from this disorder. Confirmation of the disorder by an acceptable expert may present a defense to an allegation of refusing to provide a urine sample for analysis.

III

PRE-TRIAL

8

ANALYSIS AND ARRAIGNMENT

§8.3   The Arraignment

§8.3.2   Double Jeopardy

Page 599. In last full paragraph, replace State v. Eckert citation with:

186 Neb. 134, 181 N.W.2d 264 (1970)

Page 601. Replace third full paragraph with:

Three years later, the United States Supreme Court reconsidered its decision and overruled *Grady* in *United States v. Dixon*, 509 U.S. 688 (1993), and reaffirmed the "same elements" tests as first announced in *Blockburger v. United States*, 284 U.S. 299 (1932). As such, both state and federal cases should be carefully examined before being cited as precedent to determine if the particular case was decided upon reliance of *Grady v. Corbin*, and its "same conduct" test, which is no longer good law.

Pages 601–602. Delete carryover paragraph.

Page 603. Add after first paragraph:

An interesting situation arises in circumstances in which a defendant has been observed driving across state lines in the context of whether a DUI prosecution in one state bars a DUI prosecution in the neighboring state. At least one appellate court has held that it does not. In *Commonwealth v. Stephenson*, 82

S.W.3d 876 (Ky. 2003), a high-speed police pursuit of the defendant began in Kentucky and thereafter proceeded into Indiana, where the defendant was ultimately stopped. Subsequently, the defendant was charged with DUI in both states. After pleading guilty in Indiana, the defendant moved to have the Kentucky prosecution dismissed on double jeopardy grounds. The Kentucky Supreme Court rejected the defendant's double jeopardy argument, holding that the defendant's Indiana conviction for DUI was not a double jeopardy bar to defendant's prosecution for DUI in Kentucky because the Commonwealth did not seek to punish the defendant for the same conduct for which Indiana punished him, in that the Commonwealth only sought to prosecute defendant for his criminal conduct within Kentucky, while Indiana's conviction arose out of conduct in Indiana.

10

DISCOVERY

§10.0 Discovery of DUI Evidence

§10.0.1 Objects of Discovery

Page 644. Add after first full (indented) paragraph:

If the officer has been trained with a version of NHTSA's DWI Detection and Standardized Field Sobriety Testing: Student Manual (see §4.3), the officer who destroyed his notes (or kept none) can be confronted with the following excerpts:

> ... you need a system and tools for recording field notes at scenes of DWI investigations." (Page IV-8)

> NOTE: field notes may be subpoenaed as evidence in court. It is important that any "shorthand" system you use be describable, usable, complete and consistent. (Page IV-9)

Taken together, the instructions state that notes should be taken and that they should be kept for possible defense use at trial. And a conclusion can certainly be drawn that destruction of field notes, in violation of this information concerning their later legitimate use (with the clear inference that they *should* be saved), reflects an intent to *avoid* their use at trial.

Page 644. Add after third sentence of second full paragraph:

Further, the practitioner should request the standard operating procedures of the testing laboratory relating to the substance that was tested, the calibration records for the equipment used, and the proficiency testing records of the analyst as to both the equipment and the written procedures used. See *Cole v. State,* 835 A.2d 600 (Md. 2003) (holding that a defendant is entitled to discovery of the lab's standard operating procedures, the calibration records of the equipment used to test samples, and the analyst's written procedure and equipment proficiency testing records).

Page 644. Start new paragraph after original third sentence of second full paragraph.

§10.0.2 Discovery of Computer Program in Breath Machine

Page 661. Insert at top of page:

Most of the breath machines used by law enforcement today have the capacity to store various kinds of information relevant to its use. Exactly what kinds of information are contained within the internal computer's memory is controlled by its software, which is usually customized by the manufacturer to the requirements of the agency purchasing the product. Thus, for example, the machine may store data concerning past tests, error messages, diagnostic tests, calibration checks, etc. Note: Counsel may encounter terminology such as "ADAMS" or "COBRA" in dealing with the Intoxilyzer. These are simply the names of the software used to store data such as subject tests, calibrations, quality assurance procedures, etc., and are easily downloaded and readable; COBRA is the more recent version of ADAMS.

One of many possible uses for a machine's database is to demonstrate false "refusals." The stored information can determine if a particular officer has an unusually high percentage of arrestees who "refuse"—that is, it can provide evidence that a particular officer is quick to conclude that an arrestee is not trying hard enough to provide a sample.

The following comments are presented with the kind consent of their author, Minnesota forensic toxicologist Mary Catherine McMurray (Forensic Associates, Inc.: 651-784-7721).

Computerized data capabilities

Most of the evidential breath-alcohol analyzers available today have the capability of collecting and storing data for all tests and operations performed on the test device. This data is retrievable via modem or a direct computer connection and can subsequently be stored in a database. The complete database would include:

- all **subject tests** (a test, regardless of the purpose for the test, conducted in a normal testing mode that is initiated with the start test button),
- all **calibration checks** (tests conducted in an ACA mode),
- all **diagnostics, systems,** or **circuitry tests** (at initial start-up and any diagnostic or system checks that are not a programmed part of a subject test) and
- **error messages** (instrumental and operational error messages, regardless of testing mode in which they occurred).

There may be additional database files, but these are the most basic file types that would be used for diagnostic and troubleshooting purposes. The state programs generally provide the data in a spreadsheet for each type of file (e.g. all subject tests) with each test (each subject record) comprised of data fields representing the different steps of the test and data collection process. The air blanks are generally not stored but could be. The agency that purchases the data collection program will usually specify what the various files are called and how they are formatted.

The database can be obtained on computer disc, as opposed to a printout/hard copy. When using the data directly on a computer all of the records can be presented or viewed in the same spreadsheet. This is a preferred means of receiving and working with the databases, because all tests and operations can then be viewed sequentially as they occur. Printout can be made from the computer if needed.

The computer-collected database is potentially the best source of quality assurance/quality control data available in an evidential testing program. Every test —good, bad or ugly— should be there. A complete database for a specific breath analyzer should be able to support, if not establish, the degree of accuracy of that specific test device around the time in question. By cross-referencing the records in the various data files and message logs an unbiased picture can be painted allowing the overall reliability of the testing device to be evaluated.

Control charts can be created from the database to visually demonstrate the accuracy and reliability -- or lack thereof. This all assumes that the database is in fact completely intact and that no tests are eliminated just because the overseeing agency doesn't like the data.

The database can be used for the early detection of problems, electronic or otherwise, thus assuring a higher level of confidence in the reportable test data. A well-run, scientific program will monitor and use this data as an integral part of the quality assurance and quality control program. Careful monitoring of the database for any given test device can detect many problems before they become significant enough in nature to call the integrity of the testing into question.

As an example of how the data is useful for troubleshooting consider an experience with the Intoxilyzer 5000EN. This Intoxilyzer has a "stand-by" mode that puts the unit into a low-energy use state. When a test is going to be conducted, the Intoxilyzer and the simulator have to come out of the stand-by mode and warm up to an operating temperature. The computer database showed that the first calibration check after an extended stand-by (> 1 hour) would consistently read low, usually within tolerance but on the low side. Subsequent calibration checks would demonstrate good precision and accuracy. The problem was eventually identified as being related to the simulator reaching optimum operating temperature slower than the Intoxilyzer.

As an example of how a computer database is useful as exculpatory evidence, consider the case where the test card of the accused shows absolutely no problems. The test result was high (greater than 0.20 g/210L) yet the videotape of the arrest showed a person who did not appear to be intoxicated. The maintenance history of the testing device provided by the state was rather unremarkable -- absolutely no problems being detected or reported during the months before and after the specific test in question. The client insisted he did not drink enough to achieve the test results reported. The handwritten logbook maintained at the test site showed no operational errors or instrumental malfunctions either before or after the client's test.

The complete computer database was eventually obtained and revealed that over the months preceding the test in question the occurrence of RFI flags was becoming more frequent. During the 3.5 hours immediately prior to the test in question, the test device had flagged radio frequency interference (RFI) 6 times while trying to conduct a subject test. RFI continued to be flagged intermittently throughout the evening in question on subject tests and other operational tests. The RFI flags continued to occur daily for the next 3 months then suddenly disappeared entirely after the state conducted a "routine maintenance" of the device.

RFI, if picked up in the electronics of a device but undetected as such by the RFI detector, can mimic an alcohol reading. Testing on various Intoxilyzers has shown reported alcohol results of 0.080 g/210L and higher due to nothing more than a cellular phone creating RFI but not setting off the flag. The failure of a given analyzer to flag RFI, and subsequently reporting a false alcohol concentration, can and does occur. The sensitivity of the RFI detector on most breath alcohol analyzers is adjustable. The RFI detection system needs periodic inspection and testing to assure it is functioning reliably. Any time new electrical equipment is introduced into the testing environment the system should be re-evaluated. A poorly adjusted or malfunctioning RFI detector can lead to false reporting.

It may have been a coincidence that the RFI flags disappeared entirely after a state inspection. The state inspection form showed no problems detected or reported – in other words, a routine maintenance. There were no notations of making any adjustments to any components of the device. The RFI flags just disappeared. Coincidence or not, the state had no explanation on what caused the flags or what made them disappear. The "expert" from the state who testified about the accuracy and reliability was not the person who conducted the inspection and was unable to say what exactly was done to the device. The technician who conducted the inspection was not present.

The computer data, if it records every operation, is quite useful. But be forewarned that the customized software that each state insists upon can determine what tests are stored in the database. In Arizona, the state inspections consistently showed that the Intoxilyzers never failed or produced less than desirable results. It was, apparently, the perfect machine. Then the defense learned that the state-customized software allowed the inspectors to accept, repeat or reject the analysis while they were doing the inspections.

If the inspector ran a series of calibration checks and all the numbers were numbers the inspector liked, the data would be accepted and would show up in the database. If the data was not good, in the inspector's opinion, they could reject the data and there would be no indication that any testing had been conducted. If the inspector thought they could get better numbers, they could repeat the testing and write over the data, then decide on accepting or rejecting the "new" data. A guaranteed method for assuring that the data available always looks good for the state. It made it easier for the prosecutors and law enforcement to get convictions.

Minnesota Intoxilyzers have an option that allows certain pre-programmed tests to be conducted that do not go into the database. For example, a test that is identical to a state required evidential test could be conducted using one of the function keys. The test data required, the sequencing of events and the test card printout would be identical to an evidential test, but the data would not show up in the database. Several of the programmed function key tests are similarly hidden from the database. Why it was felt important to keep some of the tests out of the database makes no sense from the troubleshooting perspective. The complete operational history gives a much better picture than an edited history.

Wisconsin, when it had Intoxilyzers, would use special citation numbers for certain types of tests, e.g.: juveniles, practice or demo tests, service checks, etc. They would then filter out and not report any or all of these other type tests. The missing tests was not something that could be easily proven, and the state position was that these tests were not evidential tests therefore they were not relevant. The refusal of the state witnesses to admit that things can and did go wrong on some of these tests was impossible to prove false until the state had to turn over a copy of all the tests for all the machines for a two year time period as the result of a Freedom of Information request. Some of the Intoxilyzers had enough exculpatory evidence that showed up in the complete download that numerous juries threw out the chemical tests.

Always get the download data – you never know what it may contain.

§10.3 The Discovery Motion

Page 701. Add at end of section:

The following is a second excellent version of a discovery motion, this one provided by noted DUI practitioner Douglas Cowan of Bellevue, Washington.* A "Notice of Non-Compliance and Motion to Compel" follows the discovery request, preparatory to a possible later demand for sanctions.

---

* Reprinted with permission.

IN THE KING COUNTY DISTRICT COURT
BELLEVUE DIVISION, STATE OF WASHINGTON

STATE OF WASHINGTON,) Plaintiff,)	NO. 123456
)	
vs.)	NOTICE OF APPEARANCE,
DEFENDANT,)	DEMAND FOR JURY TRIAL,
Defendant.)	DEMAND FOR DISCOVERY,
)	BILL OF PARTICULARS,
)	ASSERTION OF AFFIRMATIVE
)	DEFENSE, AND OMNIBUS
)	APPLICATION
)	**CLERK'S ACTION REQUIRED**

TO: Clerk of the Above-Entitled Court; and

TO: Prosecuting Attorney

PLEASE TAKE NOTICE that the below-named attorney hereby enters his appearance on behalf of the Defendant, DEFENDANT.

The defendant hereby enters a plea of Not Guilty and demands a jury trial, and demands discovery.

FURTHER, PLEASE TAKE NOTICE that, pursuant to the authority of CrR 4.7, CrRLJ 4.7, CrRLJ 6.13(c)(2), Local Rules governing dicovery, ER 705, RCW 10.58.010, 10.37.050, et seq., 46.61,502, 504 and 506, 42.17.260, the Fourth, Fifth, Sixth and Fourteenth Amendments to the United States Constitution, and art. 1, §§3, 7, 29, and 30, and the Tenth Amendment to the Washington State Constitution;

THE DEFENDANT HEREBY makes the following demands, motions, and requests for discovery in the matter(s) pending under this Cause Number:

1. Bill of Particulars

A written Bill of Particulars, including a description of all facts upon which the prosecution intends to rely to support the charge pending against the defendant, and a copy of the specific statute or ordinance under which the defendant is charged, along with a copy of any enabling legislation which adopts any other statute or ordinance by reference.

2. Assertion of Affirmative Defense

Defendant asserts that the Defendant consumed a sufficient quantity of alcohol after the time of driving and before the administration of any breath or blood test to cause Defendant's alcohol concentration to be .10 or more within two hours after driving; per *State v. Hornaday*, 105 Wash. 2d 120, 127 (1986).

3. Police Reports

Copies of any and all police or investigative reports (including field notes and/or blue book entries), and statements of all potential witnesses including *all* documentation of results of physical or mental examinations and/or scientific tests, experiments, or comparisons made in connection with the charge pending against the defendant;

4. List of Witnesses

The names and addresses of any and all persons whom the prosecution intends to call as witnesses at the hearing or trial, together with any and all written or recorded statements, and the substance of any oral statements of such witnesses, together with a summary of the expected testimony of any witness the plaintiff intends to call if the substance of the expected testimony is not contained in the materials otherwise provided;

5. Miranda Rights/242 Rights

Copies of any and all forms read to or signed by the defendant containing information regarding his rights under CrRLJ 3.1 and/or RCW 46.61.506 and 46.20.308, including information regarding the claimed basis for the arrest of the defendant and allegedly giving rise to the mandatory provisions of RCW 46.20.308;

6. Statements of Defendant/Demand for CrRLJ 3.5 Hearing

Copies of any written or recorded statements and the substance of any oral statements made by the Defendant. **Take notice that the Defendant hereby demands a hearing pursuant to CrRLJ 3.5** if the prosecution intends to offer any such statements at the time of trial;

7. Exhibits

A list of, copies of, and access to any books, papers, documents, photographs, diagrams, illustrative exhibits, or other tangible objects which the prosecution or any of its witnesses intend to use or make reference to at hearing or trial;

8. Items Seized from Defendant

A list of everything which was seized from or belonging to the defendant, regardless of whether the prosecution intends to introduce said items at hearing or trial;

9. Tape or Video Recordings, Etc.

Copies of or access to any recordings, video-tapes or tape recordings made of the defendant pursuant to the arrest of this case;

10. Prior Convictions

Any record of prior criminal conviction known to the prosecution of the defendant or persons whom the Prosecuting Attorney intends to call as witnesses at the hearing or trial;

11. Exculpatory Evidence

Disclosure of any material or information within the prosecution's knowledge which tends to negate the defendant's guilt as to the offense charged, or to any material element thereof;

12. 911 Tapes, Etc.

A copy of any "911 tapes" or other tape recordings containing information relative to this case and all radio broadcasts and tranmissions occurring between the officer(s) who detained, arrested and/or transported the defendant on the date of the alleged incident herein, and any other agency, officer, communications center or station during the course of the detention, arrest, transportation, testing and booking or charging defendant;

13. Radio Logs

A copy of all radio calls logged at the location of the breath test administered to the defendant ten minutes before through ten minutes after the time of the administration of the breath test concerned therein;

14. Photograph of DataMaster Test Machine

Timely inspection of and an opportunity to photograph the breath test machine used to test a sample of the defendant's breath herein;

15. Laboratory Procedures

A statement describing the "standard laboratory procedures" used to prepare the simulator solution as set forth in WAC 448-13-070, together with a copy of any protocol currently approved by the State Toxicologist for the preparation of simulator solutions as also described therein;

16. **Software**

A list of those versions of software currently approved for use in the BAC Verifier DataMaster as described in WAC 448-13-080;

17. **Quality Assurance Program**

A copy of the results of all tests performed pursuant to the quality assurance program described in WAC 448-13-100, together with copies of all protocols currently approved by the State Toxicologist for performing such tests;

18. **Protocols**

Copies of any protocols currently approved by the State Toxicologist for use in the administration of the breath test program as decribed in WAC 448-13-120.

19. **DataMaster Records**

A copy of the most current record of all breath tests administered on the particular machine along with the machine's evaluation, maintenance and certification records, including repairs, replacement of parts, unscheduled maintenance and reports of any malfunctions or difficulties by any person whomsoever in the history of the instrument's use, along with all documentary information relative to the machine's performance, including all records of complaints or observed problems with the machine which were reported by telephone or radio.

20. **Blood/Breath Correlation Studies**

Copies of all blood/breath correlation studies performed by the Washington State Patrol or other police agency whether formally conducted, or generated as a result of "informal drinking lab sessions";

21. **Simulator Solution Test Results**

A copy of the results of all gas chromatograph printouts of test performed on the simulator solution actually used in the test of the defendant's breath before and after the date of the test administered in this case.

22. **Radio Frequency Interference**

Any information regarding the presence of radios, microwaves, short waves, CBs and any other devices which emit radio frequency at or near the location of the breath testing instrument at or about the time of the administration of the test concerned herein, together with any and all information, test results, studies, memoranda, or other material from the manufacturer or any other source concerning the effects of "radio frequency interference" along with copies of all RFI tests performed on the machine in question known to the prosecution's expert witnesses or the Washington State Patrol crime lab personnel;

23. Interferant Studies

Copies of all experiments, studies, drinking labs, memos or other documentation of "interferants" on the DataMaster test results.

24. Mouth Alcohol Detection

Copies of all experiments, studies, drinking labs, memos or other documentation of the DataMaster's ability to detect mouth alcohol.

25. Preservation of Samples

Preservation of and access to any blood, breath, or urine samples taken from the defendant as a result of investigation of the charges pending herein for the purpose of re-testing the same;

26. Manuals

Copies of or access to the BAC Verifier DataMaster Training Manual, technical manuals, operator manuals, troubleshooting guides and maintenance manuals or bulletins and any other written materials utilized by the Washington State Patrol, State Toxicology Lab, or other law enforcement entity relating to the administration of blood or breath alcohol tests, or any written materials, including routine correspondence received by the Washington State Patrol from the current vendor of the BAC Verifier DataMaster or any supplier therefore;

27. Technician Blue Books

Copies of the "blue books" all DataMaster technicians who have worked on or maintained the machine in question over the past twelve months.

28. Mathematical Formulas

A copy of any mathematical formulas utilized in the BAC Verifier DataMaster in determining: (1) the acetone or other interferant measurement in a breath sample; (2) the alcohol content in a breath sample, or (3) any other mathematical formula or computation utilized in the BAC Verifier DataMaster at any stage of the process involved in the administration of a breath test;

29. Troubleshooting Guide
A copy of all current Troubleshooting Guides utilized by DataMaster technicians or electronic repair persons in the repair or maintenance of DataMaster machines.

30. Components in DataMaster
A list of the types and versions of the components approved for use in the relevant DataMaster machine as well as a list of those components *actually* used in the BAC Verifier DataMaster to test a sample of the defendant's breath herein, including but not limited to: Detector Board type and version; CPU Board type and version; Power Supply Board type and version; Breath Block type and version and Radio Frequency Interference Board type and version along with a copy of the document authorizing or approving the use of the component if it is different than that originally approved by the State Toxicologist.

31. Retrograde Extrapolation
The defendant demands notice if the prosecution intends to offer testimony regarding "retrograde extrapolation" and, if so, the name of the expert witnesss, his/her credentials, education, training and experience relevant thereto and disclosure of any documents, studies, reports or other materials relied on or material to any aspect of his or her testimony;

32. Widmark's Formula
The defendant demands notice if the prosecution intends to offer testimony regarding "Widmark's Formula" and, if so, the name of the expert witness, his/her credentials, education, training and experience and disclosure of any documents, studies, reports or other materials relied on or material to any aspect of his or her testimony;

33. Alcohol Impairment Testimony
The defendant demands notice if the prosecution intends to offer medical or scientific testimony regarding the effects of alcohol on driving ability, physical or mental impairment, etc., and, if so, the name of the expert witness, his/her credentials, education, training and experience and disclosure of any documents, studies, reports or other materials relied on or material to any aspect of his or her testimony;

34. Operator's Qualifications

A copy of the permit issued by the State Toxicologist to the **operator** who administered any test of the defendant's breath or blood, the effective dates of that permit, together with a description of the training taken by that operator which qualified him/her for certification, along with the dates and places that training was completed;

35. Instructor's Qualifications

A copy of the permit issued by the State Toxicologist to the instructor who trained the operator referred to in paragraph 32, above, together with a description of the training taken by that instructor which qualified him/her for certification, along with the dates and places that training was completed;

36. Technician's Qualifications

A copy of the permit issued by the State Toxicologist to any **technician** who performed maintenance, repair, adjustment, regular service, or any other work whatsoever on the DataMaster used in the administration of the breath test to the Defendant herein, together with a description of the training taken by that instructor which qualified him/her for certification, along with the dates and places that training was completed;

37. Solution Changer's Qualifications

A copy of the permit issued by the State Toxicologist to the individual **who most recently changed the simulator solution** prior to the date on which the Defendant herein submitted to a test of his/her breath on the BAC Verifier DataMaster used herein, together with a description of the training taken by that solution changer which qualified him/her for certification, along with the dates and places that training was completed;

38. Radar Demand

If the prosecution intends to offer radar evidence on any issue raised herein at motions or trial, the defense demands, pursuant to CrRLJ 6.13 and other applicable rules, the production of an electronic speed measuring device (SMD) expert at motions or trial, and objects to the introduction at motions or trial of any certificate or affidavit concerning the design, operation or construction of any such speed measuring device.

39. Experts Demanded at Trial

The defendant objects to proof of any material fact at hearing or trial by affidavit or certificate. A certified BAC Verifier DataMaster technician *and* the person(s) who conducted any quality assurance tests as well as the person(s) responsible for preparing, storing and installing the simulator solution concerned herein **IS HEREBY DEMANDED AT HEARING OR TRIAL,** including any and all records pertaining to the preparation, checking and installation of the simulator solution used in this case, including the gas chromatograph charts regarding the solution in accordance with CrRLJ 6.13 and RCW 46.61.506(6), along with a copy of his or her permit.

IF THE PROSECUTOR INTENDS TO OFFER SAID WITNESSES AS "EXPERT WITNESSES", Defendant requests discovery of his or her education and training, both general and specific to the subject of his or her testimony, experience relative to the operation, maintenance, and theory of the instrument used to test the defendant's blood or breath, or simulator solution and a description of the place, date, and subject matter of all training taken by said witnesses have participated or about which he or she may testify, and any documents, studies, reports or other materials relied on or material to any aspect of his or her testimony;

40. Any Other Experts Demanded

The disclosure and presence of any other expert witnesses **IS HEREBY DEMANDED AT HEARING OR TRIAL** along with a copy of his or her qualifications, together with all information requested in paragraph 32, above, regarding the subject matter of said witnesses' testimony.

41. Speedy Trial Demanded

Defendant objects to the date of arraignment, demands trial within the time period required by CrRLJ 3.3, objects to any trial date not so set and moves the court for an order setting a trial date within the speedy trial rule time limits;

42. Objection to Citation/Complaint

Defendant further objects to the sufficiency of the charging document, the failure of the prosecution to properly verify it, objects to the untimely filing of same and moves to dismiss all charges pending herein;

43. **Failure to Comply**
YOU ARE FURTHER NOTIFIED that failure to comply with these requests will result in the defendant moving for appropriate relief at time of hearing or trial.

Dated this 11th day of June, 1999.

_____

DOUGLAS COWAN
Attorney for Defendant
WSBA# 2146

IN THE KING COUNTY DISTRICT COURT
BELLEVUE DIVISION, STATE OF WASHINGTON

STATE OF WASHINGTON,)	
Plaintiff,)	NO. 123456
)	
vs.)	
DEFENDANT,)	NOTICE OF NON-
Defendant.)	COMPLIANCE, SECOND
)	DEMAND FOR DISCOVERY &
)	MOTION TO COMPEL

COMES NOW the Defendant by and through her attorney of record, Douglas L. Cowan, and hereby notifies the prosecuting attorney in the above-referenced case that the materials provided in response to Defendant's original Demand for Discovery are incomplete and non-responsive to the requests made therein and do not comply with the requirements of CrR4.7, CrRLJ 4.7, CrRLJ 6.13(c)(2), applicable Local Court Rules governing discovery, RCW 46.61.506 and the due process provisions of the Washington State Constitutions, to-wit: The prosecution has failed to respond to the discovery demand regarding information on retrograde extrapolation and Widmark's formula, and the name of the specific breath technician to be called in this case, together with the information demanded regarding said witness in Defendant's original Demand for Discovery.

The defendant hereby makes this Second Demand for Discovery and moves the Court for an Order compelling compliance in order to allow adequate time to prepare for the trial of the matters pending herein.

PLEASE TAKE NOTICE that failure to comply with the required information by _____, one week before trial, will result in a motion to suppress the results of the breath test herein.

DATED: _____

_____
DOUGLAS COWAN
Attorney for Defendant
WSBA# 2146

11

SUPPRESSION OF EVIDENCE

§11.0   Probable Cause to Stop, Detain, and Arrest

Page 713.   Add after first full paragraph:

An officer does not need reasonable suspicion to approach an already stopped or parked vehicle. Moreover, law enforcement officers do not violate the Fourth Amendment by merely approaching an individual on the street or in another public place and questioning him, as long as the encounter remains voluntary. For instance, a police officer may approach a car parked in a public place and ask for driver identification and proof of vehicle registration, without any reasonable suspicion of illegal activity. See *Florida v. Royer*, 460 U.S. 491, 497 (1983). However, the person approached is under no obligation to answer the questions posed by the officer and may decline to speak with the officer. See *Florida v. Royer*, 460 U.S. 491, 497 (1983), citing *Terry v. Ohio*, 392 U.S. 1, 31, 32–33 (1968). A Fourth Amendment seizure occurs only when an officer stops an individual and restrains his freedom to end the encounter and walk away. See *Terry v. Ohio*, 392 U.S. 1 (1968).

While the Fourth Amendment prohibits compelling a person to answer questions posed by officers, a state "stop and identify" statute may require such cooperation. The U.S. Supreme Court recently upheld a Nevada "stop and identify" statute. In *Hiibel v. Sixth Judicial District Court of Nevada, Humboldt County, et al.*, No. 03-5554 (2004), the defendant was arrested for refusing to identify himself during a *Terry* stop. The officer was dispatched to investigate a report of a man assaulting a woman alongside the road. When the officer approached the defendant, who fit the dispatch/description, the defendant refused to respond the officer's request for identification. *Hiibel,* No. 03-5554 at *3 (2004). The officer subsequently arrested the defendant for violating a Nevada "stop and identify" statute making it unlawful to " 'willfully resist, delay, or obstruct a public officer in discharging or attempting to discharge any legal duty of his office.' " *Id.*

Justice White, in his concurring opinion in *Terry,* stated that a detainee can be held and questioned for further investigation but is "not obliged to answer, answers may not be compelled, and refusal to answer furnishes no basis for an arrest." Nevertheless, the majority of the Court refused to hold these statements as controlling, noting:

> The passages recognize that the Fourth Amendment does not impose obligations on the citizen but instead provides rights against the government. As a result, the Fourth Amendment itself cannot require a suspect to answer questions. This case concerns a different issue, however. Here, the source of the legal obligation arises from a Nevada state law, not the Fourth Amendment. Further, the statutory obligation does not go beyond answering an officer's request to disclose a name.

Hiibel, No. 03-5554 at *7 (2004). The Court found that a state law which requires a suspect to disclose his or her name during a valid *Terry* stop is consistent with Fourth Amendment prohibitions against unreasonable search and seizure. *Hiibel,* No. 03-5554 at *7 (2004). However, an officer's request for identification must be reasonably related to the circumstances justifying the stop. *Id.* at *8 (2004).

Justice Breyer, in his dissenting opinion, noted that a lengthy history of concurring Supreme Court opinions contained "strong dicta that the legal community typically takes as a statement of the law" that a person subjected to a *Terry* stop is not obligated to answer questions and such refusal does not furnish a basis for arrest. *Id.* at *14 (2004).

Justice Stevens, in a separate dissenting opinion, further noted that a law criminalizing the refusal to identify oneself upon request violates the Fifth Amendment right against self-incrimination. *Id.* at *10 (2004). The majority rejected this argument, questioning whether disclosure of identity is testimonial and ultimately holding that "petitioner's challenge must fail because in this case disclosure of his name presented no reasonable danger of incrimination." *Id.* at *9 (2004). Justice Stevens not only found disclosure of identity to be testimonial, but also noted that such information clearly constitutes an incriminating communication and, as such, falls within Fifth Amendment protections.

> The Court reasons that we should not assume that the disclosure of petitioner's name would be used to incriminate him or that it would furnish a link in a chain of evidence needed to prosecute him. *Ante,* at 12–13. But why else would an officer ask for it? And why else would the Nevada Legislature require its disclosure only when circumstances "reasonably indicate that the person has committed, is committing or is about to commit a crime"? ... I think that, on the contrary, the Nevada Legislature intended to provide its police officers with a useful law enforcement tool, and that the very existence of the statute demonstrates the value of the information it demands.

Hiibel, No. 03-5554 at *12 (2004).

In *State v. Bond,* 74 P.3d 1132 (Or. App. 2003), the defendant was sitting in his vehicle, which was parked on the side of the road. The court held that a Fourth Amendment seizure did not occur when the officer repeatedly knocked on the defendant's window to inquire as to his well-being. Similarly, in *State v. Wilhoit,* 962 S.W.2d 482 (Tenn. Crim. App. 1997), the court found that an officer may approach a vehicle parked in a public place without reasonable suspicion of illegal activity. In such a circumstance, the court found, merely approaching a vehicle would not communicate to a reasonable person that he or she was not free to leave.

Page 713. Replace first sentence of second full paragraph with:

Reasonable suspicion to stop the driver of a motor vehicle may be an issue in any DUI case.

Page 714. Add at end of first paragraph:

Likewise, an officer may not seize or search an individual based solely on the suspect's presence in a high-crime area late at night.

See *People v. Medina*, 1 Cal. Rptr. 3d 546 (Cal. Dist. Ct. App. 2003); *Brown v. Texas*, 443 U.S. 47 (1979).

The practitioner should carefully read the statute of the charge constituting the grounds for the stop. For instance, motorists are often stopped for weaving or swerving; however, such activity may not give rise to sufficient reasonable suspicion required for a stop. In *State v. Binette*, 33 S.W.3d 215 (Tenn. 2000), the court held that while the defendant did drift and move laterally within his lane, the movement was not pronounced and did not give rise to reasonable suspicion. See also *United States v. Gregory*, 79 F.3d 973 (10th Cir. 1996); *Rowe v. State*, 769 A.2d 879 (Md. 2001); *United States v. Colin*, 314 F.3d 439 (9th Cir. 2002). The *Binette* court emphasized:

> Our legislature has stated that "[w]henever any roadway has been divided into two (2) or more clearly marked lanes for traffic, ... [a] vehicle shall be driven *as nearly as practicable* entirely within a single lane ... " Tenn. Code Ann. §55-8-123(1)(1998) (emphasis added). "[I]f failure to follow a perfect vector down the highway ... [were] sufficient reason [] to suspect a person of driving while impaired, a substantial portion of the public would be subject each day to an invasion of their privacy." *United States v. Lyons*, 7 F.3d 973, 976 (10th Cir. 1993).

Binette at 219.

Similarly, officers may not have reasonable suspicion to stop motorists for failure to use a turn signal. Many state statutes regarding the use of a turn signal require its use only in the event that other traffic may be affected by the motorist's turn or lane change. See, e.g., Mont. Code Ann. §61-8-336; Tenn. Code Ann. §55-8-143. In *Grindeland v. State*, 32 P.3d 767 (Mont. 2001), the court held that the defendant's failure to use his turn signal did not constitute reasonable suspicion for the stop. While the officer testified that other vehicles were in the vicinity when the defendant made his turn, he could not recall their exact location, and therefore, the court found, could not have reasonably determined if the other vehicles might have been affected by the defendant's turn. The practitioner should be careful to compare the municipal ordinance in incorporated areas to ensure the statutory language is not more restrictive. See, e.g., *State v. Linsey,* No. M2002-01299-CCA-R3-CD (Tenn. Crim. App., Apr. 16, 2004).

Another popular ground for a motor vehicle stop is squealing tires. In *Donaldson v. State,* 803 So. 2d 856 (Fla. Dist. Ct. App. 2002), the court held that the starting and driving of defendant's vehicle at a speed high enough to cause his tires to squeal did not demonstrate a disregard for the safety of others and did not give rise to reasonable suspicion for the stop. Likewise, in *Dora v. State,* 736 N.E.2d 1254 (Ind. Ct. App. 2000), the court held that the officer did not have reasonable suspicion to stop the defendant for squealing and spinning his tires for approximately three to four seconds because there was no evidence that this conduct placed anyone in danger.

Page 714. Add after second paragraph:

It is not uncommon, particularly in cases involving an accident, to encounter an officer who premised a detention for field sobriety testing primarily or solely on the odor of alcohol on the suspect's person or breath. Since it is not unlawful to consume alcohol and drive, it would follow that the mere presence of alcohol without any evidence of impairment would not constitute sufficient reasonable suspicion for detention/investigation. Thus, for example, in *State v. Spillers* (Ohio App. 2000), the court held that an officer who detected the odor of alcohol after stopping the suspect for a traffic infraction had insufficient information to justify the additional intrusion of ordering him out of the car to perform field sobriety tests. And in *Saucier v. State,* 869 P.2d 483 (Alaska App. 1994), the court held that the mere odor of alcohol about a driver's person, at least if it is not characterized as "strong," would not provide sufficient grounds for the intrusion of investigatory detention. Certainly, the odor of alcohol does not constitute sufficient grounds for probable cause to arrest. See, e.g., *Keehn v. Town of Torrington,* 834 P.2d 112 (Wyo. 1992).

Similarly, in *State v. Stroup,* 935 P.2d 438 (Or. Ct. App. 1997), the court held that the officer lacked objective probable cause to subject the defendant to field sobriety tests, where he observed only a slight odor of alcohol and bloodshot eyes, and the defendant admitted to drinking many hours earlier. The court emphasized that the defendant was not stopped for erratic driving and that she did not exhibit other typical signs of intoxication, such as slurred speech or impaired balance. Of course, it is important to note that the Oregon constitution requires probable cause for the administration of field sobriety tests because such tests are considered a search. See also *State v. Hurley*, No. 8-03-14 (Ohio App. 3d, Nov. 17, 2003) (holding no probable cause for arrest where officer detected an odor of alcohol on defendant's breath and slurred speech, the defendant admitted to drinking two or three beers, and the defendant passed the field sobriety tests).

The duration of the investigative stop should also be considered. The U.S. Supreme Court has found that "[i]n assessing whether a detention is too long in duration to be justified as an investigative stop, we consider it appropriate to examine whether the police diligently pursued a means of investigation that was likely to confirm or dispel their suspicions quickly, during which time it was necessary to detain the defendant." *United States v. Sharpe*, 470 U.S. 675, 686 (1985).

§11.0.1 The Citizen Informant

Page 718. Add after third full paragraph:

In *Florida v. J.L.*, 529 U.S. 266 (2000), the U.S. Supreme Court invalidated a search, holding that the information received from an anonymous caller lacked the sufficient indicia of reliability to establish reasonable suspicion for an investigatory stop. The case involved an anonymous caller who reported a young black man standing at a bus stop and carrying a gun. Officers responding to the call found a young man who matched the description and, relying solely on the information provided by the anonymous caller, frisked him and seized a gun. In invalidating the search, the Court found that the caller provided no predictive information and there was no means to test the caller's knowledge or credibility. The court further found that the information provided did not allege unlawful conduct, holding that a tip must be reliable in its assertion of illegality and not only in its tendency to identify a determinate person.

Some states have refused to extend the holding in *Florida v. J.L.* to the context of anonymous calls for erratic driving or driving under the influence, reducing the degree of corroboration necessary to uphold an investigatory stop. For instance, in *State v. Golotta*, 837 A.2d 359 (N.J. 2003), the Supreme Court of New Jersey upheld an investigatory stop based solely on information obtained from an anonymous 911 caller, relying on three factors in reaching this conclusion. First, the court stated that a call processed through 911 carries enhanced reliability because New Jersey law requires telephone companies to provide specific information for telephones used to initiate 911 calls. Next, the court looked at the nature of the intrusion and found that an investigatory stop as a result of allegation of erratic driving invoked a lesser privacy interest. Finally, the court found that an investigatory stop for erratic driving is reasonable in light of the significant risk to the public of death or injury. In addition to the consideration of these three factors, the court held that a 911 caller must "convey an unmistakable sense that the caller has witnessed an ongoing offense that implicates a risk of imminent death or serious injury to a particular person such as a vehicle's driver or to the public at large." *Golotta* at 369. A caller must also report the offense close in time to his or her observations and must provide a sufficient quantity of details so the officer stops the same vehicle that was observed/reported by the caller.

The *Golotta* court distinguished *Florida v. J.L.* because the caller in the latter case did not use 911 and no record was made of the call. The court further emphasized that while the caller in *J.L.* failed to allege any criminal activity, the caller in *Golotta* provided the officer with information of an imminent risk of danger to the public, and therefore less time to corroborate information from the anonymous tip.

Similarly, the court in *State v. Prendergast*, 83 P.3d 714 (Haw. 2004), looking at the totality of the circumstances, distinguished *J.L.*, finding that a tip regarding reckless driving is more reliable than the tip in *J.L.* and the imminence of harm is far greater. Unlike the possession of a gun, the court found that reckless conduct is open and observable to anyone nearby and therefore, the knowledge of the informant is clearly obtained from personal observation and is a crime in progress. The court further pointed out that several other jurisdictions have reached the same conclusion:

> The Supreme Court of Iowa [*State v. Walshire,* 634 N.W.2d 625 (Iowa 2001)], Kansas [*State v. Crawford,* 67 P.3d 115 (Kansas 2003)], and Wisconsin [*State v. Rutzinski,* 623 N.W.2d 516 (Wisconsin 2001)], as well as the Eighth Circuit Court of Appeals [*United States v. Wheat,* 278 F.3d 722 (8th Cir. 2001)] and the New Mexico Court of Appeals [*State v. Contreras,* 79 P.3d 1111(N.M. App. 2003)] have all held in post-*J.L.* decisions that an anonymous tip of erratic driving is sufficient to justify an investigatory stop.

Prendergast at 459–460.

Even before the decision in *Florida v. J.L.,* the law in Massachusetts and Wyoming disallowed police stops based on anonymous calls alone. The Appeals Court of Massachusetts in *Commonwealth v. Lubiejewski,* 729 N.E.2d 288 (Mass. App. Ct. 1999), held that a report from an anonymous caller, without independent observations by the officer with regards to the operation of the defendant's vehicle, was insufficient to warrant an investigatory stop.

> "Because the informant was anonymous, there was no basis for relying on previous conduct of the informant. [citations omitted] The informant's reliability, however, could be established by independent police corroboration." [citations omitted] ... [T]he information supplied by the informant did not include any specific details about the defendant which were not otherwise easily obtainable by an uninformed bystander. [citations omitted] "The corroboration went only to obvious details, not nonobvious details ... Anyone can telephone the police for any reason." [citations omitted]

Lubiejewski at 291.

In *McChesney v. State,* 988 P.2d 1071 (Wyo. 1999), an anonymous caller reported an erratic driver. Based on this reported information, the officer followed the defendant and eventually pulled him over, though he failed to observe any erratic driving or violations himself. The Wyoming Supreme Court recognized that an anonymous tip is less reliable because the caller's basis of knowledge and veracity is not known. In holding that anonymous tip of erratic driving alone was insufficient to warrant an investigatory stop, the court cautioned:

> An anonymous tip, without more, may be no more than a citizen's hunch or merely an assertion based on rumor. In addition, the potential for citizen abuse is readily apparent. Anybody with enough knowledge about a given person to make that person the target of a prank, or to harbor a grudge against the person, will certainly be able to formulate [such a] tip.

McChesney at 1077.

Page 721. Add at end of subsection before Checklist 17:

In certain circumstances, the defendant's constitutional right to confront the witness may be violated if the defendant is denied the right to confront the citizen informant. See discussion of *Crawford v. Washington*, 124 S. Ct. 1354 (2004), in §11.3.3.

§11.1 *Sobriety Checkpoints:* Sitz

Page 725. Replace second sentence of second full paragraph through list ending on page 728 with:

The National Highway Traffic Safety Administration (NHTSA) published a report that reviews recommended procedures for sobriety checkpoints. See The Use of Sobriety Checkpoints for Impaired Driving Enforcement, DOT HS-807-656 (National Highway Traffic Safety Administration, Nov. 1990). This latest version of the report claims to be consistent with court decisions, including *Michigan v. Sitz* and reviews legal issues relating to sobriety checkpoints, suggesting guidelines for the use of roadblocks in drunk driving law enforcement. Eleven suggestions are made "to ensure that sobriety checkpoints are used legally, effectively and safely":

1. *Ongoing Program to Deter Impaired Driving* — Agencies considering implementing sobriety checkpoints should

integrate them with a continuing, systematic and aggressive enforcement program. Vigorous enforcement, public information and education need to be part of this program. The purpose of the checkpoint is to maximize the deterrent effect and increase the perception of "risk of apprehension" to motorists who would operate a vehicle while impaired by alcohol or other drugs. The use of checkpoints alone will not maintain the perception of risk essential to an effective general deterrence program.

2. *Judicial Support* — When officials decide to use sobriety checkpoints, they should involve their prosecuting attorney ... in the planning process to determine legally acceptable procedures. This person can assist in identifying any legally mandated requirements and the types of evidential information that will be needed to prosecute cases emanating from checkpoint apprehension.

The jurisdiction's presiding judge should be informed of the proposed checkpoints and procedures, an essential step if the judiciary is to accept their use. The judge can provide insight on what activities would be required to successfully adjudicate such cases.

Prosecutors, judges, and other involved members of the criminal justice system can be invited to observe the actual operation of the checkpoint.

3. *Existing Policy/Guidelines* — Before using sobriety checkpoints, the agency must have specifically established procedures outlining how the checkpoints are to be conducted. The courts have been very clear in requiring the advance planning of sobriety checkpoints. Failure to do so has been used as evidence that the checkpoint techniques involved unfettered discretion. The policy should also assure that the checkpoints are conducted with a minimal amount of intrusion or motorist inconvenience.

4. *Site Selection* — Planning should assure the safety of the general public and law enforcement officers when selecting an operational site. Sobriety checkpoints must not create more of a traffic hazard than the results of the driving behavior they are trying to modify.

Planners should remember to select a site that allows officers to pull vehicles out of the traffic stream without causing significant subjective intrusion (fright) to the drivers (*United States v. Ortiz*, 422 U.S. 891 (1975)) and/or creating a safety hazard, e.g., by creating a traffic backup. Furthermore, officers' safety must be taken into account when deciding where to locate the checkpoint.

The department should objectively outline criteria used in the site selection process, e.g., an unusual incidence of alcohol/drug involved crashes or driving violations, unusual number of nighttime single-vehicle crashes or other documented alcohol/drug related vehicular incidents.

The site should permit the safe flow of traffic through the checkpoint. Consideration should be given to the posted speed limits, traffic volume, and visibility. Most jurisdictions have the capability to review the Average Traffic Volume (ATV) during the surveillance period for major roadways in their area. Once a jurisdiction has decided on possible locations for the sobriety checkpoints, the effect on traffic flow can be determined by ascertaining how long each interview takes, then multiplying that time by the number of available officers, and finally dividing that figure into the average number of vehicles that can be expected at that location. This will suggest whether all vehicles can be examined without causing a traffic build-up.

If the traffic volume precludes stopping every vehicle, a nondiscretionary scheme should be adopted, in advance, for stopping some subset of vehicles. In *Delaware v. Prouse*, 440 U.S. 648 (1979), the U.S. Supreme Court indicates that stopping all cars would be an acceptable method of conducting spot checks. In a concurring opinion, Justice Blackmun (joined by Justice Powell) suggests that other methods would also be acceptable, such as stopping every tenth car that passes a given point. If every vehicle is not stopped, the method used to determine which ones will be stopped must appear in the administrative order authorizing the use of the sobriety checkpoint.

The site should have maximum visibility from each direction and sufficient illumination for the safety of both the motorists and officers. If permanent lighting is unavailable, ensure that adequate portable lighting is provided. Planners should also ensure that sufficient adjoining space is available to pull vehicles off the traveled portion of the roadway. Any other conditions that may pose a hazard should be taken into consideration.

5. *Warning Devices* — Special care should be taken to warn approaching motorists of the sobriety checkpoint. Such notice can be accomplished using warning signs indicating the upcoming checkpoint; flares or fuses (if weather permits) and safety cones or similar devices for marking and/or closing lanes on the roadway; permanent or portable lighting to illuminate the checkpoint area; and, marked patrol vehicles with warning lights flashing.

A sign or device should be placed to provide advance warning stating why motorists are stopped. The U.S. Supreme Court has found that visible signs of the officers' authority generate less concern and fright on the part of lawful travelers, and are therefore less of a subjective intrusion (*United States v. Martinez-Fuerte*, 428 U.S. 643 (1976)).

The placement and types of traffic control devices used should comply with federal, state or local transportation codes. Planners should check with appropriate agencies administering the location and placement of signing devices.

6. *Visible Police Authority* — The visibility of uniformed officers and their marked vehicles makes the police presence obvious. It also serves to reassure motorists of the legitimate nature of the activity. This is an important aspect of the sobriety checkpoint and part of the effort to reduce the intrusion to the passing motorists affected by the checkpoint.

A sworn, uniformed officer should be assigned to provide onsite supervision of the checkpoint operation. This officer should be responsible for the overall operation and should be well versed in contingency planning for the checkpoint. The checkpoint should be staffed by a sufficient number of uniformed personnel to assure a safe and efficient operation, based on traffic volume, roadway size, type of location, etc.

7. *Chemical Testing Logistics* — Since impaired-driving arrests are anticipated at the selected location, the logistics

of chemical testing must also be included. If possible, a mobile breath-testing unit with a qualified operator could be physically located at the checkpoint. If one is not available, a system for expeditiously transporting suspected violators to chemical test sites should be established. In applicable locations, a Drug Recognition Technician (DRT) should be available, at a suitable location, to examine subjects who may be impaired by drugs other than or in combination with alcohol.

8. *Contingency Planning* — Any deviation from the predetermined plan for stopping vehicles should be thoroughly documented and the reason for the deviation given (e.g., traffic backing up, intermittent inclement weather). Courts have allowed this as long as documentation of the reason requiring the deviation from the interview sequence is kept (*United States v. Prichard*, 645 F.2d 854). If such an event occurs, jurisdictions should have prepared an alternative plan, in advance, to handle the checkpoint.

9. *Detection and Investigation Techniques* — An agency considering the use of sobriety checkpoints should ensure that the participating officers are properly trained in detecting impaired drivers. The use of sobriety checkpoints that allow impaired drivers to pass through undetected will not achieve the desired deterrence effect. Officers should look for the following indicators of impairment during initial contact with a driver at a checkpoint: odor of alcoholic beverages or other drugs (marijuana, hashish, some inhalants); bloodshot eyes; alcohol containers or drug paraphernalia; fumbling fingers; slurred speech; admission of drinking or drug use; inconsistent responses; detection of alcohol by a passive alcohol sensor; etc. It is highly desirable that officers assigned to conduct the sobriety checkpoint receive the DWI Detection and Standardized Field Sobriety Testing (SFST) training. Police are using these techniques taught in the SFST course to quickly detect whether a driver is impaired.

Once an officer's suspicion is raised, further investigation can take place out of the traffic lane without impeding the flow of traffic. If an officer believes it is necessary to move a suspect's car after he or she has reasonable suspicion of impairment, it should be moved by someone other than the suspect.

The officer should then continue the investigation using non-incriminating divided attention questions (e.g., by the officer simultaneously asking for driver's license and vehicle registration, requiring the subject to do two things at once) and the administration of the SFST battery, which includes the Walk and Turn test, One-Leg Stand test, and Horizontal Gaze Nystagmus. After the completion of the SFST, the officer may use a portable breath-testing device (PBT), if permissible in that jurisdiction. An evidential test to determine the blood alcohol concentration (BAC) should then be administered.

If the officer determines the subject is impaired and obtains a low BAC, a DRT should be utilized for further investigation. If a DRT is not available, normal departmental procedures regarding drug-impaired drivers should be followed.

10. *Operational Briefings* — The success of a sobriety checkpoint depends greatly upon smooth and efficient operations. The persons selected as supervisors of the operation should be briefed thoroughly on all procedures. This includes maintaining as little delay to the motoring public as possible and keeping records of any deviation from the original operational plan.

Persons selected to staff the checkpoint should be briefed on both its purpose and operation. They should understand the necessity for standard and uniform questions asked of drivers to avoid subjectivity. The use of an operational briefing is one way to accomplish this.

11. *Data Collection and Evaluation* — A systematic method of data collection and evaluation should be used to monitor and ensure standardization and consistency of sobriety checkpoints. This may be done by measuring the reaction of the public to the checkpoint and administrative evaluation of collected data.

Public reaction: This can be measured by immediate feedback received by officers at the site of the sobriety checkpoint. Also, a short questionnaire, which includes an explanation of why the checkpoint is conducted, given to drivers stopped at the checkpoint, can provide data. It may ask of the driver such questions as; Does the driver believe the checkpoint is fair? Did the driver mind being stopped briefly? Did the driver feel checkpoints help deter driving while impaired? The response can be completed later and mailed back to the agency. If the jurisdiction has the resources, a stamped, self-addressed postcard can be used as the questionnaire.

Evaluation: This concerns the extent to which the program's implementation, operation and efficiency meets targets set for the program. The following items may be addressed:

- Number of vehicles passing through the checkpoint
- Average time delay to motorists
- Number of motorists detained for field sobriety testing
- Number and types of arrests
- Identification of unusual incidents such as safety problems or other concerns
- Reaction of police officers participating in the sobriety checkpoint, including degree of support and effect on morale
- Perception of the quality of checkpoint cases brought before prosecutors and judges, including special problems
- Change in number of impaired-driving arrests
- Change in number of impaired-driving–related nighttime crashes
- Other information deemed necessary by individual agencies

In *State v. Mitchell*, 592 S.E.2d 543 (N.C. 2004), a field officer relied upon "standing permission" from his supervisor to set up a driver's license checkpoint. Such permission was given as long as the checkpoint was conducted pursuant to his supervisor's oral guidelines. The defense argued that too much discretion was afforded to the officers in the field because supervisory permission was not obtained for this particular checkpoint and the department did not have written guidelines to govern such checkpoints. The North Carolina Supreme Court upheld the checkpoint as constitutional because the "police officers are not constitutionally mandated to conduct driver's license checkpoints

pursuant to written guidelines," "standing permission" constitutes sufficient supervisory authority, and "the officers stopped
all oncoming traffic at the checkpoint."

Page 728. Add after numbered list:

Since the *Sitz* decision, the Supreme Court has come to a seemingly contradictory result in a case involving *drug* road-blocks.
In *City of Indianapolis v. Edmond*, 531 U.S. 32 (2000), the Court
in a 6-3 decision found a violation of the Fourth Amendment
when police stopped cars at a checkpoint, looked into them,
examined the drivers' licenses/registration, and led drug-sniffing
dogs around them. The distinction from *Sitz*, the majority
explained, was that the "primary purpose" of the drug roadblock
was "to uncover evidence of ordinary criminal wrong- doing" — as
opposed to the sobriety checkpoint the purpose of which is to
"protect public safety." Query the logic of that distinction. Interestingly, Justice Thomas in his dissent wrote, "I am not convinced
that *Sitz* and *Martinez-Fuentes* were correctly decided. Indeed, I
rather doubt that the Framers of the Fourth Amendment would
have considered 'reasonable' a program of indiscriminate stops of
individuals not suspected of wrongdoing."

The Supreme Court recently refused to apply *Edmond*,
upholding an "information-seeking checkpoint" in *Illinois v. Lidster*, 124 S. Ct. 885 (2004). In *Lidster*, police set up a checkpoint in
an attempt to obtain information about a hit-and-run accident
that had occurred approximately one week earlier at the same
time and place. Justice Breyer, delivering the opinion of the
Court, distinguished the *Lidster* checkpoint, finding that, unlike
Edmond, the checkpoint was not presumptively unconstitutional
and recognizing that "[t]he stop's primary law enforcement purpose was *not* to determine whether a vehicle's occupants were
committing a crime, but to ask vehicle occupants, as members
of the public, for their help in providing information about a
crime in all likelihood committed by others. The police expected
the information elicited to help them apprehend not the vehicle's
occupants, but other individuals." *Lidster* at 889. Rather, the Court
held that the same balancing test announced in *Sitz* should be
applied, in that the public interest served by the seizure should
be weighed against the interference with individual liberty.

Page 729. Add at end of third full paragraph:

As of this writing, the following states prohibit the use of sobriety checkpoints: Louisiana, Michigan, Minnesota, Oregon, Rhode Island, Texas, Washington, Wisconsin and Wyoming.

Page 730. Delete last line of third full paragraph, which cites to State v. Church.

Page 731. In first sentence of last (carryover) paragraph, replace State v. Wagner *citation with:*

821 S.W.2d 288 (Tex. App. 1991)

Page 732. In fourth full paragraph, replace People v. Banks *citation with:*

6 Cal. 4th 926, 836 P.2d 769 (Cal. 1993)

§11.1.1 Evasion of Sobriety Checkpoints

Page 735. Add at end of carryover paragraph:

See also *Ingersoll v. Palmer,* 43 Cal. 3d 1321, 1336 (1987); *U.S. v. Ogilvie,* 527 F.2d 330 (9th Cir. 1975).

Page 735. Add at end of subsection:

More recently, the U.S. Court of Appeals for the Ninth Circuit, dealing with a California border patrol checkpoint case, has similarly responded in the negative. In *U.S. v. Montero-Camargo,* 208 F.3d 1123 (9th Cir. April 11, 2000, #97-50643), border patrol agents were tipped that two cars with Mexicali license plates had turned around south of a checkpoint at El Centro. The drivers were stopped and taken back to the checkpoint, where searches of the cars produced two bags of marijuana. The defendant's motion to suppress on the grounds that there was no reasonable suspicion of criminal activity to justify the initial stop was denied.

The Ninth Circuit Court began by noting the general rule that "avoidance of a checkpoint, without more, is insufficient to support a finding of reasonable suspicion," citing *U.S. v. Ogilvie (supra)*. The court then went on, however, to find that there were additional factors in the case before them that did support "reasonable suspicion": the cars had Mexican plates, the drivers were Hispanic, the area was a common one for drug deals and "turnarounds." The dissenting opinion found these other factors dubious.

Clearly, then, in the drunk driving case the officer must be able to point to something more than an apparent avoidance of the checkpoint, such as making an illegal U-turn.

§11.1.2   "Electronic Roadblocks"

Page 736. In second full paragraph, replace State v. Donis *citation with:*

157 N.J. 44, 723 A.2d 35 (1998)

§11.3   Incriminating Statements

Pages 741–742. Delete last (carryover) paragraph.

§11.3.1   *Miranda* and the DUI Case

Page 752. Add at end of subsection:

What if the defendant remains silent and refuses to answer any questions? Can the silence be used against him or her in court? *Miranda* prohibits the use of a defendant's *post*-custodial silence as substantive evidence of guilt, but does not address *pre*-custodial silence. In *Jenkins v. Anderson*, 447 U.S. 231, 238 (1980), the Supreme Court held that pre-custodial silence may be used as impeachment evidence, recognizing that "impeachment follows the defendant's own decision to cast aside his cloak of silence and advances the truth-finding function of the criminal trial." Courts are divided on the issue of how to address a defendant's pre-custody silence as substantive evidence.

The First, Sixth, Seventh and Tenth Circuits and the Guam Territory have held that such an admission is a violation of the Fifth Amendment. See *Coppola v. Powell*, 878 F.2d 1562 (1st Cir. 1989); *Combs v. Coyle*, 205 F.3d 269 (6th Cir. 2000); *United States ex rel. Savory v. Lane*, 832 F.2d 1011 (7th Cir. 1987); and *People v. Muritok*, No. CRA02-001, slip. op. (Guam 2003).

The Fifth, Ninth, and Eleventh Circuits, on the other hand, have held that pre-custodial silence may be introduced as substantive evidence. For instance, in *United States v. Oplinger*, 150 F.3d 1061 (9th Cir. 1998), the court held that the use of a defendant's pre-arrest silence as substantive evidence did not violate the Fifth Amendment, relying on Justice Stevens's concurrence in *Jenkins v. Anderson:*

> The fact that a citizen has a constitutional right to remain silent when he is questioned has no bearing on the probative significance of his silence *before he has any contact with the police.* . . . When a citizen is under no official compulsion whatever, either to speak or to remain silent, I see no reason why his voluntary decision to do one or the other should raise any issue under the Fifth Amendment. For in determining whether the privilege is applicable, the question is whether petitioner was in a position to have his testimony compelled and then asserted his privilege, not simply whether he was silent. A different view ignores the clear words of the Fifth Amendment.

Oplinger at 1066 (Emphasis added).

It should be noted that both *Oplinger* and *Jenkins* can be distinguished from most issues of pre-custodial silence that may arise in a DUI case. In *Oplinger* and *Jenkins,* the defendants' silence did not result from questioning from law enforcement. The defendant in *Oplinger* refused to answer potentially incriminating questions from his employer, while the *Jenkins* defendant's silence consisted of his failure to report a crime.

Page 755. Add the following new subsection before Checklist 19:

§11.3.3   *Crawford* and the DUI Case*

In *Crawford v. Washington,* 124 S. Ct. 1354 (2004), Justice Scalia, writing on behalf of the Court, rejected the longstanding precedent of *Ohio v. Roberts,* 448 U.S. 56 (1980), which had permitted a judicial determination of reliability to govern the admissibility of out-of-court "testimonial" evidence. The vagaries of the Rules of Evidence and the amorphous notions of reliability are no longer the only deciding factors governing the admissibility of testimonial statements. See *Crawford,* 124 S. Ct. 1370. Instead, the Supreme Court has recognized that the ultimate goal of the confrontation clause is to ensure the reliability of evidence by testing the evidence in the "crucible of cross-examination." *Crawford* at 1370. The bedrock procedural guarantee that the accused may confront the witnesses against him or her applies to both federal and state prosecutions. *Pointer v. Texas,* 380 U.S. 400, 406 (1965). The Supreme Court holds in this opinion that the prosecution's ability to satisfy the hearsay requirements is no guarantee that the confrontation clause requirements have been satisfied.

Crawford proclaims that the Sixth Amendment guarantee of confrontation means that out-of-court "testimonial" statements are inadmissible at trial absent a prior opportunity to cross-examine the witness. However, the Court admits that the question of what is meant by the term "testimonial" is being left for another day. Of course, it is this very issue that is critical to DUI and other criminal defense practitioners.

The definition of testimonial evidence used by Scalia, albeit admittedly vague, is as follows: (1) "ex parte in-court testimony or its functional equivalent — that is, material such as affidavits, custodial examinations, prior testimony that the defendant was unable to cross-examine, or similar pre-trial statements that declarants would reasonably expect to be used prosecutorially" or (2) "statements that were made under circumstances which

---

*The authors wish to express their gratitude to Bruce Kapsack, Esq., Regent of the National College for DUI Defense, for his insights and contributions to this section.

would lead an objective witness reasonably to believe that the statements would be available for use at a later trial." *Crawford* at 1364.

The first definition is rather simple in scope. This definition includes any statement that is made inculpating the accused, orally or in writing, to any government official where the accused was not given the opportunity to cross-examine the declarant. If presented during grand jury proceedings, coroner investigation, preliminary hearing, or even police interrogation, such evidence is precluded no matter how "reliable" it may be.

The second definition is the troubling one. Under the old *Roberts* rule, if hearsay were shown to be "reliable," i.e., within a hearsay exception, it would be admitted. This is no longer true under *Crawford*. "Admitting statements deemed reliable by a judge is fundamentally at odds with the right of confrontation." *Crawford* at 1370.

Once one determines what constitutes "testimonial" evidence, the issue then becomes whether the defendant has had an adequate opportunity to cross-examine or question the "witness." Counsel should have the opportunity to cross-examine the witness, whether a person or a computer. If the witness is a computer, for instance, counsel should have the opportunity to discover what the computer is doing before determining the blood or breath test results.

Whereas *Roberts* stated that an unavailable witness's out-of-court statement may be admitted so long as it had an adequate indicia of reliability (that it fell within a "firmly rooted hearsay exception" or bore "particularized guarantees of trustworthiness"), the Supreme Court in *Crawford* recognized that leaving the regulation of out-of-court statements to the law of evidence would render the confrontation clause powerless to prevent even the most flagrant inquisitorial practices. The Court recognized that the framers of our Constitution would not have allowed admission of testimonial statements of a witness who did not appear at trial unless he was unavailable to testify, *and* the defendant had had a prior opportunity for cross-examination.

Thus, the Supreme Court indicates in this opinion that even the prosecution's ability to satisfy the hearsay requirements is no guarantee that the confrontation clause requirements have been satisfied. The issue then is whether the defendant has had an adequate opportunity to cross-examine or question what is going on inside the computers that analyze the blood, breath, or urine.

Looking at this issue purely from a hearsay point of view, when the prosecution attempts to admit a laboratory report, which appears to be trustworthy under a hearsay exception, *Crawford* demands the higher standard of compliance with the confrontation clause requirements. In this circumstance, the testing device, and its results, are clearly testimonial. The printout from the testing device is precisely the type of modern evidence with which the framers of our Constitution were concerned. This consideration should not evaporate when evidence happens to fall within some broad, modern hearsay exception that might be justifiable in other circumstances.

Therefore, with the possible exception of dying declarations as discussed in footnote 6 of the opinion, the Court holds in this case that the Sixth Amendment guarantee of confrontation in criminal cases means that out-of-court "testimonial" statements are inadmissible at trial absent a prior opportunity to cross-examine the witness. The unanswered issue is determining what evidence is "testimonial." Justice Scalia opines that where non-testimonial hearsay, such as business records, is at issue, the State's development of hearsay law would not amount to a constitutional violation. Where testimonial evidence is at issue, however, the Sixth Amendment demands both unavailability and a prior opportunity for cross-examination.

Therefore, at first blush, counsel may want to consider *not* cross-examining a witness at a preliminary hearing, administrative hearing, or the like if good reason exists to believe the witness may be unavailable at trial. If cross-examination were to take place, it may leave open the possibility of the prosecution using the witness's prior testimony at trial. However, counsel should be cautious with this approach, as the court may distinguish such a scenario from *Crawford*, finding that the defense waived the opportunity to cross-examine the witness, for the Sixth Amendment requires only a prior *opportunity* to cross, not an actual cross-examination of the witness.

As the term "testimonial" is defined by later case law, the *Crawford* case may change the law relating to informants who call the police to report a drunk driver, and to the computer programs and algorithms used in chemical testing devices. In sum, the *Crawford* case may ultimately mean that even though the prosecution may be able to admit evidence through a hearsay exception, the evidence may be inadmissible unless the confrontation rights of the defendant are satisfied.

§11.4 Refusal Evidence

§11.4.1 Self-Incrimination: *Neville*

Page 758. Add after carryover extract:

Nevertheless, the following year the South Dakota Supreme Court rethought its position in *State v. Hoenscheid,* 374 N.W.2d 128 (S.D. 1985). The court explained:

> This case presents an opportunity to correct the error we made in State v. Neville, 312 N.W.2d 723 (S.D. 1981) (Neville I); and in State v. Neville, 346 N.W.2d 425 (S.D.1984) (Neville II). That error was our holding that "Neville's refusal to submit to a blood test is evidence of a testimonial nature and thus within the protection of the privilege against self-incrimination." 346 N.W.2d at 429. We should have limited our holding to the ground relied upon by the United States Supreme Court, i.e., that the statute requiring a motorist to choose between agreeing to submit to a chemical test of his blood and thereby giving evidence against himself or refusing to take the test and suffering the consequences of that refusal does not involved unconstitutional coercion within the meaning of the Fifth Amendment.

Page 758. In first full sentence of carryover paragraph, change "See also" to "But see."

§11.4.3 Refusal to Take Field Sobriety Tests

Page 765. Add at end of second paragraph:

Washington law similarly concludes that a defendant may not be arrested solely for refusing to participate in field sobriety tests. See *State v. Reid,* 988 P.2d 1038 (Wash. Ct. App. 1999).

§11.5   Field Evidence

§11.5.1   Verbal Field Sobriety Tests: *Muniz*

Page 768. In second full paragraph, replace **Allred v. State** *citation with:*

622 So. 2d 984 (Fla. 1993)

Page 768. Add at end of third full paragraph:

The State of Texas, however, does not follow this logic. In *Gassaway v. State,* 957 S.W.2d 48 (Tex. Crim. App. 1977), the court found that the field sobriety tests of requiring the defendant to recite the alphabet and counting backwards were not testimonial in nature for purposes of the defendant's right to be free from self-incrimination. But see *State v. Vickers,* 878 S.W.2d 329 (Tex. App. 1994).

§11.5.2   Field Sobriety Tests

Page 769. In second full paragraph, replace **Kumho Tire v. Carmichael** *citation with:*

526 U.S. 137, 149–152 (1999)

Page 772. Add at end of page, after indented paragraph:

In 2002, a federal court was asked to rule on the admissibility of field sobriety tests and, if they were admissible, in what form. In an intelligent and well-reasoned 72-page opinion, the court in *United States v. Horn,* 185 F. Supp. 2d 530 (2002), held that a proper foundation must be presented—i.e., deficiencies go to the *admissibility* and not merely to the *weight* of the evidence—and concluded:

> . . . The results of properly administered WAT [walk-and-turn], OLS [one-leg-stand] and HGN [horizontal gaze nystagmus] SFSTs [standardized field sobriety tests] may be admitted into

evidence in a DWI/DUI case only as circumstantial evidence of intoxication or impairment but not as direct evidence of specific BAC.... Officer Jarrell ... must first establish his qualifications to administer the test. Unless qualified as an expert witness under Rule 702 to express scientific or technical opinions regarding the reliability of the methods and principles underlying the SFSTs, Officer Jarrell's foundational testimony will be limited to the instruction and training received and experience he has in administering the tests and may not include opinions about the tests' accuracy rates. If Officer Jarrell testifies about the results of the HGN test, he may testify as to his qualifications to detect exaggerated HGN, and his observations of exaggerated HGN in Horn, but he may not, absent being qualified under Rule 702 to do so, testify as to the causal nexus between alcohol consumption and exaggerated HGN....

The court then added that (as in the *Becker* case) the officer may not use quasi-scientific terms in describing the subject's performance on the tests:

... When testifying about Horn's performance of the SFSTs, Officer Jarrell may describe the SFSTs he required Horn to perform and describe Horn's performance, but Officer Jarrell may not use language such as "test," "standardized clues" or express the opinion that Horn "passed" or "failed," because the government has not shown, under Rule 702 and the *Daubert/ Kumho Tire* decisions, that these conclusions are based on sufficient facts or data and are derived from reliable methods or principles....

... Assuming the government can establish the elements of Rule 701, Officer Jarrell may give lay opinion testimony that Horn was intoxicated or impaired by alcohol. Such testimony must be based on Officer Jarrell's observations of Horn and may not include scientific, technical or specialized information.

In an interesting comment earlier in the opinion (note 3), the federal court observed:

Expedient as it may be for courts to take judicial notice of scientific or technical matters to resolve the crush of DWI/DUI cases, this cannot be done in the face of legitimate challenges to the reliability and accuracy of the tests sought to be judicially noticed.

As will be seen, there is a place in the prosecutor's arsenal for SFST evidence, but it must not be cloaked in an aura of false reliability, lest the fact finder, like the protagonist in the Thomas Dolby song, be "blinded by science" or "hit by technology."

Page 773. Add at end of subsection:

Law enforcement agencies across the country have begun using so-called standardized field sobriety tests (FSTs). These consist of a battery of three tests (walk-and-turn, one-leg stand, and nystagmus), which must be given exactly as set forth by the National Highway Traffic Safety Administration (NHTSA); the tests are objectively scored. All other tests previously used by various agencies have been found to be ineffective.

Prosecutors and law enforcement agencies in some states have resisted this clear trend. While actually copying NHTSA's techniques for the three tests in many of their own manuals, officers pretend to be ignorant of any standardized method of testing — thus permitting continued subjective scoring and the use of such discredited tests as finger-to-nose, "modified position of attention," alphabet recitation, etc. Many law enforcement and prosecution agencies prefer the absence of any standards in drunk driving investigations. The only legal grounds for the continued admissibility of non-standardized tests (including standardized tests performed in a non-standardized manner), however, appears to be "We've always done it that way"

That situation must change, as it is changing in other states. In *State v. Homan*, 732 N.E.2d 952 (Ohio 2000) (subsequently superseded by Ohio Legislature, see Ohio Rev. Code Ann. §4511.19(D), (4)(b)) for example, the Ohio Supreme Court has ruled that "(i)n order for the results of a field sobriety test to serve as evidence of probable cause to arrest, the police must have administered the test in strict accordance with standardized testing procedures." In that case, the state trooper actually gave the three NHTSA standardized FSTs that are now required in that state — but he failed to administer them in strict accordance with the standards, resulting in suppression of all tests. The court noted with approval NHTSA's conclusion that "field sobriety tests are an effective means of detecting legal intoxication 'only when: the tests are administered in the prescribed, standardized manner, the standardized clues are used to assess the suspect's performance, (and) the standardized criteria are employed to interpret that performance.'"

Specifically, the court found the following flaws in the trooper's administration of the FSTs—flaws which would be considered common among most law enforcement officers:

> During cross-examination, Trooper Worcester testified that, in administering to appellee the HGN and walk-and-turn tests, he at times deviated from established testing procedures. With respect to the HGN test, for example, Trooper Worcester testified that, in observing appellee's eyes for nystagmus at maximum deviation, he did not hold appellee's eyes at maximum deviation for a full four seconds as standardized procedures require. In addition, in determining at what angle appellee's eyes began to exhibit nystagmus, Trooper Worcester did not, as recommended, move the stimulus at a pace that would take a full four seconds to move appellee's eyes from a forward gaze to the right. It took Trooper Worcester only one to two seconds to make the pass.
> Trooper Worcester also admitted to deviating from established police practice by conducting the walk-and-turn test between his patrol car and appellee's car. In addition, Trooper Worcester gave appellee the option of turning either to the right or the left after completing the required number of steps. Police procedure requires that the suspect turn to the left.... The record also indicates that the walk-and-turn test was conducted on a gravel covered, uneven surface of road when a flat surface is required to perform the test.

The *Homan* case may represent a growing trend. On July 2, 2001, the Supreme Court of Hawaii ruled that FSTs should be excluded if the prosecution fails to lay a foundation as to test reliability and officer qualifications. *State v. Ferrer,* 95 Hawaii 409 (2001).

Despite suppression of FST results, an officer's observations of a defendant's performance of the FSTs may be admissible as lay testimony. For instance, in *State v. Schmitt,* 801 N.E.2d 446 (Ohio 2004), the Ohio Supreme Court limited its earlier *Homan* decision, holding that even if FSTs are not administered in strict compliance with NHTSA guidelines, an officer may testify regarding his or her observations made during a defendant's performance of such tests. The court found that an officer's perceptions gathered during the performance of FSTs "may easily reveal to the average layperson whether the individual is intoxicated." *Id.* at 450.

It should be apparent that as the NHTSA standardized tests become widely accepted — and non-standardized tests fall from use — a new *Kelly-Daubert* standard for admissibility is being created for field sobriety tests. The old tests are no longer "widely accepted" as a valid means of detecting impairment or intoxication, and the old methods of administering approved tests are no longer up to the professional standard. It remains only for attorneys to begin challenging the admissibility of the tests in court.

The following material will give the reader a firm understanding of the theory and development of the standardized field sobriety tests in arguing for suppression. (For a more detailed discussion of the administration of the tests themselves, see §4.3.) The author is grateful to George L. Bianchi of Seattle, Washington, for his kind permission to reproduce this edited version of his excellent work.

In June of 1975, the Southern California Research Institute was commissioned by NHTSA to study and evaluate the then currently used "field sobriety tests" to determine their alcohol sensitivity, develop more sensitive and reliable tests, and attempt to standardize the administration of "field sobriety tests." In this regard, they were looking to physical coordination tests associated with a DUI investigation to determine, if possible, their relationship to intoxication and possibly driving impairment. The goal was to develop alcohol-sensitive tests that would provide more reliable evidence by standardizing the tests themselves and the observations to be made. The end result was *Psycho-Physical Tests for DWI Arrests,* DOTHS 802 424, (Burns & Moskowitz, June 1977). Some of the original sixteen "tests" considered were AGN, walk-and-turn, Romberg-balance, finger-to-nose, one-leg- stand, and finger-count or finger-dexterity. Reciting the alphabet and counting backwards were not ever considered. To make the tests more reliable and objective (as opposed to subjective), the authors pursued the development of a "test battery" which would provide statistically valid and reliable indications that a driver's breath alcohol concentration (BrAC) level was at or above 0.10, rather than indications of driver impairments. *Validation of the Standardized Field Sobriety Test Battery at BAC's Below 0.10 Percent,* DOTHS —— at page 28 (Stuster & Burns, August 1998). Certain tests were originally eliminated because they were determined to not be alcohol sensitive. The result was a pilot program that studied a six-test battery (one-leg-stand, walk-and-run, finger-to-nose, finger-count, Gaze Nystagmus and tracing) with three alternates (Romberg-balance, subtraction, counting backwards and letter cancellation). The original data in the 1977 study suggested that it was unrealistic to attempt to use behavioral tests to discriminate BrAC's in a plus or minus 0.02 margin around the given BrAC level of 0.10 percent. *Psycho-Physical Tests for DWI Arrests,* at page 41. The authors also noted an obvious unacceptable error rate of 47 percent in "arresting" individuals who were under a BrAC of 0.10 percent. *Id.* at page 28, 30 and Appendix 6, page 102. Some of the sources of error were determined to be the failure of officers to heed the lack of test evidence, impairment which was *not* alcohol related and officers who did *not* score the tests properly. *Id.* at page 28. The study resulted in a three-test battery that included alcohol Gaze Nystagmus, the one-leg-stand, and the walk-and-turn test. The authors stated:

> It became apparent during field visits that this objective [standardization of the tests and observation procedures] is highly important. There are wide differences between officers in using tests to assess a driver's state of intoxication, and they may exist within the department as well as between agencies and locales. These differences seriously detract from reliability as well as from credibility of the officers in court proceedings.

Id. at page 59.

The standardization of the three-test battery occurred in 1981 with *Development and Field Tests of Psycho-Physical Tests for DWI Arrests,* DOTHS 805 864, (Tharp, Burns & Moskowitz, March 1981). The authors defined a standardized test as:

> One which the procedures, apparatus and scoring have been fixed so that precisely the same testing procedures can be followed at different times and locations.

Id. at page 3.

From August of 1978 until March of 1981 when the final report was concluded, Tharp, Burns and Moskowitz worked to standardize the administration and scoring procedures associated with the three-test battery (walk-and-turn test, the one-leg-stand test and Horizontal Gaze Nystagmus). Their results were evaluated in the laboratory and to a *limited* extent, in the field. *Development and Field Tests for DWI Arrests,* DOTHS 805 864 (Tharp, Burns & Moskowitz, March 1981).

As it relates to the walk-and-turn test, the authors noted that requesting people to "watch their feet" while performing this test increased its sensitivity to alcohol, but made the test difficult for people with monocular vision (i.e., poor depth perception). Performing the walk-and-turn test with the eyes open and enough light to see some frame of reference was determined to be essential if sober individuals were to perform the test without difficulty. *Id.* at page 4. Certain individuals were noted to have difficulty with the walk-and-turn test when sober, including people over 65 years of age, people with back, leg or middle ear problems, and people with high-heeled shoes (over 2 inches). *Id.* at page 5. The authors determined that the test required a line which the police officer could manufacture. They also recommended that the walk-and-turn test be performed on a dry, hard, level, non-slippery surface and under relatively safe conditions. If those requirements could not be met at the roadside, that the suspect be asked to perform the test elsewhere or that only the Nystagmus test be used. *Id.* at page 5.

As it relates to the one-leg-stand test, the authors ascertained that the suspect must be able to see in order to orient himself or herself and the police officer must stand back from the suspect in order not to provide an artificial reference frame which could distract the suspect. Generally, if the suspect could not see or orient with respect to a perpendicular frame of reference, then the test was determiend to be difficult even if sober. *Id.* at page 5. Again, the authors noted that certain individuals would have difficulty performing the one-leg-stand test under sober conditions, including people over the age of 65, people with leg, back or middle ear problems, and people who are overweight by 50 or more pounds. Lastly, the authors recommended that the one-leg- stand test be performed only on a hard, dry, level, non-slippery surface and under relatively safe conditions and if those requirements could not be met at the roadside, that the suspect be asked to perform the test elsewhere or that only the Nystagmus test be used. *Id.* at page 5.

As it relates to the Gaze Nystagmus, the author noted that approximately half of the "sober" people tested showed a slight Nystagmus in at least one eye when their eyes were deviated maximally. *Id.* at page 7. The authors recommended that corrective lenses should be removed prior to the administration of this test. *Id.* at page 7. They also recommended that in looking for the onset of Nystagmus, the stimulus be moved fairly slowly (i.e., at about 10 degrees per second), otherwise normal oscillation of the eyeball may be mistaken for Nystagmus. *Id.* at page 7. On the second movement of the stimulus in each direction, the recommendation was that the stimulus be moved faster (about 20 degrees per second) and that the observer should note whether or not the suspect can follow smoothly and how distinct the Nystagmus is at the maximum lateral deviation. *Id.* at page 9. The authors concluded that the Gaze Nystagmus test may not be applicable to individuals wearing contact lenses, since hard contacts prevent extreme lateral eye movements. *Id.* at page 9. Also of note is that the authors indicated that Gaze Nystagmus could be seen in 50 to 60 percent of all individuals if their eyes were deviated to the extremes and that Gaze Nystagmus occurs with some types of brain damage. *Id.* at page 92.

In discussing alcohol and balance, the authors noted that other variables, in addition to alcohol, could increase body sway, such as sleep loss, increasing of room temperature and eating. *Id.* at 83. They also concluded that one of the most important parameters in tests of balance and muscular coordination is vision. In their opinion, closing the eyes makes all of the balance tests much more difficult for sober and intoxicated individuals. *Id.* at 83. The data, to them, suggested that peripheral vision plays a particularly important role in maintaining balance. *Id.* at 84.

The end result of the 1981 study was an indication that the Gaze Nystagmus could correctly classify individuals at or above a BrAC of 0.10 seventy-seven percent (77%) of the time, that the walk-and-turn test could properly classify individuals as being at or above a BrAC of 0.10 sixty-eight percent (68%) of the time and the one-leg-stand test could properly classify individuals at or above a BrAC of 0.10 sixty-five percent (65%) of the time. When they combined the results of the Gaze Nystagmus with the walk- and-turn test, there was determined to be an 80 percent accurate classification of a person at or above a BrAC of 0.10 level. The authors also noticed a 32 percent false arrest rate in the overall statistics.

In 1983 the NHTSA commissioned Anderson, Schweitz and Snyder to develop standardized practical and effective procedures for police officers to use in reaching an arrest/no arrest decision. *Field Evaluation of Behavioral Test Battery for DWI*, DOTHS 806 475 (Anderson, Schweitz & Snyder, September 1983). The study tested the feasibility of using the three-test battery in the operational conditions by police officers and was to secure data to help determine if the three-test battery would discriminate as well in the field as it had previously in the laboratory. The end results of this study mirrored the statistical results of the laboratory testing previously summarized in 1981 by Tharp, Burns and Moskowitz in *Development and Field Tests for DWI Arrest.*

Jack Stuster and Marcelline Burns were commissioned by the National Highway Traffic Safety Institute to evaluate the accuracy of the standardized field sobriety test battery to assist officers in making arrest decisions for DWI at alcohol concentrations below 0.10 percent. In August of 1998, their report was submitted to the National Highway Traffic Safety Administration. *Validation of the Standardized Field Sobriety Test Battery at BAC's Below 0.10 Percent*, DOTHS _____ (Stuster & Burns, August 1998). As the authors noted:

> During the past sixteen years, NHTSA's SFSTs largely have repaced the invalidated performance tests of unknown merit that once were the patrol officers only in helping to make post-stop DWI arrest decisions. Regional and local preferences for other performance tests still exists, even though some of the tests have never been validated. Despite regional differences and what tests are used to assist officers in making DWI arrest decisions, NHTSA's SFSTs presently are used in all 50 states. NHTSA's SFSTs have become the standard pre-arrest procedures for evaluating DWI in most law enforcement agencies.

Id. at 3. The authors also found that prosecutors who were interviewed suggested that the optimum situation would be for all law enforcement agencies to restrict their field sobriety evaluations to the same standardized battery of three tests. *Id.* at 24. The 1998 study showed that the Gaze Nystagmus test had the highest correlation of accuracy when compared to the actual measured breath test level. In this regard the Gaze Nystagmus test showed a 65 percent correlation to the actual measured alcohol level. The walk-and-turn test resulted in a 61 percent correlation to the actual measured alcohol concentration level, with the one-leg-stand test showing a 45 percent correlation with the actual measured alcohol level. *Id.* at 17. Approximately 10 percent of the individuals were determined to be falsely arrested by law enforcement in that their alcohol level was estimated to have been greater than 0.08 percent, but later found to be below that level. *Id.* at 18. Of interest is the range of BrAC that is *not* measured and correlated in the 297 individuals tested. The range of BrAC tested is from a .038 for 8 underage females to a 0.07 for 2 underage females. There were no individuals whose measured BrAC level reflected 0.08 up to approximately 0.13 percent in the study. Thus, no individuals were tested at BrAC levels ranging from what appears to be a 0.08 up to and including a 0.13 which resulted in the above-listed statistical analysis. *Id.* at 16.

As a result of the above studies, the National Highway Traffic Safety Administration published both student and instructor manuals to be used by law enforcement agencies for the detection and arrest of DWI suspects. *DWI Detection and Standardized Field Sobriety Testing.* The first set of manuals were printed in 1981 with subsequent publications in 1992 (PB 94-780228 Student Manual, PB 94-780210 Instructor Manual), 1995 (AVA- 19911BB00 Student Manual, AVA-19910BB00 Instructor Manual) and 2000 (AVA 20839-BB0 Student Manual, AVA 20838-BB0 Instructor Manual). These manuals provided to law enforcement do *not* incorporate the statistical results of Stuster and Burns wherein they attempt to validate the three tests SFST battery to alcohol levels below 0.10 percent. These manuals incorporate and instruct law enforcement on the statistical results of the three studies leading up to and including *Field Evaluation of Behavioral Test Battery for DWI,* DOTHS 806 475 (Anderson, Schweitz & Snyder, September 1983).

SUMMARY OF NATIONAL HIGHWAY TRAFFIC SAFETY ADMINISTRATION STUDENT AND INSTRUCTOR MANUALS FOR DWI DETECTION AND STANDARDIZED FIELD SOBRIETY TESTING

The National Highway Traffic Safety Adminstration has defined DWI detection as:

> The entire process of identifying and gathering evidence to determine whether or not a suspect should be arrested for a DWI violation.

1995 SFST Student Manual (AVA-19911BB00) at page IV-1; 1995 SFST Instructor Manual (AVA-19910BB00) at page IV-1. DWI detection is divided into three phases. Phase one being the vehicle in motion, phase two being personal contact and phase three being pre-arrest screening. 1995 SFST Student Manual at IV-2-5, 1995 SFST Instructor Manual at IV-1-5.

Phase one involves observing the vehicle in motion and deciding whether there is sufficient cause to command the driver to stop. 1995 SFST Student Manual at IV-3-5, V-1-12, 1995 SFST Instructor Manual at IV-1-2, V-1-15.

Phase two is personal contact with an individual. At this time the officer is to observe and interview the driver, face to face, in order to decide whether there is sufficient cause to instruct the driver to step from the vehicle for further investigation. 1995 SFST Student Manual, IV-3-4, IV-1-14. It is at this point the officer makes observations to determine whether or not it is appropriate to order the individual to exit his vehicle to perform the standardized field sobriety testing.

Phase three is defined as "pre-arrest screening" to determine if there is probable cause to arrest the suspect for DWI by the use of the standardized field sobriety testing (psycho-physical tests) which have been identified and *validated* through NHTSA's research program. 1995 SFST Student Manual IV, Section VII & VIII. 1995 SFST Instructor Manual, Section VII & VIII.

Proper training of a law enforcement officer under the *NHTSA DUI DETECTION AND STANDARDIZED FIELD SOBRIETY TESTING* curriculum consists of 16 sessions that span 22 hours, 45 minutes of instruction, *excluding* breaks. While NHTSA recognizes there may be some need of flexibility in the curriculum, they state that:

> It is the IACP (International Association of Chiefs of Police) and NHTSA's position that students cannot be assured of achieving proficiency in using and interpreting the standardized field sobriety testing if the sessions dealing with that topic are curtailed in scope or duration.

1995 SFST Instructor Manual at page 6.

> THE STANDARDIZED FIELD SOBRIETY TESTS ARE NOT AT ALL FLEXIBLE. THEY MUST BE ADMINISTERED EACH TIME, EXACTLY AS OUTLINED IN THIS COURSE.

1995 SFST Instructor Manual at page 10.
NHTSA emphasizes that the results of the three studies they commissioned validated the standardized field sobriety tests, yet emphasized one final and major point.

> THIS VALIDATION APPLIES *ONLY* WHEN THE TESTS ARE ADMINISTERED IN THE PRESCRIBED STANDARDIZED MANNER; AND *ONLY* WHEN THE STANDARDIZED CLUES ARE USED TO ASSESS THE SUSPECT'S PERFORMANCE; AND, *ONLY* WHEN THE STANDARDIZED CRITERIA ARE EMPLOYED TO INTERPRET THAT PERFORMANCE.
> IF ANY ONE OF THE STANDARDIZED FIELD SOBRIETY TEST ELEMENTS IS CHANGED, THE VALIDITY IS COMPROMISED.

1995 SFST Student Manual, VIII-12 (see also 1995 SFST Instructor Manual, VIII-8, where it is stated that "if any of the standardized elements of the test are changed, their validity will be threatened.")

CONCLUSION
In the absence of foundation testimony establishing the reliability and relevance of field sobriety tests and physical observations to show alcohol-induced impairment of the ability to drive a motor vehicle, such test results and observations should

be excluded from use as that type of evidence. In any trial which does not involve a breath test, it is evident from the above-discussed studies that the standardized field sobriety tests are not relevant and should not be admissible in the DUI trial.

Before such testimony should be introduced it must be shown to be relevant and more probative than prejudicial. In order to show this requisite probative value, a foundation must be laid showing that there is a physiological relationship between the consumption of alcohol and the decreased ability to perform the specific physical tests requested by the officer. In the absence of such showing, the prosecution should be precluded from making any reference to said tests. In the absence of a proper foundation, the tests are either irrelevant or unduly prejudicial. The court went on further to state that there must be *strict* compliance by the law enforcement officer with the NHTSA standards. (This is as opposed to substantial compliance.) In ruling the need for *strict* compliance, The Ohio Supreme Court stated:

> In the substantial-compliance cases, the minor procedural deviations that were at issue in no way affected the ultimate results. In contrast, it is well established that in field sobriety testing even minor deviations from the standardized procedures can severely bias the results. Moreover, our holdings in the substantial-compliance cases were grounded, at least in part, on the practical impossibility of strictly complying with the applicable adminstrative regulations. In contrast, we find that strict compliance with standardized field sobriety testing procedures is neither unrealistic nor humanly impossible in the great majority of vehicles stops in which the police choose to administer the tests.

Homan at page 426. Attached as Appendix C is the case of *State v. Homan*.

We, as attorneys, should demand that courts analyze "field sobriety tests," question their relevance and rule on their admissibility or use in light of the numerous scientific studies commissioned by the National Highway Traffic Safety Administration. Until the required foundational training and background of the arresting officer is presented, the results of standardized field sobriety tests as well as any reference to them as "sobriety tests" must be suppressed.

Page 774. Add after the third complete paragraph:

A federal bankruptcy court has found occasion to apply the Rule 702/*Daubert* standards to the admissibility of nystagmus and retrograde extrapolation as evidence. In *Boone v. Barnes*, No. 00-6105WM (Bankr. 8th Cir., Sept. 10, 2001), the bankruptcy appellate panel addressed the dischargeability of a debt for civil liability arising out of a Missouri vehicular accident, the issue being whether the debtor was intoxicated at the time of the incident. At trial, the creditor offered the testimony of the State Trooper concerning the results of a nystagmus test he administered—while the debtor was lying down—in the course of investigating the accident; he also testified that, applying an alcohol elimination rate of .02 percent per hour, the blood test result of .05 percent indicated a probable blood-alcohol level of .11 percent at the time of the accident. The bankruptcy court ruled that the creditor had failed to prove that the debtor had been intoxicated at the time of the accident.

In affirming, the appellate court noted that Rule 702 and *Daubert* applied to the federal proceeding—and that the creditor had not shown the Trooper to qualify as an expert on either subject. She had "produced no evidence as to the reliability of the HGN test in general or its application to the specific facts of this case." Specifically, the test should not have been given to a subject while lying down, there was no evidence as to the effects on nystagmus of injuries sustained in the accident, and no testimony established the training and experience of the Trooper in administering and interpreting an HGN test. As to the blood-alcohol testimony, the creditor "did not offer any evidence concerning (the Trooper's) skill, training, knowledge, expertise, or education concerning his ability to testify to the rate at which alcohol dissipates in the blood stream."

§11.5.3 Nystagmus

Page 782. Add after indented material in carryover paragraph:

Since the publication of the fifth edition of *Drunk Driving Defense*, the author's summary of the growing consensus on admissibility of nystagmus seems to be generally holding, with variations: Nystagmus satisfies the *Frye* test ("general acceptance") and, if the officer is qualified and properly administered the test, is admissible to (1) help establish probable cause to arrest, and (2) to indicate presence of alcohol and, along with other field sobriety tests and observations, as a basis for an opinion as to possible intoxication. Nystagmus is inadmissible to help prove an actual blood-alcohol concentration. A brief sampling of decisions from across the country follows. Note that a number of jurisdictions require expert testimony to establish compliance with 702/*Frye-Daubert* requirements before HGN will be admitted. The frequency of this requirement can be expected to decrease in time as courts come to accept the test and recognize the difficulties in re-establishing the general scientific acceptance/reliability of the test for each individual case; foundational requirements as to the officer's qualifications and procedures used should, however, continue.

> *Malone v. City of Silverhill*, 575 So. 2d 101 (Ala. Crim. App. 1989), *rev'd on other grounds, Ex Parte Malone*, 575 So. 2d 106 (1990): HGN is admissible, but foundation of officer's qualifications and proper administration of the test is required.
> *Ballard v. State*, 955 P.2d 931 (Alaska App. 1998): HGN satisfies *Frye* for limited purpose of showing consumption of alcohol and potential impairment.
> *State v. City Court of City Mesa*, 799 P.2d 855 (Ariz. 1990): HGN complies with *Frye* and is admissible if the proper foundation is laid.
> *State v. Russo*, 773 A.2d 965 (Conn. App. Ct. 2001): Nystagmus is admissible only after the proper foundation is laid in accordance with *Daubert.*
> *Williams v. State*, 710 So. 2d 24 (Fla. App. 1998): HGN is accepted in the scientific community. Expanding on this, in *Bowen v. State*, 745 So. 2d 1108 (Fla. App. 1999), there must be a confirming blood, breath, or urine test before HGN evidence is admitted.
> *State v. Ito*, 978 P.2d 191 (Haw. App. 1999): Nystagmus is sufficiently reliable, but foundation required of officer qualifications and proper administration. In *State v. Ferrer*, 23 P.3d 744 (Haw. 2001), however, court held that

nystagmus was not scientific in nature and and that officer could not use testify defendant "passed" or "failed" without a proper foundation.

People v. Basler, 740 N.E.2d 1 (Ill. App. 2000): Absent contrary defense evidence, HGN satisfies *Frye* but foundation as to officer's training and administration of the test is necessary.

State v. Chastain, 960 P.2d 756 (Kan. 1998): Nystagmus is *not* generally accepted within the scientific community and exclusion at trial was appropriate.

State v. Armstrong, 561 So. 2d 883 (La. Ct. App. 1990): HGN complies with *Frye* and is admissible with the proper foundation that the officer was properly trained, was certified in the administration of HGN, and properly administered the test.

State v. Taylor, 694 A.2d 907 (Maine 1997): The test is admissible if the officer is qualified and gave the test as required.

Shultz v. State, 664 A.2d 60 (Md. App. 1995): HGN is admissible if the test is properly administered by a qualified officer to prove presence of alcohol.

Commonwealth v. Sands, 675 N.E.2d 370 (Mass. 1997): Admissibility depends on expert testimony that *Frye/Daubert* standards are met and officer's testimony as to qualifications and administration of the test.

State v. Berger, 551 N.W.2d 421 (Mich. App. 1996): HGN complies with *Frye;* admissibility only requires evidence that officer is qualified and properly performed the test.

State v. Klawitter, 518 N.W.2d 577 (Minn. 1994): Nystagmus satisfies the *Frye* standard and is admissible if a sufficient foundation is laid.

Young v. City of Brookhaven, 693 So. 2d 1355 (Miss. 1997): Nystagmus is *not* accepted within the scientific community and is inadmissible except to prove probable cause to arrest.

State v. Fisken, 909 P.2d 206 (Or. App. 1996): HGN evidence is admissible with proper foundation, but officer cannot testify that the results indicated a BAC over .10 percent.

Duffy v. Director of Revenue, 966 S.W.2d 372 (Mo. App. 1998): HGN is scientific in nature and should have been excluded because officer was unaware of proper administration and interpretation procedures.

State v. Baue, 607 N.W.2d 191 (Neb. 2000): Nystagmus complies with *Frye* and is admissible to show possible impairment but not BAC.

State v. Duffy, 778 A.2d 415 (N.H. 2001): HGN is a scientifically based test and must comply with New Hampshire's version of Fed. R. Evid. 702.

State v. Doriguzzi, 760 A.2d 336 (N.J. App. 2000): Nystagmus is scientific in nature and so a *Frye* foundation is required.

State v. Torres, 976 P.2d 20 (N.M. 1999): *Daubert* applies and so officer cannot testify until expert establishes scientific reliability of the test; judicial notice is inappropriate.

State v. Helms, 504 S.E.2d 293 (N.C. 1998): A proper foundation, such as expert testimony, is required for admissibility of HGN evidence.

State v. Murphy, 953 S.W.2d 2000 (Tenn. 1997): Expert testimony is required for admissibility of nystagmus evidence.

Salt Lake City v. Garcia, 912 P.2d 997 (Utah App. 1996): Nystagmus is admissible as another field sobriety test, given a foundation of the officer's training, experience, and observations.

State v. Zivcic, 598 N.W.2d 565 (Wis. App. 1999): HGN test evidence is admissible if the officer is properly qualified.

§11.5.5 Preliminary Breath Tests

Page 789. Add the following citation in the second line of the carryover paragraph, following the word "see":

Commonwealth v. Marshall, 824 A.2d 323 (Pa. Super. Ct. 2003);

Page 789. Add at the end of the third complete paragraph:

See also *Boyd v. City of Montgomery*, 472 So. 2d 694 (Ala. Ct. App. 1985).

Attorney John Tarantino of Providence, Rhode Island, points out that this is consistent with the decision in *Rock v. Arkansas*, 483 U.S. 44, 97 L. Ed. 2d 37 (1987) where the U.S. Supreme Court held that evidence of hypnosis offered by the defendant was admissible — even though not admissible if offered by the prosecution. The Court reasoned that prohibiting such evidence effectively precluded the defendant from presenting a defense. In other words, an accused's constitutional right to present evidence in his or her defense rises to a higher level than the prosecution's right to present evidence against the defendant, and thus the standards for admissibility should reflect this. For excellent discussions of the issue, read Mr. Tarantino's articles, Exculpatory Preliminary Breath Test Results, 14(7) The Champion 40 (1990) and Using Preliminary Breath Testing Results to Obtain an Acquittal, 3(9) DWI Journal 4 (1988).

§11.5.6 Videotapes, Audiotapes, and Photographs

Page 792. In third full paragraph, replace State v. Shaw *citation with:*

264 N.W.2d 397 (Minn. 1978)

§11.5.7 "Spoliation": Lost and Erased Tapes

Page 799. Add at end of section:

What if the defendant has made a demand for preservation or discovery before the tapes were lost, erased, or destroyed? In *State v. Benton*, 737 N.E.2d 1046 (Ohio App. 2000), involving erased DUI tapes, the court held that "where a defendant moves to have evidence preserved and that evidence is none theless destroyed by the state in accordance with its normal procedures, the appropriate remedy is to shift the burden to the state to show that the evidence was not exculpatory."

§11.6   Blood-Alcohol Evidence

§11.6.2   Defective Implied Consent Advisement

Page 803. In first full paragraph, replace Nelson et al. v. City of Irvine *citation with:*

143 F.3d 1196 (9th Cir. 1998)

Page 805. Add before last paragraph of subsection:

What if the suspect does not speak English? Language barriers sometimes make it difficult for officers to communicate the implied consent laws to a suspect. In *State v. Begicevic,* 678 N.W.2d 293 (Wis. Ct. App. 2004), the suspect immediately informed the officer that his primary language was Croatian and that he spoke some English and German. Despite this knowledge, the officer did not attempt to locate an interpreter and proceeded to convey the implied consent warnings in English. The Wisconsin Court of Appeals held that under these circumstances, the officer failed to use reasonable methods to reasonably inform the suspect of the implied consent warnings.

§11.6.3   Denial of Access to Counsel

Page 808. Delete first full paragraph and first sentence of second paragraph.

§11.6.4   Denial of Choice of Tests

Page 814. In second paragraph, replace Nelson et al. v. City of Irvine *citation with:*

143 F.3d 1196 (9th Circ. 1998)

§11.6.6   Forceful Seizure of Blood Sample: *Rochin — Schmerber*

Page 817. Add after fourth full paragraph:

Officers must have a clear indication that evidence of driving under the influence will be obtained by a forceful seizure of a blood sample. In *Duncan v. State,* 799 N.E.2d 538 (Ind. Ct. App. 2003), the defendant was forced to provide a blood sample following a fatal accident. The officer was unable to specifically describe his observations of intoxication. The court held:

> In making an exception to the warrant requirement in *Schmerber,* thereby allowing police to draw their own inferences, the Supreme Court held that probable cause must be *clearly* indicated, and that the officer in that case plainly had demonstrated probable cause through his testimony. Here, there is insufficient evidence of probable value to support the trial court's denial of [the defendant's] motion to suppress.

Duncan at 544.

Obviously, drawing of blood is considered a seizure that must comply with the Fourth Amendment of the federal Constitution. See *Schmerber v. California,* 384 U.S. 757, 767 (1966). In order for a warrantless, non-consensual removal of blood to be constitutional, there must be a finding of both probable cause and exigent circumstances. See, e.g., *State v. Aguirre,* 295 N.W.2d 79, 81 (Minn. 1980). In determining whether exigent circumstances are present, courts have considered factors such as the evanescent nature of alcohol in the blood, the passage of time, and the potential unavailability of a defendant once taken to a hospital for treatment. See *State v. Oevering,* 268 N.W.2d 68, 74 (Minn. 1978) (finding exigent circumstances because four hours had passed since the collision occurred and defendant was taken to the hospital where blood was drawn, and "normal physiological functions eliminate the alcohol content from an inebriate's blood"). The court's inquiry, however, may include an examination of the totality of the circumstances. See *State v. Lohnes,* 344 N.W.2d 605, 610 (Minn. 1984).

Page 818. Add after second full paragraph:

Similarly, in *State v. Worthington,* 65 P.3d 211 (Idaho Ct. App. 2003), the court held that the force was reasonable where the defendant was held down by three police officers and two nurses and handcuffed with a belly restraint:

> In the present case, it is our conclusion that the force used to draw a blood sample from Worthington did not violate constitutional

standards. Worthington was described as "very combative." All the evidence showed that the force used was necessary to restrain him so that a blood sample could be taken. The police did not strike Worthington or otherwise engage in violence or physical abuse. Worthington refused any less intrusive testing method, such as a breath test. We agree with the district court's conclusion that the force used was reasonable. *Id.* at 214–15.

Page 819. Add after first full paragraph:

Likewise, in *State v. Faust,* 672 N.W.2d 97 (Wis. Ct. App. 2003), after submitting to a breath test where the defendant registered a 0.09, in excess of the prohibited blood alcohol level, the officer requested the defendant to also submit to a blood test. Although the defendant refused to consent to a second test, a blood sample was forcibly taken. The officer acknowledged that he had no reason to believe that the defendant was under the influence of a controlled substance and did not request the test for the purpose of detecting the presence of controlled substances. Affirming the lower court's ruling to suppress the blood test results, the Wisconsin Court of Appeals held that "after an individual arrested on probable cause for drunk driving has provided a satisfactory and useable chemical test, the exigent circumstances justifying a warrantless and nonconsensual blood draw no longer exist." *Faust* at 102.

In light of the *Fiscalini* and *Faust* cases, both of which hailed from multiple-test states and ruled that a second, forced sample was inadmissible absent a search warrant, counsel should consider requesting the court to suppress any second sample. While such requests may ultimately result in an implied consent violation, the results of the second test may be inadmissible if obtained in violation of the defendant's right against an unreasonable search and seizure.

§11.6.7   The Physician-Patient Privilege (Blood)

Page 823. Delete first full paragraph.

Page 824. Delete last sentence of second full paragraph.

Page 825. Change citation in fourth full paragraph:

42 U.S.C. §290dd-2.

Page 825. Replace last sentence of fourth full paragraph with:

Subdivision (a) of that statute makes it a federal offense (42 U.S.C. §290dd-2(f)) to disclose, absent limited exceptions noted in subsection (b)(2), without the patient's consent

> records of the identity, diagnosis, prognosis, or treatment of any patient which are maintained in connection with the performance of any program or activity relating to substance abuse ... treatment, rehabilitation ... which is conducted, regulated, or directly or indirectly assisted by any department or agency of the United States....

Page 826. In last line of carryover paragraph, replace "substance abuse" with "alcohol abuse".

Page 826. Add before last paragraph of subsection:

What if the defendant was treated in State A, but prosecuted for DUI in State B? Does State B have to recognize the physician-patient privilege of State A? The Second District Appellate Court of Illinois examined this precise issue in *People v. Allen,* 784 N.E.2d 393 (Ill. App. Ct. 2d Dist. 2003). In *Allen,* the defendant was involved in an accident in Illinois, but transported to a hospital in Iowa, where he was treated and a blood sample was taken. The Iowa Code codifies the physician-patient privilege, while Illinois recognized an exception to the privilege for emergency medical treatment. The court applied the Restatement (Second) of Conflict of Laws, which provides:

> Evidence that is privileged under the local law of the state which has the most significant relationship with the communication but which is not privileged under the local law of the forum will be admitted unless there is some special reason why the forum policy favoring admission should not be given effect.

Allen at 394.

The court further looked to the Restatement, which provides the following four factors to be applied when determining whether such a special reason exists:

(1)   The number and nature of the contacts that the state of the forum has with the parties and with the transaction involved,

(2)   The relative materiality of the evidence that is sought to be excluded,

(3)   The kind of privilege involved, and

(4)   Fairness to the parties.

Id. at 395.

After applying the factors, the court found that the first two factors favored the admission of the test results and the latter two favored the defendant. Weighing all factors, the court held that the evidence should be admitted because it found no "special reason" to supersede the Illinois law.

§11.6.8   Noncompliance with Testing Regulations

Page 829. Add after first carryover paragraph:

In *People v. Hanna*, 773 N.E.2d 178 (Ill. App. Ct. 5th Dist. 2002), the court affirmed the suppression of the breath test results because the Breathalyzer machines had not been properly tested by the Illinois Department of Public Health, as required by Illinois regulations. While the State argued that the machines had been tested and approved by the National Highway Traffic Safety Administration, the court found that the language of the regulation was unambiguous and did not allow reliance on the testing conducted by NHTSA.

Page 833. Add after carryover paragraph:

In *State v. Burnside*, 797 N.E.2d 71 (Ohio 2003), the Supreme Court of Ohio held that the State's failure to produce evidence of compliance with regulations requiring a solid anticoagulant in the tube when procuring a blood sample was not a de minimis error and failed to meet the substantial compliance standard. The court rejected the State's argument that the blood alcohol test should be admissible because the use of the anticoagulant was not necessary to ensure the reliability of the test, recognizing that

> [t]his argument is properly directed not to us but to the Director of Health, whose charge it is to promulgate regulations that will ensure the reliability of alcohol-tests results. To hold otherwise would be to speculate, with neither the requisite expertise nor the statutory authority, whether the failure to use a solid anticoagu-lant affected the reliability of the alcohol-test results in the instant case.

Burnside at 78.

Note: Counsel should always consider a foundational chal-lenge to any blood test where the sample was taken at a medical facility. If the blood was simply turned over to law enfor-cement authorities, there may not have been any preservative or anticoagulant in the vial; it is common practice to analyze the blood at the hospital and so standard hospital procedures do not usually require such additives. If the blood was analyzed at the hospital, an argument can possibly be made that the addition of preservative and anticoagulant is still required — that is, that no exceptions in the regulations exist for medical analysis. Further, blood analyzed at a hospital is done for the purpose of assisting the physician in assessing the patient's condition, not for determining blood-alcohol concentration. Consequently, the blood sample is centrifuged — the liquid (serum or plasma) is separated from the solid — and the liquid portion alone is ana-lyzed. Because alcohol is suspended in the liquid, not in the solids, the sample is smaller — but contains the same amount of alcohol. The result: a larger percentage of alcohol (somewhere around 15 percent or more higher BAC). See §7.0.4. This casts doubt on the accuracy of the BAC result, but also provides grounds for a foundational challenge as to admissibility on *Frye/Daubert* grounds: Analysis of blood using centrifuged plasma/serum is a widely accepted medical technique — but not for precise alcohol analysis. Put another way, the test result may be *impeachable* because it may be 15 percent high, but it may also be *inadmissible* because it is not scientifically accepted for the purpose for which it is offered.

Page 834. Add at end of third full paragraph:

This decision was subsequently reversed and remanded with instruction to apply a harmless error standard of review, and on remand the court reached the same conclusion under that standard. *Atkinson v. State,* 934 S.W.2d 896 (Tex. App. 1996).

§11.6.9   Lack of Pre-Test Observation Period (Breath)

Page 835. Insert at beginning of section:

A breath test is generally considered invalid if the subject burps, belches, regurgitates, etc., within 15 to 20 minutes prior to providing a sample. To avoid this contamination of the breath sample, the officer is required to keep him under observation for this period of time. The majority of jurisdictions, however, view noncompliance with this requirement as going to the weight of the evidence rather than to its admissibility — that is, the lack of observation can be raised in cross-examination to discredit the results of the test but it cannot be the basis for exclusion of the results.

Some states, however, view this pre-test procedure as sufficiently important that non-compliance will affect the test's admissibility. In *State v. Gardner,* 967 P.2d 465 (N.M. App. 1998), for example, the arrestee was permitted to go to the bathroom alone about 15 or 20 minutes before the test; the officer watched her continuously thereafter. In reversing the trial court, the appellate court held that "the test results were improperly admitted into evidence due to the violation, by as much as five minutes, of the twenty-minute continuous observation period." The court specifically rejected the "goes to the weight" argument, held that no showing of prejudice was required, refused to accept the state's argument that the doctrine of "substantial compliance" should be applied, and found the error was not clearly "harmless."

Counsel may encounter the prevalent practice of arresting officers including the transportation of the arrestee to the station as part of the pre-test "observation" period — despite the obvious difficulties in trying to constantly "observe" a suspect handcuffed in the back seat while trying to concentrate on the road ahead. For an example of this increasingly common practice, see *State v. Carson*, 988 P.2d 225 (Idaho App. 1999), where

> ... Officer Miller testified that he had conducted the necessary observation while transporting Carson.... According to Miller, he placed Carson in the backseat of the passenger side of the police cruiser and turned on a light over the rear door so that Carson was illuminated. He also handcuffed Carson's hands behind his back so that he could not place anything in his mouth. As Officer Miller drove to the Washington County Sheriff's office, he intermittently observed Carson in the rearview mirror and listened for any indication of belching or regurgitation. Miller testified that, because of the late hour, he encountered no other traffic on the road and his police radio was quiet throughout the trip. Under examination by Carson's counsel, however, Officer Miller acknowledged that during the drive rain was falling and the vehicle's windshield wipers were operating. He also acknowledged that he wore a hearing aid in his left ear.... [988 P.2d 226.]

The trial court admitted the breath evidence, finding there was compliance with the 15-minute observation requirement because the arrestee remained in the officer's immediate presence and the officer was able to drive the vehicle and observe the arrestee simultaneously. The appellate court reversed this denial of the suppression motion:

> ... Officer Miller's attention necessarily was devoted primarily to driving.... Evidence presented at the hearing and common experience tell us that the officer's ability to use his hearing as a substitute for visual observation was impeded by noise from the automobile engine, tires on the road surface, rain and windshield wipers.... In our view, the State's foundational evidence did not demonstrate a mode of observation that would be likely to detect belching, regurgitation into the mouth, or the like.... 988 P.2d 227.

Faced with a similar fact pattern, a California court reached an opposite conclusion. In *Manriquez v. Gourley*, 130 Cal. Rptr. 2d 209 (Cal. 4th Dist. Ct. App. 2003), the officer testified that during the 15-minute observation period, the defendant was confined to the back of the police car and did not eat, drink, smoke, or vomit.

He further testified that while driving, he watched the defendant and engaged him in conversation and that before administering the breath test, he asked the defendant if he had burped in the last 20 minutes. The court held that continuous observation under the regulations does not require an officer to keep his or her eyes focused on the defendant during the entire observation period.

> Observation is not limited to perception by sight; an officer may perceive a subject has eaten, drank [sic], smoked, vomited or regurgitated by sound or smell and the perception by senses other than sight can be sufficient to comply with the regulation. Further, the regulation should be interpreted with reference to its purpose, which is to determine whether the test subject has smoked, ingested food or drink, or suffered physical symptoms that would adversely affect the test results. In our view, uninterrupted eye contact is not necessary (and may not always be sufficient by itself) to determine whether the proscribed events have occurred, so long as the officer remains present with the subject and able by the use of all his or her senses to make that determination.

Manriquez at 216.

If the officer is not able to type without looking at the keyboard, an obvious line of questioning can be developed to show the officer could not have observed your client for the requisite waiting period to ensure your client did not burp, belch, etc., by questioning the officer about the information he was required to type into the device prior to obtaining the breath sample. Of course, counsel will need to be familiar with the protocol of the machine that was used. An example follows:

Q. Officer, when you arrived at the police station, you were seated about 10 feet away from my client?
A. Yes.
Q. You were filling out paperwork during that time, weren't you?
A. I was talking to the defendant. If he said anything, I would jot it down, but I was watching him.
Q. You were watching him?
A. As far as my eye contact, I was watching the defendant while we were there.
Q. And you were listening to him?
A. Yes.

Q. And you were taking notes?

A. Yes, if it was something worthy of note-taking, I did.

Q. After watching the defendant for 20 minutes while you took notes, you got up and left this room?

A. Yes, we went to another room to administer the breath test.

Q. You have to leave the roll call room?

A. Yes.

Q. You went down the hall?

A. Yes.

Q. How many rooms down is the room where the breath test machine is located?

A. About three rooms down.

Q. How far was it for you to get from where you and my client were originally seated to the hallway?

A. Probably 10 to 12 feet.

Q. When you reached the hallway, did you turn?

A. You come out of the roll call room and you turn left.

Q. You turned left and walked how many feet?

A. From there to the third shift office, 20 or 25 feet, somewhere around there.

Q. It is three offices down, right?

A. Our station is not that big, sir.

Q. Then, which way did you turn into the room?

A. Left.

Q. Then how far to where the machine was located?

A. About 5 feet.

Q. Who was walking in front and who was walking behind?

A. I was walking behind the suspect—

Q. Okay.

A. And Officer Smith, I think, was in front. I'm not real sure, but I know I was right behind him.

Q. As you were walking out of the roll call room, turning left, walking down the hallway, turning left again and telling my client to have a seat, you weren't watching his mouth, were you?

A. No.

Q. Then you got to the breath test machine and you asked my client to have a seat behind the table, right?

A. After I removed his cuffs and put them in front, yes.

Q. He was cooperative with you, wasn't he, sir?

A. Yes.

Q. After removing the handcuffs, you sat him down?

A. Yes.

Q. Then you went over to the breath test machine, right?

A. Right.

Q. This machine was an Intoximeter EC/IR, correct?

A. Yes.

Q. On this Intoximeter EC/IR, was does the EC/IR stand for?

A. I know the name of the machine, but as far as the exact words, I'm sorry.

Q. You don't know?

A. The exact words? No, I don't.

Q. Okay. Now, this is a computer, right?

A. Yes, sir.

Q. This computer has a display on it?

A. Yes.

Q. What does that display say on it?

A. It's got a little screen down there that tells you that the machine has to be purged and blanked. Then you put the information in — type the information after it purges and blanks itself.

Q. Right, but the first thing you have to do, though, when you sit down is press "ENTER," in order for it to start, right?

A. Right.

Q. Then the screen came up and it said "SUBJECT NAME"?

A. Right.

Q. And then you had to type it in?

A. Yes, sir.

Q. You typed my client's name, right?

A. Yes, sir.

Q. You didn't know how to spell his name, did you?

A. After I got the "run back" on his name, I did, sir.

Q. Okay, you had to look at it?

A. Yes.

Q. Was it on a piece of paper?

A. Right.

Q. So, you had to look at the piece of paper?

A. Yes.

Q. And then you had to type it in?

A. Yes, sir.

Q. Are you what we call a touch typist, where you can type without looking at the keyboard?

A. Short words, yes; but long words, no.

Q. My client's name is not a short word, is it, sir?

A. No.

Q. So, you had to look at the keyboard while you were typing it in, didn't you, sir?

A. Yes, sir.

Q. You had to type in his full name, didn't you?
A. Yes.
Q. After you typed in his name, another screen popped up and it said "SUBJECT DATE OF BIRTH"?
A. Right.
Q. And you had to type in the birth date?
A. Yes, sir.
Q. And then you had to hit "ENTER" again to get to the next screen?
A. Yes.
Q. When the next screen popped up, it said "SUBJECT DRIVER'S LICENSE NUMBER"?
A. Yes, sir.
Q. Then you had to look at another piece of paper to get the driver's license number, didn't you?
A. Yes, sir.
Q. And then you typed in the driver's license number?
A. Yes.
Q. You weren't looking at my client when you typed in his name, were you, sir?
A. No, sir, I wasn't.
Q. And you weren't looking at him when you typed in his date of birth, were you?
A. No, sir.
Q. And you weren't looking at him when you typed in his driver's license number, were you, sir?
A. No, sir.
Q. After you hit "ENTER" after the driver's license number, another screen popped up, didn't it?
A. Yes, sir.
Q. The screen stated "ARRESTED" and you had to put in the time, correct?
A. Yes, sir.
Q. You had to type that in, didn't you?
A. Yes.
Q. You didn't look at my client when you typed that in, did you, sir?
A. No, sir.
Q. After all of those screens, you had to hit "ENTER" again?
A. Yes, sir.
Q. You had to then put in your name?
A. Yes.
Q. Now, you know your name, but you still had to look at the keyboard, didn't you, sir?
A. Right.

Q. Then you had to hit "ENTER" again?

A. Yes.

Q. That was so you could verify whether the data was correct or whether you needed to go back and edit it, right?

A. Yes, sir.

Q. And you hit "Y," so you could enter that, right?

A. Yes, sir.

Q. And then there was a diagnostic check, right?

A. Right, sir.

Q. You had to hit "ENTER" so it would do the diagnostic check?

A. Yes.

Q. Then for about 30 to 60 seconds, it runs this check?

A. It will purge itself out, yes, sir.

Q. No, not for the purge. The diagnostic check?

A. Yes, sir.

Q. Because only after the diagnostic check can it purge?

A. Yes.

Q. After the diagnostic check, you had to hit "ENTER" again, so it would start purging?

A. Yes.

Q. While it was purging, you had to watch it to make sure it was purging right?

A. Yes, sir.

Q. You had to watch the screen, didn't you?

A. Yes, sir.

Q. And during that time, you weren't watching my client, were you?

A. No, sir, I was not.

Q. After it purged, it came up and ran at least one blank check, right?

A. Right, sir.

Q. It may run two, right?

A. It may, yes.

Q. It's automatic, correct?

A. Yes.

Q. And when the blank check came up, you had to look at the screen to make sure that the blank was accurate?

A. Right, sir.

Q. And when that happened, you were not looking at my client, were you?

A. Not at that point in time, no, sir.

Q. Then after the blank came up there was another screen, and it said "PLEASE BLOW," right?

A. Yes, sir.

Q. It's only at that point that my client blew into the machine, right?
A. Yes, sir.
Q. And then the machine evaluated the sample and you got a printout?
A. Yes, sir.

§11.6.10 Denial of Independent Sample

Page 841. Add after last full paragraph:

Not all states are so careful to protect a suspect's right to an independent test. For instance, in *State v. Greeley*, 834 A.2d 1016 (N.J. 2003), after submitting to a breath test, the defendant requested an independent blood test. He was informed that the test could be performed by a doctor or local hospital, but that he could be released only into the custody of a friend or family member. The defendant attempted to reach someone to assist him, but since he was from out of state, he was unsuccessful. Police officers made no alternate arrangements for the defendant to obtain an independent test and released him four hours later.

The New Jersey Supreme Court held that the defendant's right to an independent test was not violated by the police department's policy to release the defendant only to the custody of a friend or relative.

> A police policy of releasing a DWI arrestee only to a responsible relative or friend is reasonable in light of the risks posed by an intoxicated person to himself and the public. In the absence of such a policy, so long as a defendant is informed of the right to an independent test, police conduct will warrant suppression of BAC test results only if that conduct affirmatively interferes with or thwarts a defendant's good-faith attempt to obtain an independent test.

Greeley at 1020.

Page 843. Add at end of first carryover paragraph:

See also *Commonwealth v. Long*, 118 S.W.3d 178 (Ky. Ct. App. 2003).

* Reprinted with permission.

§11.6.11   Noncompliance with Discovery

Pages 845–846. Delete text beginning with second sentence of last paragraph and ending with carryover paragraph on page 846.

Page 846. In first sentence of first full paragraph, replace "In a similar vein" with "On this issue."

§11.6.12   Chain of Custody

Page 852. Add new section after checklist:

§11.7   The Suppression Motion

The laws and pleading requirements concerning motions to suppress evidence vary widely from state to state. Usually, there will be a focus on one issue, such as the lack of probable cause to stop the client, and extensive argument and case law will be presented. The following sample motion, however, represents an "omnibus" approach applicable with some modification to most jurisdictions: a succinct yet comprehensive motion addressing a broad number of typical pretrial issues in a DUI case — addressing *both* suppression *and* discovery. The motion, authored by Douglas Cowan of Bellevue, Washington,* should keep any prosecutor busy for some time.

---

* Reprinted with permission.

IN THE KING COUNTY DISTRICT COURT
BELLEVUE DIVISION, STATE OF WASHINGTON

STATE OF WASHINGTON,	))	NO. 123456
Plaintiff,	))	
vs.	)	
DEFENDANT,	)	DEFENDANT'S PRETRIAL
Defendant.	)	MOTIONS AND ORDERS
	)	THEREON
	)	**NOTE FOR MOTION HEARING**

COMES NOW the Defendant, DEFENDANT, by and through his attorney, and hereby files for hearing the following motions:

I. SUPPRESSION/DISMISSAL.

1. Mandatory Filing

To dismiss based on the failure to comply with mandatory filing requirements of CrRLJ 2.1(d)(1) and (2), *State v. Greenwood*, 120 Wash. 2d 585 (1993) and *Seattle v. Bonifacio*, 127 Wash. 2d 482 (1995).

Motion is: granted _____
denied _____
reserved _____

2. Portable Breath Test

To suppress any breath test results performed on a portable breath test machine. *Frye v. United States*, 293 F.2d 1013 (D.C. Cir. 1923); *Seattle v. Peterson*, 39 Wash. App. 524 (1985); *State v. Cauthron*, 120 Wash. 2d 879 (1993); *State v. Riker*, 123 Wash. 2d 351 (1994); *Bokor v. Department of Licensing*, 74 Wash. App. 523 (1994); RCW 46.61.506(3).

Motion is: granted _____
denied _____
reserved _____

3. Gaze Nystagmus

To suppress the results of any nystagmus "gaze test" adminis-tered to the Defendant in this matter. *Frye v. United States*, 293 F.2d 1013 (D.C. Cir. 1923); *Seattle v. Peterson*, 39 Wash. App.

524 (1985); *State v. Cissne,* 72 Wash. App. 677 (1994); RCW
46.61.605(3).

Motion is: granted   _____
            denied   _____
            reserved _____

4. Speed Measuring Device

To suppress all evidence gathered following the use of any
speed measuring device (SMD) and/or as a basis for the stop of
the defendant. *Frye v. United States,* 293 F.2d 1013 (D.C. Cir.
1923); *Seattle v. Peterson,* 39 Wash. App. 524 (1985); *State v.
Cauthron,* 120 Wash. 2d. 879 (1993); *State v. Riker,* 123 Wash.
2d 351 (1994); CrRLJ 6.13(d).

Motion is: granted   _____
            denied   _____
            reserved _____

5. SMD Certificates

For production of an electronic speed measuring device
(SMD) expert at motions and trial herein and objects to the
admission of any certificate or affidavit in lieu of live testimony
concerning the design, operation or construction of any such
speed measuring device at motions hearing or trial. CrRLJ 6.13.

Motion is: granted   _____
            denied   _____
            reserved _____

6. Pupil Dilation

To suppress any testimony regarding pupil dilation and/or
reaction to light observations. *Frye v. United States,* 293 F.2d
1013 (D.C. Cir. 1923); *Seattle v. Peterson,* 39 Wash. App. 524
(1985); *State v. Cauthron,* 120 Wash. 2d. 879 (1993); *State v.
Riker,* 123 Wash. 2d 351 (1994).

Motion is: granted   _____
            denied   _____
            reserved _____

7. Probable Cause

To suppress evidence based on a violation of RCW 46.64.015,
RCW 46.61.021 and Art. 1, §7 of the Washington State
Constitution in that there was a lack of probable cause to stop,
detain, or arrest the defendant herein. *Terry v. Ohio,* 392 U.S. 1

(1968); *State v. Thornton,* 41 Wash. App. 506 (1985); *State v. Michaels,* 60 Wash. 2d 638 (1962); CrRLJ 3.6.

> Motion is: granted _____
>   denied   _____
>   reserved _____

8. Consent to FSTs

To suppress physical tests for failure to obtain a valid consent from the defendant prior to the administration of said tests. *Seattle v. Personeus,* 63 Wash. App. 461 (1991); *Seattle v. Mesiani,* 110 Wash. 2d 454 (1988).

> Motion is: granted _____
>   denied   _____
>   reserved _____

9. Admissibility of FSTs

To suppress all evidence obtained in the course of "field sobriety" or other physical agility tests administered to the Defendant herein. Washington Const. Art. 1, § 7; U.S. Const. Amend. IV, *Frye v. United States,* 293 F.2d 1013 (D.C. Cir. 1923); *Seattle v. Peterson,* 39 Wash. App. 524 (1985); *State v. Cauthron,* 120 Wash. 2d. 879 (1993); *State v. Riker,* 123 Wash. 2d. 351 (1994).

> Motion is: granted _____
>   denied   _____
>   reserved _____

10. Testimonial FSTs

To suppress those physical tests which were testimonial in nature, not preceded by Miranda Warnings. CrRLJ 3.5 and *Pennsylvania v. Muniz,* 110 S. Ct. 2638, 110 L. Ed. 2d 528 (1990).

> Motion is: granted _____
>   denied   _____
>   reserved _____

11. Corpus Delicti

To dismiss the charge on the grounds that the prosecution is unable to prove the required element of identification of the defendant as the driver, in that there is insufficient evidence of the *corpus delicti* of the crime independent of the defendant's statements, pursuant to *State v. Hamrick,* 19 Wash. App. 417 (1978), et al.; *Bremerton v. Corbett,* 106 Wash. 2d 569 (1986).

Motion is: granted ＿＿＿＿＿
                         denied ＿＿＿＿＿
                         reserved ＿＿＿＿＿

12. Defendant's Statements

To suppress all statements attributed to the defendant at the time of arrest. *Edwards v. Arizona,* 451 U.S. 477 (1981); *State v. Johnson,* 48 Wash. App. 681 (1987), and for a pretrial hearing pursuant to CrRLJ 3.5.

Motion is: granted ＿＿＿＿＿
                         denied ＿＿＿＿＿
                         reserved ＿＿＿＿＿

13. Right to Counsel

To dismiss or, in the alternative, suppress evidence due to violation of the right to counsel based on Wash. Const. Art. 1, §22; U.S. Const. Amend. VI; *State v. Fitzsimmons,* 93 Wash. 2d 436 (1980); *Arizona v. Holland,* 711 P.2d 592 (1985); and *Spokane v. Kruger,* 116 Wash. 2d 135 (1991); *State v. Prok,* 107 Wash. 2d 153 (1986); *Seattle v. Box,* 29 Wash. App. 109 (1981); *Seattle v. Koch,* 53 Wash. App. 352 (1991), *State v. Easter,* 130 Wash. 2d 228 (1996).

Motion is: granted ＿＿＿＿＿
                         denied ＿＿＿＿＿
                         reserved ＿＿＿＿＿

14. Refusal

To suppress any alleged refusal to perform any test pursuant to ER 403 and *State v. Long,* 113 Wash. 2d. 266, (1989); *State v. Parker,* 16 Wash. App. 632 (1976); *Seattle v. Personeus,* 63 Wash. App. 461 (1991) and *Seattle v. Loyd Stalsbroten,* COA#40677-9-I (Div. One May 26, 1998).

Motion is: granted ＿＿＿＿＿
                         denied ＿＿＿＿＿
                         reserved ＿＿＿＿＿

15. Implied Element

To dismiss the charges and/or suppress the breath test on the grounds of the State's inability to establish the "Implied Element" of non-consumption of alcohol following the time of driving per *State v. Crediford,* 130 Wash. 2d 747 (1996).

Motion is: granted ＿＿＿＿＿
                         denied ＿＿＿＿＿
                         reserved ＿＿＿＿＿

16. Implied Consent Warnings
To suppress the breath test on the grounds of failure to comply with the requirements of RCW 46.20.308 (Implied Consent Warnings).

Motion is: granted _____
denied _____
reserved _____

17. Implied Consent/Erroneous Warnings
To suppress the breath test results on the grounds that the Implied Consent Warnings read to the defendant were erroneous and inaccurate in that no probationary license is conferred upon minors following a test result of .02 or above, pursuant to *State v. Bartels*, 112 Wash. 2d 882 (1989); *Spokane v. Holmberg*, 50 Wash. App. 317, (1987), *Cooper v. DOL*, 61 Wash. App. 525 (1991).

Motion is: granted _____
denied _____
reserved _____

18. Implied Consent/Additional Language
To suppress results of the breath test on the grounds of inclusion of additional advisements in violation of the requirements of RCW 46.61.308 and the holdings of *State v. Bartels*, 112 Wash. 2d 882 (1989); *Spokane v. Holmberg*, 50 Wash. App. 317 (1987) and *Cooper v. DOL*, 61 Wash. App. 525 (1991); *State v. Bostrom*, 127 Wash. 2d 580 (1995).

Motion is: granted _____
denied _____
reserved _____

19. Improper Breath Test Procedure
To suppress the breath test for failure to follow the requirements of the Washington Administrative Code (WAC 448-13 *et seq.*) and the protocols established by the Washington State Toxicologist.

Motion is: granted _____
denied _____
reserved _____

20. Independent Tests
To dismiss for interference with Defendant's right to obtain an independent test. RCW 46.20.308 and *Blaine v. Suess*, 93 Wash. 2d 722 (1980).

Motion is: granted   _____
denied   _____
reserved   _____

21. Simulator Solution

To suppress breath test for failure to comply with the requirements of the Washington Administrative Code (WAC 448.13 *et seq.*) and the protocols established by the Washington State Toxicologist. WAC 448-13.

Motion is: granted   _____
denied   _____
reserved   _____

22. Defective Charging Document

To dismiss based on a defective charging document. *Auburn v. Brooke,* 119 Wash. 2d 623 (1992); *State v. Leach,* 113 Wash. 2d 679 (1989); *State v. Kjorsvik,* 117 Wash. 2d 93 (1991).

Motion is: granted   _____
denied   _____
reserved   _____

23. Insufficient Evidence

To dismiss for lack of facts sufficient to support a finding of guilt beyond a reasonable doubt of all elements necessary to convict the defendant of the charge(s) pending herein. *State v. Knapstad,* 107 Wash. 2d 346 (1986).

Motion is: granted   _____
denied   _____
reserved   _____

24. 3.1 Motion

To dismiss, or in the alternative, suppress based on a violation of the right to counsel based on CrRLJ 3.1.

Motion is: granted   _____
denied   _____
reserved   _____

25. Double Jeopardy

Motion to dismiss based on the statute's violation of double jeopardy in violation of Wash. Const. Art. 1, §9, and U.S. Const. Amend. V.

Motion is: granted   _____
denied   _____
reserved   _____

II. DISCOVERY MOTIONS

1. 911 Tapes, etc.
To compel production of any recording, video tape, or tape recordings, including any radio transmissions between officers and dispatch, between officers, or 911 tapes, or to issue a subpoena duces tecum for same.

Motion is: granted _____

denied _____

reserved _____

2. Documentary Materials
To compel disclosure of those evidentiary materials and documents set forth in defendant's Demand for Discovery previously filed herein. CrRLJ 4.7;*State v. Dunnivan*, 65 Wash. App 728 (1992); CrRLJ 4.7(a)(d).

Motion is: granted _____

denied _____

reserved _____

3. Police Reports/Field Notes
To compel production of any and all police or investigative reports, including field notes made by the involved officers, and statements of all potential witnesses, including production of *all* documentation of results of physical or mental examinations and/or scientific tests, experiments, or comparisons made in connection with the charge pending against the Defendant. CrRIJ 4.7 and *State v. Campbell*, 103 Wash. 2d 1 (1984).

Motion is: granted _____

denied _____

reserved _____

4. DataMaster Records
To compel production of all documents and records of certifications, evaluations, maintenance, repairs, and telephone complaints for the DataMaster machine in question. RCW 46.61.506(6) and CrRLJ 4.7(d).

Motion is: granted _____

denied _____

reserved _____

5. Radio Frequency Interference
To compel disclosure of any information regarding presence of radios, microwaves, short waves, CB's, and any other transmitters

or other such devices at or near the location of the DataMaster at the time of the test.

Motion is: granted _____
            denied _____
            reserved _____

6. Widmark's Formula

To compel disclosure of whether or not the prosecution intends to offer testimony regarding "retrograde extrapolation," or "Widmark's Formula," and, if so, to compel disclosure of the name(s) of the expert witness(es), his/her credentials, qualifications, education, training and experience, and disclosure of any documents, studies, reports, or other materials relied on or material to any aspect of such testimony, and for a summary of their testimony. RCW 46.61.506, CrRLJ 4.7(d).

Motion is: granted _____
            denied _____
            reserved _____

7. Identity of Experts

To compel disclosure of the identity of the specific breath test technician, simulator solution changer, and state toxicology lab technician the prosecution intends to call at trial, the subject of their testimony, the basis of their expertise, including qualification, education, training and experience, and disclosure of any reports, documents, or studies upon which they intend to rely or make reference to in any aspect of their testimony. CrRLJ 4.7(d).

Motion is: granted _____
            denied _____
            reserved _____

8. DataMaster Operator's Manual

To compel production of a copy of the BAC Verifier DataMaster Operator's Manual of the officer who administered the breath test, and any manual received or used by the officer who administered field tests, during training for administration of same or for issuance of subpoena duces tecum for said manuals for trial.

Motion is: granted _____
            denied _____
            reserved _____

9. Subpoena Duces Tecum

For issuance of a Subpoena Duces Tecum directed to the Communications Division, Washington State Patrol Breath Test Section or any other applicable division or person within the Washington State Patrol for production of all records of complaints of malfunctions, operator error, or other communication in the Patrol's possession concerning operation of the BAC Verifier DataMaster used to test the Defendant's breath herein, CrRLJ 4.8(b).

Motion is: granted _____
denied _____
reserved _____

10. Expert/Breath or Blood Test

For discovery of the identity of any state expert witness concerning evidence of the defendant's alleged breath or blood alcohol concentration. U.S. Constitution, Fourth and Fourteenth Amendments, Washington Constitution, Art. 1 §3. *State v. Dunnivan,* 65 Wash. App. 728 (1992), CrRLJ 4.7.

Motion is: granted _____
denied _____
reserved _____

11. Expert Physiological Effects

For discovery of the identity of any state expert witness concerning evidence of the physiological effects of alcohol or any drug on the defendant's ability to operate a motor vehicle. U.S. Constitution, Fourth and Fourteenth Amendments; Washington Constitution, Art. 1 §3, *State v. Dunnivan,* 65 Wash. App. 728 (1992), CrRLJ 4.7.

Motion is: granted _____
denied _____
reserved _____

12. Expert's Credentials

Defendant requests discovery of the education and training of any expert witness the prosecution intends to offer, both general and specific to the subject of his or her testimony, experience relative to the operation, maintenance, and theory of the instrument used to test the defendant's blood or breath, or simulator solution and a description of the place, date, and subject matter of all training taken by said witnesses regarding the instrument in question or the effects of alcohol or drugs on the human body and a full description of any experiments in which said witnesses have participated or about which he or she may testify, and any documents, studies, reports or other materials relied on or material to any aspect of his or her testimony.

Motion is: granted _____

denied _____

reserved _____

13. Objection to Certificates

Defendant hereby notes an objection to proof of any material fact at hearing or trial by affidavit or certificate. A certified BAC Verifier DataMaster technician *and* the person(s) who conducted any quality assurance tests as well as the person(s) responsible for preparing, storing and installing the simulator solution concerned herein **IS HEREBY DEMANDED AT HEARING OR TRIAL,** including any and all records pertaining to the preparation, checking and installation of the simulator solution used in this case, including the gas chromatograph charts regarding the solution in accordance with CrRLJ 6.13 and RCW 46.61.506(6), along with a copy of his or her permit.

Motion is: granted _____

denied _____

reserved _____

IT IS HEREBY ORDERED, ADJUDGED AND DECREED that the prosecution shall comply with all granted motions to compel no later than 4 p.m. on the ____ day of _____, 199__.

DONE IN OPEN COURT this ____ day of _____, 199__.

_____
JUDGE

Presented by:

_____
DOUGLAS COWAN
Attorney for Defendant
WSBA# 2146

IV

TRIAL

13

CROSS-EXAMINATION

§13.0   The Arresting Officer

§13.0.4   Undermining the Field Sobriety Tests

Page 926. Add after fifth full paragraph:

In considering the defendant's emotional state at the time of the field sobriety tests, the jury should be made clearly aware of the *psycho-physiological effects of anxiety* on test performance. The following materials, provided the author from noted DUI practitioner Steven Oberman of Knoxville, Tennessee,* present the issue clearly:

———————

One factor that is not given enough attention, in the opinion of the author, is the role of anxiety on a person's ability to perform the field sobriety tests satisfactorily. This is not discussed in much detail in the NHSTA manuals, but is assumed to have been considered, at least to some extent, in the underlying research for the standardized tests. We may all recall from our schooling that the human autonomic nervous system is divided into two divisions, the sympathetic and the parasympathetic.

An easy way to remember the most important roles of the two autonomic nervous system divisions is to think of the parasympathetic division as the "D" (Digesting, Defecation, and Diuresis (Urination)) division, and the sympathetic division as the

———————

*Reprinted with permission.

"E"(Exercise, Excitement, Emergency, and Embarrassment) division.[1]

The sympathetic division is often referred to as the "fight-or-flight" system.[2] Its activity is evident when we are excited or when we find ourselves in an emergency or threatening situation.[3] When this threat or emergency is perceived by the individual, the hypothalamus stimulates the sympathetic fibers as the body prepares for "fight-or-flight."[4] Within a few minutes, the chemicals epinephrine and norepinephrine are released, which cause the anxiety to be manifested through a person's verbal responses, as well as clinical signs, which include perspiration, tremulousness, and rapid pulse and breathing.[5] Equally characteristic are changes in brain wave patterns and in the electrical resistance of the skin (galvanic skin resistance), which are events that are frequently recorded during polygraph examinations.[6] When the body is activated to this "fight-or-flight" status by some short-term stressor or emergency, the sympathetic nervous system is mobilized, causing blood to be diverted from temporarily non-essential organs to the brain, heart, and skeletal muscles.[7] This results in the exhibition of the anxiety symptoms.

Anxiety is a psychological response to stressors that have both physiologic and psychologic components. Anxiety results when a person perceives a threat to the self, either physically or psychogically (such as self-esteem, body image, or identity). The level of anxiety engendered and its manifestations depend on the individual's maturity, understanding of need, level of self-esteem, and coping mechanisisms.[8] The behavioral reactions to anxiety are

---

[1] Elaine N. Marieb, R.N., Ph.D., Human Anatomy and Physiology, 463 (3d ed. 1995).

[2] Elaine N. Marieb, R.N., Ph.D., Human Anatomy and Physiology, 463 (3d ed. 1995).

[3] Elaine N. Marieb, R.N., Ph.D., Human Anatomy and Physiology, 463 (3d ed. 1995).

[4] Judith Haber, Ph.D, RN, CS, FAAN, et al., Comprehensive Psychiatric Nursing, 166 (5th ed. 1997).

[5] Judith Haber, Ph.D, RN, CS, FAAN, et al., Comprehensive Psychiatric Nursing, 166 (5th ed. 1997).

[6] Elaine N. Marieb, R.N., Ph.D., Human Anatomy and Physiology, 463 (3d ed. 1995).

[7] Elaine N. Marieb, R.N., Ph.D., Human Anatomy and Physiology, 570 (3d ed. 1995).

[8] Medical-Surgical Nursing, 172 (Wilma J. Phipps, Ph.D., R.N., FAAN, et al. eds., 5th ed. 1995).

influenced by psychosocial-cultural factors, basic personality development, past experiences, values, and economic status.[9]

While mild anxiety may result in increased alertness, anxiety can increase to a stage where the subject would suffer from the recognized psychological signs of anxiety such as decreased attention span, decreased ability to follow directions, and increase in the number of questions, and need to seek reassurance.[10] Those who suffer from a severe stress response may actually exhibit immobility.[11] These are the very symptoms that may cause a person who is not under the influence to perform poorly on the standardized field sobriety tests.

Those who regularly practice in the field of DUI defense are aware of officers' frequent testimony that our clients were not acting normally because our client "wanted to fight," "couldn't understand the instructions for the field sobriety tests," "wouldn't shut up," or simply "wouldn't cooperate." In many instances, it is not an intoxicant that causes such behavior from the suspect, but it is rather the suspect's autonomic nervous system response to anxiety resulting from the stressor of the confrontation with the police and fear of going to jail. The changes in bodily functions that provide what the body considers to be optimal physiological conditions in response to the threat of incarceration may be the same factors that convince the officer that the driver is chemically impaired.[12]

§13.2 Illustrative Cross-Examination of Arresting Officer

Page 989. Add at end of section:

The following represents an excellent illustration of an effective cross-examination of the officer, particularly as to field sobriety tests. The examination, modeled largely after the tactics

[9] Medical-Surgical Nursing, 172 (Wilma J. Phipps, Ph.D., R.N., FAAN, et al. eds., 5th ed. 1995).
[10] Medical-Surgical Nursing, 174 (Wilma J. Phipps, Ph.D., R.N., FAAN, et al. eds., 5th ed. 1995).
[11] Medical-Surgical Nursing, 174 (Wilma J. Phipps, Ph.D., R.N., FAAN, et al. eds., 5th ed. 1995).
[12] See Elaine N. Marieb, R.N., Ph.D., Human Anatomy and Physiology, 463 (3d ed. 1995).

and techniques presented in this book, is the work of noted DUI practitioner Mark Gardner of Cleveland, Ohio.*

The Polite Lead-In

Q. Officer, if I ask you any question that offends you, or make you feel uncomfortable, please let me know. Will you do that?
A. Yes.
Q. Now, is there any portion of your testimony, where you may have made a mistake, or may have innocently misled the jury, where in all fairness to you, you now want to correct?
A. No.

Importance of Not Guessing During Testimony

Q. Now Officer, you understand that this is a criminal trial, don't you?
A. Yes.
Q. And you understand the seriousness of the charge you've leveled against my client?
A. Yes.
Q. And because these charges are so serious, are you willing to promise now, before this jury, that you're going to testify to those things that you are 100 percent sure about?
A. Yes.
Q. So that you will not be guessing, or speculating or making any inferences. You are only going to testify to those things that you know for certain?
A. Yes.

Cop's Prior Experience at Testifying (Very Optional)

Q. Now, from looking at your uniform, it is obvious that you are a police officer. Correct?
A. Yes.
Q. And it is true that you attended a police academy or training school before you were allowed to become a police officer?
A. Yes.
Q. And at that academy, you studied a number of different subjects?
A. Yes.
Q. And one of those subjects was how to testify?
A. I believe so.

*Reprinted with permission.

Q. In fact, the course was how to testify convincingly so as to get the jury to believe you?

A. [Who cares what his answer is.]

Q. And part of this training was how to anticipate certain questions?

A. [Who cares what his answer is.]

Q. And how to respond to certain answers?

A. [Who cares what his answer is.]

Q. In fact, you were trained in a classroom setting how to present yourself as a believable-sounding witness?

A. [Who cares what his answer is.]

Q. Do you agree that your demeanor on the stand today is more polished than when you first started testifying?

A. [Who cares what his answer is.]

Q. And that's because you have had experience at testifying?

A. [Who cares.]

Cop's Memory of Events

Q. Is the night you arrested my client the first time you ever met him?

A. Yes.

Q. You did prepare an arrest report for your arrest of D?

A. Yes.

Q. I assume your report was prepared at around the time of your contact with my client as well as shortly thereafter?

A. Yes.

Q. Prior to testifying today, have you had an opportunity to review this report?

A. Yes.

Q. Has reading this report refreshed your memory, or do you need more time to review it?

A. I remember it well.

Q. Now concerning your memory, would you agree that your memory of the events that occurred that night were better at the time that you wrote the report than now, some three months later?

A. Maybe a bit.

Q. Well, could you tell me the average number of persons you ticket monthly?

A. Twenty.

Q. How about the number of persons you arrest for DUI?

A. Four.

Q. How about the name of the person you ticketed before you arrested D?

A. I don't recall.

Q. How about the name of the person you ticketed after D?

A. I don't recall.

Q. How about the name of the person you arrested for DUI before you arrested D?

A. Don't recall.

Q. How about the name of the person you arrested for DUI after you arrested D?

A. Don't recall.

Q. How about the total number of tickets written since you arrested D?

A. Don't know.

Q. How about the total number of DUI arrests since you arrested D?

A. Don't recall.

Q. Officer, will you admit to this jury that you have forgotten things in the past?

A. Sometimes.

Q. Will you also admit to this jury that you have sometimes incorrectly remembered some events in the past?

A. Rarely.

Q. Officer, isn't it a fact that you sometimes mix up the facts of one case with those of another case?

A. [Who cares what his answer is.]

If cop appears to be guessing as to anything, ask the following

Q. Is it true that you are just as sure about _____ as you are about my client being under the influence?

A. [Who cares what his answer is.]

Duty to Accurately Complete the Arrest Report

Q. Now concerning your report, you were taught at the police academy the reasons for filling out an arrest report, weren't you?

A. Yes.

Q. You were taught that you must fully and accurately complete the report so that, if a trial takes place some months after the arrest, you would be able to remember the details of the arrest, is this correct?

A. Yes.

Q. And the reason for this is that you were taught that observational evidence — first, could you explain to the jury what observations evidence is?

A. Blah, blah, blah.

Q. You were taught at the academy that observation evidence is shortlived evidence?

A. Yes.

Q. Another reason for fully completing this form is that the state's attorney may review your arrest report, evaluate the case, and develop an appropriate strategy to get a conviction?

A. Yes.

Q. At the academy, you were taught to include all significant and material information in your report?

A. Yes.

Q. When you reviewed your report, did you note any inaccuracies? Is there anything in the report you wish to change some three months after writing it?

A. No.

Q. Then may I presume that you properly discharged your duty and carefully and completely recorded all significant aspects of what you observed?

A. Yes.

Q. Then, after reviewing your report this morning, are you now going to testify that you omitted any information that you should have included in your report?

A. No.

Length of Time Before Writing Report (Very Optional)

Q. Now about this arrest report—you wrote it at the police station?

A. Yes.

Q. So that means you wrote your report sometime after pulling D over on the road, is that correct?

A. Yes.

Q. And that you wrote your report sometime after D exited his vehicle?

A. Yes.

Q. And your report was written after you asked D to perform the various coordination and balance exercises?

A. Yes.

Q. And it was written after you had already made up your mind as to how D performed on these exercises?

A. Yes.

Q. And it was written after, in your opinion, you were dissatisfied with how D performed on these exercises?

A. Yes.

Q. In fact, you wrote your report after D was placed under arrest?

A. Yes.

Q. And it was written after you placed D in handcuffs?

A. Yes.

Q. And you wrote it after you had called various information back to dispatch?

A. Yes.

Q. And still after a tow truck had been called by dispatch?

A. Yes.

Q. In fact, you wrote your report after the tow truck arrived on scene?

A. Yes.

Q. And it was written after the tow truck towed away D's car?

A. Yes.

Q. In fact, it was written sometime after you arrived back at the station with D in the back seat?

A. Yes.

Q. Now, one of the first things you did upon arriving at the station with D was read D his rights, correct?

A. Yes.

Q. So you were taking care of business other than writing your report at this time?

A. Yes.

Q. And at some point, you read D something called the Implied Consent Law?

A. Yes.

Q. And again, that was prior to you sitting down and writing your arrest report?

A. Yes.

Q. All told, you finally sat down to write out your report some two hours after you pulled D over and arrested him?

A. Yes.

Q. So you wrote your report out in a manner that would tend to justify your actions in arresting D?

A. I wrote down what I witnessed.

Selectivity of Report/Cop's Predisposition to Slant Report

Q. Officer, I believe you testified earlier that in writing out your report, you were careful and complete in recording all significant and material aspects of what you observed. Is that correct?

A. Yes, that's true.

Q. Would you consider information tending to prove D innocent as "significant" and "material"?

A. I would guess so.

Q. Then is it fair to say that you included in your report observation tending to prove D was not intoxicated? That the charges you filed against him may be wrong?

A. I'm not sure what you mean.

348

Q. Well, did you write down in your report that it took D an extremely long time to pull his car over to the side of the road after you activated your overhead lights and siren?

A. No.

Q. Would you please check your report to make sure of this?

A. No, I did not write that down.

Q. Is it safe to assume that you did not write this information in your report because D pulled his car over within a normal amount of time?

A. I guess so.

Q. If D had driven on for miles after you activated your lights and siren, completely ignoring your order to pull over, would you have written that in your report?

A. Yes.

Q. And you would have written that information because it is both significant and material?

A. Yes.

Q. In fact, you would have treated that as an indication that the amount of alcohol D had consumed had affected his ability to both observe and respond to your commands, correct?

A. Yes.

Q. Now, people who are driving drunk, they have problems with dividing their attentions, correct?

A. Yes.

Q. For instance, they can focus on what's happening straight in front of them, but they won't notice sirens and strobe lights flashing behind them?

A. That's correct.

Q. So, taking an unreasonably long time to pull your car over after being signaled to by a police officer is a common phenomenon associated with intoxicated drivers, is it not?

A. Yes.

Q. Then the opposite must be true. Pulling your car over within a reasonable amount of time is at least one sign that the driver of this vehicle is capable of properly dividing his attention, and is not intoxicated. His mind and body were responding in the same manner as a sober and law-abiding person's mind and body would respond?

A. Some drunk people pull over fast, too.

Q. Well, the truth of the matter is, you did not write in your report a fact that proves that D was able to control his car in a fashion consistent with a perfectly sober person? Then his driving ability was not affected?

A. Like I said, that's not conclusive proof that he was sober.

Q. But the fact is, my client's actions, reactions, and mental processes were functioning in a manner consistent with a sober person?

A. I guess so.

Q. Did you write in your report that when D pulled his car over, he slammed on his brakes, or almost drove off the road, or left half of his car on the road instead of pulling it onto the shoulder?

A. No.

Q. Would you please check your report to make sure of that?

A. As I said, I did not write that in my report.

Q. If he would have done any of these things, is there any question in your mind that you would have written that in your report as proof that, in your opinion, D was too intoxicated to properly operate his car?

A. I probably would have.

Q. Is it safe to assume that because you did not write in your report that D did any of these things, that in fact, D pulled over his car in a safe and reasonable manner?

A. I guess so.

Q. Now, people who are driving drunk, they have problems with their fine motor skills, is that correct?

A. Yes.

Q. For instance, problems steering, braking, judging distance?

A. Yes.

Q. So, pulling your car over in an unsafe and reckless manner is a common phenomenon associated with intoxicated drivers, is it not?

A. Yes.

Q. Then, once again, the opposite must be true. Pulling your car over in a safe and reasonable manner is another sign that D was not intoxicated. In fact, my client's actions, reactions, and mental processes responded in the same way a sober person's would have responded?

A. As I said before, that is not proof that D was sober.

Q. Now, you've testified at an earlier hearing that when you arrested my client, you read him his Miranda rights?

A. Yes.

Q. There are four or five sentences that comprise the Miranda rights that you are required to read to individuals you arrest, correct?

A. Yes.

Q. You read them from a card you probably have right now in your wallet or shirt pocket?

A. Yes.

Q. And your testimony is that my client waived his Miranda rights and agreed to talk to you without an attorney present?

A. Yes.

Q. And he did speak with you, and answered your questions?

A. Yes.

Q. From your police training, you understand, do you not, that for a Miranda waiver to be effective, the person waiving them must fully understand exactly what his Miranda rights are?

A. Yes.

Q. And that he can only waive his Miranda rights by making a knowing, intelligent, and voluntary decision to give up those rights?

A. Yes.

Q. Officer, did you violate my client's constitutional Miranda rights on the night you arrested him?

A. No.

Q. Are you saying then that you feel confident that my client made a knowing, intelligent, and voluntary waiver of his Miranda rights?

A. Yes.

Q. And you're saying that my client understood these rights?

A. Yes.

Q. And you're saying that my client waived these rights?

A. Yes.

Q. And you understood my client's response, that he was willing to waive these rights?

A. Yes.

(Probably don't ask this question — save for argument)

Q. Then you are telling this jury that whatever amount of alcohol my client consumed — whether mild or potent — did not affect his normal mental processes. His ability to comprehend his rights and make an intelligent decision was not impaired by any alcohol?

A. Not much.

Q. Isn't it true that in your report, you only wrote down information that supports yourself, information that puts another DUI arrest under your belt?

A. I wrote down what I believed to be important.

Q. So, facts that would tend to show that D is innocent — that he did not violate the law — that information is not important to you?

A. I wrote down what I considered to be good evidence.

Q. Well, seeing as you needed to read your report to remember what happened, and in your report you only wrote down your opinions that tend to make D look guilty, aren't you testifying as to only a portion of what happened? Only that part that brings you a step closer to making Sergeant?

A. I'm trying to tell you what I saw.

On the other hand, if the cop tries to add facts not written in his report

Q. Officer, you just testified that D failed to pull over in a reasonable and safe manner?

A. Correct.

Q. Now, pulling over in an unsafe fashion is pretty significant and material in a drunk driving case, isn't it?

A. Yes.

Q. And you have testified that you were trained to record in your report all significant and material observations?

A. Yes.

Q. And you have testified that the reason you record these observations is because observational evidence is short-lived?

A. Yes.

Q. And you also testified earlier that you properly discharged your duty and carefully and completely recorded all significant aspects of what you observed?

A. Yes.

Q. You also testified earlier that there were no omissions in your report?

A. Yes.

Q. In fact, you even swore under oath that "you are not now going to testify that you omitted any information that you should have included in your report."

A. Yes.

Q. So what you previously swore to under oath wasn't exactly accurate and true?

A. [Who cares.]

D's Scared/Fragile/Embarrassed Mental Condition

Q. You pulled D's car over at around two o'clock in the morning?

A. Yes.

Q. Is it your experience that citizens that you pull over are somewhat nervous and scared at being pulled over?

A. Not always.

Q. But the vast majority of the time, they are embarrassed?

A. Yes.

Q. Distressed quite a bit?

A. Yes.

Q. Tense?

A. Sometimes.

Q. And this is how the average citizen appears when talking to you while sitting in the driver's seat and you outside his car?

A. Yes.

Q. Well, in this case, you ordered D to get out of his car because you believed he was DUI, is that correct?

A. Yes.

Q. Certainly, the prospect of being arrested and jailed must have made D quite scared?

A. I would guess so.

Q. Embarrassed.

A. Probably.

Q. Nervous, tense?

A. Probably.

Preliminary Questions Cop Should Ask D

Q. There came a point in time where you asked D to step out of the car?

A. Yes.

Q. The purpose of that was to have D perform various coordination and dexterity exercises, which you like to call sobriety tests?

A. Yes.

Q. Will you agree with me that as individuals, people differ substantially in their abilities, skills, and talents?

A. Yes.

Q. People do have different athletic abilities?

A. Yes.

Q. And all people do not have the same coordination and balance skills, do they? I mean, we've both seen people in circuses that can walk tightrope wires 100 feet up in the air. You and I can't do that, can we?

A. I know I can't.

Q. In your opinion, would it be important to know about any physical limitations that D has, prior to asking him to perform these exercises?

A. It could help.

Q. Okay, so let's talk about some of the things that can affect a person's ability to perform balance and coordination exercises.

A. Okay.

Q. How about a painful back? Would a painful back likely affect a person's performance of these coordination and balance exercises?

A. I guess it could have an impact.

Q. How about knee problems?

A. Yes. But D never told me that he had any physical problems or injuries.

Q. Did you ask D if he had any injuries before you had him start these exercises?

A. No.

Q. Didn't you just testify that you wanted to be fair to D, that he had a fair opportunity to perform these exercises to your satisfaction?

A. Yes. And I did give him a fair opportunity to pass the sobriety tests.

Q. But you never bothered to ask him if he had an injury or other problems that would hinder him in performing your exercises?

A. No.

Q. Never asked him about sore joints or arthritis?

A. No.

Q. Wouldn't that sort of information have been relevant in judging how D performed the coordination and balance exercises?

A. Maybe just a bit.

Q. But you never did bother to ask these few simple questions that could have helped you form a more intelligent and informed opinion about D?

A. No.

Q. Would you agree with me that if D had any of the physical ailments that we just discussed, that judging D by how he performed on these difficult exercises is a bit unfair?

A. Maybe. But as I said, D didn't tell me he had any physical problems.

Q. You know, of course, that a person's balance is determined in large part by the fluid in his inner ear?

A. I believe that is true.

Q. But you didn't bother to ask D if he had a cold, did you?

A. No.

Q. You didn't ask him if he had sinus congestion?

A. No.

Q. Didn't ask him if he was taking medication for his sinuses, did you?

A. No.

Q. Did you ask him if he was taking an over-the-counter medication for any illnesses or injuries?

A. No.

Q. Do you know if he was taking over-the-counter medications?

A. No.

Q. If he was taking over-the-counter medications, can it be that these perfectly legal, everyday medications were what caused D to have performed the coordination and balancing exercises the way he did?

A. I don't know.

Q. You don't know, because you never bothered to ask D if he was taking over-the-counter medications?

A. I guess so.

Q. And the same holds true for any prescription medicines D was taking. You have no way of ruling out his prescription medications as the cause of how D performed on these exercises, do you?

A. No.

Q. Now, you are a police officer, aren't you?

A. Yes.

Q. When you stopped D, you were investigating the possibility of a drunk driver on the road?

A. Yes.

Q. Are you telling this jury that your investigations are only concerned with technicalities that tend to make people look guilty, but that you ignore investigating details that may prove that people are innocent?

A. No. That's not what I'm saying.

Q. But the fact is, you never bothered to ask D a few simple questions about his physical condition?

A. No.

Q. Well, the fact of the matter is, you're here trying to get D convicted of a very serious crime based on both your opinion and a half-completed investigation. Isn't that so?

A. I'm telling you what I believe is true.

Q. Okay, before you stopped D, how long had he been driving for?

A. I don't know.

Q. Well, isn't it a common phenomenon to be rather stiff, and have poor lower body circulation, after having sat in the same position for long periods of time?

A. Sometimes.

Q. When you told D to perform these exercises, did you tell him to walk around a bit to get any stiffness out of his joints, or to get his blood circulating?

A. No.

Q. Would that have been a little more fair to D to give him the opportunity to move around a bit before giving him these exercises?

A. I really don't think that it matters.

Q. According to your report, you pulled D over at around two o'clock in the morning.

A. Yes.

Q. Do you know for how many hours D had been up that day?

A. No. I didn't ask him that.

Q. Didn't you think that was an important fact to know?

A. No. Not really.

Q. Well, let me ask you this hypothetical. There are two people. Both have no alcohol or drugs in their body. The first person has worked a long day, he's been up for 18 hours and is exhausted. The second person has been up for five hours and is well rested. It is your opinion, under oath, that the first person is likely to perform these exercises as well as the second person?

A. The sobriety tests are designed so that anyone can pass them.

Q. So, you're telling this jury under oath, that the first person should be able to do every bit as good on your exercises as the second person?

A. Maybe not as good, but good enough to pass.

Q. Isn't it a fact that you conducted this investigation with the view of making D look guilty? You were not interested in D's innocence, were you?

A. That's not right.

Q. But the fact is, you didn't ask a couple of simple questions that would have helped you make a more intelligent and informed decision?

A. I just forgot to ask a couple of questions.

When Probable Cause Arose (the Sobriety Test "Lock")

Q. Now, you've already testified as to how D was driving that night. Correct?

A. Yes.

Q. You didn't arrest him for driving DUI as soon as you pulled him over, did you?

A. No.

Q. And the reason why is because, based on his driving alone, you had not formed the opinion that D was intoxicated?

A. Correct.

Q. And that means you did not believe that you had probable cause to arrest D for DUI?

A. Correct.

Q. Now, you've testified about a number of observations you made of the defendant upon pulling him over. Specifically, you told this jury about a slurred speech, a strong odor of an alcoholic beverage, disheveled appearance and eyes that were bloodshot and glassy.

A. That's correct.

Q. Did you arrest D for DUI upon making these observations?

A. No.

Q. And again, that is because, in your opinion, you had not yet formed the opinion that my client was intoxicated?

A. Not at that point.

Q. And because you weren't sure at that point, you correctly determined that you did not have probable cause to arrest him for DUI?

A. Correct.

Q. Now building upon that point, you had D step out of his car. Correct?

A. Yes.

Q. And you say that he had stumbled getting out of the car, and that he had to lean against the car door to maintain his balance?

A. Correct.

Q. Again, you did not arrest him at this point?

A. Correct.

Q. And the reason that you didn't arrest him for DUI at this point is that you still had not yet formed opinion that my client was intoxicated?

A. I wanted more information on which to base my decision.

Q. And because you didn't have all the information you needed to determine if my client was intoxicated, you correctly decided that you did not have probable cause to arrest him for DUI?

A. Correct.

Q. And that is why you wanted to administer what you called "field sobriety tests"?

A. Correct.

Q. Because to reach "probable cause" of intoxication, you need to have my client perform certain balance and coordination exercises?

A. Yes.

Q. And without having my client perform these physical tests, today, in front of this jury, you stand by your decision you made on this particular night. That based just upon your observations of my client's driving and his appearance, and how he spoke and how he smelled, you did not have probable cause to arrest him for DUI?

A. I guess so.

Q. So your "probable cause" to arrest D for drunk driving was based on how he performed on these "field sobriety tests"?

A. Yes.

Q. And these exercises were all important to you in forming your opinion as to whether D was driving intoxicated?

A. Yes.

Q. So if D had performed the coordination and balance exercises to your satisfaction, that means that you would not have arrested D. Is that correct?

A. Correct.

Q. Now, in having D perform your tests, you were trying to be as fair as possible to D, were you not?

A. I was.

Q. The first test you gave D was the HGN. Is that correct?

A. Yes.

Q. The next test was the Walk and Turn?

A. Yes.

Q. The last test was the one-leg stand?

A. Yes.

Q. You evaluated D on how he performed on each test?

A. Yes.

Q. You formed an opinion as to how D performed each test?

A. Yes.

Q. You were sure not to make any quick or snap decisions as to how D performed these tests?

A. Yes.

Q. After D performed the HGN, you did not arrest him for DUI at that point. Did you?

A. Not at that point.

Q. And the reason for that is that you had not yet completed your investigation?

A. Correct.

Q. You wanted additional information?

A. Correct.

Q. In fairness to D, you wanted additional information to base our decision of intoxication or not?

A. Correct.

Q. And that is because you still had doubt about D being DUI after the HGN?

A. I was trying to be open-minded, out of fairness to your client.

Q. Okay. You were open-minded as to whether my client was intoxicated or not after he performed the HGN. Correct?

A. Correct.

Q. And you were still open-minded as to whether my client was intoxicated or not after he performed the Walk and Turn. Correct?

A. Correct.

Q. And it was only after the one-leg stand that you made up your mind and decided that you had probable cause to arrest my client for DUI. Correct?

A. Correct.

Q. Okay. So it was only after the one-leg stand was complete did you form the opinion that you had probable cause to arrest D for DUI?

A. That's correct.

Odor of Alcohol

Q. You testified earlier to smelling the "strong odor of alcohol" about my client. Is that correct?

A. Yes.

Q. And the inference that you're trying to make is that a "strong odor of alcohol" somehow relates to a person who is intoxicated?

A. I believe so.

Q. Isn't it true, and haven't you been taught, that alcohol has no odor? Rather, that it's the beverage that the alcohol is in, and not the alcohol, that creates the odor?

A. True.

Q. Well, from this strong odor you say you smelled, could you tell the jury what type of beverage D drank?

A. I believe it was beer.

Q. Did you write this down in your report?

A. No.

Q. From the odor, could you tell where D had consumed the beverage?

A. No.

Q. Could you tell when D had consumed the beverage?

A. No.

Q. Could you tell how much or how little of the beverage that D had consumed?

A. No.

Slurred Speech

Q. During the course of your investigation, you spoke with my client?

A. Yes.

Q. And from what you've testified to, my client spoke back to you. Correct?

A. Yes.

Q. In fact, my client spoke hundreds of words to you on that night?

A. Maybe.

Q. Could you tell us one word that my client said in a slurred manner?

A. No. [leave it at that]

Or

A. Yes.

Q. Then can you tell us what word it is that my client slurred?

A. Blah, blah, blah.

Q. Can you demonstrate for the jury exactly how he slurred that word?

A. Blah, blah, blah.

Q. Isn't it true that on every DUI arrest you make, you always say that the suspect slurs his words?

A. [Who cares what his answer is.]

Specific Instructions Given to D

Q. You've testified that you have made numerous arrests for DUI throughout your career, is that correct?

A. Yes.

Q. And that means that you have given the instructions to perform the coordination and balance exercises many times?

A. Yes.

Q. I'm holding in my hand a tape recorder. What I would like you to do is to repeat the instructions to the exercises that you gave to D, and that I assume you gave to all the other people you arrested for DUI.

A. Right now?

Q. Yes. And please, I want you to say it just like you did on the evening you arrested D.

A. Blah, blah, blah.

Counsel: Your Honor, I wish to mark the recording just made by Officer Bullethead as Defendant's Exhibit 1.

Judge: It will be marked as such.

Test Site Conditions

Q. You pulled D over off to the side of the highway?

A. Yes.

Q. Is this where you administered the coordination and balance exercises?

A. Yes.

Q. At two o'clock in the morning?

A. Yes.

Q. The highway where you pulled D over is not a lighted highway, is it?

A. No.

Q. According to the ticket you wrote, you say that there was moderate traffic driving on the highway at the time?

A. Yes.

Q. And that the traffic was in both the oncoming and same-direction lanes?

A. Yes.

Q. The speed limit on the highway is 55 mph?

A. Yes.

Q. And being as it was late at night, these cars must have had their headlights on?

A. I assume so.

Q. So the headlights of cars whizzing by were in D's eyes as he was trying to perform your exercises?

A. I guess so.

Q. And the pressure waves of these 55-mph cars were also hitting D as he was trying to balance himself?

A. I don't believe they affected him.

Q. Is it possible that any of these cars that were passing you and D were exceeding the speed limit? Could you tell if any of the cars were doing, say 75 mph?

A. I couldn't tell.

Q. With all these cars driving by, were you at all afraid of being rear-ended?

A. It's always a concern.

Q. Did you have the overhead lights of your cruiser on, as a way of notifying other drivers that you were pulled over?

A. Yes.

Q. The overhead lights that you're talking about are the red and blue flashing lights?

A. Yes.

Q. Both strobes and halogen lights flashing?

A. Yes.

Q. So the red and blue flashing lights were also in D's face while he was trying to perform the exercises?

A. Well, yes. But it didn't affect him.

Q. Did you notice his footwear?

A. I believe he was wearing sneakers.

Q. Sneakers have soft soles, don't they? I mean they're softer than your normal dress shoe?

A. Yes.

Q. You had D perform the exercises on the shoulder of the highway?

A. Yes.

Q. It it safe to assume that this highway shoulder is just like every other highway shoulder in this state, covered with small pebbles and gravel?

A. No. Actually, it was clear.

Q. Okay, so this small strip of highway is very unique within this state. It has no pebbles, gravel, or other small obstructions. Well, is it then like every other highway shoulder in this state in that it slopes down away from the highway for drainage purposes?

A. I didn't notice any sloping.

Q. And, as you said earlier, D did appear to be a little nervous and embarrassed.

A. Yes.

Q. Okay, D had to perform these difficult exercises under these unique conditions, or else you were going to say that D was drunk and arrest him?

A. Yes.

Q. And under these circumstances, D had to perform various coordination and balance exercises?

A. Yes.

Q. Are these conditions we just spoke about fair to D?

A. I believe that a sober person should have been able to perform the sobriety tests properly under these conditions.

Q. Fair enough that you would have a member of this jury perform them under the same conditions if you pulled one of them over?

A. Yes.

Q. And if one of the jurors paused while performing the Walk and Turn, or put his foot down during the one-leg stand, you would also arrest them for drunk driving?

A. If I believed they were intoxicated, yes.

Q. You've testified that you have been a cop for the past eight years. Is that correct?

A. Yes.

Q. During that time, you have written hundreds, maybe thousands of traffic tickets?

A. Yes.

Q. A lot of these tickets have been written to individuals pulled over on the side of the road?

A. Yes.

Q. Is it fair to say that you've become pretty used to standing on the side of a busy freeway with cars whizzing by at 60 mph?

A. I'd say so.

Q. How long did it take you to get used to that?

A. Not long.

Q. Longer than you gave my client to get used to it?

A. [Who cares what his answer is.]

Q. Tell me, after you arrested D, you took him back to the police station?

A. Yes.

Q. Are there other officers at the station?

A. Yes.

Q. You had him sit across a table from you as you filled out various paperwork?

A. Yes.

Q. Was this room lighted?

A. Yes.

Q. Nice bright fluorescent lights?

A. Yes.

Q. Was the floor covered with tiling?
A. Yes.
Q. I take it the tiled floor is flat and smooth?
A. Yes.
Q. Is it also true that there are no wind gusts in this room?
A. Yes.
Q. This room's temperature is just right; not too cold, not too hot?
A. Yes.
Q. In other words, all the environmental conditions were as good as they could be in the booking room?
A. I guess so.
Q. These conditions were a lot better than what my client had to put up with on the highway when you had him do the exercises.
A. I told you: I don't think any of that affected how he performed.
Q. Would it have been at all possible for you to allow D to repeat any of these exercises under fair and decent conditions?
A. I guess I could have.
Q. But you absolutely, positively did not allow D the opportunity to perform your exercises at the station under optimal conditions?
A. No.
Q. And it is not your practice to allow people you arrest for DUI to perform the exercises at the station?
A. No, it's not.
Q. Have you ever performed any of these same exercises?
A. Yes. When I went through DUI training school.
Q. I take it the training class was conducted in a classroom setting?
A. Yes.
Q. Have you ever performed these exercises under circumstances other than for training purposes?
A. No.
Q. Then you don't know what it feels like to perform these exercises when you're nervous?
A. No.
Q. When you're embarrassed?
A. No.
Q. Under a lot of stress?
A. No.
Q. In short, you've never performed these exercises in a suspect situation?
A. No.

Was D Told What He Would Be Graded On?

Q. You've already told us specific instructions you gave D regarding each test, is that correct?

A. Yes.

Q. Considering the Walk and Turn, did you tell D that if he started before you finished giving the instructions it would count against him?

A. No.

Q. And you didn't tell him that raising his arms even a little bit was going to be counted against him?

A. No.

Q. In fact, you never told him anything about what he was going to be graded on, did you?

A. I gave him instructions and he had to follow them.

Q. You're not answering my question. You never told him what he was going to be graded on, did you?

A. No.

Q. You gave D what you want to call a "test," but you never told him what he was going to be graded on?

A. Yes.

Q. Does it strike you as fair that you "failed" D on parts of the exercises that he had no way of knowing he was being graded on?

A. Like I said, I gave him instructions and he had to follow them.

Q. Could you have told D what you were going to grade him on?

A. Yes.

Q. But you didn't?

A. That's not how I was taught to do it.

Q. Isn't it true that if you told more people what they were going to be graded on, that more people would do better on these exercises?

A. Maybe.

HORIZONTAL GAZE NYSTAGMUS (HGN)

Lack of Officer's Qualifications/Understanding of HGN

Q. One of the so-called "tests" you say you performed on D was the Horizontal Gaze Nystagmus?

A. Yes.

Q. Are you claiming to be an expert in diagnosing and interpreting the medical conditions of human eyes?

A. I was taught to detect the nystagmus related to alcohol consumption.

Q. Please tell the jury the name of the doctor who taught you how to diagnose the various conditions of the human eyes?

A. I wasn't taught by a doctor.

Q. The fact is, you were taught by another police officer?

A. Yes.

Q. And that police officer wasn't a doctor, was he?

A. I don't know.

Q. Well, if he was a doctor, he sure didn't claim to be one, did he?

A. No.

Q. And you didn't address him as doctor, did you?

A. No.

Q. Of course, you don't hold any degrees in the field of medicine or human physiology, do you?

A. No.

Q. You don't have any licenses related to the practice of medicine or human physiology?

A. No.

Q. No higher studies in the fields of ophthalmology, or neurology or pharmacology?

A. No.

Q. But you feel certain that you can medically diagnose ocular nystagmus?

A. Yes.

Q. Please explain to the jury how, in your mind, alcohol causes nystagmus?

A. I don't know. I was just taught that it did.

Q. [Having a medical dictionary nearby] Could you explain to the jury the difference between Nystagmus and Saccadic Intrusions?

A. No.

Q. Do you know what a Saccadic Intrusion is?

A. No.

Q. Could you please read from this medical dictionary the definition of a Saccadic Intrusion?

A. Blah, blah, blah.

Q. Now, please explain to the jury the differences between Nystagmus and Saccadic Intrusion?

A. I don't know.

Q. [Still with the medical dictionary nearby] Then could you explain to the jury the differences between Nystagmus and Saccadic Ocular Oscillations and Oscillopsia?

A. No.

Q. Could you please read from this medical dictionary the definitions of Saccadic Ocular Oscillations and Oscillopsia?

A. Blah, blah, blah.

Q. Now, having just read the definitions, please explain to the jury the differences between Nystagmus and Saccadic Ocular Oscillations and Oscillopsia?

A. I can't.

Q. So what you're saying is, that you have no idea what Saccadic Intrusions and Ocular Oscillations look like?

A. Yes.

HGN Option #1

Q. Now, concerning Nystagmus—have you ever heard of Acquired Fixation Nystagmus?

A. No.

Q. I take it then that if you've never heard of it, you do not know what it looks like?

A. Correct.

Q. Well, if you don't know what it looks like, how do you know that what you actually saw was Acquired Fixation Nystagmus?

A. I guess I don't.

Q. Have you ever heard of Anticipatory Induced Nystagmus?

A. No.

Q. I take it then that if you've never heard of it, you do not know what it looks like?

A. Correct.

Q. Well, if you don't know what it looks like, how do you know that what you actually saw was Anticipatory Induced Nystagmus?

A. I guess I don't.

[If the attorney wishes to truly punish the testifying cop, run all 47 different types of Nystagmus through the same three monotonous questions. Of course, the same thing can be done for the 16 different types of Saccadic Intrusions and Oscillations.]

HGN Option #2

Q. Officer, are you aware of how many different types of nystagmus and saccadic intrusions there are?

A. Not exactly. I heard there were a lot.

Q. I'm going to read to you just some of the different types of nystagmus and saccadic intrusions. Please tell me if you have heard of any of them. OK?

A. Yes.

[Read as many of them as you like.]

Q. You don't recognize any of the ones I've just read?

A. No.

Q. The reason you don't recognize any of them is that you're not an eye doctor. Correct?
A. Yes.
Q. You can't explain to the jury what the causes of these conditions are?
A. No.
Q. Or what brings them on?
A. No.
Q. Or even how they look?
A. No.
Q. You don't know if any of these conditions look exactly like what you're calling HGN?
A. I know what I was taught.
Q. Please answer my question. You don't know if any of these conditions look exactly like what you're calling HGN?
A. I guess not.

Administration of the HGN to the Defendant

Q. You were taught, were you not, that to administer this examination, the subject must keep his head still and follow an object only with his eyes. Is that correct?
A. Yes.
Q. And it takes approximately one-and-a-half minutes to conduct this examination?
A. Yes.
Q. And you believe you performed this procedure correctly?
A. Yes.
Q. Well, didn't you write in your report and testify that D was extremely impaired?
A. Yes.
Q. That he couldn't keep his balance?
A. Yes.
Q. That he was staggering?
A. Yes.
Q. That he was swaying?
A. Yes.
Q. And that this condition persisted from the time you first observed D until the time you turned him over to the jailer?
A. Yes.
Q. So your testimony now is that for about two hours, D didn't stop swaying, staggering, and stumbling, except for one-and-a-half minutes during which time he kept his body and head perfectly still?
A. Yes.

Q. You administered the HGN out on the highway?

A. Yes.

Q. You testified earlier that you had your overhead lights on, as well?

A. Yes. They were on.

Q. By your overheads, we're talking about your red and blue flashing strobe lights and halogen lights?

A. Yes.

Q. Now, these lights are designed to be seen by others from miles away, correct?

A. Yes.

Q. You're not going to tell us that these flashing lights were not in D's eyes when you were performing the eye check?

A. As I said, I don't believe they affected him.

Q. Tell me, have you ever been to the eye doctor?

A. Yes.

Q. For an examination?

A. Yes.

Q. When the doctor was conducting the examination of your eyes, did he have red and blue strobe lights flashing in your eyes?

A. No.

Q. How about flashing halogen lights? Did he have these types of lights flashing about while conducting an examination of your eyes?

A. No.

Q. How about car headlights shining in your eyes during the examination?

A. No.

Q. Do you think that there might be a good reason why eye doctors do not have obnoxious and distracting colored lights flashing on and off during their eye examinations?

A. [Who cares what his answer is.]

Q. By the way, don't strobe lights tend to make smooth movements look choppy, like at a disco?

A. They can.

Q. And you were examining D's eyes under pretty similar conditions?

A. As I said, I don't believe the flashing lights inferred with my evaluation.

WALK AND TURN (WAT)

Q. You also asked D to perform a Walk and Turn exercise?

A. That's correct.

Q. And you instructed him how to perform this exercise?

A. Yes.

Q. But as you said, you did not tell him what factors you were going to grade him on?

A. No.

Q. We spoke earlier about cars driving by while D was trying to do your exercises.

A. Yes.

Q. And we've already spoken about how these cars driving by at high speeds tend to create wind disturbances, correct?

A. Yes.

Q. I recall many instances in which my car was actually moved as a result of wind blasts created by passing cars and trucks. Has that ever happened to you?

A. Yes.

Q. You will agree that performing a balancing exercise can be difficult while cars are zooming by creating wind blasts that can actually move cars weighing over a ton?

A. I don't recall if cars were actually driving by when D was doing the Walk and Turn.

Q. Passing cars and trucks also tend to be distractions, don't they?

A. I guess they could be.

Q. Headlights and all?

A. Yes.

Q. And D performed this exercise on the road shoulder?

A. Yes.

Q. The shoulder off the highway?

A. That's correct.

Q. The shoulder that is not flat and level?

A. Yes.

Q. But there are no straight lines marked on the shoulder of the highway?

A. I had him walk an imaginary straight line.

Q. Not an actual line?

A. No.

Q. Not a visible line?

A. No.

Q. So this imaginary line that you saw in your head, D was supposed to figure out where that line was?

A. Yes.

Q. Now, could you please assume the starting position of this exercise?

A. [Bullethead stands up, places heel to toes and keeps his hands by his sides.]

Q. Is the posture you're in now a normal driving posture? In other words, is how you look now the way you look when you're behind the wheel of a car driving?

A. No.

Q. Exactly. Sitting in a comfortable car seat is completely different from walking heel to toe on a windblown highway with your arms by your sides, isn't it?

A. I'm trying to test his ability to drive a car safely.

Q. Driving is a normal function that most people do with regularity, correct?

A. Correct.

Q. Walking with your heel against your toe and your arms down by your side, is that something that most people do with regularity?

A. No.

Q. Well, D did walk from his car over by your cruiser, right?

A. Yes.

Q. In your report, you don't mention anything about D stumbling or falling down, do you?

A. No.

Q. Then is it safe to assume that D did not stumble or fall down when given the opportunity to walk like an ordinary human?

A. Yes.

Q. In fact, if you wanted to be fair to D, you could have had him walk—in a normal manner—up and down the whole highway shoulder to see if he was sure on his feet, couldn't you have?

A. I guess so.

Q. So in other words, on a dark night, with cars driving by, on a sloping highway shoulder not scattered with gravel and other debris, not knowing what he was being evaluated on, walking in an abnormal manner, and thinking that he could be arrested and thrown in jail, you claim that D did not follow the imaginary line you had in your mind and therefore he is drunk?

A. Yes.

Q. Instead of giving D negative points for each thing you say he did wrong, is it possible to give him positive points for things he does right?

A. I guess so. Yes.

Q. For instance, you said D stepped off your imaginary line twice, didn't he touch his heel with his toe three times, and made an improper turn. A total of six infractions. Is that correct?

A. Yes.

Q. So D didn't lose his balance during the instructions or start before being told to begin?

A. No. That's not how this test is graded.

Q. But if D had done either of those two things, you would have scored it against him as being proof that he was drunk.

A. That's the way I was taught to do it.

Q. As part of this exercise, you had D walk 18 steps: nine in one direction and then nine back. Correct?

A. Yes.

Q. And during each one of those 18 steps, D could have done something that you would have counted against him? Correct?

A. I don't know what you mean.

Q. Well, if D would have paused after his first step, would you have counted that as a point against D?

A. Yes. If the subject pauses once he starts walking, it is counted as a point tending to prove intoxication.

Q. Is it possible that D could have paused after each one of his 18 steps?

A. Yes.

Q. But he didn't.

A. No.

Q. Did you then score him 18 positive points as proof that he was not intoxicated?

A. No.

Q. But you could have?

A. That's not the way I was trained.

Q. You also required D to walk heel-to-toe for 18 steps. Correct?

A. Yes.

Q. And out of those 18 steps, his heel of one foot did not touch that of his other foot on three occasions?

A. Correct.

Q. That means on 15 occasions it was done perfectly?

A. I guess so.

Q. Did you give him 15 positive points showing he was not intoxicated?

A. No.

Q. And out of 18 chances to stepping on your imaginary line, D stepped off it twice?

A. Yes.

Q. That means on 16 occasions, it was done perfectly?

A. Yes.

Q. And of course, you didn't give him 16 positive points, did you?

A. No.

Q. If D would have raised his arms more than six inches from his side to balance himself while walking, you would have counted that as a point against him. Is that correct?

A. Yes.

Q. And he could have raised his arms during each of the 18 steps you required him to take. Correct?

A. Yes.

Q. But he didn't raise his arms, not even once?

A. Yes.

Q. And, of course, you didn't give him 18 positive points?

A. No.

Q. You say that D did, in your opinion, make an improper turn? Correct?

A. Yes.

Q. And there was only one turn that was required during this exercise?

A. Yes.

Q. And you did count this one improper turn against D?

A. Yes.

Q. You would also grade a point against D for taking the wrong number of steps. Is that correct?

A. Yes.

Q. But he walked the correct number of steps?

A. Yes.

Q. He walked 18 steps?

A. Yes.

Q. Did you give him 18 positive points?

A. No.

Q. Adding up all the negative points you give D, that totals 6 points. Is that correct? Two points off for stepping off your imaginary line, three points off for not touching heel-to-toe and one point off for making an improper turn. Correct?

A. Yes.

Q. Now let's add up all of D's positive points. One point for keeping his balance during instructions: One point for not starting too soon. Eighteen points for not stopping during the exercise; fifteen points for touching his heel-to-toe; sixteen points for walking dead straight on your imaginary line; 18 points for not using his arms for balancing; and eighteen points for taking the correct number of steps. That comes out to a total of 87 positive points. Correct?

A. That's not the way I compute the test.

Q. Well I know that's not how you normally do it, but that's the way we're doing it here and now. Okay?

A. Yes.

Q. Now, D had 87 positive points and six negative points. That means D was being graded on 93 separate actions. Correct?

A. I guess you could look at it that way.

Q. With my calculator, could you please divide 87 by 93 [= 0.935]. When you get the answer, multiply it by 100 to put it in proper percentage form (= 93.5 percent). Please tell the jury what percent the number 87 is of 93?

A. 93.5 percent.

Q. Isn't a scoring in the 90s generally considered an "A"?

A. I guess so.

Q. Have you ever failed a class in your life because you scored a 93.5 percent?

A. No.

Q. But even though D scored a 93.5 percent, he failed your test?

A. Yes.

ONE LEG STAND (OLS)

Q. You also asked D to perform a One Leg Stand test?

A. That's correct.

Q. And you instructed him how to perform this exercise?

A. Yes.

Q. But as with the other exercises you had D perform, you did not tell him what factors you were going to grade him on?

A. No.

Q. We spoke earlier about cars driving by while D was trying to do your exercises?

A. Yes.

Q. Where do you think it's easier to balance yourself on one leg, on an uneven highway shoulder as cars go screaming by at high speeds at night with their headlights shining in your eyes, or in a police station?

A. Easier.

Q. Yes. Easier. Also fairer. Where would that be at?

A. I guess at the police station.

Q. Did you have D perform this exercise, or any other exercise, at the police station?

A. No.

Q. Could you have?

A. I guess so.

Q. So you only had him perform an exercise that he was totally unfamiliar with at a place, and under conditions, that you agree are not the most fair?

A. Maybe.

Q. Now, could you please assume the starting position of this exercise?

A. [Bullethead stands up, places his hands by his sides, lifts one foot six inches off the ground and looks down at it.]

Q. Is the posture you're in now a normal driving posture? In other words, is how you look now, the way you look when you're behind the wheel of a car driving?

A. No.

Q. Exactly. Again, sitting in a comfortable car seat is completely different from imitating a flamingo standing on one leg. Isn't it?

A. I was trying to test his ability to drive a car safely.

Q. Driving is a normal function that most people do with regularity, correct?

A. Correct.

Q. Balancing yourself on one leg with your arms down by your side, is that something that most people do with regularity?

A. No.

Q. Could you possibly operate a car in the position you're in right now?

A. Obviously, no.

Q. In fact, there is not one driving skill that requires a person to balance himself in this awkward position?

A. No.

Q. But based on this unfamiliar, awkward, and unrelated-to-driving exercise that you had D perform, under unfair conditions, you claim that D was drunk?

A. That is my opinion.

Q. Well, let's count all the positive points that you could have given D, shall we?

A. Okay.

Q. For instance, you said that D put his foot down twice, and used his arms to maintain balance. Correct?

A. Yes.

Q. If you look through your report, you don't write down for how many seconds D was using his arms for balance, do you?

A. I really cannot recall exactly how long he used his hands for.

Q. But if D had used his arms for all 30 seconds of this exercise, that surely would have been significant enough for you to write that in your report, would it not?

A. I think so.

Q. And the same would hold true if he used his arms for 15 seconds — half the time. That definitely would have been significant enough for you to write that down, would it not?

A. I guess so.

Q. Well, the fact that you didn't write down how long he used his arms for balance, the amount of time that he used his arms to balance himself must have been relatively insignificant. As you said earlier, you were taught to write down all significant facts. Correct?

A. Yes.

Q. Let's go through your exercise, shall we?

A. Okay.

Q. To begin the exercise, D was required to stand at attention with his feet together and hands by his sides?

A. Yes.

Q. And he did that?

A. Yes, to start the exercise.

Q. Did you give him one positive point for correctly following your instructions?

A. No.

Q. But, again, you could have?

A. Yes.

Q. Now, this exercise required D to stand on one foot for a total of 30 seconds?

A. Yes.

Q. And you say D put his foot down twice. Correct?

A. Yes.

Q. That means that for 28 seconds, D performed this exercise correctly in this regard?

A. I guess so.

Q. Did you score D 28 positive points?

A. No.

Q. There was nothing to prevent you from scoring D in this matter, is there?

A. It's just not the way I was taught.

Q. Under your standards, if D would have swayed at any time during the exercise, you would have graded that against D. Correct?

A. Yes.

Q. But you don't claim that D was swaying, do you?

A. No. He wasn't swaying.

Q. He wasn't swaying for all 30 seconds?

A. Yes.

Q. Well, did you give him 30 positive points for not swaying?

A. No.

Q. And as far as D using his arms for balancing, you will agree that because you left any mention of it out of your report, that he must have only used his arms for some small amount of time?

A. I guess so.

Q. We can only guess on this one, but let's give you the benefit of the doubt. D used his arms for about five seconds?

A. Okay.

Q. That leaves 25 positive points.

A. Under the way that you are scoring him, yes.

Q. If D would have hopped around during the exercise, that would have counted against him. Correct?

A. Yes.

Q. And he didn't hop around during this exercise?

A. No.

Q. Well, that's another 30 positive points in D's favor?

A. Like I said, it's only in his favor the way you're scoring it.

Q. And D also counted all the way to 30 before putting his foot down?

A. Yes.

Q. And D could have skipped numbers, or have mixed them up if he were drunk. Couldn't he?

A. Yes.

Q. But he didn't?

A. No.

Q. So let's give D another 30 positive points.

A. That's not the way it's done.

Q. Adding up all the negative points you gave D on this exercise, that totals seven points. Is that correct? Two points off for putting his foot down, and approximately five points off for using his hands. Correct?

A. Yes.

Q. Now let's add up all of D's positive points. One point for following your instructions regarding the positioning of his feet and hands; 28 points for keeping his foot in an unnatural position for so long; 30 points for being steady as a rock and not swaying; 25 points for balancing and not swaying; 30 points for being sure-footed and not hopping around; and another 30 points for having the mental faculties to count properly while under extremely difficult circumstances. That comes out to a total of 114 positive points. Correct?

A. That's not the way I compute the test.

Q. Well, I know that's not how you normally do it, but it's how we're doing it today. Okay?

A. Yes.

Q. Now, D had 114 positive points and seven negative points. That means D was being graded on 121 separate actions. Correct?

A. I guess you could look at it that way.

Q. With my calculator, could you please divide 114 by 121 [= 0.942]. When you get the answer, please multiply it by 100 to put it in proper percentage form [= 94.2 percent]. Please tell the jury what percent the number 114 is of 121?

A. 94.2 percent.

Q. Isn't scoring in the 90s generally considered getting an "A"?
A. I guess so.
Q. Have you ever failed a class in your life because you scored 94.2 percent?
A. No.
Q. But even though D scored a 94.2 percent, he failed your test?
A. Yes.

Opportunity to Practice the SFST before "Grading"

Q. You testified earlier that your opinion that D was drunk came from how he performed on the coordination and balance exercises, what you called "sobriety tests."
A. Yes, that's true.
Q. Is it your testimony that a person who is intoxicated cannot perform these exercises?
A. Yes.
Q. No matter how hard they try?
A. Yes.
Q. Well, after you told D what you wanted him to do, did you give him a chance to practice these exercises before you graded him?
A. No. That's not the way it's done.
Q. Yes. But you could have allowed D a practice run before you graded him?
A. I guess it could be done.
Q. And according to what you just said, no matter how many times you practice, it would not reflect the results?
A. I don't believe so.

Politeness and Cooperation Proving Sobriety

Q. You've testified that you told D that you wanted him to perform certain coordination and dexterity exercises?
A. Yes.
Q. Is there any law that says that D has to perform those exercises?
A. No, not that I know of.
Q. But D did agree to perform them?
A. Yes.
Q. So he was being cooperative. He wasn't one of those people that "stand on their rights." He agreed to perform these exercises, even though by law, he didn't have to?
A. Well, yes.
Q. Now, you have indicated to me that my client was being cooperative that evening?

A. Yes.

Q. And I assume that is because he complied with all of your orders and demands?

A. Yes.

Q. And he didn't give you any hassles?

A. No.

Q. Isn't it true that people who are impaired by alcohol are contentious and belligerent and difficult to deal with?

A. Well, a lot of the time. But not always.

Q. Well, as you just agreed with me, D was not any of those. He agreed to perform these difficult balancing and coordination exercises. Isn't being cooperative a mannerism that is more associated with a person who is sober, rather than drunk?

A. Yes, but not conclusively.

Q. But my client was a perfect gentleman?

A. Well, yes.

Q. Now, can you turn to the jury and tell them why else my client was a perfect gentleman?

A. Blah, blah, blah.

Q. Now officer, you have also indicated that my client was polite?

A. Yes.

Q. And I assume that is because he said "yes sir" and "no sir."

A. Yes.

Q. And he spoke politely in other ways?

A. Yes.

Q. Could you turn and face and tell the jury what else you say my client did that was polite and respectful?

A. Blah, blah, blah.

The Self-Comparison Issue

Q. Now, you've testified earlier that you have never met D before the night you arrested him?

A. That's correct.

Q. Could you tell the jury how D normally responds to stressful situations?

A. I can only tell you what he was like on the night I arrested him.

Q. Is D a type of person who gets flustered easily?

A. I don't know.

Q. Does he normally get embarrassed easily?

A. I don't know.

Q. Do you normally know how he deals with these feelings?

A. I don't know.

Q. How smart is D?
A. I don't know.
Q. Is he normally a klutz?
A. I don't know.
Q. How about athletic ability? Is he generally athletic?
A. I don't know.
Q. So you have no idea how D would perform on your exercises if he had absolutely no alcohol in his body?
A. No.
Q. Wouldn't you agree that all people are different? They have different abilities?
A. Yes.
Q. Differences in strength?
A. Yes.
Q. Differences in muscle development?
A. Yes.
Q. Differences in their coordination?
A. Yes.
Q. Differences in their balancing abilities?
A. Yes.
Q. Differences in height?
A. Yes.
Q. Differences in weight?
A. Yes.
Q. Differences in the speed with which they learn new things?
A. Yes.
Q. Differences in their speech and manner of talking?
A. Yes.
Q. Differences in their memory ability?
A. Yes.
Q. Differences in their ability to learn and recall the instructions to strange and unusual exercises?
A. Possibly.
Q. Wouldn't you agree that people generally get better at performing exercises with more practice?
A. Generally.
Q. Do you know what my client's normal physical abilities are?
A. No.
Q. Do you know what his normal mental faculties are?
A. No.
Q. How about the judge's?
A. No.
Q. How about the prosecutor's?

A. No.

Q. How about juror # _____'s normal mental faculties?

A. No.

Q. How about any other member of the jury?

A. No.

Q. How about any other person in this courtroom, other than yourself?

A. No.

Conclusion

Q. Hypothetically speaking, if you pulled over some members of the jury on the highway, you smelled a strong odor of alcohol, you had them perform the same exercises you had D perform, and they performed them as well as D did, would you arrest them for drunk driving?

A. Yes.

Q. How about if they came back a day later with no alcohol in their bodies, and still couldn't perform your exercises. Would you still want them prosecuted for drunk driving?

A. No.

Q. Well, how about if you performed the same tests on some of the members of the jury, and they were completely sober — no alcohol whatsoever in their bodies — but they still performed your exercises as well as D, would you still arrest them for drunk driving?

A. I'm not sure.

Q. By the time you asked D to submit to a breath test back at the station, you already had D under arrest for being DUI, isn't that so?

A. Yes.

Q. And that was your opinion, that he was DUI?

A. Yes.

Q. Did you ever tell D that if he submitted to your breath test and tested under the legal limit, that you would unarrest him, apologize to him, and let him go?

A. No.

Q. And you made that quite clear to him by your actions and your words. He was under your arrest, and no matter what reading would have come out of your machine, he was going to remain under your arrest on DUI charges?

A. Yes.

Q. So he could have tested under the legal limit, but he was still going to remain under your arrest and have to go to trial, in front of this jury?

A. Yes.

Q. In fact, he could have tested .03 percent and he was still going to have to come to court and defend himself against you and your charges, isn't that true?

A. Yes. [Attorney could then respond, "Then this machine that your department relies upon all the time to get drunk drivers off the road would have been wrong and you, of course, would have been right".]

A. No. [Attorney could respond, "Then you are willing to concede that you do not trust your own judgment or your exercises; you are willing to defer to a machine to make your decision for you".]

Q. Attorney: Nothing further.

§13.3   The Breath Operator and/or Blood-Alcohol Expert: Strategy and Techniques

Page 1002. Add after first full paragraph:

Counsel should never overlook the potential value of the prosecution's blood-alcohol expert or laboratory technician for getting into evidence scientific articles relating to blood-alcohol analysis. Confronted with articles counsel has obtained that are favorable to the defense theory of the case, the witness must either confess ignorance or acknowledge his having either read it or being authored by a reliable authority in the field.

When the witness invariably testifies on direct examination as to his expert opinion concerning impairment, etc., keep in mind that most states permit him to be questioned concerning scientific literature in the field. California's Evidence Code §721(b) is a fairly typical example:

> If a witness testifying as an expert testifies in the form of an opinion, he or she may not be cross-examined in regard to the content or tenor of any scientific, technical, or professional text, treatise, journal, or similar publication unless any of the following occurs:
>> (1) The witness referred to, considered, or relied upon such publication in arriving at or forming his or her opinion . . . .
>> (3) The publication has been established as a reliable authority by the testimony or admission of the witness or by other expert testimony or by judicial notice.

If admitted, relevant portions of the publication may be read into evidence but may not be received as exhibits.

A tactic used by the author with some success is to mail copies of relevant articles to the toxicologist/technician before trial, if he is known, and suggest that he read it—with the advisory that he will be asked about it on the stand. If he still claims not to have read the article(s), he can be presented to the jury as an "expert" who is uninterested in the literature of leading experts in his field.

§13.4   Illustrative Cross-Examination of Operator/Expert

Page 1050. Add after end of material on "Blood Analysis":

In a trial involving direct analysis of the blood, counsel should consider the following illustrative cross-examination of a law enforcement blood-alcohol expert by Charles J. Unger, of Glendale, California.*

Q. Good morning, Mr. Ting.
A. Good morning.
Q. Mr. Ting, you mentioned you have been with the sheriff's crime lab for the last six years; is that correct?
A. Yes.
Q. With respect to the blood alcohol section, you've been with that section for the last four years; is that right?
A. Yes.
Q. You mentioned you testified in court before, approximately 200 times; is that correct?
A. Yes.
Q. Would it be fair to say that all but a handful of those times you were called as an expert by the prosecution?
A. Yes.
Q. Mr. Ting, you mentioned you have your—you got your bachelor's degree in chemistry and biology at Irvine; is that correct?
A. Yes.
Q. That you're currently seeking your master's at Cal State, L.A.; correct?
A. Well, I've been enrolled in the program.

*Reprinted with permission.

Q. In fact, you have been enrolled in that program for a considerable period of time, haven't you?

A. Yes.

Q. You enrolled in that program in 1981; is that correct?

A. That's correct.

Q. So for eight years you have been enrolled in the master's program; correct?

A. Yes.

Q. Mr. Ting, you indicated that — I think the quote was — you had had trouble with the gas chromatograph and you overcame it; is that correct?

A. Yes.

Q. The trouble occurred in February of 1986, didn't it?

A. Yes.

Q. And at that time your supervisor — you have a supervisor over at the crime lab, don't you?

A. Yes, I do.

Q. And his name is Dan Nathan?

A. Yes.

Q. And in February of 1986 Mr. Nathan took you off the gas chromatograph because you couldn't get the duplicate analyses, the two analyses that you did, to agree with each other?

A. That's correct.

Q. And Mr. Nathan indicated to you at that time, did he not, that as soon as you discovered what you were doing wrong, what the problem was, that he would put you back on the gas chromatograph; correct?

A. Yes.

Q. Did you discover what you were doing wrong later in that month, in February?

A. No.

Q. March?

A. No.

Q. April?

A. No.

Q. It wasn't until August, was it?

A. August, September.

Q. Okay. Approximately six or seven months; correct?

A. Yes.

Q. And six or seven months later, you determined that you weren't sealing the vials tightly enough; is that correct?

A. It wasn't tightly enough, it was properly. I was — after the sample is dispensed into the three-inch glass vial using the automatic dispenser, an aluminum cap is placed onto the vial and a vise grip is used to seal that cap around the vial. And I was not properly sealing the vials with the vise grip. I was not making a good airtight seal using the vise grip on the aluminum caps.

Q. Mr. Ting, back in September, then, of 1986, Mr. Nathan let you go back to the gas chromatograph; correct?

A. Yes.

Q. With respect to your lab and their use of the gas chromatograph, you are allowed to run up to 45 samples per run, aren't you?

A. Yes.

Q. In fact, I think you indicated you did 43 in this case; is that correct?

A. Forty-three on that particular date, 4/13/89. Yes.

Q. Okay, thank you. Your laboratory permits the run to count if there are fewer than seven errors on the run; correct?

A. Well, fewer than seven what are called "rejects," and rejects being the duplicate analyses differing from one another from the same blood sample by greater than plus or minus 5 percent of the average of the two results.

Q. So in other words, if 39 out of 45 agree with each other, the run will count and those 39 that agree will be used, and six that don't agree will be tossed or thrown out or not used or rerun; is that correct?

A. Well, the six to seven that do not agree would then be rerun.

Q. Okay, and if in fact 38 of them do agree within the plus or minus 5 percent and there are seven rejects, then the whole run is scrapped; correct?

A. Yes.

Q. But if there are 39 that would get through without a little "R" to show you — to indicate a reject —

A. Yes, a little "R" shows up on the computer-generated summary sheet on the right-hand side — far right-hand margin of the sheet.

Q. All right, if you get six out of every 45 rejects, the other 39 are permitted to remain and count — that's not a good word — are permitted to remain and the remainder of the run counts; correct?

A. Yes.

Q. And is there anything different done in your analysis of the 39 where you didn't get an "R" as opposed to the six where you did get an "R" to indicate a reject?

A. Generally, the causes of rejects are in the — are due to the improper sealing of the blood vials — or the three-inch glass vials with the aluminum caps.

Q. But the laboratory does not require you to reanalyze those other 39 that are going to count and be considered valid; is that correct?

A. That's correct.

Q. Mr. Ting, I take it — or I think you indicated you base part of your expertise on the knowledge of the literature; is that correct?

A. Yes.

Q. Mr. Ting, are you familiar with an article by Dr. Sheldon Plotkin entitled "Most Direct Blood Testing for Alcohol Content Is in Error"?

A. No, I'm not.

Q. All right, do you know the rules — I can only question you about articles that you have read and relied upon.

   Mr. Ting, have you read and relied upon an article by Dr. Sidney Kay entitled "The Collection and Handling of the Blood Alcohol Specimen?"

A. No.

Q. Mr. Ting, have you read and relied upon an article entitled "The Stability of Ordinary Blood-Alcohol Samples Held for Various Periods of Time Under Different Conditions" by Drs. Glenn, Denning, and Waugh?

A. I don't believe so.

Q. How about one entitled "Determination of Fluoride in Blood Samples for Analysis of Alcohol" by N. K. Shajani?

A. I don't believe so.

Q. And lastly, "Effects and Mechanisms of Sodium Fluoride in Forensic Alcohol Samples" by Heude, John Heude?

A. I don't believe so.

Q. Well, then let me ask it a different way: What have you read and relied on that pertains to blood-alcohol testing specifically?

A. Specifically, I've read approximately 20 to 25 articles with respect to the proper preservation and handling of blood samples. And probably an additional maybe 50 to 100 other articles pertaining directly with the analysis of samples with respect to blood-alcohol determinations.

Q. All right, with respect to blood tests specifically, can you give me the name of a couple of articles that you've read, please.

A. Not by — not by title alone, no.

Q. Can you give me perhaps one title of something you've read pertaining to blood alcohol tests?

A. Well, one of the most extensive articles I've read covers almost all aspects of alcohol, alcohol and driving and also alcohol and the impaired driver.

Q. That's put out by the American Medical Association; correct?

A. Yes.

Q. I'm talking about articles specifically that go to blood testing as opposed to more generalized articles that talk about alcohol and the effects on the human body.

A. By title alone, I could not give you a title alone.

Q. Mr. Ting, fermentation is a process by which sugar converts into alcohol; correct?

A. Yes.

Q. Sugar is present in the blood of all humans; is that right?

A. Yes.

Q. The vials that are used in these type of cases are supposed to have a certain amount of preservative in them, aren't they, to prevent fermentation?

A. Yes.

Q. They are also supposed to have a certain amount of anticoagulant in them to prevent coagulating; correct?

A. Yes.

Q. The preservative used in these types of vials is called sodium fluoride; is that correct?

A. Yes.

Q. At any time—well, does your laboratory prepare the vials itself? Does it put the preservative or anticoagulant in it?

A. No, it does not.

Q. In fact, the laboratory orders these vials en masse from a company called Terumo; is that correct?

A. Yes.

Q. And your laboratory—your laboratory orders these vials several thousand at a time; is that correct?

A. Probably.

Q. All right. And when your laboratory gets these vials in, are any of them tested at that time to determine whether or not there's a proper amount of preservative in the vials?

A. Not to my knowledge.

Q. Well, how about when you analyze the vial for blood-alcohol content, do you test it for preservative level at that time?

A. No.

Q. A proper amount of preservative is in fact necessary to flow or prevent fermentation; correct?

A. Yes.

Q. Mr. Ting, the literature also indicates that refrigeration is important with respect to fermentation, doesn't it?

A. Well, refrigeration is one way to ensure proper preservation of a blood sample, and the addition of a sufficient amount of preservative would be another.

Q. All right, now, you analyzed this blood nine days after it was drawn, correct?

A. That I don't know.

Q. All right. Do you have your slip up there with you, Mr. Ting?
A. I have a Xerox copy of the laboratory receipt and also the computer-generated summary sheet, which indicates the day I would have analyzed the sample.
Q. All right, this is what I'm looking for. May I?
A. Sure.
Q. Thank you. Mr. Ting, this indicates an analysis date of April thirteenth, correct?
A. Yes.
Q. Now, this April fifth date, does that indicate that that's the day when your lab received this blood?
A. No, actually April sixth, the date headed by the box. The date on the laboratory receipt being 4/6/89.
Q. All right. So you—this blood basically sat in the laboratory from 4/6/89 until you analyzed it on 4/13/89; correct?
A. Well, actually, it sat a little longer. Because it was not until 4/19/89 that I returned the sample to the evidence control section or evidence locker at the crime lab.
Q. All right, I'm talking about the time it sat before you analyzed it would be from 4/6 to 4/13?
A. In the crime lab, yes.
Q. All right. In the crime lab you don't refrigerate the vials, do you?
A. No, we do not.
Q. All right. So assuming that the evidence was first placed in an unrefrigerated locker at Whittier P. D. and then put in your crime lab refrigerator, we have a nine-day period of unrefrigerated blood from the time the blood was drawn to the time it was analyzed; is that correct?
A. I don't know what date the sample was drawn.
Q. Mr. Ting, in your reading, in your reliance upon the literature, is time important as far as the time from when the sample was drawn to when in fact you do your analysis?
A. Not really, if the sample is properly preserved.
Q. Okay, that's really what it comes down to, isn't it, whether the sample was properly preserved?
A. Yes.
Q. Mr. Ting, police officers, well, they don't have an opportunity themselves to measure preservative, but they can look inside a vial and see if there is at least something in there, can't they?
A. Yes.
Q. Well, assuming that there's something in there of an unknown quantity, what would a police officer expect to see?
A. A powder inside of the vial—unused blood vial.

Q. And what color would that powder be?

A. That depends. The older blood vials, the preservative and anti-coagulant used to appear as a white powder. As of about 1986, the vials since 1986 purchased by the sheriff's crime lab, the preservative and anticoagulant appears as a light pink, light purple color.

Q. So then basically for the last four years, if an officer were to see what is in fact preservative and anticoagulant, he would look in and see something pink or purple in color?

A. Depending whether or not a new blood vial versus an old blood vial are used.

Q. Are blood vials ordered from 1985 still being used?

A. Occasionally.

Q. That would be a four-year-old vial?

A. Yes.

Q. Would it be fair to say that 90 percent of the time or so new vials are in fact used?

A. Well, I don't know of an exact number, but the vast majority of the vials submitted to the crime lab currently would be the newest blood vials. Every now and then, occasionally, a very old blood vial is submitted to the crime lab.

Q. All right, when you say every now and then, I take it that would be a rare or unusual occurrence; is that correct?

A. I would say a rare occurrence.

Q. All right. Mr. Ting, when you analyzed the blood, you analyzed a quarter of a milliliter; is that correct?

A. The automatic dispenser places into each three-inch glass vial a quarter of a milliliter of blood so that is then done in duplicate. So at least a half milliliter of blood is removed from the blood vial, the original blood vial, when the sample is collected from the subject.

Q. All right. So you're analyzing a quarter, two different times, to equal a half then; correct?

A. Yes.

Mr. Unger. All right, thank you. Thank you. I have nothing further.

The Court. Redirect.

REDIRECT EXAMINATION

By Ms. Felix.

Q. You testified that earlier in your training you had some difficulties. Now, you are now working on the gas chromatograph at the sheriff's lab; is that correct?

A. Yes.

Q. Who is your supervisor there?

A. Mr. Dan Nathan.

Q. Is that the same Mr. Dan Nathan that defense counsel referred to as having taken you off from doing work on the gas chromatograph back in 1986?

A. Yes.

Q. Thank you. Are you familiar with Title 17 of the California Code —?

A. Yes.

Q. — in reference to refrigeration of blood samples?

A. I don't believe Title 17 directly addresses refrigeration. Title 17 requires that samples be properly preserved. I don't believe it necessarily states that there is a need to refrigerate samples.

Q. Thank you. Now when you went to do your tests on the vial that you received around nine days after the blood sample was supposed to have been taken, was the blood coagulated?

A. I have no indication of such.

Q. Based on your training and experience in biology and blood analysis, would you have been able to see if the blood had been coagulated?

A. With the exception of very, very small minute clots, because generally blood clots are big enough to be seen by the naked eye.

Q. Now, the run you did — the runs you did on April thirteenth, 1989, which you show on the calibration sheet there, was that an acceptable run?

A. Yes, it was.

Q. So would you say that in your opinion when you received that vial of blood on October — or April thirteenth, 1989, to begin doing a blood-alcohol analysis, there was no coagulation that you could determine? The evidence envelope was intact, you had no difficulty doing the analysis using the gas chromatograph, and the gas chromatograph was in proper working order; is that correct?

A. Yes.

Q. Has anything the defense questioned you about where you've given your answer about — changed your opinion of what a person with a blood-alcohol level of .14 would be considered as under the influence, in your opinion?

A. No.

Ms. Felix. Nothing further, Your Honor.

The Court. Mr. Unger.

Mr. Unger. Thank you, Your Honor.

RECROSS-EXAMINATION

By Mr. Unger.

Q. Mr. Ting, we have no quarrel with the .14. In fact, it is your opinion, just to make sure that's clear, that all people at .10 or above are under the influence of alcohol for purposes of driving, you'd agree with that, wouldn't you?

A. Yes.

Q. All right. Mr. Ting, you answered counsel's questions with respect to whether you saw any — anything occurring with respect to coagulant. My question to you would be, at no time did you or anyone with your lab, either when the vials came in or when you analyzed it for alcohol content, test the vial to determine how much, if any, preservative was in it, did you?

A. To the best of my knowledge, that's correct.

Q. All right. Mr. Ting, Title 17, which was referred to by counsel, gives a list of steps with respect to how blood is supposed to be drawn by a nurse or a lab technician, doesn't it?

A. Nurse, lab technician or other qualified personnel drawing blood samples, yes.

Q. All right, it talks about blood samples by venepuncture?

A. Yes.

Q. It also indicated that alcohol or other volatile organic disinfectants should not be used to clean the skin where a specimen is to be drawn, correct?

A. Yes.

Q. It also indicates that blood samples should be collected using sterile, dry hypodermic needles and syringes?

A. Yes.

Q. It basically gives a road map on how the nurse or lab technician or qualified individual should draw the blood; correct?

A. Yes.

Q. These procedures are the law in this state, aren't they?

A. Yes.

Mr. Unger. Thank you. I have nothing further.

The Court. Ms. Felix.

FURTHER REDIRECT EXAMINATION

By Ms. Felix.

Q. Do you have anything or has anything been indicated to you that the blood was not properly drawn in this case?

A. No.

Q. When you did your analysis on the blood, was there anything in there that would indicate to you that possibly the blood may have been drawn incorrectly?

A. Not that I was aware of.

Ms. Felix. Thank you. Nothing further, Your Honor.

The Court. Anything else, Mr. Unger?

Mr. Unger. Briefly, Your Honor.

FURTHER RECROSS-EXAMINATION

By Mr. Unger.

Q. Mr. Ting, you don't know anything about how the blood was drawn in this case, do you?

A. No.

Q. And in fact if there were problems, you wouldn't necessarily expect to see something in the vial, would you? I mean, it is possible that you would. But you wouldn't necessarily expect to, would you?

A. If for instance, an improper swabbing agent had been used to cleanse the arm, I would not be able to see that in the blood sample itself. So in that regard, yes.

Q. All right. And if fermentation or some sort of degeneration had occurred, that's not something you would visually be able to determine whether or not it had occurred, correct?

A. Right, that's something you cannot see.

Mr. Unger. Thank you very much. Nothing further.

The Court. Ms. Felix?

Ms. Felix. Nothing further, Your Honor.

The Court. May Mr. Ting be excused, Counsel?

Mr. Unger. Yes, Your Honor.

The Court. Ms. Felix, may Mr. Ting be excused?

Ms. Felix. Yes, Your Honor.

The Court. Thank you, Mr. Ting.

The Witness. Thank you.

14

THE DEFENSE

§14.1 *The Defense Blood-Alcohol Expert*

Page 1073. Add after carryover paragraph:

Confronted with a trial judge who feels that attacks on the machine are "speculative" without evidence that specific problems did, in fact, exist, the language of the U.S. Supreme Court's decision in *California v. Trombetta* should be pointed out. 467 U.S. 479, 491 (1984). In rejecting respondent's argument that the state must preserve breath samples for defense discovery, the Court noted that he was free to attack the validity of the breath test before a jury on numerous possible grounds, including radio frequency interference — that he could, for example, have introduced evidence "that the test was conducted near a source of radio waves." Clearly, it can never be proven that RFI (see §6.3.10) actually did affect a given breath test result; any such evidence would, of necessity, be speculative. In other words, the Supreme Court indicated that a defendant may offer evidence that something *could* have happened to affect the machine's reading.

For an excellent discussion of a defendant's constitutional right to present expert testimony, see Imwinkelried, The Recognition of an Accused's Constitutional Right to Introduce Expert Testimony Attacking the Weight of Prosecution Evidence: The Antidote for the Supreme Court's Mistaken Assumption in California v. Trombetta, 33 Arizona Law Review 59 (1991).

§14.3   Should the Defendant Testify?

Page 1091. Add after first full paragraph:

A survey reported at 29 Massachusetts Lawyers Weekly 1025 (Jan. 8, 2001) reported that jurors place too much emphasis on the testimony of criminal defendants. Many jurors who were surveyed said they wished that defendants who did not take the witness stand*had* testified. Where defendants did testify, however, jurors often noted the witnesses' "character," "mannerisms," and "potential to commit a crime." Perhaps the most important lesson to be learned from this survey is the need for counsel to emphasize whenever possible to the jury its responsibility to determine whether the prosecution has met its burden of proof.

RESOURCES

NHTSA Manuals

Page 1143. Please note the following corrections:

NHTSA SFST Instructor Manual (PB94-780210)	$225.00
NHTSA SFST Student Manual (PB94-780228)	$150.00
NHTSA SFST Video — Part 1 (PB94-780236)	$70.00
NHTSA SFST Video — Part 2 (PB94-780244)	$70.00
"Psychophysical Tests for DWI Arrest," Burns and Moskowitz (PB 269309)	$41.00
"Development of Field Test of Psychophysical Tests for DWI Arrests," Tharp, Burns and Moskowitz (PB 81203721)	$34.00
"Pilot Test of Selected DWI Protection Procedures for Use At Sobriety Checkpoints," Compton (PB86-170-958)	$34.00

Organizations

Page 1144. Replace paragraph with:

The National College for DUI Defense. Any attorney having a significant practice in the drunk driving field should seriously consider applying for membership in the National College for DUI Defense. The College consists of a Board of Regents of the most prominent DUI attorneys in the country, 100 founding members, a sustaining membership, and unlimited general membership. Among its seminars, the College sponsors an intensive three-day seminar/workshop held annually in July at Harvard Law School, as well as an annual seminar in the winter. The College also maintains an Internet Web site (*http://www.ncdd.com*), with access to various resources and listings of members available to the public. The College listserv maintains an active discussion relevant to the issues of DUI defense. The College is in the process of applying for authority from the ABA to certify attorneys as specialists in drunk driving litigation. Information can be obtained from Executive Director Dee Dee Trichter at (713) 654-3055.

The National Association of Criminal Defense Lawyers (NACDL). NACDL is the preeminent organization in the United States advancing the mission of the nation's criminal defense lawyers to ensure justice and due process for persons accused of a crime or other misconduct. This professional bar association was founded in 1958 and has more than 10,000 direct members. The DUI Advocacy Committee maintains an active forum on its Internet site (www.nacdl.org) and an extensive brief bank for the benefit of its members. NACDL, in conjunction with the National College for DUI Defense, sponsors the largest DUI seminar in the nation. Additional information about the organization and its seminars may be obtained by contacting the Washington, D.C. headquarters at (202) 872-8600.

Expert witnesses

Page 1146. Note the following correction:

Dr. Richard Jensen's telephone number has been changed to
(651-784-7721) (fax: 651-784-7250).

Page 1146. Add to the list of blood-alcohol experts:

Joe Citron, MD, JD, Atlanta, GA (404-261-2911)
Edward F. Fitzgerald, JD, Mesa, AZ (480-699-9334, 480-688-0831)
Forensic Associates, Shoreview, MN (651-784-7721)
Francis Gengo, Pharm.D., Ph.D., Williamsville, NY (716-634-0915)
Ken Habben, Columbia, SC (803-731-8420, 888-793-4675)
Dr. Robert Middleberg, Pharm.D., Ph.D., Willow Grove, PA (215-657-4900)
Alfred E. Staubus, Pharm.D., Ph.D., Columbus, OH (614-451-5367)
Toxicology Associates, Inc., Columbus, OH (614-459-2307)
J. Robert Zettl, Littleton, CO (303-886-4498)
Medical & Toxicological Information (MTI), Alexandria, VA (703-684-4636, *www.medtoxinfo.com*)

Page 1146. Add to the list of experts on the subject of field sobriety tests:

Joe Citron, MD, JD, Atlanta, GA (404-261-2911)
Forensic Associates, Shoreview, MN (651-784-7721)
David (Dave) Fries, Live Oak, FL (386-658-3464)
Robert (Bob) LaPier, Rigby, ID (208-754-4632, 800-257-4643)
Bill Taylor, Gainesville, GA (770-534-1501)

Resources

Page 1146. Add at end of Resources material:

The following are experts in the field of breath-alcohol:

Joe Citron, MD, JD, Atlanta, GA (404-261-2911)
Edward F. Fitzgerald, JD, Mesa, AZ (480-699-9334, 480-688-0831)
Forensic Associates, Shoreview, MN (651-784-7721)
David (Dave) Fries, Live Oak, FL (386-658-3464)
Francis Gengo, Pharm.D., Ph.D., Williamsville, NY (716-634-0915)
Robert (Bob) LaPier, Rigby, ID (208-754-4632, 800-257-4643)
Dr. Robert Middleberg, Pharm.D., Ph.D., Willow Grove, PA (215-657-4900)
Alfred E. Staubus, Pharm.D., Ph.D., Columbus, OH (614-451-5367)
David Sweeney, Conway, SC (843-347-1855)
Bill Taylor, Gainesville, GA (770-534-1501)
J. Robert Zettl, Littleton, CO (303-886-4498)

The following are accident reconstruction experts:

Bob Awtrey, LaGrange, GA (706-645-1643)
William C. Fischer, Endicott, NY (607-785-5766)

The following is a polygraph expert:

Richard Rackleff, Gainesville, GA (770-718-1975)

BIBLIOGRAPHY

Books and Pamphlets

Biasotti, A.A., et al., Marijuana and Alcohol: A Driver Performance Study, California Office of Traffic Safety Project No. 087902 (Sept. 1986)

Biasotti, A.A., et al., The Effects of Alcohol and Marihuana on Driver-Controlled Behavior in a Driving Simulator, Phase I, DOT-HS-806-414 (Sept. 1986)

Lafave & Scott, Handbook on Criminal Law (1972)

National Highway Traffic Safety Administration, Improved Sobriety Testing, DOT-HS-806-512

National Highway Traffic Safety Administration, DWI Detection & Standardized Field Sobriety Testing: Student Manual, DOT-HS-178-R10/95 (1995)

National Highway Traffic Safety Administration, DWI Detection & Standardized Field Sobriety Testing: Student Manual, DOT-HS-178-R2/00 (2000)

National Highway Traffic Safety Administration, DWI Detection & Standardized Field Sobriety Testing: Student Manual, DOT-HS-178-R1/02 (2002)

National Highway Traffic Safety Administration, Special Testing for Possible Alcohol Carry-over Effects Using the Intoximeters, Inc. Alco-Sensor IV at 10 degrees C, DOT-HS-809-424 (Mar. 2002)

National Highway Traffic Safety Administration, The Use of Sobriety Checkpoints for Impaired Driving Enforcement, DOT-HS-807-656 (Nov. 1990)

Tharp, V., et al., Psychophysical Tests for DUI Arrest, NHTSA DOT-HS-8-01970 (1981)

Whited & Nichols, Drinking/Driving Litigation Criminal and Civil (2d ed.)

Articles

Arnold, John, Hypoglycemia: Driving Under the Influence, 8 Medical & Toxicological Information (MTI) Review 1 (Sept. 2003)

Bode, et al., Effects of Cimetidine Treatment on Ethanol Formation in the Human Stomach, 19(6) Scandinavian Journal of Gastroenterology 853 (1984)

Booker, J.L., End Position Nystagmus as an Indicator of Ethanol Intoxication, 40(2) Sci. & Just. 113

Bosch, Xavier, Using Asthma Inhalers Can Give False Positive Results in Breath Tests, 324 British Medical Journal 756 (Mar. 30, 2002)

Dell'Osso, L.F., Nystagmus, Saccadic Intrusions/Oscillations and Oscillopsia, 3 Current Neuro-Ophthalmology 147 (1989)

Ericson, Effects of Antacids on Alcohol's Reaction, 5(5) Alcoholism 28 (1985)

Falvey, Wolfman & Maroney, Staring Down Both Barrels in a Corporate Fraud Case: Can a Civil Stay Help the Defense?, 8 No. 22 Andrews' Bank & Lender Liab. Litig. Rep. 15 (Apr. 3, 2003)

Hassman, Phillip E., Annotation, When Intoxication Deemed Involuntary so as to Constitute a Defense to Criminal Charge, 73 A.L.R.3d 195 (1976)

Jones & Neri, 24 Canadian Society of Forensic Sciences Journal 165 (1991)

Kalfus, Suzanne, Alcohol Prohibitions for Pilots and Flight Instructors, Air Line Pilot 26 (Apr. 2003)

Labianca, D.A., How Specific for Ethanol Is Breath-Alcohol Analysis Based on Absorption of IR Radiation at 9.5 microns?, 16 Journal of Analytical Toxicology 404 (1992)

Labianca, D.A., The Flawed Nature of the Calibration Factor in Breath-Alcohol Analysis, 79 Journal of Chemical Education 1237 (Oct. 2002)

Labianca & Simpson, Medicolegal Alcohol Determination: Variability of the Blood- to Breath-Alcohol Ratio and Its Effect on Reported Breath-Alcohol Concentrations, 33 European Journal of Clinical Chemistry 919 (1995)

McKinney, W. Troy, Challenging and Excluding HGN Tests, The Champion (Apr. 2002)

Moskowitz, Burns & Ferguson, Police Officers' Detection of Breath Odors from Alcohol Ingestion, 31(3) Accident Analysis and Prevention 175 (May 1999)

Oberman, Steve, Drunk or Drowsy? How Fatigue Can Be Mistaken for Intoxication, The Champion 56 (Jan./Feb. 2001)

Saunders, News of Science, Medicine and Technology: Straight Talk, 21(10) Discover (Oct. 2000)

Scheff, Coffina & Baisinger, Taking the Fifth in Civil Litigation, 29 Litig. 34 (Fall 2002)

Simpson, The New "Direct Breath" Statutes: Both Bad Law and Bad Science, 6(4) DWI Journal 1 (1991)

Stafford, David T., Drugs Other Than Alcohol: Marijuana, 17 No. 3 For the Defense 5-6 (May-June 2003)

Strayer, Drews & Crouch, Fatal Distraction? A Comparison of the Cell-phone Driver and the Drunk Driver, Second International Driving Symposium on Human Factors in Driver Assessment, Training & Vehicle Design (Univ. of Utah, Salt Lake City, July 2003)

Stutts, et al., The Role of Driver Distraction in Traffic Crashes, AAA Foundation for Traffic Safety (2001)

Tasman & Jager, eds., 2 Duane's Clinical Ophthalmology 20 (1989)

Umeda & Sakata, Alcohol and the Oculomotor System, 87 Annals of Otology Rhinology 69 (1978)

Vythilingum, Stein & Soifer, Is "Shy Bladder Syndrome" a Subtype of Social Anxiety Disorder? A Survey of People with Paruresis, 16 Depression and Anxiety 84 (May 2002)

TABLE OF CASES

References are to sections.

Table of Cases

INDEX